AT COLD WAR'S END

AT COLD WAR'S END

Editor
Benjamin B. Fischer

GOVERNMENT REPRINTS PRESS
Washington, D.C.

© Ross & Perry, Inc. 2001 All rights reserved.

No claim to U.S. government work contained throughout this book.

Protected under the Berne Convention. Published 2001

Printed in The United States of America
Ross & Perry, Inc. Publishers
717 Second St., N.E., Suite 200
Washington, D.C. 20002
(202) 675-8300

SAN 253-8555

Government Reprints Press Edition 2001
Government Reprints Press is an Imprint of Ross & Perry, Inc.

Library of Congress Control Number: 2001091650

http://www.GPO.reprints.com

ISBN 1-931641-04-8

All rights reserved. No copyrighted part of this publication may be reproduced, stored in a retrieval system, or transmitted, in any form or by any means, electronic, photocopying, recording, or otherwise, without the prior written permission of the publisher.

Contents

	Page
Foreword	v
Preface	vii
Chronology	xlv
Appendix	lvii

Documents: A Compendium of National Intelligence Estimates and Assessments

The Soviet Crisis: Gorbachev and the Perils of *Perestroika*

1.	NIE 11-23-88, December 1988, *Gorbachev's Economic Programs: The Challenges Ahead*	1
2.	SOV 89-10077, Central Intelligence Agency, Office of Soviet Analysis, September 1989, *Gorbachev's Domestic Gambles and Instability in the USSR*	27
3.	NIE 11-18-89, November 1989, *The Soviet System in Crisis: Prospects for the Next Two Years*	49
4.	NIE 11-18-90, November 1990, *The Deepening Crisis in the USSR: Prospects for the Next Year*	83
5.	Central Intelligence Agency, Office of Soviet Analysis, April 1991, "The Soviet Cauldron"	111
6.	NIE 11-18-91, July 1991, *Implications of Alternative Soviet Futures*	121
7.	NIE 11-18.3-91, November 1991, *Civil Disorder in the Former USSR: Can It Be Managed This Winter?*	141

The End of Empire I: Eastern Europe

8.	NIE 11/12-9-88, May 1988, *Soviet Policy Toward Eastern Europe Under Gorbachev*	151
9.	NIE 12-90, April 1990, *The Future of Eastern Europe* (Key Judgments only)	179

The End of Empire II: National Secession and Ethnic Conflict in the USSR 180

    10.   SNIE 11-18.2-91, September 1991, *The Republics of the Former USSR: The Outlook for the Next Year*   185

"New Thinking": Soviet Foreign Relations

    11.   SNIE 11/37-88, March 1988, *USSR: Withdrawal From Afghanistan* (Key Judgments only)   215

    12.   SNIE 11-16-88CX, November 1988, *Soviet Policy During the Next Phase of Arms Control in Europe* (Key Judgments only)   221

    13.   NIE 11-4-89, April 1989, *Soviet Policy Toward the West: The Gorbachev Challenge*   227

    14.   SNIE 11/37-89, November, 1989, *Afghanistan: The War in Perspective* (Key Judgments only)   255

    15.   NI IIM 91-10006, November 1991, *Soviet Tactical Nuclear Forces and Gorbachev's Nuclear Pledges: Impact, Motivations, and Next Steps* (Key Judgments only)   259

The Military Balance I: Conventional Forces in Europe

    16.   NIE 11-14-89, February 1989, *Trends and Development in Warsaw Pact Theater Forces and Doctrine Through the 1990s*   265

    17.   M/H NIE 4-1-84, September 1989, *Warning of War in Europe: Changing Warsaw Pact Planning and Forces* (Key Judgments only)   289

    18.   NIC M 89-10002, September 1989, *The Post-CFE Environment in Europe*   297

    19.   NIC M 89-10003, October 1989, *Status of Soviet Unilateral Withdrawals*   303

    20.   NIC M 89-10005, November 1989, *Soviet Theater Forces in 1991: The Impact of the Unilateral Withdrawals on Structure and Capabilities* (Key Judgments only)   315

    21.   NIC M 90-10002, April 1990, *The Direction of Change in the Warsaw Pact*   319

The Military Balance II: Strategic Nuclear Weapons

22. NIE 11-3/8-88, December 1988, *Soviet Forces and Capabilities for Strategic Nuclear Conflict Through the Late 1990s* (Key Judgments and Executive Summary) — 341

23. NIE 11-3/8-91, August 1991, *Soviet Forces and Capabilities for Strategic Nuclear Conflict Through the Year 2000* (Key Judgments only) — 359

24. NIE 11-30-91C, December 1991, *The Winter of the Soviet Military: Cohesion or Collapse?* — 369

Foreword

The Center for the Study of Intelligence (CSI) of the Central Intelligence Agency and the George W. Bush Center for Presidential Studies at Texas A&M University co-sponsored a conference on "US Intelligence and the End of the Cold War" on the Texas A&M University campus at College Station from 18 to 20 November 1999. As a contribution to the conference, CSI prepared a compendium of newly declassified US intelligence documents covering the years 1989-1991. This period encompassed events in the USSR and Eastern Europe that transformed the postwar world and much of the 20th century's geopolitical landscape. It was a time when the tempo of history accelerated so rapidly that, as one historian put it, events seemed to be moving beyond human control, if not human comprehension.

Benjamin B. Fischer of CIA's History Staff selected, edited, and wrote the preface to the National Intelligence Estimates and other intelligence assessments included in this companion volume.[1] In conjunction with the conference, the Intelligence Community will release to the National Archives and Records Administration (NARA) the records reprinted in this compendium and those listed in the Appendix.

The declassification and release of these documents marks a new stage in the CIA's commitment to openness. The Agency has only rarely declassified and made available to the public and to scholars Cold War records of such recent vintage. The new release complements and supplements the previous declassification of more than 550 National Intelligence Estimates (NIEs) and Special National Intelligence Estimates (SNIEs) on the Soviet Union and Eastern Europe from 1946 to 1985. CIA continues to review and declassify finished intelligence on these countries. These records are available at NARA's Archives II facility in College Park, Maryland, in Records Group 263 (Central Intelligence Agency Records).[2]

Two of the documents reprinted in this volume originated with CIA's Office of Soviet Analysis (SOVA). Both have been cited in accounts of

---

[1] For a review of previous CSI publications on national intelligence topics and their tie-in with conferences sponsored by CIA, see Benjamin Franklin Cooling, "The Central Intelligence Agency and the Policy of Openness," *The Public Historian* 20:4 (Fall 1998), pp. 60-66.

[2] See "Declassified National Intelligence Estimates on the Soviet Union and International Communism, 1946-1984," (Washington, DC: Central Intelligence Agency, 1996). This is a list of all NIEs and SNIEs declassified and released to date to NARA.

US-Soviet relations during the Bush administration and have been discussed elsewhere.[3] The complete texts appear here for the first time.

Mr. Fischer tried to identify and release the most important analysis available for this period. His selection is comprehensive. Some of the documents, especially those on military-strategic subjects, were only partially declassified, since they contain data from still-sensitive sources and methods. Readers should understand, however, that even the portions reprinted here contain information that until recently was highly classified. We want to note, in addition, that we have selected only estimates and assessments prepared during the Bush administration. We realize that, in some cases, estimates and other forms of finished intelligence issued before 1989 may have addressed some of the same issues and even reached some of the same conclusions as those that came later, but our focus is exclusively on what was written during 1989-1991.

Mr. Fischer and I would like to thank all those responsible for making this compendium and the conference possible. Above all, we would like to thank former President George Bush and his staff for enthusiastically endorsing the conference and Director of Central Intelligence George J. Tenet for his support and cooperation. We also would like to thank CIA's Executive Director, David W. Carey, for his assistance in releasing the documents. Closer to home, we want to thank CIA's Office of Information Management, headed by Edmund Cohen, and in particular James Oliver, chief of the Historical Review Program, Howard Stoertz, John Vogel, and James Noren. We also would like to thank readers who took the time to examine this volume in draft and to make comments, and Michael Warner, Deputy Chief of the History Staff, who worked closely with us on this project.

Gerald K. Haines
Chief Historian
September 1999

---

[3] See Robert M. Gates, *From the Shadows: The Ultimate Insider's Story of Five Presidents and How They Won the Cold War* (New York: Simon & Schuster, 1996), pp. 514, 520; Michael R. Beschloss and Strobe Talbott, *At the Highest Levels: The Inside Story of the End of the Cold War* (Boston: Little, Brown, and Company, 1993), p. 360; Kirsten Lundberg, "CIA and the Fall of the Soviet Empire: The Politics of 'Getting It Right,'" Case Study C16-94-1251.0, Harvard University, 1994, pp. 36-37; Don Oberdorfer, *From the Cold War to a New Era: The United States and the Soviet Union, 1983-1991* (Baltimore: The Johns Hopkins Press, 1998), pp. 450-451; and Bruce D. Berkowitz and Jeffrey T. Richelson, "The CIA Vindicated," *National Interest* 41 (Fall 1995), pp. 41-42. Lundberg's case study was written for the Harvard Intelligence and Policy Project of the John F. Kennedy School of Government and was funded by CIA.

Preface

The last great drama of the Cold War—the collapse of communism in the Soviet Union and Eastern Europe and the end of the four-decade-old East-West conflict—unfolded in three acts between 1989 and 1991. Even as the story began, Soviet leader Mikhail Gorbachev already had made the largest opening to the outside world in Russian history. To convince the West, and above all the new administration in Washington, of his sincerity, Gorbachev had made major concessions on arms control, withdrawn Soviet troops from Afghanistan, pledged to reduce Soviet ground forces by half a million, and rejected class warfare in favor of "pan-human values" as the basis of Soviet foreign policy. Initially skeptical because of past disappointments with détente, President George Bush and his foreign policy team gradually convinced themselves that Gorbachev was ready for dialogue and compromise. They set a high price for cooperation, however, and were gratefully surprised to find that the Soviets were willing to pay it.

The second act of the drama began in the fall of 1989 with peaceful revolutions in Eastern and Central Europe (except Romania) and the fall of the Soviet "outer empire." The *de facto* collapse of the Warsaw Pact (it would formally dissolve itself a year later) plus a new treaty that substantially reduced Soviet superiority in conventional forces in Europe resulted in a stronger Western alliance—so strong that the US could redeploy forces from Europe to the Persian Gulf for use against Iraq. East Germany, the USSR's main prize from World War II, was united with West Germany and integrated into NATO.

The third and final act closed with the 1991 dissolution of the USSR. The centrifugal forces in the "outer empire" stimulated and accelerated those in the "inner empire" as the Soviet republics sought sovereignty and then independence from Moscow. At the same time, Gorbachev's domestic reforms ran into serious trouble, and the economy went into a tailspin. Gorbachev's struggle with the old imperial elite in the communist party, the armed forces, and the military-industrial complex culminated in the August 1991 coup, which, when it failed, finished off the USSR—and Gorbachev himself. On Christmas Day 1991, at 7:35 p.m., the Soviet flag flying over the Kremlin was lowered and replaced by the new Russian banner. The USSR officially ceased to exist on 31 December. The Cold War was over.

The National Intelligence Estimates and other intelligence assessments reprinted below reveal publicly for the first time how the US Intelligence Community interpreted and predicted the rapidly unfolding events that led to the collapse of communism and the end of the Cold War. The Bush administration's stewardship of American foreign policy coincided with some of the most momentous changes of the 20th century. For a brief span of time, the extraordinary became an almost daily event. Estimates that seemed premature or pessimistic or alarmist often turned out to be too conservative in their forecasts within six months or a year. Some key events, such as Soviet acquiescence in German unification within NATO, happened so quickly and unexpectedly that they do not even appear in any of the Estimates. The Estimates, in fact, often accurately anticipated an event or development but misjudged the time it would take for it to materialize—an indication of the acceleration of history in this period.

Readers of the Estimates that follow may find the terms of discussion familiar, since they generally paralleled contemporary discussions in the press and academe. They may be surprised, however, to discover that the Intelligence Community early on took a pessimistic view of Gorbachev's chances for success in reforming the Soviet system when that was not a popular view inside or outside the government. The Estimates also predicted the impending implosion of the Soviet system and anticipated some of the problems for internal, regional, and international stability that the collapse of Soviet power would create. Fortunately, the direst predictions of widespread famine and civil war proved wrong. Although some readers may be familiar with the Estimates that describe political and economic issues surrounding the collapse of communism and the end of the Cold War, they should find the Estimates on military-strategic issues unique. Estimates and intelligence memoranda on Soviet and Warsaw Pact military forces—especially the NIE 11-3/8 series on *Soviet Forces and Capabilities for Strategic Nuclear Conflict*, the bible on Soviet strategic nuclear weapons for US military planners, weapons program managers, and arms control specialists—reveal facts and interpretations that were once among the Intelligence Community's most highly classified secrets. While these Estimates helped the United States maintain its defenses, they also made it possible for US policymakers to engage the Soviet Union in conventional and strategic arms talks that led to the end of the arms race even before the Cold War itself had ended.

The Road to Malta

President George Bush entered office in January 1989 determined to put his own stamp on America's foreign policy and make US-Soviet relations its main focus.[1] He intended to build on the legacy of his predecessor without reprising Ronald Reagan's policy. On 15 February 1989 the President ordered a review of US policy toward the USSR and Eastern Europe, which, for a variety of political and bureaucratic reasons, took longer and proved more complicated than expected.[2] In behind-the-scenes discussions, the new foreign policy team quickly divided into those who wanted to open an immediate dialogue with Gorbachev and those who took a skeptical view of the new-style Soviet leader.[3]

The first Soviet challenge to the new Bush administration arrived even before the President's inauguration. To reverse the foreign policy course inherited from his predecessors and to relieve tensions that had accumulated in US-Soviet relations in the 1970s and 1980s, in 1987 Gorbachev signed the US-Soviet Treaty on Elimination of Intermediate-Range and Shorter-Range Missiles (INF), the first nuclear arms reduction (actually an arms destruction) accord in history. Then in 1988, he announced his intention to withdraw Soviet forces from Afghanistan within a year.[4] Addressing the United Nations General Assembly in December 1988, Gorbachev went further, delivering the most important foreign policy speech of his career. He renounced class warfare as the basis of Soviet foreign policy, embraced "pan-humanist values" and "global interdependence," and pledged to convert an "economy of armaments into an economy of disarmament." He invited the US to cooperate in ending the Cold War by halting the arms race and seeking settlements of regional conflicts. Then he made dramatic unilateral concessions, pledging to reduce Soviet ground forces by 500,000 and to withdraw 50,000 troops from Eastern Europe, as well as 10,000 tanks, 8,500 artillery systems, and 800 combat aircraft, over a two-year

---

[1] See George Bush and Brent Scowcroft, *A World Transformed* (New York: Knopf/Distributed by Random House, 1998), pp. 15-16; and James A. Baker III, *The Politics of Diplomacy: Revolution, War, and Peace, 1989-1992* (New York: G. P. Putnam's Sons, 1995), p. 68.

[2] Bush and Scowcroft, *A World Transformed*, p. 40; and Baker, *The Politics of Diplomacy*, p. 68.

[3] For a discussion of the range of views among the "core group" of policymakers, see Bush and Scowcroft, *A World Transformed*, pp. 41-44; and Baker, *The Politics of Diplomacy*, pp. 68-70.

[4] To get the INF agreement, Gorbachev had made major concessions that Brezhnev and his two successors had flatly rejected, including asymmetrical reductions and intrusive on-site inspections.

period.[5] The speech had a stunning impact in Western Europe—and not just there. The *New York Times*, not normally given to hyperbole, wrote:

> Perhaps not since Woodrow Wilson presented his Fourteen Points in 1918 or since Franklin Roosevelt and Winston Churchill promulgated the Atlantic Charter in 1941 has a world figure demonstrated the vision Mikhail Gorbachev displayed yesterday at the United Nations.[6]

The question of Gorbachev's intentions animated policy discussions in the White House and in the US Intelligence Community. The leading skeptic was national security adviser Brent Scowcroft, a White House veteran with a broad background in Soviet affairs. His skepticism was rooted in the experience of the 1970s and 1980s, when America's initial euphoria over détente turned sour, leading to the renewal of the Cold War at the turn of the decade. Scowcroft now worried that the USSR could induce the US to disarm while leaving its own military structure intact. "I was suspicious of Gorbachev's motives and skeptical of his prospects," Scowcroft wrote.[7] Still, much of the administration's planning "depended heavily on Gorbachev," on his intentions, and on his domestic and foreign policy:

> To oversimplify, I believed that Gorbachev's goal was to restore dynamism to a socialist political and economic system and revitalize the Soviet Union domestically and internationally to compete with the West. To me, especially before 1990, this made Gorbachev potentially more dangerous than his predecessors, each of whom, through some aggressive move, had saved the West from the dangers of its own wishful thinking about the Soviet Union before it was too late.[8]

---

[5] The Red Army had about 5.2 million men under arms at the time, and the withdrawal from Eastern Europe represented about ten percent of the total stationed there. The USSR also had about 53,000 tanks, 29,000 artillery systems, and 4,880 combat aircraft. Gorbachev's reductions and withdrawals were significant, since the INF Treaty could have been fully implemented without affecting the overall Soviet force structure poised toward Europe. See William E. Odom, *The Collapse of the Soviet Military* (New Haven: Yale University Press, 1998), p. 147. Poland, Hungary, East Germany, and Czechoslovakia later gave Gorbachev's declaration an added boost by announcing a reduction of 56,000 troops, 2,000 tanks, 130 aircraft, and thousands of artillery pieces and mortars as well as a "13.6 percent" reduction in defense spending. (Defense budget data were still classified, so the figure was meaningless.) See Vladislav Andreyevich Drobkov, *Kommunist* 6 (April 1989), p. 125.

[6] "Gamble, Showman, Statesman," *New York Times*, 8 December 1988, p. 34.

[7] Bush and Scowcroft, *A World Transformed*, p. 134.

[8] *Ibid.*, p. 13.

1989: The Year That Changed the World

Even in retrospect it is hard to grasp how much and how quickly the world changed in 1989. In a mere twelve months, the face of Cold War Europe changed forever. Columnist George Will called it Europe's Second Reformation—the "most startling, interesting, promising and consequential year *ever*."[a] Neal Ascherson of the *Observer* (London) labeled 1989 the "pivotal year of the 20th century."[b] Soviet President Mikhail Gorbachev, in his 1990 New Year's address, declared 1989 the "year of ending the Cold War." This was the year when:

The USSR withdrew its last soldier from Afghanistan. Gorbachev demanded that the retreat be orderly and dignified—he didn't want television images reminiscent of the chaotic 1975 US pullout from Vietnam. "We must not appear before the world in our underwear or even without any," he told the Politburo inner circle.[c] "A defeatist position is not possible." The withdrawal was intended as a sign of conciliation toward the West and reassurance to the East Europeans, but it encouraged the national minorities to challenge Soviet power.

The communist party lost its monopoly of power. In the USSR, multi-candidate elections were held for the first time.[d] In Poland, Solidarity emerged from underground to win a stunning electoral victory over the communists and form the first coalition government in Eastern Europe since 1948. In Hungary, the communists agreed to multi-party elections, which occurred the next year.

Communism collapsed in Eastern Europe. The USSR renounced the "Brezhnev doctrine" and condemned the 1968 invasion of Czechoslovakia. As one historian noted, in Poland communism took ten years, in Hungary ten months, in East Germany ten weeks, and in Czechoslovakia ten days to disappear.[e] In Romania—the bloody exception to the rule of peaceful transition—the end came with the execution of Nicolae Ceausescu and his wife on Christmas Day.

Nationalism trumped communism. The Soviets believed they had solved the problem of nationalism and ethnic conflict within their multinational state. But nationalism was in fact the gravedigger of the Soviet system. As the center disintegrated and Gorbachev opened up the political process with *glasnost* (openness), the old communist "barons" in the republics saw the handwriting on the wall and became nationalists; they "first of all attacked the USSR government . . . and subsequently destroyed the USSR."[f] Asked when he decided to secede from the USSR, Ukrainian party boss Leonid Kravchuk replied: "1989."

The Soviets pondered the fate of their revolution as the French celebrated the bicentennial of theirs. The Soviets considered their revolution both the heir to and a superior version of the French Revolution of 1789 because it had solved the problem of class inequality by eliminating private property and the irrationality of the business cycle by replacing the market with the plan. But as historian François Furet wrote: "It is 1917 that is being buried in the name of 1789."[g] A protest banner summed up the Soviet experiment: "72 Years on a Road to Nowhere." The system's failure was evident. Then *perestroika* (restructuring) turned into *katastroika*, a neologism that was heard more and more on Moscow streets as Gorbachev's reform program faltered and then failed. The next year, a Soviet citizen could ask, only half-jokingly: "If there were socialism in the West, whom would we buy food from? The Ethiopians perhaps?"[h]

The Berlin Wall, the paramount symbol of the Cold War and the division of Europe, fell. When Gorbachev visited East Berlin in October (ironically to celebrate the 40th anniversary of the East German state), his mere presence rocked the foundations of the Stalinist regime. Young marchers, handpicked and bussed in from the countryside to present an image of unity and conformity, spontaneously chanted: "Gorby! Gorby! Help us!" German unification a year later accelerated the Soviet political and military withdrawal from Europe. When it was over, Russia's borders had been pushed back to those of 1653, undoing more than 300 years of Tsarist and Soviet advance toward the West and leaving behind a country that was more Eurasian than European.

Gorbachev introduced glasnost (openness) to create popular support for his reforms. By doing so, however, he opened a Pandora's box of revelations about the Gulag, the Great Terror, genocidal famines, mass deportations, and killing fields that had turned the USSR into one large charnel house in Stalin's time. *Glasnost* underscored Gorbachev's key dilemma: by allowing the truth to emerge, it destroyed the foundation of lies on which the communist system was built. One example: After releasing a map showing that the government had covered up the actual extent of contamination caused by the 1986 Chornobyl' nuclear reactor catastrophe, Moscow confiscated dosimeters from civil defense units so that people in the affected areas could not measure radiation levels.

---

[a] George F. Will, "Europe's Second Reformation," *Newsweek*, 20 November 1989, p. 90.
[b] Neal Ascherson, "1989 stands out as pivotal year in 20th century; Chain reaction ends Cold War," *Washington Times*, 26 April 1999, p. A17.
[c] Dmitri Volkogonov, *Autopsy for Empire: The Seven Leaders Who Built the Soviet Regime* (New York: The Free Press, 1998), p. 105. The author cites the minutes of a Politburo meeting held 18 April 1988.
[d] The USSR did not formally rescind the communist party's monopoly of power until March 1990, but that was a culmination of a trend that began in 1989.
[e] Timothy Garton Ash.
[f] Michael Ellman and Vladimir Kantorovich, "The Collapse of the Soviet System and the Memoir Literature," *Europa-Asia Studies* 49:2 (1997), p. 268.
[g] Francois Furet, "From 1789 to 1917 & 1989," *Encounter* 75:2 (September 1990), p. 5.
[h] P. Yemelin, "The Army and Politics," *Literaturnaya Rossiya*, 14 December 1990, p. 8.

Scowcroft was not the only skeptic on the Bush foreign policy team. Secretary of State James A. Baker III observed that "Gorbachev's strategy, I believed, was premised on splitting the alliance and undercutting us in Western Europe."[9]

Gorbachev's UN speech caught the US off guard. In late 1988, Douglas MacEachin, the chief of Soviet analysis at CIA, told Congress straightforwardly that, despite Gorbachev's initiatives in domestic and foreign policy, the Agency had "never really looked at the Soviet Union as a political entity in which there were factors building which could lead to at least the initiation of political transformation that we seem to see [at the present time]." He added:

> Moreover, had [such a study] existed inside the government, we never would have been able to publish it anyway, quite frankly. And had we done so, people would have been calling for my head. And I wouldn't have published it. In all honesty, had we said a week ago that Gorbachev might come to the UN [in December 1988] and offer a unilateral cut of 500,000 in the military, we would have been told we were crazy.[10]

Two intelligence Estimates, both written in late 1988, give a "before" and "after" picture of the Community's thinking. SNIE 11-16-88, *Soviet Policy During the Next Phase of Arms Control in Europe*, November 1988 (Document 12), which appeared on the eve of the Gorbachev speech, concluded that the Kremlin had substantial political, military, and economic motives to engage in conventional force reduction talks; but it also observed that Moscow would prefer "mutual" reductions in order to maintain the Warsaw Pact's numerical advantage. An agreement acceptable to the USSR "could take years—and might not even be possible."

The second Estimate, issued just after Gorbachev's UN speech, was more upbeat on prospects for favorable agreements with the USSR. NIE 11-23-88, *Gorbachev's Economic Programs: The Challenges Ahead*, December 1988 (Document 1), dealt mainly with internal economic reforms, which, it concluded, were not working and would almost certainly fail to produce marked improvement over the next five years. Even that turned out to be too optimistic. This Estimate was the first one to underscore the connection between the USSR's domestic vulnerabilities and its new foreign policy face. It stated that "Gorbachev needs

---

[9] Baker, *The Politics of Diplomacy*, p. 70.

[10] Cited in Kirsten Lundberg, "CIA and the Fall of the Soviet Empire: The Politics of 'Getting It Right,'" Case Study C16-94-1251.0, Harvard University, 1994, pp. 30-31.

the many benefits of a non-confrontational international environment," adding that this would give the US and its allies

> considerable leverage in bargaining with the Soviets over the terms of that environment on some security issues such as regional conflicts and arms control and on some internal matters such as human rights and information exchange. The margins of this leverage will be set by Moscow's determination not to let the West affect the fundamental nature of the Soviet system or its superpower status.

NIE 11-23-88 was still cautious, however, depicting Soviet weaknesses as an opportunity for the West to achieve marginal bargaining advantage—not to end the Cold War and the arms race.

Over the spring of 1989, moreover, there was some "new thinking" in the policy and intelligence debates. Divergent views were reflected in NIE 11-4-89, *Soviet Policy Toward the West: The Gorbachev Challenge* (Document 13), which appeared in April as the administration was completing its policy review. The Estimate included an unusual section labeled "Disagreements" in the main text rather than relegating dissents to a footnote:

> There is general agreement in the Intelligence Community over the outlook for the next five to seven years [i.e., that the US could reach favorable agreements with the USSR], but differing views over the longer term prospects for fundamental and enduring change toward less competitive behavior:
>
> - Some analysts see current policy changes as largely tactical, driven by the need for breathing space from the competition. They believe the ideological imperatives of Marxism-Leninism and its hostility toward capitalist countries are enduring. They point to previous failures of reform and the transient nature of past "détentes." They judge that there is a serious risk of Moscow returning to traditionally combative behavior when the hoped-for gains in economic performance are achieved.
>
> - Other analysts believe Gorbachev's policies reflect a fundamental rethinking of national interests and ideology as well as more tactical considerations. They argue that ideological tenets of Marxism-Leninism such as class conflict and capitalist-socialist enmity are being revised. They consider the withdrawal from Afghanistan and the shift toward tolerance of power sharing in Eastern Europe to be historic shifts in the Soviet definition of national interest. They judge that Gorbachev's changes are likely to have sufficient momentum to produce lasting shifts in Soviet behavior.

The NIE concluded that the USSR would remain an adversary for the foreseeable future and would pose serious challenges to NATO unity. It was sanguine, however, about Gorbachev's chances for survival and did not anticipate major changes in Soviet policy even if he left the scene.

On 12 May 1989, President Bush delivered a speech at Texas A&M University that incorporated the results of his policy review and redefined US policy toward the Soviet Union. It did not attract a lot attention at the time—Gorbachev's dramatic gestures were still grabbing headlines—but it remains important to understanding the end of the Cold War. Its theme was that the US should "move beyond containment" by bringing the USSR into the international community.[11] While offering to cooperate on mutually beneficial issues, President Bush made it clear that Washington had lingering doubts about Soviet intentions: "[A] new relationship cannot simply be declared by Moscow or bestowed by others; it must be earned. It must be earned because promises are never enough." In effect, the President was challenging Gorbachev to back up his attractive words with bold deeds.

Gorbachev's pronouncements fed Cold War weariness at home and abroad. In April, George Kennan, the *doyen* of American Soviet-watchers, told the Senate Foreign Relations Committee that the USSR no longer posed a military threat to the United States. During February and March, the *New York Times* had run a series of op-ed columns by leading experts under the rubric "Is the Cold War Over?" The paper's answer was an unqualified yes. In Europe, many began complaining that the United States, for reasons that were either naive or sinister, was ignoring an opportunity to end the Cold War. "Everyone was tired of the Cold War, and some leaders such as British Prime Minister Margaret Thatcher were now declaring it over," Scowcroft noted.[12]

The White House was worried that "Gorbymania" would lull the West into a false sense of security. Gorbachev's well-received pronouncements gave the impression that the Cold War had already ended. But saying so didn't make it so. Third World conflicts were still a contentious issue. Scowcroft believed the Soviets had "narrowed" their priorities while intensifying efforts to hold key positions. "Soviet recalcitrance in the Third World deepened my reservations about Gorbachev," he wrote.[13] This was especially the case with Afghanistan, where the Kremlin's handpicked ruler, Najibullah, was still in power thanks to massive Soviet aid, and in Nicaragua and El Salvador, where

---

[11] The full text of the speech is in *Public Papers of the Presidents of the United States: George Bush 1989*, Book I: January 20–June 30, 1989 (Washington, DC: Government Printing Office, 1990), pp. 540-543.

[12] Bush and Scowcroft, *A World Transformed*, p. 14.

[13] *Ibid.*, p. 134.

Cuba and East Germany had taken up some of the Soviet slack.[14] Such trouble spots led Scowcroft to comment that *perestroika* looked like a "Brezhnev system with a humanitarian paint job."[15]

Of all the questions raised by *perestroika*, however, none from the White House's perspective was more important than its impact on Soviet military power—above all its implications for strategic nuclear weapons targeted on the US. In his Texas A&M speech, President Bush had emphasized that deterrence would remain the basis of US defense policy—and with good reason. NIE 11-3/8-1988, *Soviet Forces and Capabilities for Strategic Nuclear Conflict Through the 1990s*, December 1988 (Document 22), concluded that "in terms of what the Soviets spend, what they procure, how their strategic forces are deployed, how they plan, and how they exercise, *the basic elements of Soviet defense policy and practice thus far have not been changed by Gorbachev's reform campaign*" [emphasis added]. The Estimate projected that, based on current development and deployment efforts, the Soviets would continue to modernize their strategic forces into the late 1990s. The bottom line—no observable changes here: "To date, as demonstrated in the strategic forces programs and resources commitments we have examined, we have not detected changes under Gorbachev that clearly illustrate that either new security concepts or new resource constraints are taking hold."[16] This did not surprise the estimators, since it would have required a long leadtime for Gorbachev's "new thinking" to make an impact on deployments, plans, exercises, and major programs in Soviet strategic forces. For this reason, as noted below, changes in Soviet conventional forces were better indicators of a change in military policy. The Estimate noted the apparent economic need to reduce military expenditures (most of which were spent on relatively much more

---

[14] SNIE 11/37-88, *USSR: Withdrawal from Afghanistan*, March 1988, (Document 11), correctly assessed the Kremlin's domestic and foreign policy reasons for quitting Afghanistan, noting that withdrawal would be seen both as a defeat for the "Brezhnev doctrine" and a "triumph for Western policy." The Estimate also stated confidently that Najibullah's regime "will not survive the completion of Soviet withdrawal even with continued Soviet assistance." But it did not collapse, partly because the USSR began pouring in aid in the summer of 1989. The next Estimate, *Afghanistan: The War in Perspective*, SNIE 11/37-38, November 1989 (Document 14), came to a different conclusion, asserting that the Kabul regime, though "weak, unpopular, and factionalized," would "probably remain in power over the next 12 months." The SNIE included an unusual *mea culpa* in a page-one footnote, stating that the previous SNIE, 11/37-88, had "incorrectly forecast that the Najibullah government would not long survive the completion the Soviet withdrawal and that the regime might even fall before the withdrawal was completed."

[15] Bush and Scowcroft, *A World Restored*, p. 155.

[16] In his 1988 UN address, Gorbachev had used the term "defensive sufficiency" to describe the proper goal of the Soviet military posture.

costly conventional forces) and the resulting incentive to achieve foreign policy goals through arms control agreements; but it noted that the USSR remained "more strongly influenced by the requirement to meet military and political objectives than by economic concerns." This assessment jibed with Brent Scowcroft's reaction to Gorbachev's UN speech. He remarked that it contained "little of military significance" but had, as intended, put the United States on the psychological defensive, creating a "heady atmosphere of optimism."[17]

Gorbachev's ability to move beyond promises soon became clear. His mission and that of the *perestroishchiki*, his brain trust of pro-reform advisers, was to reorganize and revitalize the Soviet system; but to do so they needed to create a favorable international situation that would enable them to relieve the material burden of arms competition with the West. That was their minimum goal. Their maximum objective was to win Western—and especially American—diplomatic and economic support for *perestroika* while trying to maintain—even enhance—the USSR's superpower status. *Perestroika*, in Gorbachev's view, was the strategic mission of both foreign and domestic policy.

Gorbachev had entered office determined to scrap old assumptions about Soviet foreign policy. He, like Scowcroft, had drawn lessons from the return of Cold War tensions in the early 1980s—and they scared him.[18] One of his first decisions in 1985 was to kick the veteran Soviet foreign minister, septuagenarian Andrei Gromyko, upstairs to the ceremonial post of Chairman of the Supreme Soviet.[19] Gromyko was the preeminent symbol of "old thinking"—an advocate of the view that the USSR would emerge victorious in the Cold War if it continued building up its arsenal and fostering "progressive" regimes in the Third World in places like Angola, Ethiopia, and especially Afghanistan.

To replace Gromyko, Gorbachev had chosen Eduard Shevardnadze, a Georgian *apparatchik* with virtually no foreign affairs experience but with a strong committment to "new thinking." Like Gorbachev and the other *perestroishchiki*, Shevardnadze saw a close correlation between

---

[17] Bush and Scowcroft, *A World Transformed*, p. 46.

[18] In the first rough draft of "new political thinking" (his attempt to revise the precepts of the Soviet foreign and defense policy), Gorbachev told the 27th Congress of the Communist Party of the Soviet Union (CPSU) in 1986: "Never, perhaps in the postwar decades, was the situation in the world as explosive and hence, more difficult and unfavorable, as in the first half of the 1980s." See "The Political Report of the Central Committee of the CPSU to the Party Congress of the CPSU, Moscow, February 25, 1986," in Mikhail S. Gorbachev, *Toward a Better World* (New York: Richardson & Steirman, 1987), pp. 158-159.

[19] See Dmitri Volkogonov, *Autopsy for Empire: The Seven Leaders Who Built the Soviet Regime* (New York: The Free Press, 1988), p. 491.

> **National Intelligence Estimates**
>
> National and Special National Intelligence Estimates (NIEs and SNIEs) are prepared for the President, his Cabinet, the National Security Council, and senior policymakers and officials. NIEs focus on strategic issues of mid- or long-term importance to US policy and national security, and SNIEs address near-term issues of more urgent concern. Both types of Estimates are prepared under the auspices of the National Intelligence Council (NIC), which serves as a senior advisory panel to the Director of Central Intelligence. The NIC is an Intelligence Community organization that draws on CIA and other intelligence agencies as well as outside experts for staffing and for preparing estimates. During 1989-1991, it was composed of a chair, vice chair, 11 National Intelligence Officers responsible for a number of geographical and functional areas, and several staffs and production committees.
>
> Estimates are issued over the signature of the DCI in his capacity as the head of the US Intelligence Community and represent the coordinated views of the Community's member agencies. The final product bears the statement: *This National Intelligence Estimate represents the views of the Director of Central Intelligence with the advice and assistance of the US Intelligence Community.*

foreign and domestic policy, especially in the elimination of fear—the foundation of the regime at home and in Eastern Europe. When, for example, the Polish dissident Adam Michnik asked Shevardnadze why Soviet foreign policy had changed, he replied: "Why has our relationship to other nations changed? Because our relationship to our own people has changed."[20]

Gorbachev and Shevardnadze knew that they could not immediately challenge the traditional Cold War advocates in Moscow, especially the powerful Soviet military-industrial establishment (the so-called "metal-eaters") that Nikita Khrushchev had tried and failed to control during the early 1960s.[21] In the short run, they maneuvered around it—as well as the hidebound Foreign Ministry—by holding foreign policy close to the vest. But they understood that the source of their domestic problems as well as their foreign policy dilemmas was the neo-Stalinist political

---

[20] Adam Michnik, "Why Has Our Relationship to Other Nations Changed?—Because Our Relationship to Our Own People Has Changed," *Gazeta Wyborcza*, 27-29 October 1989, p. 4.

[21] After the Soviet collapse, Shevardnadze told Secretary of State Baker that he and Gorbachev realised when *perestroika* began that sooner or later they would have change the Soviet state but claimed they had no schedule for doing so. See Baker, *The Politics of Diplomacy*, p. 568.

system and its arsenal state, which had led the USSR into a dead end of low living standards and dangerous military confrontation with the West. *Perestroika, glasnost,* and "new thinking" put Gorbachev and Shevardnadze on a collision course with diehard supporters of the Soviet political-military empire.

The impact of Gorbachev's and Shevardnadze's new policies, however, was seen first in Eastern Europe. The mounting turbulence in Eastern Europe was both homegrown and imported from the USSR. As *Soviet Policy Toward Eastern Europe*, NIE 11/12-9-88, May 1988 (Document 8) noted, Gorbachev's efforts to push *perestroika* on the other communist countries had "increased the potential for instability in Eastern Europe." The Estimate envisioned three "extreme" scenarios: popular upheaval in Poland, Romania, or Hungary with challenges to party supremacy and Soviet control; sweeping reform in Hungary or Poland that might go beyond *perestroika*; and conservative backlash in the form of repudiation of Gorbachev's reform policy in East Germany and/or Romania. In fact, all three scenarios materialized, but with national variations and in more sweeping forms than NIE 11/12-9-88 had anticipated. With the exception of Romania, the transitions to post-communist governments were peaceful, largely because of an innovative power-sharing model developed in Poland and then adopted in East Germany, Czechoslovakia, and Hungary. Roundtable talks between communist leaders and the still amorphous opposition groups enabled the two sides to reach a mutual understanding: the Communists would eschew violence and relinquish their monopoly of power in return for "amnesty" and a share of political power (plus, of course, pensions and perks[22]). There would be no White terror but no Red repentance either.

The peaceful transitions rested on the fact, noted in the 1988 NIE, that Gorbachev faced "greater constraints than did his predecessors against intervening militarily in Eastern Europe." That judgment was tempered by the qualification that "in extremis" he would "intervene to preserve party rule and decisive Soviet influence in the region." Former foreign policy adviser Sergei Tarasenko claims, however, that his boss, Eduard Shevardnadze, made the renunciation of force—beginning with Afghanistan—the centerpiece of Soviet foreign policy from his first day at Smolensk Square.[23] "Some people fought Gorbachev on this," he claims, because it tied Soviet hands. "But the plight of the country

---

[22] See Charles S. Maier, *Dissolution: The Crisis of Communism and the End of East Germany* (Princeton: Princeton University Press, 1997), pp. 182-183.

[23] Smolensk Square is the site of the former Soviet (now Russian) Foreign Ministry.

meant that the use of force might have precipitated violent collapse. Far from maintaining the empire, it would have ended in blood."[24] Gorbachev, however, seems to have believed that the question of using force to hold the "outer empire" together would not arise, since the East Europeans would embrace *perestroika*. According to Anatoly Dobrynin, Gorbachev's former Ambassador to the US:

> I believe that Gorbachev never foresaw that the whole of Eastern European would fly out of the Soviet orbit within months or that the Warsaw Pact would crumble so soon. He became the helpless witness to the consequences of his own policy.[25]

The withdrawal of Soviet troops from Afghanistan had been meant to reassure the West and the East Europeans that they "would not be sent into another country."[26] For East Europeans, this meant that the so-called "Brezhnev doctrine" on the permanence of communist rule was a dead letter.

With the momentous events in Eastern Europe in the summer and fall and a possibility of ending the Cold War suddenly in sight, the Bush administration's focus shifted to Gorbachev's domestic policy and the perils of *perestroika*. For Scowcroft the key questions became:

> What was the internal situation in the Soviet Union? What were his relations with the conservatives, and what was his staying power? These questions further complicated an already complex calculation, adding to the difficulty of assessing a tolerable pace of reform, and they remained at the forefront of every policy decision related to Eastern Europe.[27]

The administration was not always pleased by the answers it received from the Intelligence Community, especially on the touchy issue of Gorbachev's prospects.[28] One of the first studies prepared for it that raised the possibility of Gorbachev's failure was a CIA intelligence assessment written by the Office of Soviet Analysis (SOVA) in September 1989 and titled *Gorbachev's Domestic Gambles and Instability in the USSR* (Document 2). It argued that the reform program was based on "questionable premises and wishful thinking" and that the "unrest that has punctuated Gorbachev's rule is not a transient phenomenon.

---

[24] David Pryce-Jones, *The Strange Death of the Soviet Empire* (New York: Metropolitan Books/Henry Holt and Company, 1995), p. 115.

[25] Anatoly Dobrynin, *In Confidence: Moscow's Ambassador to Six Cold War Presidents* (New York: Times Books/Random House, 1995), p. 632.

[26] Stanislav Kondrashov, "Turbulent End to the Year Heralding the Start of a New Era," *Izvestiya*, 31 December 1989, p. 5.

[27] Bush and Scowcroft, *A World Transformed*, p. 39.

[28] Bruce D. Berkowitz and Jeffrey T. Richelson, "The CIA Vindicated," *National Interest* 41 (Fall 1995), pp. 36-47.

Conditions are likely to lead in the foreseeable future to continuing crises and instability on a larger scale." Further: "By putting economic reform on hold and pursuing an inadequate financial stabilization program, Gorbachev has brought Soviet internal policy to a fateful crossroads, seriously reducing the chances that his rule—if it survives—will take a path toward long-term stability." SOVA noted that labor unrest and food riots posed a serious challenge to the regime and its reform effort but nevertheless argued that the severest challenge to the Kremlin would come from ethnic violence or secessionist movements. The study anticipated that a Kremlin crackdown "is most likely in the Baltic region, but could also come in the Caucasus, Moldavia, or—down the road—even in the Ukraine."

The emphasis on national and ethnic tensions as the Achilles' heel of the Soviet empire was prescient. Even Gorbachev, according to virtually every account by former Soviet leaders, failed to see the explosive potential of ethnic nationalism. Shevardnadze, a Georgian and therefore more attuned to the problem, repeatedly warned Secretary Baker of the danger that *perestroika* and *glasnost* might unleash nationalistic passions and tensions. He was much more concerned with nationality than economic issues; with Gorbachev it was just the opposite.[29]

The Intelligence Community as a whole did not yet share SOVA's pessimism about Gorbachev's chances. *The Soviet System in Crisis: Prospects for the Next Two Years*, NIE 11-18-89 (Document 3), which appeared in November 1989, was actually optimistic:

> Community analysts hold the view that a *continuation and intensification of the current course is most likely* and believe that, despite the obvious difficulties, the turmoil will be manageable without the need for repressive measures so pervasive that the reform process is derailed [emphasis in original].

Whereas the earlier SOVA assessment was impressed with Gorbachev's problems, the NIE focused on his still considerable strengths, particularly his increased "power and political room to maneuver." The NIE did not ignore problems facing Gorbachev or their seriousness and complexity; rather it judged that, based on his track record to date, he would persevere. It also offered an alternative scenario, which it deemed "less likely," in which Gorbachev might use force to hold the country together.

---

[29] Baker, *The Politics of Diplomacy*, p. 78.

Deputy Director for Intelligence John Helgerson argued in CIA's dissent to the NIE that, even assuming Gorbachev were able to avoid a crackdown, he would still be faced with increasing instability and unrest. Helgerson added that

> . . . we believe there is a significant chance that Gorbachev, during the period of this Estimate, will progressively lose control of events. The personal political strength he has accumulated is likely to erode, and his political position will be severely tested.
>
> The essence of the Soviet crisis is that neither the political system Gorbachev is attempting to change nor the emergent system he is fostering is likely to cope effectively with newly mobilized popular demands and the deepening economic crisis.

The dissent concluded that Gorbachev would have to give up his "still authoritarian vision in favor of a truly democratic one, or recognize his vision as unreachable and try to backtrack from democratization." In contrast to the Community consensus, CIA believed that, come what may, *perestroika* was *"certain to make the next few years some of the most turbulent and destabilizing in Soviet history"* [emphasis in original].

It was not easy for CIA to take such a pessimistic view of Gorbachev's future in late 1989. Many in the West euphorically considered him the only hope for ending the Cold War. "Gorbymania" had become a worldwide phenomenon. Polls in Europe showed that Gorbachev's popularity exceeded that of any Western leader of the 20th century. *Time* chose him Man of the Decade, and he received the Nobel Peace Prize for 1990—a token of the West's gratitude for his helping to end the Cold War. Critical assessments in the media and the scholarly journals were rare.

By late 1989 the Bush administration had reached a consensus on Gorbachev and US policy goals. First, Gorbachev was for real; one could "do business with him," as British Prime Minister Thatcher had once put it. Second, the United States should pursue two agendas—one bilateral and focused on issues of mutual concern such as arms control, regional conflicts, and economic assistance; and the other unilateral, aimed at reducing the Soviet presence in Eastern Europe and unifying the two Germanys inside NATO. The administration had doubts about Gorbachev's staying power but saw this uncertainty as a reason to move quickly rather than to wait. The Soviet leader was seen as offering concessions ("moving in our direction" per Scowcroft) because he needed to stabilize the international sector in order to concentrate on the home front. His successor might not be so inclined. The goal of US policy therefore was to lock in as many agreements as possible that would endure even if a change of leadership occurred.

Some in the White House began to think outside the box, wrestling with the implications of Gorbachev's paradoxical role as both the would-be savior and the potential destroyer of the Soviet system. On the one hand, Gorbachev's determination to end the Cold War and restructure the Soviet system appeared to make possible even more dramatic progress "across the entire US-Soviet agenda." Scowcroft credits NSC Soviet affairs director Condoleezza Rice with this idea. "It was," he notes, "both an ambitious goal and a distinct and positive departure for US policy."[30] On the other hand, pessimism inspired the NSC to begin considering a future without Gorbachev and the Soviet Union as it was then constituted. Thus, according to Scowcroft's deputy, Robert M. Gates, the CIA's and the Intelligence Community's pessimistic assessment inspired the creation of a secret "contingency planning group," chaired by Rice, to study the implications of a Soviet collapse.[31] Washington, it seemed, was in the advantageous position of hoping for the best while being able to prepare for the worst.

The first Bush-Gorbachev summit, held at Malta on 2-3 December 1989, permitted President Bush to use what Sir Michael Howard calls his "genius for friendship" and "most important of all his friendship with Mikhail Gorbachev" to advance US and Western interests.[32] ("I *liked* him," the President later wrote of Gorbachev.[33]) At Malta, Secretary Baker noted, the "relationship became human and personal, and through the spring of 1990, as we worked to bring a unified Germany into NATO, the President's personal relationship with Gorbachev was critical."[34] According to Scowcroft, it was a "good start," and President Bush noted that the summit "made me confident that Gorbachev was sincere in his efforts to match his words with actions."[35] The so-called shipboard summit opened the way for the successful conclusion of the Conventional Forces in Europe (CFE) Treaty in 1990 and the Strategic Arms Reduction Talks (START) in 1991. Gorbachev's press spokesman declared: "We buried the Cold War at the bottom of the Mediterranean." Back in the USSR, however, the diehards were trying to resuscitate it.

As 1990 opened, Shevardnadze's aide, Sergei Tarasenko, said that Gorbachev and Shevardnadze felt that they had "to accomplish a huge

---

[30] Bush and Scowcroft, *A World Transformed*, p. 41.

[31] "CIA and the Cold War," an address by DCI Robert M. Gates at the University of Oklahoma, International Program Center, 12 September 1997.

[32] Michael Howard, "The Prudence Thing: George Bush's Class Act," *Foreign Affairs* 77:6 (November/December 1998), p. 131.

[33] Bush and Scowcroft, *A World Transformed*, p. iv.

[34] Baker, *The Politics of Diplomacy*, p. 170.

[35] Bush and Scowcroft, *A World Transformed*, pp. 205, 207.

maneuver without losing time." The USSR was in "free fall," and its "superpower status would go up in smoke unless it was reaffirmed by the Americans." They hoped to reach "some kind of plateau that would give us time to catch our breath and look around."[36]

The Bush administration was "cautiously optimistic" at first. National security adviser Scowcroft thought that 1990 might be the year in which "we could achieve a fundamental shift in the strategic balance."[37] (He was right.) The United States would continue to recognize the USSR as a superpower but less out of respect for its strength than for concern over the security implications of its weakness. As Secretary Baker put it, the task of US policy now was to create a "soft landing" for a collapsing empire.

1990 was the year in which the CFE Treaty, signed in November, changed the military face of the Warsaw Pact forever.[38] A series of NIEs and NIC memoranda that appeared during 1989 and early 1990 predicted the strategic implications of political and military changes in Eastern Europe—changes that transformed the geopolitics of the Cold War.[39] By now the implications of the 1989 Velvet Revolution in Eastern Europe were clear. In April 1990, NIE 12-90, *The Future of Eastern Europe*, (Document 9), stated flatly that "Communist rule in Eastern Europe is finished, and it will not be revived." It added: "The Warsaw Pact as a military alliance is essentially dead, and Soviet efforts to convert it into a political alliance will ultimately fail."

The strategic implications for the Pact as well as for NATO were profound. NIE 11-14-89, *Trends and Developments in Warsaw Pact Theater Forces and Doctrine Through the 1990s,* February 1989 (Document 16), measured the most significant change in Soviet general purpose forces since Khrushchev's 1960 announcement of a 30-percent

---

[36] Michael R. Beschloss and Strobe Talbott, *At the Highest Levels: The Inside Story of the End of the Cold War* (Boston: Little, Brown, and Company, 1993), p. 152.

[37] Bush and Scowcroft, *A World Transformed*, p. 205.

[38] The CFE talks began on 9 March 1989; an agreement was signed in Paris on 19 November 1990. The talks, which included all 23 members of the two alliances, were held under the auspices of the Conference on Security and Co-operation in Europe. The treaty set limits on five categories of weapons, including tanks, armored combat vehicles, artillery pieces, combat aircraft, and helicopters. In May 1989, the USSR accepted NATO's proposal for equal force ceilings, which meant that the Warsaw Pact would have to destroy far more weapons than NATO.

[39] NIC M 89-10002, *The Post-CFE Environment in Europe*, September 1989 (Document 18); NIC M 89-10003, *Status of Soviet Unilateral Withdrawals*, October 1989 (Document 19); and NIC M 89-10005, *Soviet Theater Forces in 1991: The Impact of the Unilateral Withdrawals on Structure and Capabilities,* November 1989 (Document 20).

reduction of the Soviet army.[40] Based on an assessment of planned reductions in force levels, defense spending, and military procurement, the Estimate concluded that a 25-year period of continuous growth in Soviet ground forces had ended, that reductions beyond those already announced were possible, and that a "resumption of growth . . . [is] highly unlikely before the turn of the century." The result: a "drastic alteration in our forecast of future . . . forces," since trends, including reductions in force levels and in defense spending and defense production levels, necessitated by *perestroika*, were beginning to diverge sharply from existing force development trends. Nevertheless: "For the period of this Estimate, Warsaw Pact forces . . . will remain the largest aggregation of military power in the world, and the Soviets will remain committed to the offensive as the preferred form of operations in wartime." (Billboards in Moscow still proclaimed: "The Main Goal of *Perestroika* Is To Strengthen Military Preparedness!"[41])

But the impact of the cuts was already making itself felt. In 1985, for example, the Intelligence Community had estimated that the Pact logistic structure in Central Europe could support an offensive against NATO for 60 to 90 days. By 1989, that Estimate was reduced to 30 to 45 days, on the assumption that NATO could hold Pact forces at bay for at least two weeks. This, in turn, affected one of the most critical intelligence issues, warning of war or surprise attack by the opposing side. *Warning of War in Europe: Changing Warsaw Pact Planning and Forces*, M/H NIE 4-1-84, September 1989 (Document 17) concluded that:

> The warning time we associate with possible Warsaw Pact preparations for war with NATO in Central Europe have increased significantly from those set forth in 1984 . . . . We should be able to provide about four to five weeks of warning [of the four-front attack that Warsaw Pact planners would prefer].

A NIC memorandum, NIC M 90-10002, *The Direction of Change in the Warsaw Pact*, April 1990 (Document 21) concluded that:

> Recent political events in Eastern Europe will further erode Soviet confidence in their allies. Moscow can *not* rely upon non-Soviet Warsaw Pact forces; it must question its ability to bring Soviet reinforcements through East European countries whose hostility is no longer disguised or held in check [emphasis in original].

---

[40] As one reason for doing so, Khrushchev cited the USSR's increasing reliance on strategic nuclear weapons, in particular on intercontinental ballistic missiles (ICBMs). At the time, the USSR had only four operational ICBMs.

[41] Stephan Sestanovich, "Did the West Undo the East?" *National Interest* 31 (Spring 1993), p. 29.

The NIC stated that, in light of the scheduled unilateral withdrawals, "We now believe that the capability to conduct an unreinforced conventional Pact attack on NATO would be virtually eliminated." If pending CFE cuts were taken into account, then Pact forces would be incapable of conducting a "theater strategic offensive *even after full mobilization of reserves and deployment of standing forces within the Atlantic-to-the-Urals (ATTU) Zone*" [emphasis in original]. Eastern Europe, in effect, had been eliminated as a staging area or buffer zone in Soviet military plans.

Many consider the Soviet Union's sudden about-face on German unification in mid-1990 a surprise, a miracle, or a mystery that still eludes a convincing explanation.[42] An inter-agency assessment issued in February 1990, for example, did not even consider the possibility of unification, though an April 1990 Estimate anticipated the impact of a united Germany on Eastern Europe (see Document 9). When asked why Moscow surrendered its most strategically significant dependency without a fight, the Central Committee's Valentin Falin, answered: "We are still waiting for the answer to that from Gorbachev. . . . He confided in no one."[43] Of all Gorbachev's decisions, this was the most fateful.[44]

The decisive moment came at the White House on 31 May 1990 during the second Soviet-American summit, when Gorbachev unexpectedly agreed that in principle the Germans had the right to decide their own future. In his memoirs, Gorbachev claims credit for the idea, but it actually resulted from prodding by President Bush over the preceding months. When the President asked whether the Germans had a right to choose their own alliance, Gorbachev unexpectedly agreed.[45] "I could

---

[42] Wisla Suraska, *How the Soviet Union Disappeared: An Essay on the Causes of Dissolution* (Durham: Duke University Press, 1999), p. 83.

[43] Pryce-Jones, *The Strange Death of the Soviet Empire*, p. 292.

[44] According to Suraska:
> The unification of the two Germanies was the most important event shaping international relations in the second half of the twentieth century. The Soviet Union's dissolution can be considered its most immediate geopolitical consequence; the Soviet loss of a key strategic position in Europe triggered the process of territorial retrenchment, pushing the range of Moscow's domination back to the East. Suraska, *How the Soviet Union Disappeared*, p. 83.

[45] For accounts of the White House session, see Bush and Scowcroft, *A World Transformed*, p. 282; and Baker, *The Politics of Diplomacy*, pp. 252-253.

scarcely believe what I was witnessing, let alone figure what to make of it," Scowcroft wrote later.[46] Gorbachev's inadvertent concession—the biggest he would ever make—set off a "firestorm" within his delegation. When Gorbachev tried to pass the buck to Shevardnadze, he refused, handing it back to his boss.

It was West German Chancellor Helmut Kohl, however, who finally nailed down Gorbachev's concession. Kohl was reportedly stunned, when, during a *tête-à-tête* with Gorbachev in the Caucasian village of Arkyhz in mid-July 1990, the Soviet leader dropped all conditions on German unification and NATO membership. As Secretary Baker recalled, it was "too good to be true." German unification was a result of *perestroika*, the collapse of the East German economy, and "George Bush's determination to make German unity one of the crowning achievements of his presidency."[47] President Bush, according to Scowcroft, was the first inside the administration and the first Western leader "to back reunification unequivocally . . . a point Kohl never forgot."[48]

The Empire Strikes Back

For the West, these dramatic changes signified a big reduction—if not the elimination—of the Soviet military threat in Europe. For diehard Soviet opponents of the Gorbachev-Shevardnadze foreign policy line, however, they were disastrous. Soviet compromises, or "blunders" as the diehards called them, had destroyed the political, geostrategic, and material basis of Soviet security in Europe and altered the balance of power. "We have lost virtually all our allies. The lines of our defense have been moved directly to the lines of our state borders," complained one critic.[49] In Washington, NSC staffers wondered how far Gorbachev could retreat before crossing some invisible line that would force him to turn back to the right or risk being overthrown. Now it seemed, he was close to or already over that line.

The collapse of communist power in Eastern Europe was a windfall for the United States, especially in the military-strategic area. But the consequences were also ironic. As much as the East Europeans had hated

---

[46] Bush and Scowcroft, *A World Transformed*, p. 282.

[47] Martin McCauley, *Gorbachev* (London: Longman, 1998), p. 197.

[48] Bush and Scowcroft, *A World Transformed*, p. 188.

[49] USSR People's Deputies N. S. Petrushenko, V I. Alksnis, and Ye. V. Kogan, "We Cannot Interpret This as an Accomplishment of Our Foreign Policy," *Literaturnaya Rossiya*, 12 November 1990, pp. 18-19.

the political-military alliance system Moscow had imposed on them, it had the virtue of keeping ethnic and other destructive tendencies in check. Now things were far less certain. The withdrawal of Soviet troops placed a tremendous burden on the already strained domestic economy, where there were neither jobs nor housing for those being mustered out. The Soviet Army's presence in Eastern Europe and especially East Germany was a symbolic and tangible reminder of its victory in World War II, and now the troops were returning home without having been defeated in battle.[50] Foreign Minister Aleksandr Bessmertnykh, a former ambassador to the United States and Shevardnadze's successor who would side with the diehards during the August 1991 coup, said simply that the decision to let Germany unite and join NATO was "one of the most hated developments in the history of Soviet foreign policy, and it will remain so for decades."[51]

The Bush administration now had to worry about too much rather than too little success in wresting concessions from Moscow. Gorbachev needed "face and standing," President Bush said, especially as everything around him—the empire, the economy, and the Soviet Union itself—was "falling to pieces."[52] Summing up the past year, NIE 11-18-90, *The Deepening Crisis in the USSR: Prospects for the Next Year*, November 1990 (Document 4), stated flatly that the "old communist order is in its death throes" and that the crisis of *perestroika* was now threatening "to tear the country apart." Gorbachev had even become the target of popular anger and ridicule. (Even though it was still considered impermissible to attack him by name in the media, Soviet citizens in Red Square jeered him off the Lenin Mausoleum reviewing stand during the traditional May Day parade.) The NIE added: "No end to the Soviet domestic crisis is in sight, and there is a strong probability that the situation will get worse—perhaps much worse—during the next year." The NIE overestimated the extent to which poor economic performance would result in "serious societal unrest and breakdown of political authority"—as did most of its predecessors—but it also identified Boris Yel'tsin in the Russian republic as a rising figure to watch.

NIE 11-18-90 was as remarkable for its candor as for its dire predictions:

> In such a volatile atmosphere, events could go in any number of directions. Because of this, the Intelligence Community's uncertainties about the future of the Soviet system are greater today than at any time in the 40 years we have been producing Estimates on the USSR. Accordingly, our projections for the next year will be highly tentative.

---

[50] See Dobrynin, *In Confidence*, pp. 626-627.

[51] Beschloss and Talbott, *At the Highest Levels*, p. 240.

[52] Bush and Scowcroft, *A World Transformed*, p. 276.

The Estimate envisioned four possible scenarios for the coming year: deterioration short of anarchy; anarchy; military intervention; and "light at the end of the tunnel." It concluded that the first scenario was the most likely, followed by scenario four, i.e., more muddling through without a breakdown of law and order and without resolving the crisis. Scenarios two and three, though less likely, were still possible and would pose the most problems for US-Soviet relations and US efforts to end the Cold War through negotiated compromises.

For the United States, 1990 was a spectacularly successful year. The Bush administration had accomplished most of the goals it had set for both its unilateral and bilateral agendas either through negotiations with Moscow or as a result of the collapse of the Soviet empire in Eastern Europe. For Moscow, however, it had been a disaster—"one of the most difficult years in our history," Gorbachev lamented in the traditional New Year's address. But 1991 would be worse—the year the USSR entered its death spiral.

The implications for US-Soviet relations were obvious to observers on both sides. Scowcroft observed as early as March 1991: "After so much rapid progress, the window of opportunity appeared to be closing. It was time to consolidate our gains."[53] Or as Baker put it, "The stock market was heading south; it was time to sell."[54] Pro-Gorbachev reformers in the Soviet Union took a remarkably similar view. Wrote senior *Izvestiya* commentator and pro-reformer Aleksandr Bovin:

> If you look at the Soviet Union through the eyes of an "average" US observer, you get the following picture. A dangerously ailing, weakening giant. Refusal to take medicine based on democratic prescriptions is rendering the situation virtually hopeless. . . . Gorbachev has fallen hostage to conservatives of yesteryear who are sharply criticizing his "pan-human" approaches to foreign policy and his "pro-US" foreign policy course. . . . The White House in general is being advised to return to the "pre-Malta era" and play a waiting game rather than submitting new initiatives and to be more energetic, despite Moscow's dissatisfaction, in working with the republics. [In these circumstances] the maximum we can aim for [in US-

---

[53] *Ibid.*, p. 500.

[54] Baker, *The Politics of Diplomacy*, p. 478.

Soviet relations] is not to slide backwards and to hang on to the things we have already agreed on.[55]

Open attacks in the Soviet Union on "Shevardnadze's foreign policy" began in October 1990—everyone understood that critics really meant Gorbachev—and continued to escalate during the next year. (Shevardnadze resigned in December, warning of an approaching dictatorship.) Spearheading the attack was a new parliamentary group called *Soyuz* ("Union"), an unlikely alliance of communists, nationalists, and even monarchists united by "Soviet patriotism" and a common desire to preserve the empire at all costs.

The two most vocal critics were Col. Nikolay Petrushensko and Lt. Col. Viktor Alksnis. They were Russian *pieds-noirs* not unlike the French Algerian settlers who brought down the French Fourth Republic and later plotted against President Charles de Gaulle. Petrushenko is a Russianized Belorussian from Kazakhstan, and Alksnis is a Russianized Latvian born in Siberia.[56] (The reform press dubbed the duo the "black colonels" *apropos* of their nationalistic and chauvinistic views.) They spoke for the millions of ethnic Russians living outside historic Russian lands who now feared that, with rising nationalist and separatist sentiments and acts of violence directed at Russians, power would devolve from the center to the republics, leaving them to the tender mercies of national minorities who considered them alien occupiers. *Soyuz* and the colonels were given to apocalyptic visions and supported the idea of martial law—by constitutional decree if possible or by force if necessary. Thus, Alksnis in December 1990:

> I would compare the present situation to October 1941 near Moscow [when the German army had reached the suburbs]. There is nowhere to retreat further. We are faced with a catastrophe—economic, political, and

---

[55] Aleksandr Bovin, "Political Observer's Opinion: Time Out?", *Izvestiya*, 28 March 1991, p. 4. In late 1991 Gorbachev appointed Bovin ambassador to Israel, after restoring diplomatic ties that had been severed in 1967. As the USSR began disintegrating, the United States expanded its political contacts, both with "opposition" leaders such as Yelt'sin in Moscow and with republic officials. By late 1992, it was clear that Gorbachev's days were over, and power had devolved to the republic and local level. See Baker, *The Politics of Diplomacy*, pp. 472, 531.

[56] Alksnis's uncle was commander of the Red Air Force in 1938, when Stalin ordered his execution as part of the purge of the Soviet military establishment on the eve of World War II.

interethnic. And this is explained largely by the mistakes of the country's leadership.[57]

Western observers tended to dismiss *Soyuz* as a fringe group with little clout. But it wasn't.[58] It had some 560 adherents in the Supreme Soviet, and, in alliance with the Communist delegates, represented the overwhelming majority (700 plus) of members of parliament. More important, *Soyuz* was a mouthpiece for diehards in the party, the military, and the military-industrial complex. As one pro-reform journalist put it, as "amorphous though *Soyuz* is," the real power behind it was the "imperialist-militarist circles connected to the military-industrial complex, the conservative section of the party apparatus, and the national-patriots."[59] The "black colonels" were perfectly representative in this regard. Petrushenko was a *zampolit*, one of 80,000 political officers engaged in *agitprop* work in the armed forces, and Alksnis was an engineer assigned to an aircraft maintenance facility.

Soyuz's rise paralleled the resurgence in 1990 of the armed forces and the military-industrial complex and their increased influence on US-Soviet relations in general and arms control negotiations in particular. In 1988, when challenged from the right, Gorbachev had lurched leftward. In 1990, he moved in the opposite direction. Gavrill Popov, the radical reform Mayor of Moscow, said that after Gorbachev returned from his summer home at Foros in the Crimea in August 1990, the "*apparat* resumed pressing him every day. Mainly it was the military-industrial complex, which gave him an ultimatum. Gorbachev didn't desire a confrontation."[60] Gorbachev himself admitted as much in an off-the-record interview as he was preparing to resign:

> [In June 1990], it would have seemed natural to conclude an alliance with the democratic forces inside and outside the party and to wage a final battle against the reactionaries. And this would have been, in fact, reasonable from a strategic point; but not from a tactical one. It was too soon. The

---

[57] Yemelin, "The Army and Politics," *Literaturnaya Rossiya,* 14 December 1990, p. 8

[58] Gorbachev took Alksnis seriously enough to order a KGB tap on his office phone. See "Direct Line: Deputy's Request by Viktor Alksnis," in *Krasnaya Zvezda,* 27 December 1992, p. 3.

[59] A. Kiva, "'Union' of Obsessives: Political Portrait of a Deputies Group Aspiring to a Serious Social Role," *Izvestiya*, 12 May 1991, p. 3.

[60] Interview with Moscow City Soviet Chairman Gavrill Popov by Yegor Yakovlev, "The Times are Getting Tougher," *Moscow News*, 28 October–4 November, 1991, p.7.

balance of forces in the Politburo and the Central Committee was not good. The military-industrial complex was still too strong.[61]

The diehards put the brakes on arms talks, citing both political and "technical" reasons, and threatened to re-open or even unilaterally circumvent both the INF and CFE treaties. The Soviets also demanded revisions and changes in the draft version of the START agreement. US officials noted that all negotiating teams now included senior military officers and defense industry representatives, and, in Moscow, arms proposals were reviewed by committees that included members representing the corporate interests of the military-industrial complex.[62]

The diehards attacked Gorbachev's policy on both conceptual and practical grounds as a surrender to the United States and a sellout of Soviet interests. His commitment to "pan-human interests" and a "common European home," for example, were derided for undermining the *raison d'être* of the state and the military establishment—hostility toward the West and expansion of Soviet power and influence. Virtually every compromise, concession, and negotiated agreement Gorbachev and Shevardnadze had made to jump-start détente came under fire, ranging from destruction of the SS-23 missile[63] to dismantling of the Krasnoyarsk radar[64] to even minor accords, such as the US-Soviet Bering Strait agreement on demarcation of national boundaries.[65]

---

[61] Andrei S. Grachev, *Final Days: The Inside Story of the Collapse of the Soviet Union* (Boulder, CO: Westview Press/A Division of HarperCollins Publishers, 1995), p. 170.

[62] *Ibid.*, pp. 26-27.

[63] Gorbachev and Shevardnadze agreed to destroy all SS-23 short-range missiles—even though the terms of the INF Treaty did not require them to do so—without consulting with the Ministry of Defense.

[64] In 1988, when the Reagan administration complained that a large, phased-array radar located near Krasnoyarsk (Siberia) violated the 1972 US-Soviet ABM Treaty, the Soviet military denied the US charge, falsely claiming that the radar's sole purpose was to track artificial Earth satellites and other space objects. Shevardnadze's 1989 decision to admit the truth made him an enemy of the military establishment, which considered the decision to dismantle the radar as capitulation to the United States and a threat to Soviet security.

[65] Diehards claimed that the Kremlin had made unacceptable territorial and economic concessions by accepting the new demarcation line.

President Bush's Open Skies proposal, made in May 1989, was condemned for allegedly permitting the United States to monitor Soviet foreign economic activity and economic "potential," i.e., weaknesses.[66]

More sinister allegations followed. *Soyuz* representatives and even KGB chief Vladimir Kryuchkov charged that the *perestroishchiki* were in fact agents of influence recruited by Western intelligence in the 1970s to destroy the USSR from within, that Shevardnadze had received subsidies disguised as royalties and speaking fees for his pro-US policy, and that the United States intended to Balkanize the Soviet Union by fomenting secession.[67]

The diehards drew several conclusions from the events of 1989-1990. They saw that *perestroika* in Eastern Europe had not led to communism's reform but its rejection, jeopardizing their own future. Then there was the boomerang effect in the USSR. Gorbachev, an ethnic Russian, seemed oblivious to it, but Shevardnadze and Tarasenko, both ethnic minorities, were not. When Solidarity defeated its Polish communist opponents at the polls in June 1989, they immediately realized

> [t]hat inevitably we will lose our allies—the Warsaw Pact. These countries will go their own ways. And we even acknowledged between ourselves that the Soviet Union would not manage to survive. The logic of events would force the breakup of the Soviet Union, specifically the Baltics....[68]

With the Baltic republics in ferment and civil wars being fought in the Transcaucasus, the diehards had more to worry about than just their loss of allies in Eastern Europe. This is why they eventually resorted to force in Lithuania and Latvia, a move that was intended to reassert Moscow's

---

[66] President Dwight Eisenhower made the original proposal in 1955; Khrushchev rejected it. President Bush revived Open Skies in his 1989 Texas A&M speech. His plan called for surveillance overflights of unarmed aircraft over the United States and the USSR to monitor compliance with arms control treaties and military developments. In 1992, the sixteen NATO countries, all members of the former Warsaw Pact, and Russia, Ukraine, and Belarus signed an agreement permitting 42 surveillance overflights per year by aircraft equipped with photographic and electronic intelligence collection gear.

[67] Kryuchkov made his allegations about agents of influence during a closed session of the Supreme Soviet, but the KGB leaked a tape of his remarks to the Leningrad television program "600 Seconds." See Sergei Roy, "The Crash of an Empire," *Moscow News*, 7 April 1999, p. 4.

[68] William C. Wohlforth, ed., *Witnesses to the End of the Cold War* (Baltimore: The Johns Hopkins Press, 1996), p. 113.

National Intelligence and the Soviet Economy

The US Intelligence Community and CIA in particular made a sustained effort, beginning in the 1950s, to gauge the strength and growth of the Soviet economy. CIA began reporting on declining growth rates in the 1960s and analyzing their implications in Estimates. That effort continued, with mixed but mostly positive results, until the USSR disintegrated. The Intelligence Community recorded the Soviet economy's stagnation and decline in the 1980s, and anticipated the failures of *perestroika* and the break-up of the USSR in a timely and accurate manner, even though the message was not always welcome.[a]

The NIEs and SNIEs reprinted here pay heed to economic factors in the Soviet collapse without putting them at the center of the story. Most—certainly not all—Western and Russian experts agree that Gorbachev's reforms caused the economy to collapse, not the other way round.[b] When Gorbachev took office, the economy was stagnant—though not in crisis—and most observers expected it to "muddle through" for at least another decade or two. As one former Soviet economist put it: "This 'economic' explanation [of collapse] . . . is, at best, incomplete. Poor economic performance is commonplace in the world, while the peacetime collapse of a political system is quite rare."[c]

Finally, two ironies. First, in the 1970s, Soviet economists told their leadership that the final stage of the "crisis of capitalism" had begun. Leonid Brezhnev's belief that "capitalism is a society without a future" led him to step up the arms race and expand Soviet influence in the Third World—to give history a push in the direction he believed it was headed.[d] That, not Gorbachev's *perestroika*, was the real beginning of the final decline. Second, the Central Committee regularly translated (and then classified) published CIA studies of the Soviet economy, especially those studies on growth rates and defense spending.[e] In one case, a CIA study on the petroleum industry may have led the Soviet leadership to change an economic policy headed for disaster. One is left wondering what would have happened if Soviet leaders had taken more CIA studies to heart.

---

[a] Bruce D. Berkowitz and Jeffrey T. Richelson, "The CIA Vindicated," *National Interest* 41 (Fall 1995), pp. 36-47.

[b] See, for example, Myron Rush, "Fortune and Fate," *National Interest* 31(Spring 1993), pp. 19-25; Vladimir Kantorovich, "The Economic Fallacy, in *Ibid.*, pp. 35-45; and Lilla Shestsov, "Was the Collapse of the Soviet Union Inevitable?", in Anne de Tinguy, *The Fall of the Soviet Empire* (Boulder, CO: East European Monographs/Distributed by Columbia University Press, 1997), p. 76.

[c] Kantorovich, "The Economic Fallacy," p. 36.

[d] Richard B. Day, *Cold War Capitalism: The View from Moscow 1945-1975* (Armonk, NY: M.E. Sharpe, 1995), p. 275.

[e] Vladimir G. Treml, *Censorship, Access, and Influence: Western Sovietology in the Soviet Union* (Berkeley: The University of California at Berkeley, 1999), pp. 36-37.

imperial domination while destroying *perestroika* and derailing détente with the United States. Indeed, Washington felt torn between its support for Baltic independence and the overriding objective of ending the Cold War, which now meant keeping Gorbachev in power at almost any price. Lithuania's demand in January 1990 for immediate independence briefly imperiled the second Bush-Gorbachev summit and German unification. Gorbachev's decision in April 1990 to halt oil and natural gas deliveries to the Baltic republic cost him rapid Congressional action on Most-Favored-Nation trade status and an opportunity to address Congress during the Washington summit the next month. (Lithuania and then Latvia would cast even bigger shadows over relations in January 1991, when Soviet paratroops and the elite KGB Alfa detachment—plus the so-called OMON or Black Berets[69]—assaulted and killed peaceful demonstrators.)

The Persian Gulf crisis was the last straw for the diehards. US-Soviet joint opposition to Iraq's occupation of Kuwait was heralded in Washington as the first test of a new post–Cold War relationship (the so-called "new world order"). Secretary Baker visited Moscow after the 1991 war specifically to salute Gorbachev and the Soviet government for their support, but Soviet policy was anathema to the diehards and many Soviet citizens.[70] (It is not accidental that Shevardnadze had resigned in December 1990 just three weeks after endorsing UN Resolution 678, which called for using "all necessary measures" to force Iraq out of Kuwait.) *Sovetskaya Rossiya*, one of *Soyuz*'s favorite press outlets, asserted that cooperation with the United States "had ended the USSR's existence as superpower."[71] According to the diehards, the Kremlin had betrayed the USSR's traditional Arab allies, insulted its 50 million Muslim citizens in Central Asia, allowed the United States to deploy substantial military forces within 700 miles of the USSR's southern borders, and served US oil companies while ignoring Soviet state interests.[72]

---

[69] Special detachment militia units of the Interior Ministry. In this case, the OMON squads were composed of renegade ethnic Russians and Poles from the Latvian Interior Ministry.

[70] In his memoirs, however, the former Secretary of State noted that "once the air war began in January 1991, Soviet efforts to avoid a ground war became without question our greatest political impediment." Baker, *The Politics of Diplomacy*, p. 396.

[71] Cited in Beschloss and Talbot, *At the Highest Levels*, p. 334.

[72] Teresa Cherfas, "Iron Man," *New Statesman* (London), 5 April 1991, p. 12.

The Soviet military establishment was even more disturbed. The US-led war had destroyed much of the Soviet advanced weaponry sold to Saddam Husayn over the previous decade, making Moscow a silent partner in Baghdad's humiliation. As the chief of the Soviet General Staff noted, the Gulf campaign was in effect a US testing ground for weapons that would eventually be aimed at the Soviet Union.[73] The Soviet military withdrawal from Eastern Europe and the CFE Treaty had added insult to injury moreover, by making it possible for the United States to redeploy troops, armor, and matériel from Germany to the Middle East for Operation Desert Storm. Most important, as Defense Minister Dmitri Yazov concluded, the Gulf war and the CFE Treaty taken together signified a basic shift in the "correlation of forces" between the NATO and the USSR in the West's favor—a dangerous situation if Gorbachev's revised threat assessment of Western intentions was wrong (something of which Yazov was firmly convinced.[74]) The "new world order" Washington was talking about was really "American command in the world arena," in the diehards' eyes.

Even professional diplomats, who had supported *perestroika* at first, turned on Gorbachev, suggesting that by 1991 a broad section of the Soviet establishment—those who were oriented toward saving the USSR and its superpower status without sharing more extreme views—no longer supported official policy. Some of the bitterest attacks on Gorbachev appear in memoirs written later by Georgy Kornienko, formerly number two in the Foreign Ministry, who considered Soviet cooperation with the United States during the Gulf crisis "craven."[75] Even former Ambassador Dobrynin, whom Gorbachev used as a special envoy to President Bush on several occasions, was angry and resentful:

> The Soviet Union that Gorbachev inherited in 1985 was a global power, perhaps somewhat tarnished in that image, but still strong and united and

---

[73] For more than a decade, some senior military officers had been warning of the need to develop new hi-tech conventional weapons in emulation of the US before it was too late. Now, their worst nightmare had come true, since the Gulf war had been a one-on-one engagement of US and Soviet weaponry, and it was clear who had won.

[74] USSR Defense Minister Marshal of the Soviet Union D. Yazov, "Greatness of the People's Feat: Victory, Memory and Truth," *Pravda*, 9 May 1991, p. 3.

[75] See G. M. Kornienko, *Kholodnaia voina: svidetel'stvo ee uchastnika* (Moscow: Mezhdunarodnyee Otnosehniya, 1995), especially Chapter x.

one of the world's two superpowers. But in just three years, from 1989 to 1991, the political frontiers of the European continent were effectively rolled eastward to the Russian borders of 1653, which were those before Russia's union with the Ukraine.[76]

The Soviet diehards blamed the loss of superpower status on Gorbachev's and Shevardnadze's "blunders" and give-away foreign policy. The *perestroishchiki* countered that it was not foreign policy but the "universal crisis of socialism" that had undermined the USSR. Tempers flared as the domestic situation worsened in the Soviet Union.

The Empire Collapses

The most prescient assessment of the late Gorbachev period was a CIA/SOVA "typescript," an informal rather than fully coordinated assessment prepared at the request of the National Security Council (Document 5). "The Soviet Cauldron," completed on 25 April 1991, anticipated that "anti-Communist forces are breaking down the Soviet empire and system of governance" and laid out conditions in which diehards would move to reassert control "with or without Gorbachev." It predicted, accurately, that a coup probably would fail. The authors analyzed the significance of Boris Yel'tsin's rise, predicting that he was about to become the first popularly elected leader in Russian history and would challenge the old order. This assessment was especially forward-leaning on the nationality question, seeing the drive for independence and separatism as the most immediate threat to the Union, especially in the Ukrainian, Belorussian, Georgian, and Baltic Republics. It played down the economic crisis as a determining factor, although it noted that the centrally planned economic system had

---

[76] Dobrynin, *In Confidence*, p. 615. The loss of empire had a profound effect on the diehards and many Soviet citizens of diverse political views. One experienced observer recently noted that during a 1994 symposium Russian participants tried to explain how:
> their deep sense of national pride in the Soviet Union as a superpower, equal in terms of military potential to the United States, served as psychological compensation for their material shortages and very low standard of living. Jan Nowak, "Russia: Isolation or Co-operation?", unpublished paper delivered to The Jamestown Foundation Conference, Washington, DC, 9-10 June 1999, p. 4.

broken down and was being replaced by a mixture of republic and local barter arrangements—adding to already strong centrifugal forces.[77]

The United States watched the summer's events with increasing concern. *Implications of Alternative Soviet Futures,* NIE 11-18-91, July 1991 (Document 6), the last in the series before the coup, began: "The USSR is in the midst of a revolution that probably will sweep the Communist Party from power and reshape the country within the five-year time frame of this Estimate." In fact, this would happen within the next six months—an incredible period that witnessed the outlawing of the Communist Party of the Soviet Union (CPSU), the break-up of the Soviet Union, the formation of the Commonwealth of Independent States, Gorbachev's resignation, and the triumph of Boris Yel'tsin. As in other cases, the tough part was not anticipating what would happen but when.

NIE 11-18-91 outlined four possible scenarios—chronic crisis; system change (with Gorbachev holding power in a more pluralistic and voluntary union of the republics); "chaotic and violent" fragmentation into many separate states; and regression (a coup)—without assigning probabilities. The authors did, however, agree that scenarios two and three were the most likely and that most propitious scenario for the West would be "system change." Fragmentation and repression would pose challenges to efforts to the end the Cold War, either because the United States would have to deal with several new states and a new kind of nuclear proliferation or because the ascendancy of hard-liners who would put the brakes on arms control and negotiations.

The August coup in the Soviet Union and the disintegration of the center posed new problems for the US Intelligence Community.[78] The first post-coup assessment was SNIE 11-18.2-91, *The Republics of the Former USSR: The Outlook for the Next Year*, September 1991

---

[77] According to one account, even though the NSC had requested the paper, it dismissed its conclusions as having a pro-Yel'tsin bias. Beschloss and Talbott, *At the Highest Levels*, p. 360. See also Berkowitz and Richelson, "The CIA Vindicated," p. 43. Gates notes that the paper clearly warned the White House that serious trouble was brewing but does not comment on its final impact. See Robert M. Gates, *From the Shadows: The Ultimate Insider's Story of Five Presidents and How They Won the Cold War* (New York: Simon & Schuster, 1996), p. 520.

[78] John M. Broder, "CIA Scrambles to Evaluate Breakaway Soviet Republics," *Los Angeles Times*, 12 December 1991, p. 14.

(Document 10). It concluded that the "USSR and its communist system are dead. What *ultimately* replaces them will not be known within the next year, but several trends are evident" [emphasis in original]. The SNIE then spelled out three possible scenarios for the post-Soviet future, including:

- One: Political and economic "confederation" in which the republics would coordinate economic, defense, and foreign policies, while continuing to pursue economic reform. Control over nuclear weapons would remain centralized, and the West could continue pursuing improved relations and arms control with the successor republics.

- Two: A "loose association" in which several key republics would break away but maintain a common market. Russia and several others would attempt to coordinate foreign and military policies, although a tendency to go it alone and pursue independent policies would prevail.

- Three: "Disintegration" and collapse of the center. Rising nationalism and continuing economic problems would pave the way for authoritarian governments in some republics. Republics would fight over operational control of nuclear weapons, and the threat of such weapons falling into terrorist hands would increase.

The SNIE concluded that the second scenario was the most likely and the third the least likely over the coming year—three months before the final breakup. It was right and wrong at the same time. Its authors did not envision the death of the USSR and the birth of 15 new countries, although it did project that Russia would play the leading role in whatever happened next and that—if Ukraine went its own way—it would change the equation even more. One reason the drafters may not have seen what was coming was their tendency to overestimate the impact of economic problems and underestimate the impact of resurgent nationalism. It also overlooked the Yel'tsin-Gorbachev duel as a factor motivating the Russian leader to finish off his rival by finishing off the USSR, Gorbachev's last power base.

"A Battle to the Death"

When Gorbachev finally lashed out at *Soyuz* and, by name, Alksnis and Petrushenko in mid-1991, he was really engaging proxies rather than principals. The "power ministers," Dmitri Yazov (defense), Boris Pugo (interior), and Vladimir Kryuchkov (KGB) as well as Gennadi Yanaev, his vice president, were the real threat, as became clear when they emerged as the ringleaders of the August coup. Gorbachev was not able to attack them openly not only because the ministers were his appointees but also because they were "his last remaining power base."[79] Avoiding a political shakeup on the eve of the G-7 summit in Paris, where Gorbachev hoped to obtain Western economic aid, was another consideration. In Moscow, Gorbachev had been their political hostage, but at Foros in August 1991 he became a real hostage. The coup plotters hoped to prevent the break-up of the Soviet empire by putting an end to the Novo-Ogarevo agreements for a new Union of Soviet Sovereign Republics, Gorbachev's last-ditch effort to keep the Soviet state intact as a confederation. (They also knew that Gorbachev was planning to replace them and hoped to keep their positions.[80])

Time was running out. The coup not only failed but produced the opposite of its intended effect, setting the stage for Yel'tsin's final blow of 8 December 1991 (the Minsk agreement), which finished off the USSR and created the Commonwealth of Independent States. The failure of the August coup decided the fate of the CPSU, the USSR, and, of course, Gorbachev and Yel'tsin. But the coup itself was not only about who would rule the USSR but it was also about the fate of the revolution and the empire. At stake was whether *perestroika* would succeed in creating a civil society, one that would live in peace with its own citizens and the rest of the world, or return to authoritarianism at home and Cold War abroad. The situation was, if anything, more polarized than most Western observers realized. As Bovin wrote: "All crucial fronts are now within the country. Either *perestroika* triumphs—and we create a democratic, open, economically efficient society—or we have the inevitable return to the 'cold war' and the arms race."[81] Gorbachev saw the situation in the same terms, describing his struggle with the anti-reform forces as a "battle to the death."[82] It was, but no one expected it to end in mutual annihilation.

Ironically, the arms control momentum continued even after the August coup. The Intelligence Community published the latest version of NIE 11-3/8, *Soviet Forces and Capabilities for Strategic Nuclear Conflict*

---

[79] See Roy, "The Crash of an Empire," p. 4.

[80] In April 1991, Gorbachev met with the leaders of nine Soviet republics and Boris Yel'tsin at Novo-Ogarevo, the Soviet version of Camp David, to draft a new treaty for a Union of Soviet Sovereign Republics. Gorbachev was forced to agree to the removal of the "power ministers" as the price of support from Boris Yel'tsin and the Kazakh republic leader for the Union treaty. The KGB head of his security detail had bugged the presidential dacha at Novo-Ogarevo and given the tapes to Kryuchkov. It was the impending approval of this treaty that prompted the hardliners to attempt to seize power and maintain the Soviet empire. See Boris Yel'tsin, *The Struggle for Russia* (New York: Random House, 1994), p. 39.

[81] Bovin, "Political Observer's Opinion: Time Out?"

[82] Grachev, *Final Days*, p. 170.

Through the Year 2000 (Document 23) in August 1991. NIE 11-3/8-91 noted that Soviet superpower status was more dependent than ever on nuclear weapons. (Even "liberal" commentator Bovin admitted that the "fact we can destroy the United States is kind of comforting and encouraging in the wake of the Gulf war."[83]) The Estimate predicted that that the USSR would retain and modernize "powerful, survivable forces through the next decade." For example, there were five strategic ballistic missiles in development as well as two land- and three sea-based missiles. Although the Soviet economy would be unable to support a sustained, across-the-board buildup comparable to the 1980s, even for strategic forces, there would be no appreciable impact on the production or deployment of such forces.

The good news, according to the Estimate drafters, was still the CFE Treaty, which, by reducing the risk of war in Europe, reduced the risk of nuclear war growing out of a conflict between the United States and the USSR. The Estimate nonetheless took a clear-eyed view of the new and disturbing nuclear realities in an empire facing implosion. The wild card was separatism. The center might lose control over nuclear-weapons production, R&D facilities, and test sites. The rebellious republics were withholding or reducing payments to Moscow, which portended problems affecting deployment and operation of strategic forces. Ballistic missile early warning was another issue: five of the eight early-warning radar sites were located outside the Russian Republic—one of the most important was in Latvia. Then there was the looming problem of central civilian control to prevent unauthorized use by renegade military officers or nationalists. NIE 11-3/8-91 gave Soviet security measures high marks, while adding that, in the event of a military coup, collapse of the central government, or civil war, all bets were off.

In September, President Bush announced his decision to remove or destroy all tactical nuclear weapons deployed in Europe and Asia and on US warships. He also canceled plans to deploy the mobile MX and Midgetman missiles. US bombers and missiles that were scheduled for destruction under START were taken off 24-hour alert status.[84] The

---

[83] Bovin, "Political Observer's Opinion: Time Out?"

[84] Presidents Bush and Gorbachev signed the START I Treaty during the Moscow summit of 29-31 July 1991. Gorbachev and Shevardnadze made three major concessions (over the objections of the military, the military-industrial complex, and some top diplomatic officials) to get an agreement. They agreed to complete a treaty without insisting on restrictions on the US anti-missile-defense program (Strategic Defense Initiative or SDI); they agreed to dismantle the Krasnoyarsk radar; and they accepted a 50-percent reduction in "heavy" SS-18 missiles—the backbone of the Soviet nuclear deterrent. The two sides agreed to reduce deployed strategic warheads to no more than 6,000 and launchers (missiles and bombers) to maximum of 1,600. The USSR also accepted a 50-percent reduction in throw weight for its intercontinental and sea-launched ballistic missiles.

President also called on the USSR to adopt additional arms control measures, including elimination of all land-based ICBMs with multiple warheads.

Gorbachev responded by announcing his intention to dismantle all tactical nuclear weapons. (See *Soviet Tactical Nuclear Forces and Gorbachev's Nuclear Pledges: Impact, Motivations, and Next Steps,* November 1991 (Document 15.) He described this as "racing downhill" with the United States in arms control. But it also was a race against time. As President Bush noted, the international security situation had changed for the better—especially with the elimination of the threat of surprise attack in Europe—and it was time to "seize the opportunity" to reduce nuclear weapons further and stabilize US and Soviet forces at lower levels.[85] But the subtext, on both sides, was the looming possibility of Soviet imperial implosion and the chance that terrorists or renegade military officers might seize nuclear, particularly tactical nuclear, weapons for use in local conflicts or civil wars. (The administration's worst fear was "Yugoslavia with nukes," a Soviet empire torn apart by civil war and descending into regionalism and warlordism.[86]) The United States (and Gorbachev and his supporters in the USSR) wanted to reach binding agreements while there was still a central political authority in the Kremlin.

The fate of the Soviet Union can be traced out in the title and content of NIE 11-18.3-91, November 1991 (Document 7), *Civil Disorder in the Former USSR: Can It Be Managed This Winter?* Some of the dire predictions had come true, and now the US Intelligence Community was rushing to assess the consequences—rather than the causes—of *perestroika's* failure. The impending death of the Soviet empire was raising a host of problems that exceeded the old imperial arrangements in their capacity for threatening to disrupt regional and international stability. Those problems—fragmentation of the armed forces, control over nuclear weapons and technology, ethnic tensions and open conflicts, food and fuel shortages, economic stagnation, and the high potential for domestic strife and even civil war—made some nostalgic for the empire. Nightmare scenarios, such as a clash between Russia and Ukraine, were considered. The pessimistic prediction of the "most significant civil disorder in the former USSR since the Bolsheviks consolidated power" fortunately did not happen. For once it was good to be wrong.

---

[85] The US and USSR agreed to even deeper reductions in their nuclear arsenals in the START II Treaty, which was signed with Russia in January 1993 but to date has not been ratified by the Duma.

[86] Baker, *The Politics of Diplomacy*, p. 562.

The Cold War Ends

American statesmanship, aided at times by perceptive Estimates, was instrumental in identifying and seizing an opportunity to end the Cold War and the arms race. Presidents Bush and Gorbachev grappled with the enormous issues of the day as well as the legacy of the past in an effort to change US-Soviet relations and, in the process, the postwar international system. They met three times at bilateral summits and twice at multilateral sessions.[87] In between, they kept up contact through correspondence and phone calls. Secretary Baker met more than 20 times with Foreign Minister Shevardnadze and worked closely with his successor. This intensively personal diplomatic activity produced numerous formal agreements and informal understandings that, in effect, led to the end of the Cold War. Most important, perhaps, was the tacit US-Soviet partnership that helped Gorbachev and Shevardnadze in downsizing the overly militarized Soviet state. Some have attributed the end of the Cold War to impersonal forces rather than skillful diplomacy or to luck rather than judgment, but the historical record reveals the main factor to have been a giant effort involving a handful of statesmen on both sides of the US-Soviet relationship and recorded in the agreements they reached.

Did the end of the Cold War entail the end of the Soviet system?[88] Or was it the other way around? It is possible to imagine a cold war without the USSR, but it is difficult to imagine a Soviet Union without the Cold War. "The Soviet empire was created and built for the arms race, confrontation, and even war with the rest of the world," according to civilian defense expert and Duma deputy Aleksey Arbatov.[89] As long as it existed, a return to the Cold War was still possible and perhaps inevitable.

The ultimate paradox was that détente rather than confrontation led to the collapse of Soviet power and the breakup of the Soviet Union. As soon as Gorbachev succeeded in gaining the West's trust in the later 1980s, he began undermining the Soviet system. That system, noted

---

[87] US and Soviet leaders held 16 bilateral summits from 1961 to 1991.

[88] Historian Eric Hobsbawm poses this question in *The Age of Extremes: A History of the World, 1914-1991* (New York: Pantheon, 1994), p. 250.

[89] Aleksey Arbatov, "The National Idea and National Security," *Mirovaya Ekonomika i Mezhdunarodnyye Otnosheniya*, 5 (May 1998), p. 8.

Gen. Dmitri Volkogonov, a reform-minded military officer and historian, "could exist only by watching its opponents through the cross hairs of a gunsight, only by digging deeper and stronger defenses, only by feverishly competing for military superiority."[90] Once the perceived Western military threat to Russia was eliminated or was redefined out of existence, the USSR's last remaining state purpose disappeared with it. The Cold War ended when the diehards finally realized that they could not revive it, and it became irreversible sometime between the August '91 coup and the December collapse. If the coup had not failed, or if a subsequent coup—better planned and better executed than the first—had succeeded, the diehards might well have been able to torpedo the new détente and restart the Cold War, as they almost succeeded in doing.

The Estimates and the End of the Cold War

An objective reading of the NIEs and other documents reprinted below refutes the allegation that readers of the intelligence assessments at the time of their publication would have come away misinformed about the direction of events and shape of policies in the Soviet Union. They also reject the idea that the Intelligence Community ignored the impending collapse of communism and breakup of the Soviet Union. In fact, the community was probably ahead of most analysis on this issue. The Estimates' focus on *perestroika* and *glasnost* as forces that would probably destroy rather than save the Soviet Union system tracks well with today's emerging scholarly consensus on the causes of the Soviet collapse.[91] While most of the world was still seeing Gorbachev as a miracle worker, the Estimates portrayed him more as a sorcerer's apprentice.

The Estimates clarified the debate on Soviet intentions that was ongoing early in the Bush administration, and they made the appropriate connection between Gorbachev's need for stability on the international front and the opportunity for the United States to negotiate favorable arms

---

[90] Dmitri Volkogonov, *Lenin: A New Biography* (New York: The Free Press, 1994), p. 484.

[91] See Robert Strayer, *Why Did the Soviet Union Collapse? Understanding Historical Change* (Armonk, NY: M. E. Sharpe, 1998), p. 83, which argues that Gorbachev's reform program was the "primary and independent cause" of the Soviet collapse. Other historians have argued, however, that the Soviet system contained "fatal flaws" that doomed it from the outset. See, for example, Martin Malia, *Russia Under Western Eyes: From the Bronze Horseman to the Lenin Mausoleum* (Cambridge: The Belknap Press of the Harvard University Press, 1999), pp. 406-407.

reduction agreements. The Estimates, like many other commentaries, may have assigned too much weight to economic factors as a cause of the Soviet crisis. On the other hand, they perceived earlier than Gorbachev himself the essence of the nationality problem as a critical factor as well as portraying Eastern Europe as the soft underbelly of the Soviet empire. The military Estimates also documented and anticipated the profound changes occurring in Eastern Europe as a result of arms control and political disintegration, giving American policymakers the confidence they needed to bring the Gulf crisis to a successful conclusion and reach new agreements with Moscow. The strategic Estimates provided vital information on the absence of basic change in Soviet strategic programs despite *perestroika* and, later, on the fundamental changes resulting from the START Treaty and the host of new problems raised by the Soviet collapse. All in all, the Estimates stand up well in the light of what we now know.

Chronology

1989

10 January — Central Committee of the Communist Party of the Soviet Union (CC/CPSU) nominates candidates for the Congress of People's Deputies (CPD).

18 January — Estonia adopts law requiring minorities (i.e., Russians) to learn its native language within four years. [Lithuania, Latvia, Tajikistan, Kyrgyzstan, Moldavia, Uzbekistan, and Ukraine later follow suit.]

20 January — George Bush inaugurated as 41st President of the United States.

3 February — Soviet troop withdrawals from Czechoslovakia begin.

6 February — Solidarity and Polish Government start roundtable talks.

15 February — Last Soviet troops leave Afghanistan. [Najibullah regime survives until 1992.]

18 February — Polish Government declares USSR, not Nazi Germany, was responsible for 1940 Katyn Forest massacre.

9 March — Conventional Forces in Europe (CFE) talks begin.

26 March — National elections for CPD; many communist candidates are defeated; Baltic popular fronts sweep elections; Boris Yel'tsin wins 90 percent of vote in Moscow.

29 March — Gorbachev claims that defeat of CPSU candidates shows USSR does not need multiparty system.

7 April — Solidarity legalized, signs agreement on elections in which it can contest 35 percent of seats in Sejm, all in Senat.

9 April — Soviet forces attack nationalist demonstrators in Tiblisi, Georgia.

25 April — Soviet forces begin leaving Hungary.

2 May — Hungarian Government lifts "iron curtain" along border with Austria.

15-19 May	Gorbachev is first Soviet leader in 30 years to visit China.
18 May	Lithuania and Estonia declare sovereignty; Latvia follows on 29 July.
25 May	First session of CPD carried live on television; elects Gorbachev chairman; next day elects Supreme Soviet (standing parliament) from among members.
3 June	Chinese Army suppresses dissidents in Tiananmen Square.
4 June	Interior Ministry (MVD) troops dispatched to quell clashes between Uzbeks and Meskhetian Turks in Fergana Oblast, Uzbekistan; Solidarity wins landslide victory, communists are defeated.
10 June	First session of Supreme Soviet opens; Gorbachev visits West Germany, says of Berlin Wall "Nothing is eternal in this world."
4 July	Gorbachev visits France.
6 July	Gorbachev tells Council of Europe (Strasbourg) that USSR will not block East European reform.
7 July	Gorbachev tells Warsaw Pact leaders they can choose own road to socialism.
10 July	Coal miners strike in Kuzbass (Siberia), then later in Donbass (Ukraine).
23 July	Aleksandr Yakovlev, chairman of CPD commission investigating Soviet-German agreements of 1939, acknowledges that secret protocols divided Poland and ceded Baltic states to USSR.
22 August	Gorbachev urges Polish communists to join coalition government with Solidarity.
23 August	Two million Balts form human chain linking Vilnius, Riga, and Tallin to protest Soviet occupation.
24 August	First non-communist government in Eastern Europe since 1948 elected in Poland.
September	More than 17,000 East Germans flee to Austria via Czechoslovakia and Poland.
10 September	Hungary opens border with Austria, allowing East Germans to flee.

22-23 September	Secretary of State Baker, Foreign Minister Shevardnadze meet at Jackson Hole, Wyoming.
7 October	Gorbachev visits East Germany, urges Erich Honecker to adopt reforms.
7 October	Hungarian Communist Party becomes a socialist party.
9 October	100,000 East Germans march in Leipzig, demand democracy.
18 October	Egon Krenz replaces Honecker as East German leader.
27 October	Warsaw Pact members endorse right of self-determination, renounce Brezhnev doctrine.
9 November	Berlin Wall opens.
19 November	Georgian Supreme Soviet declares sovereignty; 10,000 attend Civic Forum rally in Czechoslovakia.
27 November	Supreme Soviet bans censorship of press.
28 November	Czechoslovakia abandons leading role of party.
2-3 December	Bush and Gorbachev meet at Malta.
3 December	East German government resigns.
4 December	Warsaw Pact condemns 1968 invasion of Czechoslovakia.
10 December	Non-communist government elected in Czechoslovakia.
20 December	Lithuanian Communist Party declares independence from CPSU.
24 December	USSR Supreme Soviet declares secret protocol to Molotov-Ribbentrop Pact invalid but does not comment on Stalin's 1940 incorporation of Baltic states.
25 December	Nicolae Ceausescu, wife executed in Romania.
29 December	Vaclav Havel becomes first democratic president of Czechoslovakia.

1990

11-13 January	Gorbachev visits Vilnius, Lithuania, in attempt to halt independence movement, says "Our security lies here."
19 January	Soviet troops enter Baku, Azerbaijan, to quell anti-Armenian riots.
4 February	Moscow demonstrators demand acceleration of reforms.
5-7 February	Central Committee plenum approves Gorbachev's proposal to create USSR presidency.
9 February	Secretary Baker, in Moscow, proposes "Two plus Four" talks on German unification to Gorbachev.
13 February	Four powers agree on "Two plus Four" arrangement.
25 February	Demonstrators across USSR attack Gorbachev by name; in Moscow troops and KGB units stand by as 50,000 to 100,000 march through streets.
11 March	Lithuania declares independence; Gorbachev brands move illegal.
13 March	Article 6 of Soviet Constitution is amended, eliminating CPSU monopoly on power.
14 March	CPD elects Gorbachev president.
24-26 March	Gorbachev chooses new 15-member presidential cabinet with representatives from right and left.
25 March	Estonian Communist Party declares independence of CPSU.
9 April	Gorbachev announces he will use new powers to institute economic reform.
13 April	Gorbachev embargoes oil and natural gas for Lithuania; government acknowledges that NKVD, not Nazis, murdered Polish officers at Katyn, other sites in 1940.
1 May	Demonstrators jeer Gorbachev at May Day celebration.
4 May	Latvia declares independence; Gorbachev declares act illegal.
29 May	Boris Yel'tsin elected chairman of the Supreme Soviet of the Russian Republic.

30 May	Bush and Gorbachev open their second summit in Washington; Gorbachev agrees that "Germans should decide whether or not they're in NATO."
8 June	Russian parliament declares sovereignty over USSR laws.
12 June	Russian republic declares sovereignty.
30 June	Gorbachev lifts embargo against Lithuania.
2-13 July	28th CPSU Congress meets, re-elects Gorbachev general secretary.
12 July	Yel'tsin resigns from CPSU.
15 July	Gorbachev and West German Chancellor Helmut Kohl meet at Arkhyz (Caucasus); Gorbachev gives final agreement to unified German state in NATO.
16 July	Ukraine declares sovereignty.
20 July	500-Day economic reform plan to create market economy in 17 months published; Gorbachev rejects it.
27 July	Belorussia declares sovereignty.
1 August	Gorbachev and Yel'tsin agree to work on economic reform.
2 August	Iraq invades Kuwait.
3 August	Secretary Baker, Foreign Minister Shevardnadze issue joint statement condemning Iraqi invasion.
8 August	CPSU issues new program that concedes the failures and mistakes of Soviet socialism.
23 August	Turkmenistan, Armenia declare sovereignty.
25 August	Tajikistan declares sovereignty.
9 September	Presidents Bush and Gorbachev meet in Helsinki to discuss Gulf crisis, agree to try to get Saddam Husayn to withdraw; US privately agrees to Soviet proposal for a Middle East conference on the Arab-Israeli peace process.
12 September	Treaty on German unification signed; four-power control ends, and German sovereignty begins.

24 September	Gorbachev granted power to govern by decree.
3 October	German unification.
15 October	*Soyuz* parliamentary group attacks Shevardnadze's foreign policy record as a sellout to Washington.
25 October	Kazakhstan declares sovereignty.
30 October	Kirghizia declares sovereignty.
7 November	Shots fired at Gorbachev during national day celebrations.
17 November	Supreme Soviet accepts Gorbachev's proposal for a Soviet of the Federation, a new government structure with representatives from all 15 republics.
19 November	CFE Treaty signed.
23 November	Gorbachev issues draft of treaty for a new Union of Sovereign States; most republic leaders criticize it.
27 November	UN Resolution 678 authorizes use of force against Iraq to liberate Kuwait.
1 December	Gorbachev replaces a reformer with a diehard as interior minister; offers Shevardnadze position as vice president.
20 December	Shevardnadze resigns as foreign minister, warns of impending dictatorship.
22 December	KGB chief Kryuchkov claims US is masterminding breakup of USSR.

1991

2 January	OMON forces (a.k.a. the Black Berets) seize public buildings in Vilnius, Riga.
7 January	Paratroop units sent to 7 republics to enforce draft law, round up deserters.
9 January	OMON troops surround Vilnius television tower.

11 January	OMON, KGB Alpha group, paratroops, and tanks surround main printing plant, close airport and train station in Vilnius; pro-Soviet "national salvation committee" formed.
13 January	Bloody Sunday I: Army troops seize Vilnius television station, beat and fire on demonstrators, killing at least 15; MVD minister Pugo blames Lithuanians for violence.
14 January	Gorbachev denies ordering use of force in Vilnius, claims local "national salvation committee" requested assistance. V. Pavlov, former finance minister and opponent of reform, appointed chairman, USSR Cabinet of Ministers (premier) in new presidential government.
15 January	A. Bessmertnykh appointed foreign minister. [He would be fired in August for siding with coup plotters.]
17 January	Coalition air war against Iraq (Desert Storm) begins.
19 January	Pro-Soviet "national salvation committee" formed in Riga; top economic adviser to Gorbachev resigns, claiming reform is not possible in current situation.
18 January	Gorbachev demands US halt bombing of Iraq.
20 January	Bloody Sunday II: in Riga, Black Berets attack demonstrators and seize Latvian MVD headquarters, killing four; 300,000 in Moscow demonstrate in solidarity with Balts.
22 January	Gorbachev blames violence in Lithuania, Latvia on parliaments; presidential decrees order confiscation of 50- and 100-ruble notes, undermining entrepreneurs and discouraging free market.
25 January	Moscow city soviet rations meat, grain, and vodka; Defense Ministry, MVD begin joint patrols in 7 cities.
6 February	Six republics boycott referendum on Union treaty.
9 February	Lithuanians (90%) vote for independence.
18 February	Gorbachev meets Iraqi foreign minister, offers to broker agreement to avoid ground war in Kuwait.
19 February	Yel'tsin calls for Gorbachev's resignation.

24 February	US-led ground war against Iraq begins; hardliners demonstrate in Moscow.
25 February	Warsaw Pact members abrogate all military agreements, retain political ties; pro-reform demonstrators march in Moscow.
26 February	Gorbachev denounces "pseudo-democrats" for bringing country to "brink of war."
27 February	US-led coalition force liberates Kuwait, halts ground offensive.
3 March	Estonians, Latvians vote for independence.
10 March	300,000 demonstrate for Yel'tsin, who denounces Gorbachev's "constant lies and deceptions" and calls for "declaration of war against Soviet leadership."
14-16 March	Secretary Baker, in Moscow, meets Baltic, other republic leaders.
17 March	Large majority votes for Union treaty (to preserve USSR) and for executive presidency.
28 March	100,000 pro-Yel'tsin demonstrators defy Gorbachev's ban, march in Moscow.
31 March	Warsaw Pact officially dissolves.
9 April	Georgia declares independence.
23 April	Gorbachev shifts toward reformers, holds talks with 9 republic leaders at Novo-Ogarevo to speed up Union agreement, stabilize situation, and accelerate market reforms.
12 June	Yel'tsin elected president of RSFSR.
17 June	Vice president Pavlov asks Supreme Soviet to grant him special powers; with Gorbachev absent, Yazov, Pugo, and Kryuchkov secretly support attempted "constitutional coup."
20 June	Moscow Mayor Popov warns US ambassador of impending coup; President Bush passes message to Gorbachev, who dismisses it.
30 June	Last Soviet soldiers leave Czechoslovakia.

17 July	Presidents Bush and Gorbachev complete Strategic Arms Reduction (START) Treaty at London G-7 meeting; Gorbachev asks for but does not receive economic aid.
25-26 July	CPSU adopts "social democratic" program.
29 July	US-USSR sign START Treaty during Moscow summit; announce co-sponsorship of Middle East peace conference.
1 August	President Bush visits Kiev, meets independence leader Kravchuk.
18-21 August	"State Committee for the State of Emergency" attempts coup against Gorbachev, Soviet government; Yel'tsin denounces coup as illegal, organizes resistance; Gorbachev is held in seclusion at home in Foros.
20 August	Mass demonstrations in Moscow and Leningrad against coup.
22 August	Gorbachev returns to Moscow from Foros and resumes duties as head of state.
24 August	Gorbachev resigns as head of CPSU, suspends its activities; Ukraine declares independence.
25 August	Belorussian Supreme Soviet declares political and economic independence.
27 August	Moldova (former Moldavia) declares independence.
29 August	USSR Supreme Soviet bans CPSU.
30 August	Azerbaijan declares independence.
31 August	Kyrgyzstan (formerly Kirghizia), Uzbekistan declare independence.
2 September	US recognizes independent Baltic countries.
2-6 September	Fifth extraordinary session of CPD calls for new treaty on Union of Soviet Sovereign States.
6 September	Georgia severs all ties to USSR; Leningrad renamed St. Petersburg.
9 September	Tajikistan declares independence.
21 September	Armenia declares independence.
11 October	USSR State Council breaks up KGB into 5 separate organizations.

19 October	Gorbachev, eight republic leaders sign treaty on economic union.
30 October	Presidents Bush, Gorbachev meet at Madrid Middle East peace conference.
4 November	Republic leaders meet with USSR State Council, abolish all USSR ministries except defense, foreign affairs, railways, electric power, and nuclear power.
6 November	Yel'tsin abolishes Russian Communist Party, confiscates assets.
19 November	Gorbachev reappoints Shevardnadze foreign minister.
1 December	Ukraine votes for independence.
3 December	Gorbachev calls for preservation of USSR; Yel'tsin recognizes Ukraine.
7-8 December	Presidents of Russia, Ukraine, Belarus meet secretly at Belovezhskaya Pushcha (Belorussia), sign Minsk agreement abolishing USSR and forming Commonwealth of Independent States (CIS); Gorbachev brands it "dangerous and illegal."
15 December	Baker in Moscow, meets Gorbachev, Yel'tsin.
16 December	Kazakhstan declares independence.
17 December	Gorbachev, Yel'tsin agree USSR will cease to exist by 1 January 1992.
21-22 December	Eleven former republic leaders meet at Alma Ata (Almaty), agree to expand CIS.
25 December	Gorbachev resigns; Russian flag replaces Soviet over Kremlin.
31 December	USSR officially ceases to exist under international law.

Appendix

National Intelligence Estimates and Intelligence Assessments at the National Archives and Records Administration

The following declassified estimates, assessments, and memoranda may be of interest to readers. They are available from the National Archives and Records administration, Records Group 263 (Records of the Central Intelligence Agency). Much of this material is also available on the Internet at http://www.foia.ucia.gov. Click on Historical Review Program.

USSR Energy Atlas (January 1985)

SOV 85-10141, *Gorbachev's Approach to Societal Malaise: A Managed Revitalization* (August 1985)

SOV 85-10165, *Gorbachev's Economic Agenda, Promises, Potentials, and Pitfalls* (September 1985)

SOV 86-10015, *Gorbachev's Modernization Program: Implications for Defense* (March 1986)

The Soviet Economy Under a New Leader (March 1986)

SOV 86-10023, *The 27th CPSU Congress: Gorbachev's Unfinished Business* (April 1986)

SOV 86-10011X, *Defense's Claim on Soviet Resources* (February 1987)

SOV 87-10011X, *Gorbachev's Domestic Challenge: The Looming Problems* (February 1987)

SOV 87-10033, *The Kazakh Riots: Lessons for the Soviet Leadership* (June 1987)

SOV 87-10036, *Gorbachev: Steering the USSR Into the 1990s* (July 1987)

SOV DDB-1900-140, *Gorbachev's Modernization Program: A Status Report* (August 1987)

SOV 88-10040, *Soviet National Security Policy: Responses to the Changing Military and Economic Environment* (June 1988)

SOV M88-2005, *The 19th All-Union Party Conference: Restructuring the Soviet Political System* (June 1988)

DDB-1900-187, *Gorbachev's Economic Program: Problems Emerge* (June 1988)

SOV 88-10049, *The Impact of Gorbachev's Policies on Soviet Economic Statistics* (July 1988)

NIE 11-22-88, *The Prospects for Change in Sino-Soviet Relations* (August 1988)

Leadership Situation in the USSR: Prospects for a Leadership Crisis (September 1988)

SOV 88-1004U, *USSR: Sharply Higher Deficits Threaten* Perestroyka (September 1988)

SOV 88-10079, *Gorbachev's September Housecleaning: An Early Evaluation* (December 1988)

SOV 89-10017, *The Soviet Economy in Global Perspective* (March 1989)

SOV 89-10035, *USSR: Estimates of Personal Incomes and Savings* (April 1989)

SOV 8-10035, *Modeling Soviet Agriculture: Isolating the Effects of Weather* (August 1988)

SOV 89-10040, *Rising Political Instability Under Gorbachev: Understanding the Problem and Prospects for Resolution* (April 1989)

The Soviet Economy in 1988: Gorbachev Changes Course (April 1989)

NIC 0060-89, *Executive Brief: How Vulnerable Is Gorbachev?* (May 1989)

SOV 89-10020, *A Comparison of the US and Soviet Industrial Bases* (May 1989)

NIE 11-15-89, *Soviet Naval Strategy and Programs Toward the 21st Century* (Key Judgments) (June 1989)

SOV 89-10059, *Gorbachev's Assault on the Social Contract: Can He Build a New Basis for Regime Legitimacy?* (July 1989)

NIE 11/30-89, *Soviet Policy Toward the Middle East* (December 1989)

NI IIM 90-10001, *Outlook for Eastern Europe in 1990* (February 1989)

LDA 90-12598, *The USSR Presidency* (April 1990)

GI 90-10013U, *USSR: Demographic Trends and Ethnic Balance in the Non-Russian Republics* (April 1990)

DDB-1900-161, *The Soviet Economy Stumbles Badly in 1989* (May 1990)

SOV 90-10021, *Soviet Energy Data Resource Handbook* (May 1990)

LDA 90-13125, *The Soviet Banking Industry: Blueprint for Change* (May 1990)

NIC M 90-10009, *The Readiness of Soviet General Purpose Forces Through the Year 2000* (June 1990)

The USSR: Approaching Turning Point (June 1990)

IR 90-10008, *Selected Countries' Trade With the USSR and Eastern Europe* (July 1990)

SOV 90-10038, *Measuring Soviet GNP: Problems and Solutions* (September 1990)

Measures of Soviet Gross National Product in 1982 Prices *Gorbachev's Future* (May 1991)

SOV 91-10018, *Soviet Economic Futures: The Outlook for 1991* (May 1991) *Prospects for the Russian Democratic Reformers* (April 1991)

SOV 91-10026, *Yeltsin's Political Objectives* (June 1991)

DDB-190-164, *Beyond* Perestroyka*: The Soviet Economy in Crisis* (June 1991)

LDA 91-13194, *A Guide to Soviet Institutions of Power* (July 1991)

LDA 91-16344, *USSR and the Baltic States: Leading Economic Players* (December 1991)

OSE 92-10001, *The Republics of the Former Soviet Union and the Baltic States: An Overview* (January 1992)

Moscow's Defense Spending Cuts Accelerate (May 1992)

Economic Survey of Russia (March 1993)

The Soviet Crisis
Gorbachev and the Perils of *Perestroika*

1. NIE 11-23-88, December 1988, *Gorbachev's Economic Programs: The Challenges Ahead*

Director of Central Intelligence

~~Secret~~

Gorbachev's Economic Programs: The Challenges Ahead

National Intelligence Estimate

This National Intelligence Estimate represents the views of the Director of Central Intelligence with the advice and assistance of the US Intelligence Community.

~~Secret~~

NIE 11-23-88
December 1988
Copy 373

1. *(Continued)*

 **Director of Central Intelligence**

~~Secret~~
~~NOFORN NOCONTRACT~~

NIE 11-23-88

Gorbachev's Economic Programs: The Challenges Ahead (U)

Information available as of 20 December 1988 was used in the preparation of this National Intelligence Estimate.

The following intelligence organizations participated in the preparation of this Estimate:
The Central Intelligence Agency
The Defense Intelligence Agency
The National Security Agency
The Bureau of Intelligence and Research, Department of State
The Office of Intelligence Support, Department of the Treasury

also participating:
The Office of the Deputy Chief of Staff for Intelligence, Department of the Army
The Office of the Director of Naval Intelligence, Department of the Navy
The Office of the Assistant Chief of Staff, Intelligence, Department of the Air Force
The Office of the Deputy Assistant Secretary for Intelligence, Department of Energy
The Director of Intelligence, Headquarters, Marine Corps

This Estimate was approved for publication by the National Foreign Intelligence Board.

~~Secret~~
December 1988

1. *(Continued)*

Secret
NOFORN-NOCONTRACT

Key Judgments

We believe that Gorbachev's efforts at reviving the Soviet economy will produce no substantial improvement over the next five years, although his efforts to raise consumer welfare could achieve some modest results. Soviet attempts to raise technology levels will not narrow the gap with the West in most sectors during the remainder of this century.[1] (C NF)

Gorbachev's economic program has so far failed consumers, who, according to anecdotal evidence, probably feel somewhat worse off now than they did when Gorbachev assumed power in 1985. To improve consumer welfare, Gorbachev has begun to place more emphasis on housing, food processing, and light industry; and the defense industry is being told to increase its production for consumers. Gorbachev has also sought to expand the private and cooperative sectors through long-term leasing arrangements in both agriculture and industry. These initiatives are the ones that are most likely to improve the quality of life in the Soviet Union over the next five years. (C NF)

Gorbachev's effort to reform the country's system of planning and management and to improve the country's capital stock is going poorly. Ill-defined reform legislation, interference by ministries, and piecemeal implementation are creating disruptions and preventing progress. Reforms already planned in the state sector will probably be implemented slowly. Sharp moves toward a market economy would be very disruptive and would jeopardize popular support for his programs. Nevertheless, Gorbachev has often dealt with setbacks by adopting radical measures, and we cannot rule out an effort to move rapidly toward a market economy in the state sector. (C NF)

To promote growth of private enterprise, Moscow must allow more flexibility and reliance on the market for leasing and cooperative arrangements in order to increase significantly the production of goods and services for consumers. A resentful public and skeptical bureaucracy will make this difficult. Lease contracting in agriculture will remain bound by centrally directed procurement targets, reliance on state supplies, and a

---

[1] *The Director, Defense Intelligence Agency, believes that this uneven performance could include sufficient improvement in the Soviets' economic and technical base to facilitate fulfillment of future military requirements. Moreover, since the Soviets already lead in several key defense technologies, they should be able to continue assimilating technology gains in this sector.* (S NF)

1. *(Continued)*

recalcitrant bureaucracy. The comparatively high prices of privately supplied goods will spur inflation. An added problem for Moscow is that these reforms probably will be most successful, at least initially, in non-Russian areas such as the Baltic states and the Caucasus.

We do not foresee a large, sustained increase in Soviet imports from the West. The Soviets may increase borrowing to perhaps $3-4 billion net per year over the next few years. Even a much larger surge in borrowing from the West, which we think is unlikely, would not aid the overall economy substantially or ameliorate the resource competition between the military and civilian sectors. A few industries may benefit, however.

We judge Gorbachev will divert additional resources from defense—including managers, equipment designers, investment funds, and plant capacity—to his civilian programs. While we recognize there is some redundant defense plant capacity, significant increases in the production of goods for the civilian sector would require a diversion of resources from the military. Diversion from defense to civilian objectives will escalate conflicts over resource allocation because it could delay upgrades to weapons plants, thereby postponing the introduction of new systems. Clearly there are strong economic pressures for major reductions in military spending. Striking the right balance will involve many leadership arguments and decisions over the entire period of this Estimate. In any case, the large-scale modernization of Soviet defense industries in the 1970s has already put in place most of the equipment needed to produce weapon systems scheduled for deployment through the early 1990s.[2]

Moscow will press harder on Eastern Europe for more and higher quality machinery and consumer goods, for greater participation in joint projects, and for greater contributions to Warsaw Pact defense. Such demands will produce only marginal benefits for the USSR because of real economic constraints in Eastern Europe and the reluctance of its regimes to increase their help to the Soviets.

There is some chance that Gorbachev's economic programs may not survive. Disruptions, such as widespread reform-related work stoppages or a drastic drop in performance indicators, might strengthen conservative opposition. Such trends, coupled with continuing nationality turmoil, could force the leadership into a major retreat.

[2] *The Director, Defense Intelligence Agency, holds an alternative view that a critical distinction must be made between near-term resource allocation trade-offs that can be made without significantly disrupting current defense procurement, and those of the longer term where a downward turn in defense spending trends may result in reordering or stretching out of weapons procurement.*

1. *(Continued)*

Given the severity of Soviet economic problems, Gorbachev needs the many benefits of a nonconfrontational international environment. This gives the United States and its allies considerable leverage in bargaining with the Soviets over the terms of that environment on some security issues such as regional conflicts and arms control and on some internal matters such as human rights and information exchange. The margins of this leverage will be set by Moscow's determination not to let the West affect the fundamental nature of the Soviet system or its superpower status.[3]

---

[3] For a fuller discussion of these issues, see SNIE 11-16-88, *Soviet Policy During the Next Phase of Arms Control in Europe*, November 1988; NIE 11-3/8-88, *Soviet Forces and Capabilities for Strategic Nuclear Conflict Through the Late 1990s (Volume I)*, December 1988; and the forthcoming Estimates NIE 11-14-88, *Trends and Developments in Warsaw Pact Theater Forces and Doctrine, 1988-2007*; and NIE 11-4-89, *Soviet Strategy Toward the West: The Gorbachev Challenge*.

1. *(Continued)*

Contents

	Page
Key Judgments	iii
Discussion	1
The Need for Change	1
A Bold Action Plan	2
Clearing the Political Track	3
Slow Progress	6
Altering Economic Strategy	9
Outlook	10
Implications for the West	13
On Arms Control	13
For Eastern Europe and Soviet Client States	14
In Commercial Relations	14
For Western Leverage	15
Annex A. The "Kosygin Reform"	17
Annex B. The Budget Deficit	19
Annex C. Soviet Economic Reform: Signs of a Radical Economic Shift	21
Annex D. Update on Joint Ventures	23

1. *(Continued)*

Discussion[*]

The Need for Change

A simple growth formula—ever increasing inputs of labor and capital—resulted in rapid economic gains for the Soviet Union in the postwar era. This postwar system placed heavy stress on quantity rather than quality. Because there was an abundance of low-cost, readily available resources, there was little concern for efficiency and productivity. As the USSR moved out of the reconstruction phase in the 1960s, this growth formula became less effective. Labor supply growth slowed, ever larger expenditures were required to exploit natural resources, and the inefficiencies inherent in central planning became more acute as the economy grew.

Military spending also has increasingly hindered economic performance. To support the military effort, Moscow created an institutional mechanism reaching from the highest state bodies down through layers of administrative control to individual enterprises, thus ensuring priority to defense programs. As a result of this priority, the defense sector's share of national output grew and by the mid-1980s consumed 15 to 17 percent of GNP. The incentive structure—wages, bonuses, perquisites—was designed to favor those who worked in or supported the defense industry. The defense sector was given priority access to raw materials, machinery and equipment, subcomponents, scientists, engineers, and skilled workers, preempting consumption and investment in the civilian sector. The Soviet defense industry became the most technologically advanced and most effective sector of the economy. This effectiveness was due primarily to the priority that created the institutional mechanism rather than greater efficiency. The defense industry has been at least as inefficient and wasteful as the civilian sector.

As a result of these factors, GNP growth slowed from rates that were closing the economic and technological gaps with the developed West during the 1950s and 1960s to a range in the 1980s that allowed little expansion of per capita output and stymied progress in narrowing the technology gap. The large and still growing burden of defense coupled with increasing demands for investment in areas such as energy and agriculture allowed no room for major increases in the quantity and quality of consumer goods and services.

Brezhnev's successors, then, were saddled with:

- An antiquated industrial base and a defense sector that was siphoning off high-quality resources needed for economic improvement.

- An energy sector beset by rapidly rising production costs of oil, its major fuel.

- Levels of technology that, for most areas, substantially lagged those of the West.

- Inefficiencies inherent in the conflict between ever more central planning and control and an increasingly large and complex economy.

- An inefficient farm sector that, despite large investments, still employed 20 percent of the Soviet labor force compared with only 5 percent in the United States.

---

[*] General Secretary Gorbachev's efforts at reforming the political and economic fabric of the Soviet Union have been under way for more than three years. This Estimate reviews the progress of his economic strategy, identifies the conflicts inherent in his approach, and assesses the outlook for reform over the next five years. The Soviet leader has set in motion a dynamic process whose outcome cannot be predicted with confidence. There will continue to be major alterations in the game plan, and a conservative reaction to the strains unleashed by the current effort is possible. What is clear is that the very fabric of Soviet ideology and institutions is being questioned more than at any time since the revolution, and in the Soviet Union there is a general consensus that retreating to the economic and political path existing when Gorbachev took over is not tenable.

1. *(Continued)*

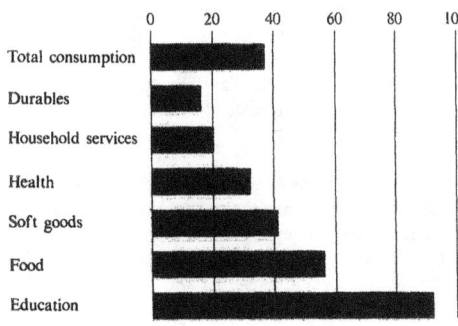

Figure 1
USSR: Low Living Standards

Soviet consumption as a percentage of US consumption, 1983

Unclassified

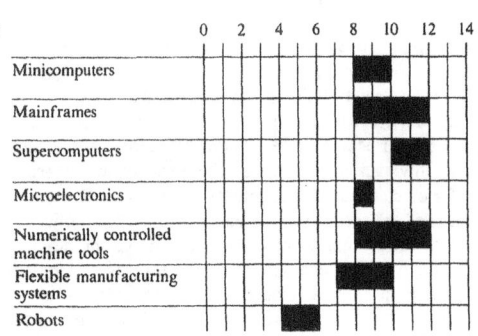

Figure 2
USSR: Lags in Key Technologies

Approximate length of US lead in years

Unclassified

- A hidebound, corrupt bureaucracy and inflexible planning system that failed to provide the proper signals for production and investment, retarded scientific-technical innovation, and encouraged high costs and massive waste of resources. (C NF)

A Bold Action Plan

Gorbachev recognized the "pre-crisis" urgency of these problems and initiated a bold strategy to deal with them. He grouped his efforts to revive the economy under the broad rubric of *perestroyka*, a term that includes three major economic elements—tighter *economic discipline*, *industrial modernization*, and *economic reform*. The goal of these actions, we believe, is to develop an economic environment capable of:
- At least containing, if not narrowing, the growing gaps in technology and economic performance with the West, thereby also enabling Moscow to maintain its military competitiveness.

- Achieving major improvements in consumer welfare to gain the cooperation and support of the masses for *perestroyka* and to maintain regime legitimacy. Gorbachev and other Soviet leaders recognize that reaching these economic goals will take years, possibly decades, and that progress toward them could be greatly facilitated by a more nonconfrontational international environment. Gorbachev's efforts in arms control, his political initiatives, and the campaign to refurbish the USSR's image are intended to achieve such an environment. (C NF)

When Gorbachev first assumed office, he concentrated on extending and intensifying Andropov's *discipline* campaign. His "human factors" initiatives—discipline, temperance, and improved work incentives—were intended to raise labor productivity and to increase economic growth for the first two or three years of the 1986-90 Five-Year Plan while industry retooled. He also removed many inept and corrupt managers and officials and attempted to rationalize

1. *(Continued)*

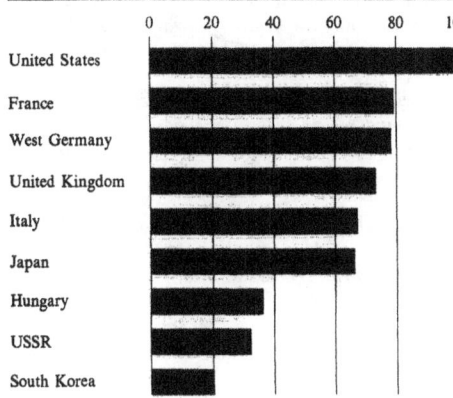

Figure 3
USSR: Per Capita Consumption in a Global Perspective, 1985

Index: US=100

the organizational structure of the bureaucracy by trimming slots and rearranging and combining functions.

Gorbachev argued that *industrial modernization* was the key to long-lasting improvement of the USSR's economic situation. His program was aimed at the massive introduction of new machinery and the rapid retirement of old equipment. This depended heavily on major improvements in the machine-building and metalworking sector that manufactures producer and consumer durables and military hardware. (See inset, "Machine Building—The Focus of Gorbachev's Modernization Plans.")

Gorbachev's boldest proposals were focused on *economic reform* of planning and management. These changes—contained in the Basic Provisions for Fundamentally Reorganizing Economic Management, the Law on the State Enterprise, and 11 decrees—were approved at the Central Committee plenum in June 1987. This set of documents, together with decrees adopted over the last three years that expanded the role of the private sector, represents a design for the most comprehensive reform of economic management in the Soviet Union since the introduction of Stalinist central planning in the late 1920s. The plan goes well beyond the "Kosygin" reforms adopted in 1965 (see annex A). The reform package is scheduled to be "almost fully" in place by the beginning of 1991—the first year of the 13th Five-Year Plan—and major parts of the package are already in effect. (See the table on pages 5 and 6.)

Clearing the Political Track

Gorbachev also proposed reforms of the political system in part because of the ability of the entrenched state and party bureaucracies to defeat past efforts at economic reform. He aims to decentralize the political system to circumvent the resistance to reform at the top and middle levels of the leadership—groups that have forced him to compromise and slow implementation of his programs. The reforms place more decisionmaking authority at the local level in hopes of making the system more responsive to local economic signals than to administrative dictates from the top. His program for "democratization" is designed to produce a more participatory political culture—encouraging local officials to take initiative to resolve problems and giving the populace a greater say in decisions.

At Gorbachev's initiative, measures were approved by the national party conference in June 1988 to reduce the size of the party apparatus, force local party chiefs to stand for election as head of the regional soviets, and give the soviets new authority. These measures aim at diminishing the ability of local party chiefs to block controversial reforms and sensitizing local leaders to popular sentiment on such economic issues as more and better food and consumer goods. *Glasnost*—an element of political reform in the broadest

1. *(Continued)*

Machine Building—The Focus of Gorbachev's Modernization Plans

Gorbachev has argued that the key to long-lasting improvement of the USSR's economic situation is the continuous introduction of increasingly productive machinery and equipment. The modernization program, therefore, depends heavily on improvements in machine building and metalworking—the sector that produces these producer durables, as well as consumer durables and military hardware. The ambitious targets of the 1986-90 plan reflect the sector's importance:

- Output is to increase by 43 percent during the period 1986-90.

- Targets for high-technology equipment are even higher. Planned growth rates are especially high for numerically controlled machine tools (125 percent), robots (225 percent), and processing centers (330 percent).

- Quality and technological levels are to improve dramatically. By 1990, 85 to 90 percent of the most important types of machinery output will be up to "world technical levels," compared with 13 to 15 percent for civilian machinery in 1986. New machinery is to be at least 50 to 100 percent more productive and reliable than previously produced equipment.

- New machinery is to be introduced more quickly than in the past—by 1990, 13 percent of machine-building output is to be in its first year of production, up from 3 percent in 1985.

- By 1990, 60 percent of the sector's own machinery is to be new—that is, brought on line during the preceding five years. To reach this goal, investment in civil machine-building ministries is to rise by 80 percent. Meanwhile, the withdrawal rate for old capital goods is to double by 1990, while the withdrawal rate for machinery is to quadruple. (S NF)

Machine building's struggle to meet these goals was hindered, in part, by the quality control program and new financial arrangements introduced in 1987:

- Production of numerically controlled machine tools showed no growth in 1987, and production of industrial robots declined.

- While newly introduced machines represent about 9 percent of output, the Soviets admit to a general lack of progress in meeting "world standards."

- The pace of both investment and machinery retirements has slowed markedly from the plan guidelines. (S NF)

Though machine builders will not reach their 12th Five-Year Plan targets, the leadership has taken steps to revitalize modernization by refocusing resources on priority areas including machinery for consumers, the food program, transportation, and construction. At the same time, the plan calls for an intensification of the development of machine tool building, instrument building, electronics, and electrical equipment—the same industries targeted for preferential development in the original 12th Five-Year Plan goals. (S NF)

1. *(Continued)*

Secret

Soviet Economic Reform: A Status Report

Reform	Major Purpose	1989 Goals	1988 Results	Final Objective
Enterprise self-financing	Enterprises will bear full economic responsibility for the results of their activity. Investment will be financed less through budget allocations and more through enterprise's own resources and bank credits.	100 percent of industry and agriculture; "hope" to complete changeover of nonproduction sphere to same principles.	60 percent of volume of output in the economy.	Same as 1989 goals.
Regional/local self-financing	Republics and local governments will have greater role in forming their own budgets and will be expected to balance revenues and expenditures. Revenues will be formed from taxes levied on enterprises within the region or locale to fund social/economic development.	Estonia, Latvia, Lithuania, Belorussia, Moscow City, Tatar ASSR, and Sverdlovsk Oblast (RSFSR).	Not yet introduced.	Expansion to unnamed regions.
Planning	Enterprises will produce a portion of their output in compliance with mandatory state orders and will be given greater latitude in determining the remainder.	All enterprises and associations. State orders are to make up an estimated 40 percent of industrial production.	State orders made up 86 percent of industrial production.	State orders are to "eventually" drop to 20 to 25 percent of total production.
Supply	Only "scarce" producer goods and supplies for state orders will continue to be rationed by the state. Other supplies will be distributed through a wholesale trade system that will allow free purchase and sale under direct contracts between providers and users.	Approximately 10 percent of total industrial production; 50 to 55 percent of sales through state supply networks.[a]	Over 4 percent of total industrial production operated under wholesale trade.	Wholesale trade reform to cover more than 70 percent of sales through state supply networks by 1992.[b]
Wages	Entire wage and salary structure in the production sector will be overhauled, but increases are dependent upon enterprise's ability to finance them and are tied to increases in labor production.	No announced goal. 1988 goal was 60 to 70 percent of the work force. (May not be expanded because of concern that wages are being increased more than increases in labor productivity.)	No information.	All industrial sectors by end of 1990.
Banking	Decentralizes bank decisionmaking somewhat and elevates the role of economic criteria in extending credit.	Codification of banking practice through new banking legislation.	Limited decentralization. Some flexibility in negotiating lending rates. Assumed role of liquidators in cases of insolvency.	After price reforms are implemented.
Foreign trade	Allows selected enterprises to engage directly in foreign trade and keep portion of foreign currency earned.	Unannounced.	Was to be 26 percent of all imports and 14 percent of all exports. (Implementation behind schedule.)	No date given.

Footnotes appear at end of table.

5 Secret

1. *(Continued)*

~~Secret~~

Soviet Economic Reform: A Status Report (continued)

Reform	Major Purpose	1989 Goals	1988 Results	Final Objective
Wholesale prices	Will be revised to better reflect resource scarcity and customer demands and will be based on contracts.	Not scheduled to be implemented.	Not scheduled to be implemented.	Industry, transportation, and communications by 1 January 1990; construction and agriculture by 1 January 1991.
Retail prices	Will be made more flexible and more fully reflective of supply and demand, probably resulting in higher prices for food, rent, and consumer services.	None; to begin only after full public discussion and before 1991 (beginning of 13th Five-Year Plan).	Not scheduled to be implemented.	Whole economy, presumably including retail by 1991.

a This goal was moved up to 1989 from 1990. In 1987, the stated 1989 goal was to be 30 percent of sales through state supply networks operating on wholesale trade.

b This goal was slightly reduced. In 1987, the stated 1992 objective was for wholesale trade to cover 80 percent of sales through state supply networks.

~~This table is~~ Confidential ~~Noforn.~~

sense—encourages the critical reexamination of economic history and the Stalinist system's ideological foundations and provides a new set of precepts that support the devolution of economic and political power. (See inset, "Challenging Accepted Norms.") (C NF)

Slow Progress

Implementation of Gorbachev's program is off to a rocky start. This is particularly true of his attempts to reform the system of planning and management. Ministries have not clearly apprised enterprise managers of their new tasks and responsibilities. Detailed instructions have not been issued, nor have chains of command in new organizations been delineated clearly. Enterprise managers remain reluctant to take risks and to focus on quality and innovation because pressure remains to meet quantitative targets set in the extremely ambitious original five-year plan. (C NF)

Loopholes in the reform legislation—the result of compromise between those who wanted a radical decentralization of economic decision making immediately and those who preferred a more traditional, cautious approach—have allowed the ministries and the planning bureaucracy to resist change and have postponed the advent of market forces:

- For example, although obligatory plan targets covering an enterprise's entire range of output have been replaced by a system of "nonbinding" control figures and mandatory state orders, during the first year of implementation, state orders levied by Gosplan and the ministries often took all of an enterprise's output. In an effort to solve this problem, ministries are prohibited from issuing state orders during 1989, and Gosplan is instructed to reduce state orders by one-half to two-thirds.

1. *(Continued)*

Challenging Accepted Norms

Initiatives	Conflicts
Initiatives to make enterprises more financially independent would inevitably result in the bankruptcy of inefficient firms.	This creates major uncertainties for workers, who face unemployment and/or retraining, and for the manager, a member of the privileged elite, who has typically spent his entire career at the same plant.
Wage reform would tie rewards more closely to individual production results and would give greater rewards to professionals and skilled workers.	This eliminates wage leveling and creates pressures to fire redundant workers, thus conflicting with the social contract.
Retail price reform would reduce government subsidies and bring supply and demand more into line.	While needed ultimately for long-term reform, it would weaken the safety net that gives the poorest segment of the population assured access to necessities such as food, housing, and health care.
Wholesale price reform would allow prices to reflect changes in resource scarcities and consumer demand.	It would allow the market more influence over Soviet economic activity, increasing the potential for its reputed evils—inflation, unemployment, "unearned" profits, and cyclical fluctuations.
Expansion of the private sector to increase the availability of consumer goods and services would unleash private initiative.	It encourages qualities previously eschewed in the making of the "new Soviet man"—self-interest, competition, and "money-grubbing"—while it chips away at state ownership of the means of production.
Workplace democratization would allow the workers to elect their managers and workers councils, giving them a greater stake in the collective's success.	Democratization violates the Lenin-ordained principle of one-man plant management and gives the workers a greater potential to challenge the role of the party in the economy.
The cooperative movement in agriculture would give the farmer a personal interest in using the land more efficiently by allowing him to contract with the farm and to pocket the profits.	It appears to be at variance with the raison d'etre for collectivization—the submergence of the individual to the group and a mechanism to transfer dividends from agriculture to other sectors.

1. *(Continued)*

- Under the new conditions of "self-financing," enterprises are to finance operating expenses and some capital expenditures out of their own revenues and bear the full economic responsibility for their actions. However, the amount of revenues they are permitted to keep and the distribution of these resources among investment and incentive funds remain under the control of the ministries. As a result, the ministries are able to juggle these accounts and use the earnings of profitable enterprises to bail out the unprofitable ones.

In the area of foreign trade, a "stage-by-stage" convertibility of the ruble is planned, starting with the currencies of the countries belonging to the Council for Mutual Economic Assistance. Enterprises also are being given broader rights to keep part of the foreign exchange earned from exports. However, they still need approval to participate directly in foreign economic activity, and Soviet economists admit that currency convertibility, even with the currencies of Eastern Europe, is far off.

Finally, implementation of Gorbachev's program is slow because only a portion of the economy has changed to the new system, and crucial elements of the reform package are not scheduled for full implementation until the beginning of the 13th Five-Year Plan in 1991. Wholesale and retail price reform is essential to make other reforms work, such as self-financing and making the ruble more convertible into both domestic goods and foreign currencies at realistic rates. Yet, wholesale price reform in the state sector will not be completed until 1991 and is likely to consist of administrative revisions rather than changes in the way prices are determined. Retail price reform has been postponed indefinitely because the regime fears that it will corrode the support of the populace for *perestroyka*. Substantial new flexibility in setting prices, as reformers originally intended, is not likely because the Soviets have seen that granting limited enterprise rights to set prices has been inflationary under monopolistic conditions. (See inset, "Backtracking on Reform.")

The modernization program has also been lagging and seems to be getting a reduced level of attention. In 1987 there was no increase in the output of machinery for the civilian sector, and the resulting shortfalls in equipment for investment caused problems throughout industry and the rest of the economy. The high targets that machine builders were tasked to achieve were overwhelming, particularly in light of the fact that they were being forced to do everything at once: retool, increase quality, conserve resources, change the product mix, and accelerate production. Despite some performance improvement in 1988, the program remains well below target.

Backtracking on Reform

Some economic reforms, particularly those that would negatively affect the consumer, have been delayed or modified:

- *Retail price reform, which was to be implemented in 1991 along with wholesale price reform, has been pushed into the indefinite future; even reform economists are expressing skepticism about its wisdom.*

- *Consumer goods remain tied to state orders in order to ensure that unprofitable goods will be produced; state orders have been reduced substantially in other sectors.*

- *A new set of price regulations on goods and services produced in the cooperative sector are in response to public complaints of price gouging.*

- *Decisions on wage increases, which were to be the preserve of the enterprise, now are monitored by Gosbank in order to ensure that they do not exceed productivity gains and add to inflationary pressures.*

- *Wholesale price reform that will be implemented beginning in 1990 is not the reform of the price mechanism itself as envisioned in the original reform decree, but another revision that will periodically need adjusting.*

1. *(Continued)*

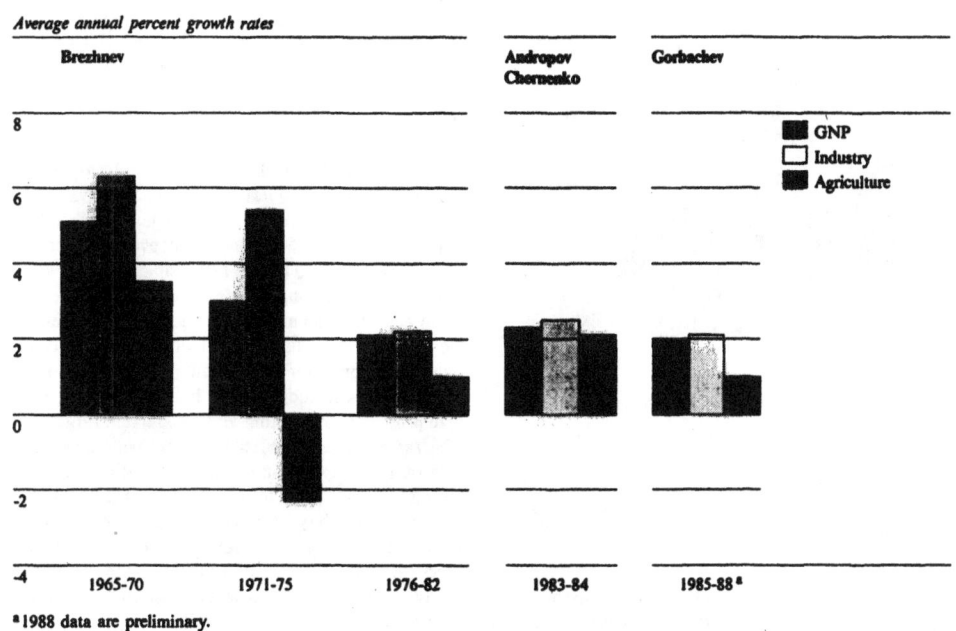

Figure 4
USSR: Economic Performance Under Gorbachev and His Predecessors

Average annual percent growth rates

ª 1988 data are preliminary.

Gorbachev's economic program has so far failed consumers. Economic performance during 1985-88 was about the same as in 1976-82—the most stagnant Brezhnev years when per capita income did not grow. The effects of this poor performance—coupled with reduced imports of consumer goods and the antialcohol campaign—mean that Soviet consumers probably felt somewhat worse off at the end of 1987 than they did in early 1985 when Gorbachev assumed the post of General Secretary. The Soviet consumer scene is still marked by lengthy queues, rationing of some goods, pervasive black-market activity, and shortages of basic necessities, especially food.

Altering Economic Strategy

Because of these mounting problems, Gorbachev has begun to alter his strategy in an attempt to revitalize his economic program and prepare for the planning decisions for the next five-year plan (1991-95). The potential problems from disgruntled consumers forced Gorbachev to alter his investment strategy to place more emphasis on housing, food processing, and light industry and to restrict growth in some other sectors. The Soviets have directed the machine-building industry to give priority to sectors that directly serve the consumer.

**Figure 5
USSR: Average Annual Growth of
Per Capita Consumption, 1956-87**

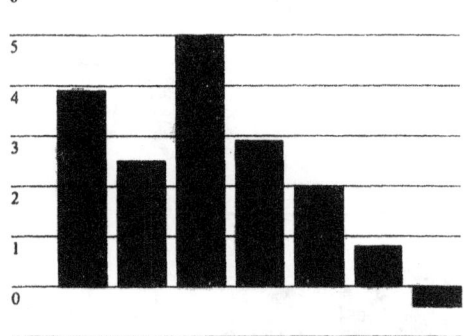

The defense industry is also being told to assume responsibility for a greater share of consumer-related production:
- Premier Ryzhkov directed the defense industry to increase deliveries of equipment to the food-processing sector.
- The Ministry of Machine Building for Light and Foods Industry and Household Appliances was disbanded and most plants resubordinated to the defense industry.
- The 1989 plan calls on the defense industry to improve the quality and increase production of consumer goods and capital equipment for consumer-related industries.
- The Minister of Medium Machine Building (the most secretive defense-industrial ministry) announced plans to increase sharply the output of equipment for the dairy industry.

Gorbachev is increasingly concentrating on expanding the private and cooperative sectors and offering long-term leasing arrangements in both agriculture and industry because those initiatives hold the best prospects for producing considerable improvements in the quality of life over the next five years. Legislation that would have levied a prohibitive tax structure on cooperatives was remanded in July by the Supreme Soviet in an unprecedented move.

Outlook

We believe that Gorbachev's efforts at reforming the economy, fostering capital renewal, and motivating labor and management will produce no substantial improvement in the Soviet economy over the next five years.[5] His efforts to devote increasing resources and attention to improving consumer welfare, however, could achieve some modest results. Still, we believe Gorbachev will be disappointed with the overall consequences. Squeezing investment growth in nonconsumer sectors, including heavy industry, will jeopardize prospects for meeting vital production targets. This same strategy resulted in serious bottlenecks and a substantial slippage in industrial growth during the period 1976-80. Plans to increase investment in light industry and to buy Western manufacturing equipment face long-drawn-out retooling and installation processes. Gorbachev's failure to deal with the already large budget deficit will intensify inflationary pressures. (See annex B.)

Soviet attempts to incorporate new technologies and create a more productive labor force will not be enough to narrow the technology gap in most sectors with the West during the remainder of this century. More important, gains in particular areas will not be self-perpetuating as long as incentives for dynamic technological change remain weak. The Soviets have undertaken a variety of measures to spur innovation and the introduction of new technologies, including: (1) raising prices for innovative products; (2) forming associations to gather research, development, and production responsibilities under one roof; (3) making

---

[5] *The Director, Defense Intelligence Agency, believes that this uneven performance could include sufficient improvement in the Soviets' economic and technical base to facilitate fulfillment of future military requirements.*

1. *(Continued)*

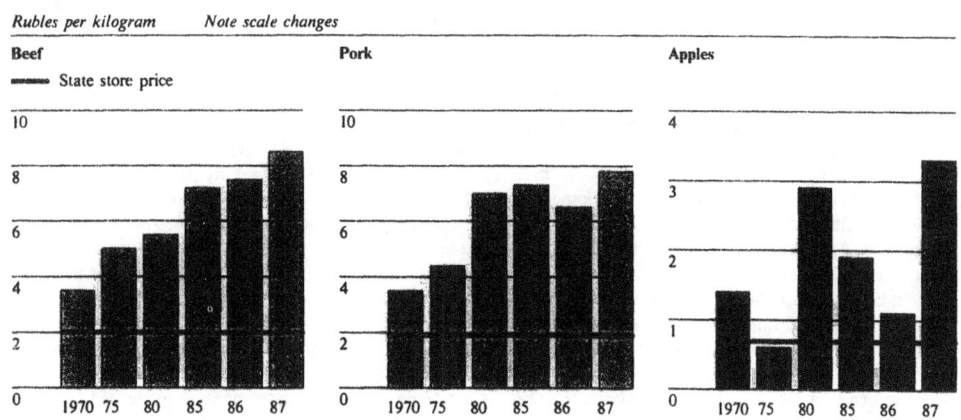

Figure 6
Moscow: Collective Farm Market Prices of Selected Goods [a]

[a] Data are for purchases made in Moscow in August or September of each year.

information more available as a result of *glasnost*; and (4) encouraging joint ventures and technical exchanges with the more advanced countries. Nevertheless, systemic obstacles remain that discourage the introduction and dispersion of new technologies at industrial enterprises.[6] Recent reforms aim at creating conditions and incentives for greater "technology pull" from below and expanding the autonomy of research and production collectives, but we believe these first faltering steps will not produce substantial results during the period covered by this Estimate. Acquisition of technology aimed toward military uses will not provide advances in Soviet industrial applications—the cornerstone of Soviet modernization. On the other hand, the new proposed forms of cooperative sharing of technology and managerial techniques with the West, particularly joint ventures, could allow for easier transfer of technology than has been the case with traditional purchases of machinery and equipment.[7]

There may be some economic benefits from the reform program that will help to prevent further deterioration in the planned economy. For example, financial pressures on enterprises should help reduce redundant labor and some waste of materials. On balance, however, we believe that such benefits will be slow in coming and that they will be outweighed by disruptions resulting from the conflicting and changing signals that piecemeal implementation of the reform program will continue to create.

[6] *The Director, Defense Intelligence Agency, believes that, since the Soviets already lead in several key defense technologies, they should be able to continue assimilating technology gains in this sector. (S NF)*

1. *(Continued)*

~~Secret~~

We see no evidence that Gorbachev currently intends to impose more radical reform in the state sector, a strategy that would include:
- Disengaging enterprises completely from ministerial control and allowing them to respond to economic levers.
- Providing much better price and profit signals by allowing prices to fluctuate in response to supply and demand.
- Creating a more competitive environment by breaking up the present huge production conglomerates and permitting competition from abroad.
- Introducing financial and capital markets.

Such moves toward a market economy at this time would be even more disruptive to the planned economy than piecemeal implementation and in particular would jeopardize Gorbachev's campaign to win popular support for his programs. We believe it most likely that reforms for the state sector will continue to be implemented slowly. Only a small number of unprofitable firms will be shut down, and price reform will entail the periodic revision of prices rather than a change in the basic pricing mechanism to allow more flexibility. Nevertheless, Gorbachev has often reacted to setbacks by proposing increasingly radical measures, and we cannot rule out an effort to move rapidly toward a market economy in the state sector. (See annex C.) (C NF)

We believe Gorbachev will continue to push forward on the moves already begun to expand private initiative by paving the way for growth in the private and cooperative sectors and by allowing long-term agricultural leases. For such reforms to work, however, Moscow must allow more flexibility and reliance on the market. We believe progress in this area will be difficult because a resentful public and skeptical local authorities are likely to continue retarding the development of the private sector. Furthermore, the lease contracting system in agriculture will probably remain bound by centrally directed procurement targets and state supplies of inputs as well as a recalcitrant bureaucracy. Goods supplied by the private sector will be costly, raising concerns over inflation. An added problem for Moscow is that these reforms probably will be most successful, at least initially, in non-Russian areas such as the Baltic states and the Caucasus. (C NF)

We believe there will be escalating conflicts over resources as the industrial modernization program falls short, consumers continue to clamor for tangible rewards, and the military perceives no reduction in its needs. In the near term, the resource allocation debate will be sharpest on investment. The present five-year plan has no slack that would permit greater investment in priority sectors without offsetting adjustments in other areas. The regime continues to balance the books on the investment program by assuming large gains in productivity in key areas such as machine building, agriculture, industrial materials, and construction. Yet, in his three-plus years in power, Gorbachev has not made any progress in reversing the long-term decline in productivity. (C NF)

As a result, the leadership will have to tap resources outside the civilian machinery-production sector to continue the high investment strategy needed to renew the USSR's capital stock and improve productivity over the long term. As a large claimant on some of the economy's most valuable and productive resources, the defense industry is the prime, but not the only, candidate that will be tasked to support Gorbachev's industrial modernization drive. The defense industry already produces civilian investment goods and is the main source of some high-technology machinery and equipment such as robots, computers, and advanced machine tools both for its own use and for the civilian economy. (S NF)

The defense industry has been given additional assignments to support the civilian sector and has been told that these civil projects must be given priority, even at the expense of some defense activities. We judge Gorbachev will divert additional resources from defense—including managers, equipment designers, investment funds, and plant capacity—to his civilian programs. The unilateral force reductions recently announced by Gorbachev could pave the way for cutbacks in weapons procurement in the near term, which will release defense industry resources for Gorbachev's civil economic agenda. While we recognize there is some redundant defense plant capacity, significant increases in the production of goods for the

1. *(Continued)*

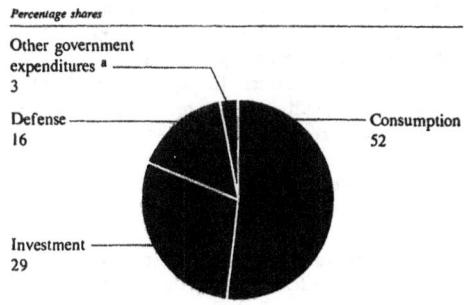

**Figure 7
Estimated Distribution of Soviet GNP by End Use**

Percentage shares

Other government expenditures ᵃ — 3
Defense — 16
Consumption — 52
Investment — 29

ᵃ Administration, other services, and civilian research and development.

Unclassified

civilian sector beyond the short term would require a diversion of resources from the military. Some members of the military have acknowledged that defense must endure some pain under *perestroyka* to help the economy and, hence, its own needs down the line. Nevertheless, diversion of resources from defense to civilian objectives will escalate conflicts over resource allocation because it could delay upgrades to weapons plants, thereby postponing the introduction of new systems. Clearly there are strong economic pressures for major reductions in military spending. The full extent of these trade-offs will be based on an ongoing decisionmaking and bureaucratic process that will continue over the scope of the Estimate. (C-NF)

The Director, Defense Intelligence Agency, holds the view that a critical distinction must be made in the discussion of resource allocation trade-offs between the resource requirements for short-term objectives and those of long-range goals. Short-term requirements will rely primarily upon existing plant capacity and inputs. The demands Gorbachev is making on the defense sector do not require significant short-term reallocations from defense to the civilian sector or the disruption of current procurement programs. In the longer term, to achieve lasting gains in productivity, significant investment resources will be required. Redirecting investment going to the defense industry would not be sufficient to meet the economy's modernization requirements since other sectors take far greater shares of total investment. While slowing the flow of investment resources into the defense sector may well result in a downward turn in defense spending trends, the Soviets probably would maintain weapons programs that are key to force modernization, while stretching some lower priority programs and phasing out early some long-established weapons production runs. (S-NF)

The accumulating economic problems and the challenges posed by the simultaneous pursuit of economic and political reform will raise the level of contention higher than it has been so far in Gorbachev's tenure. As a result of these tensions and continued struggles over resource allocation, we believe there is some risk for Gorbachev's economic program. In the area of economic reform in particular, disruptions—widespread reform-related work stoppages or a drastic drop in performance indicators—would strengthen conservative opposition and convert to opponents those who have been only lukewarm supporters of reform. Such trends—coupled with the effects of *glasnost* and continuing nationality turmoil—could force the leadership into major retreat. If this should happen, the more orthodox elements of Gorbachev's program would survive, but the reforms designed to bring about a major decentralization of economic decision making would be shelved. (C-NF)

Implications for the West

On Arms Control
Gorbachev's initiatives in the arms control arena have been supported by development of "new thinking" in the formulation of national security policy. Three leading themes of this new policy are:

- *The economic dimension of national security.* Soviet leaders have linked an improved economy to the expansion of the USSR's influence, and they have

1. *(Continued)*

contended that the challenge posed by the arms race to Moscow's superpower status is as much economic as it is military. They and the military leadership agree that significant improvements in the high-technology sector of the economy are essential to compete with future Western weapon systems.

- *The limits of military power.* Gorbachev has tried to promote a concept of "mutual security" that attaches greater weight to political factors.

- *"Reasonable sufficiency."* Gorbachev and his followers have characterized this concept as having the necessary forces to deter aggression, and they have indicated that the Soviets already have sufficient power to do so. The Party Congress in February 1986, moreover, endorsed Gorbachev's call to "restrict military power within the bounds of reasonable sufficiency." (S NF)

In addition to trying to redefine Soviet national security requirements, we believe Gorbachev has moved arms control to the forefront of the USSR's national security agenda in an effort to dampen both external and internal pressures to spend more on defense, at least until he can reap the productivity gains he hopes to achieve from his industrial modernization program. With more than 150 Soviet Ground Forces divisions, 160 Soviet Air Forces regiments, and 50 Soviet Air Defense Forces regiments west of the Ural Mountains, any type of accommodation with NATO that would allow the Soviets to reduce expenditures on modernizing these forces has the potential to result in substantial resource savings. The Soviet leadership probably hopes that the process of arms control negotiations will weaken NATO's resolve to modernize conventional and tactical nuclear weapons—thus making possible cuts in their own defense spending. (S NF)

The unilateral force reductions recently announced by Gorbachev could pave the way for cutbacks in weapons procurement in the years ahead. The amount saved will depend on the forces affected, the restructuring of remaining forces to give them what Gorbachev described as a "clearly defensive" orientation, the pace at which the reduced force is modernized, and the costs of carrying out these initiatives. (S NF)

A plausible long-term method of transferring resources would be to redirect future investment from defense industries into the civilian sector during the next five-year plan (1991-95). As a result of the large-scale modernization in the defense industries in the 1970s, the defense sector has already in place most of the equipment it needs to produce weapon systems scheduled for deployment through the early 1990s. But the high-quality machine tools, equipment, and raw materials required to retool the defense industry to produce the next generation of weapons are the same resources needed for Gorbachev's industrial modernization program. (S NF)

For Eastern Europe and Soviet Client States

Attempts at political reform in the USSR are likely to generate pressure on East European countries for similar reforms. Moscow will also increase its demands on them for more and higher quality machinery and consumer goods and for greater participation in joint projects—particularly those involving the exploitation of Soviet natural resources. East European countries will also be asked to shoulder more of the costs of the Warsaw Pact defense effort. We believe these countries—which are facing economic constraints and are anxious to do hard currency business with the West—will be able to resist most of these demands successfully.[1] (C NF)

As to relations with client states, we expect increased pressure from Moscow for those countries to adopt reforms in order to reduce the burden of Soviet support. While such support is only a limited drain on resources, Gorbachev apparently believes that it is inconsistent to continue support at past levels to countries, such as Cuba and Vietnam, that are not willing to adopt more flexible economic policies. (C NF)

In Commercial Relations

We do not foresee a large, sustained increase in Soviet imports from the technologically advanced capitalist countries. Poor Soviet export prospects mean that such an increase would have to be financed either by a

---

[1] For further details, see NIE 11/12-9-88 (Secret NF NC), May 1988, *Soviet Policy Toward Eastern Europe Under Gorbachev.* (S NF)

1. *(Continued)*

substantial runup of debt, which Soviet officials insist they will avoid, or by accelerated gold sales, which could risk significant reduction in world gold prices. In this regard, the situation facing Moscow in 1988 is far different from the USSR's position in the early-to-middle 1970s, when the Soviets could easily manage a substantial increase in their debt to the West:
- Now Moscow must contend with stable or declining oil prices and uncertainties over the quantity of oil available for export.
- Much of the debt incurred in the 1970s was formally tied to Western agreements to purchase Soviet raw materials. This option is currently being used more selectively.

Moreover, although the Soviets recognize the potential gains from increased use of Western technology and equipment, they lack the confidence in the ability of the economy—as currently configured—effectively to absorb and ultimately to diffuse imported technology on a large scale. (C NF)

We cannot rule out a temporary sharp increase in imports of consumer goods as a stopgap measure, given the leadership's concern over the lack of popular support for Gorbachev's programs. Even such an increase would only restore Soviet spending on consumer goods imports to pre-1985 levels. The Soviets cut back substantially on imports of consumer goods at that time in response to a large reduction in export earnings. In recent months Western banks have been negotiating credit lines with the Soviet Union worth between $6 billion and $9 billion—largely tied to Soviet purchases of machinery and equipment for the production of consumer goods. In the past the Soviets have arranged such lines and not used them fully, and it is currently unclear to what extent they will use these newly acquired credit lines. Unlike the mid-1970s, when credit competition among Western governments worked to the Soviets' financial as well as political advantage, the new credit lines do not offer preferential financing, nor do they otherwise materially broaden the potential base for Soviet borrowing. (C NF)

A surge in borrowing from the West would not aid the Soviet economy significantly or ameliorate the resource competition between the military and civilian sectors. For example, even borrowing as much as Western bankers would allow—perhaps $3-4 billion net annually in addition to the roughly $5 billion needed per year to refinance maturing debt—would provide only a drop in the bucket for an economy that produces roughly $2 trillion worth of goods and services annually. We believe the Soviet leadership will not undertake such borrowings for fear of the economic leverage it would give Western governments and bankers. Moreover, the Soviets recognize that plans for any debt buildup can go awry should Moscow unexpectedly confront lower oil prices, further depreciation of the dollar, or two consecutive bad harvests. (C NF)

We expect to see an intensification of Soviet foreign economic initiatives, including increased concessions to Western firms to conclude joint-venture agreements, greater efforts to learn from Western businessmen, a stepped-up campaign for GATT membership, and the possible release of more trade and financial data to facilitate improved borrowing terms. (See annex D.) Under these conditions Soviet hard currency trade will continue to be dominated by Western Europe and Japan. The Soviets also will push hard as a top priority to improve economic relations with the European Community. (C NF)

The Soviets will continue to press for trade and possibly financial concessions from the West. This will lead to increased pressures for the West to pare further the list of COCOM-controlled technologies. Such pressure will make it more difficult for the West to maintain a unified stance on current agreements—or reach a new consensus—concerning trade and financial flows to the Soviet Bloc. (C NF)

For Western Leverage
Given the severity of Soviet economic problems, Gorbachev needs the many benefits of a nonconfrontational international environment. This gives the United States and its allies considerable leverage in bargaining with the Soviets over the terms of that environment on some security issues such as regional conflicts and arms control and on some internal

1. *(Continued)*

matters such as human rights and information exchange. The margins of this leverage will be set by Moscow's determination not to let the West affect the fundamental nature of the Soviet system or its superpower status.⁹ (C NF)

⁹ For a fuller discussion of these issues, see SNIE 11-16-88, *Soviet Policy During the Next Phase of Arms Control in Europe*, November 1988; NIE 11-3/8-88, *Soviet Forces and Capabilities for Strategic Nuclear Conflict Through the Late 1990s (Volume I)*, December 1988; and the forthcoming Estimates NIE 11-14-88, *Trends and Developments in Warsaw Pact Theater Forces and Doctrine, 1988-2007*; and NIE 11-4-89, *Soviet Strategy Toward the West: The Gorbachev Challenge*. (C NF)

1. *(Continued)*

Annex A
The "Kosygin Reform"

As outlined by Kosygin, the 1965 reform program was to include an administrative reorganization of the bureaucracy, some decentralization of planning and decisionmaking functions from the ministries to the enterprises, a change in success criteria for enterprises, a revision of wholesale prices, and a reform of the industrial supply system.

In comparison, Gorbachev's reform program is much more comprehensive and integrated, encompassing other key elements. For example, his price reform, unlike previous efforts, is designed to encompass all forms of prices—wholesale, procurement, and retail—and, in theory, is intended to change the basic pricing mechanism.

The 1965 reforms were handicapped by major economic flaws and inconsistencies. But they foundered largely because of opposition from the government bureaucracy, which reacted by procrastinating, assimilating, complicating, and regulating. Implementation of the reform also suffered from a lack of strong leadership backing. Its initiator, Kosygin, became increasingly overshadowed by Brezhnev, who lacked his predecessor's commitment to reform. The climate for a decentralization of decisionmaking became even less favorable after the Czechoslovak "spring" of 1968, which underscored the political risks of reform. Consequently, the reform was never implemented as initially intended.

1. *(Continued)*

Annex B
The Budget Deficit

The Soviet state budget deficit has increased dramatically during the last three years. We calculate the 1989 deficit will be about 125 billion rubles—some 13 percent of Soviet GNP. (For comparison, the highest US Government budget deficit represented 3.5 percent of US GNP in fiscal year 1986.)

The inflationary pressures resulting from Moscow's fiscal policy are already visible. Growth of wages almost doubled in the first half of 1988. There has been a marked increase in the prices of consumer goods sold in collective farm markets, along with higher prices and increased shortages of consumer goods in state stores. Articles in the Soviet press have complained loudly about enterprises inflating the prices of new machinery products. Excess purchasing power also has probably led to an expansion of the underground economy, which results in resource diversions from the state sector and undermines attempts to spur state worker productivity through higher wages and salaries.

Gorbachev's policies are partly responsible for the deficit rise:
- State spending has risen rapidly as a result of large boosts in state investment and increases in total state subsidies on food and livestock products.
- Receipts from stiff sales taxes on alcoholic beverages are down substantially as a result of the regime's antialcohol program.
- Revenues from the large markups imposed on the retail prices of imported food and consumer goods have fallen sharply as a result of the cutback in these imports starting in 1986.
- Proceeds from enterprise profit taxes grew slowly last year because of production problems due to retooling, reforms, and quality control measures.

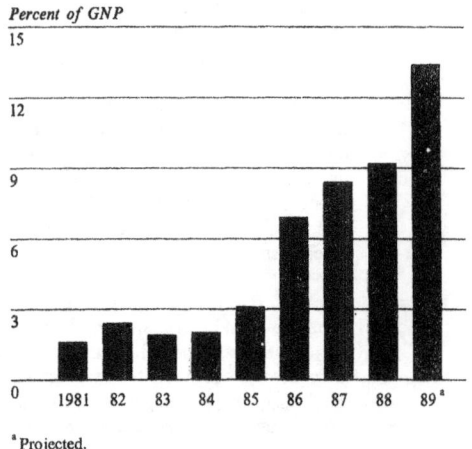

Figure 8
USSR: Estimated State Budget Deficit, 1981-89

Percent of GNP

ᵃ Projected.

19

1. *(Continued)*

Annex C
Soviet Economic Reform: Signs of a Radical Economic Shift

Indicators of forward movement toward radical, market-oriented reform would include:

- Less emphasis on the fulfillment of 1986-90 Five-Year Plan targets and the announcement of realistic 1991-95 goals. The 1989 plan already has accepted targets for produced national income and industrial production that are lower than called for in the current five-year plan.

- Strong, united commitment by the leadership not only to the general concept of economic restructuring but also to individual elements of the reform program that are particularly controversial, such as essential price changes or even price reform.

- Willingness to carry through particularly painful adjustments such as bankruptcies that close down many enterprises and wage reforms that lead to wide differentials in pay.

- Evidence of a large expansion in the number of cooperatives (and employees of cooperatives) and the playing down of resentment by the general populace over egalitarian issues.

- Promulgation of major new agricultural reforms that reduce the powers of the state and collective farms.

- Greater consolidation of economic ministries, accompanied by cuts in staff and revision of their charters to steer them away from supervising the day-to-day activities of economic enterprises.

- Continued ability of reform economists to publish controversial articles that push the limits of reform.

1. *(Continued)*

Annex D
Update on Joint Ventures

Moscow has signed 41 joint-venture contracts with Western firms in 1988, bringing the total to 61 since legislation governing such contracts took effect in January 1987. Nevertheless, Soviet leaders are discouraged by the low level of investment and technology in most of these deals and are considering changing the program to encourage more Western participation. Such changes might spur additional contracts, but primarily from firms interested in small-scale projects. (C-NF)

Moscow's relative success in negotiating joint ventures is largely the result of greater Soviet flexibility, particularly in easing restrictions on the repatriation of profits, the biggest obstacle to concluding agreements. The original legislation allowed Western firms to earn hard currency profits only by exporting finished products of the joint enterprise. Moscow is now allowing an array of options, including countertrade agreements in which the Western partners export Soviet goods to earn hard currency. In one agreement, the Soviets reportedly will also allow a consortium of six US firms to repatriate profits by pooling their hard currency earnings. (C-NF)

Despite the surge in agreements, the Soviet leadership is far from satisfied with the progress of its joint-venture program. Service and consumer-related projects, rather than high-technology deals, still dominate the list of completed contracts. (C-NF)

2. SOV 89-10077, Central Intelligence Agency, Office of Soviet Analysis, September 1989, *Gorbachev's Domestic Gambles and Instability in the USSR*

Directorate of
Intelligence

~~Secret~~
~~NOFORN-NOCONTRACT-~~
~~ORCON~~

Gorbachev's Domestic Gambles and Instability in the USSR (U)

An Intelligence Assessment

This paper was prepared by Grey Hodnett, Office of Soviet Analysis. Comments and queries are welcome and may be directed to the Director of Soviet Analysis on 482-7170 or secure ▓▓▓. (U)

Reverse Blank

~~Secret~~
SOV 89-10077X
September 1989

2. *(Continued)*

~~Secret~~
~~NOFORN-NOCONTRACT~~
~~ORCON~~

**Gorbachev's Domestic Gambles
and Instability in the USSR** (U)

Key Judgments

*Information available
as of 21 September 1989
was used in this report.*

Gorbachev and other Soviet leaders are concerned about serious future breakdowns of public order in the USSR. This concern is well justified. The unrest that has punctuated Gorbachev's rule is not a transient phenomenon. Conditions are likely to lead in the foreseeable future to continuing crises and instability on an even larger scale—in the form of mass demonstrations, strikes, violence, and perhaps even the localized emergence of parallel centers of power. This instability is most likely to occur on a regional basis, not nationwide—although overlapping crises and a linking together of centers of unrest could occur. (C NF)

Instability in the USSR is not exclusively a product of *glasnost*, and some of it is indeed a sign—as Gorbachev asserts—that reforms are taking hold. But Gorbachev's claim that instability otherwise merely reflects the surfacing of problems that were latent or repressed under Brezhnev is only partly true. The current budget deficit and consumption crisis is largely due to policies Gorbachev himself has pursued since 1985. And the prospects for further crises and expanded turmoil in the future are enhanced by key policy gambles he is taking now:

- In the *nationality* arena, Gorbachev is gambling on defusing ethnic grievances and achieving a more consensual federative union through unrestrained dialogue, some concessions to local demands aimed at eliminating past "mistakes," a constitutionalization of union/republic and ethnic group rights, and management of ethnic conflict to a substantial degree through the newly democratized soviets.

- In the *economic* arena, Gorbachev is gambling that, by putting marketization on hold through the postponement of price reform, and by pursuing a short-term "stabilization" program, he can avoid confrontation with the public *and* reengage in serious economic reform without steep costs at a later date.

- In the *political* arena, Gorbachev is gambling that, by transforming the Communist Party from an instrument of universal political, social, and economic management into a brain trust and authoritative steering organ, while empowering popularly elected soviets, he can create a more effective mechanism for integrating Soviet society and handling social tensions. (C NF)

iii

~~Secret~~
*SOV 89-10077X
September 1989*

2. *(Continued)*

~~Secret~~
~~NOFORN NOCONTRACT~~
~~ORCON~~

Gorbachev has no easy choices, and other approaches would not necessarily be safer or more successful. But these gambles, understandable and even desirable from a democratic standpoint, are based on questionable premises and wishful thinking:

- The aspirations of many non-Russians will never be satisfied within the framework of maximum rights the Soviet leadership could grant union republics or so-called autonomous ethnic formations within national republics while still preserving a strong federative USSR. Allowing these people freedom to protest without being able to redress their basic grievances is a recipe for escalating crises.

- Because the deficit reduction plan is likely to fall far short of planned targets and because it is unlikely that supply can catch up with consumer "needs" without a price-induced change on the demand side, Gorbachev's emergency financial "stabilization" program more likely than not will fail. In the meantime, circumstances for introducing marketization of the economy will have become even less propitious than they were when this program was introduced, setting the stage for continued corruption, protracted economic crisis, and retreat to the old "command-edict" methods.

- Gorbachev's attempt to reform the Communist Party is based on a visionary notion of what it could become, and is in practice undermining its ability to integrate Soviet society before new political institutions are capable of coping with mounting popular demands unleashed by *glasnost* and failing economic performance.

As Gorbachev's various critics correctly contend, his gambles are likely to generate instability over both the near and the longer term. (C NF)

The odds are high that labor unrest or ethnic strife will—perhaps even within the next six months—create strong pressures within the Soviet leadership to crack down much harder than it has to date. Soviet leaders have a broad range of instrumentalities they can employ to dampen instability, ranging from stronger threats, to new restrictions on human rights, to police intimidation, to imposition of martial law. We have evidence in at least one case of sharp disagreement within the Politburo over the use of violence. Gorbachev has sought to avoid widespread use of

2. *(Continued)*

physical force, probably calculating that the fallout from repression would endanger his entire program of *perestroyka* as well as his foreign policy, while perhaps provoking more serious disorders that could lead to loss of control. Almost certainly he would be willing to escalate coercion somewhat to maintain order and isolate nationalist or other "extremists," as he threatened to do in his report on nationality policy to the Central Committee plenum on 19 September 1989. Yet beyond a certain point, repression *would* mean abandonment by Gorbachev of his natural constituency and his entire political program. There is some evidence that he might choose to resign rather than assume responsibility for a crackdown involving a major imposition of martial law. Alternatively, the imposition of harsh measures could be associated with a coup d'etat or legal removal of Gorbachev.

Provided he manages to hold onto power, two outcomes of Gorbachev's rule are possible, depending on how successfully the economy is marketized. In both scenarios, Gorbachev's retention of power depends upon avoidance of acute polarization of political forces and progress in reinstitutionalizing means of political integration. This process would be reflected in further democratization of the political order, the emergence of some form of multiparty competition, and a loosening of the Soviet multinational empire. If political reform were complemented by effective financial stabilization and marketization, there might be high instability in the near term (two to five years), but a course could be set toward long-term (10 to 25 years) social equilibrium. Without financial stabilization and marketization, on the contrary, there would be rising instability in the near-to-medium term, high instability in the long term, and likely movement of the Soviet system toward revolution, a hard-right takeover, or "Ottomanization"—growing relative backwardness of the USSR and a piecemeal breakoff of the national republics.

Gorbachev's gambles and the centrifugal trends they have set in motion are already viewed with extreme alarm and anger by many members of the Soviet political elite. But Gorbachev's major gains in the Politburo at the September 1989 plenum of the Central Committee demonstrated once again how difficult it is to translate conservative sentiment in the ranks into effective opposition to Gorbachev's rule at the top. For the time being, his power looks secure. If, somehow, a successful challenge were mounted against him over the next year or so, the most likely outcome would be a

2. *(Continued)*

~~Secret~~
~~NOFORN-NOCONTRACT~~
~~ORCON~~

traditionalist restoration that would attempt to "draw the line" in various areas—especially with respect to democratization of the party and soviets, *glasnost* in the media, the conduct of informal groups, and expression of "nationalist" views—but would accept the need for significant change, including reduction in military spending and decentralization of management. Unless such a regime chose to move ahead vigorously with marketization (not impossible, but highly unlikely) it would obtain possible stability in the near term but suffer high medium- to long-term instability, leading toward Ottomanization or upheaval from below. If Gorbachev were not overthrown in the near term, an attempt to turn the clock back would become more difficult—given the reaction of increasingly well-entrenched pluralistic forces—and could thus also be nastier, possibly involving the armed forces and taking on a xenophobic Russian nationalist coloration. ~~(C NF)~~

Whether or not Gorbachev retains office, the United States for the foreseeable future will confront a Soviet leadership that faces endemic popular unrest and that, on a regional basis at least, will have to employ emergency measures and increased use of force to retain domestic control. This instability is likely to preoccupy Moscow for some time to come and—regardless of other factors—prevent a return to the arsenal state economy that generated the fundamental military threat to the West in the period since World War II. Moscow's focus on internal order in the USSR is likely to accelerate the decay of Communist systems and growth of regional instability in Eastern Europe, pointing to the need for post-Yalta arrangements of some kind and confronting the United States with severe foreign policy and strategic challenges. Instability in the USSR will increase uncertainty in the West about proper policies to pursue toward Moscow, reflecting nervousness about Soviet developments but nonchalance about defense, and will strain domestic and Alliance decisionmaking. ~~(C NF)~~

Domestic policy successes or failures will be the paramount factor ultimately determining Gorbachev's retention of office, but foreign policy achievements that allow him to justify further cuts in military spending on the basis of a reduction in the external "threat" would give him more room for maneuver. Western actions that could be presented by his opponents as attempts to "take advantage" of Soviet internal instability could hurt Gorbachev. ~~(C NF)~~

~~Secret~~

2. *(Continued)*

By putting economic reform on hold and pursuing an inadequate financial stabilization program, Gorbachev has brought Soviet internal policy to a fateful crossroads, seriously reducing the chances that his rule—if it survives—will take the path toward long-term stability. Over the short haul, there appears to be lack of competence among his advisers in the area of monetary and fiscal policy. A more fundamental weakness in Gorbachev's strategy that will perpetuate instability is its hesitant approach to marketization and unwillingness to face up to the necessity of real privatization of ownership of capital stock and land. He and his advisers need help with economic theory. Reduction of instability over the long haul requires the steady extension of a law-based private sector. (C-NF)

Harsh repression of labor unrest or of food riots in Russian cities are certainly contingencies that could require a response from US policymakers. But instability provoked by Gorbachev's gambles is likely to present its severest challenge to US policymaking through a crackdown in the ethnic arena—probably not in response to communal violence, but in the context of a move by Moscow to intervene in Russian-native clashes or to repress the drive for greater national autonomy. Such a crackdown is most likely in the Baltic region, but could also come in the Caucasus, Moldavia, or—down the road—even in the Ukraine. (C-NF)

Gorbachev has said he wants to create a constitutionally structured federative union, and movement toward such a system would certainly be a positive development from the US perspective. Gorbachev, however, is *not* interested in greasing the skids for dissolution of the USSR, and this is precisely what acceptance of the more radical Baltic demands would imply. Unless Gorbachev is prepared to broker a special status for the Baltic republics, and is able to win necessary political support for such an arrangement, a direct and violent confrontation between Moscow and the Baltic peoples seems likely. (C-NF)

2. *(Continued)*

Contents

	Page
Key Judgments	iii
Scope Note	xi
Introduction	1
Nationality Policy Gamble: Concessions Within Limits	1
Economic Reform Gambles	3
Postponement of Price Reform	3
The Crash Budget Deficit Reduction, Resource Reallocation, and Consumption Program	4
Selective Structural Reform	5
Political Reform Gambles	6
Transformation of the Communist Party	6
Empowering Democratized Soviets	7
Implications	8
Stability	8
Political Outcomes	10
Implications for the United States	12

2. *(Continued)*

Scope Note

This report offers a broad look at Gorbachev's domestic strategy and its implications for stability in the USSR. Descriptive sections of the report take into account the full range of classified and open-source information available, especially that dealing with Gorbachev's views, and are consistent with more detailed analysis produced by the Directorate of Intelligence. No systematic attempt is made to source the various judgments which, in the projective sections of the report, are based—as they are in all estimative writing—on a combination of extrapolation and logical inference. (C NF)

The report is a speculative paper drafted by a senior analyst in the Office of Soviet Analysis. In a period of epochal change in the USSR, anticipating the future is a hazardous undertaking, and the issues dealt with in the report hardly invite unanimity of judgment. Although there are differences among analysts on specific issues, the report's conclusions do reflect our sense of the problems and challenges that confront Gorbachev's revolution and the general direction in which it is now heading. (C NF)

2. *(Continued)*

Secret
NOFORN NOCONTRACT
ORCON

Gorbachev's Domestic Gambles and Instability in the USSR (U)

Introduction

Despite the increasingly pessimistic tenor of recent assessments in Moscow of Gorbachev's popularity and prospects, and rumors of coups or military intervention, his major gains in the Politburo at the September 1989 plenum of the Central Committee demonstrated once again great tactical political skill in transforming attacks against his line into movement forward. For the time being, at least, the future of *perestroyka* would appear to be less dependent on political struggle in the Politburo than on faltering regime performance. (C NF)

Many factors will affect this longer term performance. A key one, however, is Gorbachev's broad sense of where he wants the Soviet Union to go and how he seeks to get there—which is the focus of this paper. Western analysts disagree over the extent to which Gorbachev has a set of stable long-term objectives. Like Soviet observers, they are also uncertain whether Gorbachev's stated objectives are always necessarily his "real" objectives. The premise of this paper is that, while his positions have evolved over time, Gorbachev does have a fairly coherent "vision" (but not a "blueprint") of the future that is revealed in both classified and unclassifed sources. The existence of such a vision does not, of course, preclude tactical dissembling and ad hoc adjustment to circumstances. (C NF)

Gorbachev has insisted that the domestic revolution that he has launched in the USSR—which involves radically dismantling an existing *system* of more or less stable, if stagnant and poorly performing institutions—is the only path open. In fact, *perestroyka*, *glasnost*, and *demokratizatsiya* were not and are not the only options open to the Soviet Union: they represent the ultimate gamble on Gorbachev's part that a liberal, reformed Communism is possible and that the destabilization brought by change is containable. While denying his own fundamental responsibility for instability, Gorbachev has claimed that some measure of it is a necessary corollary of reform. And, in fact, instability arising from certain types of change undoubtedly is a sign of progress. Yet *glasnost* has accelerated the delegitimization of the present system. It has irretrievably destroyed the regime's capacity to use Marxist-Leninist doctrine as an instrument of political control. And it has weakened popular obedience to authority. (C NF)

Gorbachev is now embarked on a set of related gambles as he seeks to reform ethnic relations, the economy, and the general political system. These too are producing crises, on which Gorbachev hopes to capitalize to provide further momentum for *perestroyka*. From these crises new instability will arise, with the key questions being: how serious will manifestations of this instability be, and what types of crackdown is it likely to inspire? To call Gorbachev's choices gambles, of course, does not imply that other approaches would necessarily be safer or more successful; in each case, the trade-offs are not easy. (C NF)

Nationality Policy Gamble: Concessions Within Limits

Establishing a framework for dissolution of the USSR is not on Gorbachev's agenda. Yet he does seek solutions to the nationality problem that enjoy legitimacy, are not simply imposed by Moscow, and obviate levels of repression that would wreck his overall policy of *perestroyka*. The vision he has articulated over the past year or so—most recently at the September 1989 plenum of the Central Committee—encompasses:

- Transition of the USSR from a de facto unitary empire tempered by toleration of local boss rule to a more consensual union with real federative content.

- Constitutional delimitation of the functions of the Center and the national republics, with an increase in the authority allocated to the republics and some decentralization of operational powers within the Communist Party.

Secret

2. (Continued)

- Removal of discriminatory and provocative obstacles to the development of non-Russian languages and cultures, while preserving a strategic role for Russian as the language of interethnic communication.

- Equalization of the rights of all *nations* (including minor nationalities and Russians), balanced by equalization of the rights of *individuals* regardless of their place of residence.

- Integration of the national republics within a single unionwide economy, in which the "socialist market" harmonizes the interests of the multiethnic whole with the interests of the ethnic parts, but in which there is also some devolution of power to the republics.

The Soviet leadership confronts two quite different types of ethnic crises: the assertion of traditional nationalist demands for greater cultural, political, and economic autonomy from the Center; and rage generated by economic and social grievances that finds an outlet in communal violence. In principle, the first type of crisis can possibly be resolved, if not through political dialogue (there are many forms of autonomy and even "independence"), then at least through a type of crackdown that does not involve physical force; whereas the second type requires physical repression—utilized in a context, of course, that invites more sympathy on the part of outside observers.

In nationality policy, Gorbachev's gamble lies in the scope he has permitted for public expression of ethnic grievances and demands. He has acquiesced in a mushrooming of "informal" organizations in the non-Russian republics that, by any standard, are articulating "nationalist" views. He has tolerated substantial absorption of ethnic platforms by republic Communist Party organizations. With some exceptions, he has sought to resolve nationality problems through dialogue and has generally exercised restraint in repressing communal violence or pronational ethnic demonstrations. Indeed, there is some evidence that Moscow may be willing to go very far to meet Baltic demands, provided there is no deviation from the Center's line on foreign policy, defense policy, and—perhaps less categorically—financial-monetary policy.

Gorbachev is evidently convinced that the potential exists for the emergence of a broadly shared sense of genuine unionwide community among most Soviet citizens. Ethnic instability, he seems to believe, arises basically from past policy mistakes and mismanagement. Thus, ethnic unrest can eventually be moderated if these errors are corrected and legitimate ethnic grievances addressed. He has issued several stern warnings against "nationalism." At the September 1989 plenum of the Central Committee he observed that "the time has . . . come to talk with the clear and forcible language of law about conditions under which nationalist, chauvinist, and other extremist organizations can and should be banned and disbanded by the court." But he probably believes that attempts to "draw the line" through coercion are likely to trigger still higher levels of ethnic tension and play into the hands of opponents of *perestroyka*. And he seems to be counting heavily on the reconstituted political institutions of the USSR—especially the empowered Supreme Soviet and local soviets—to provide a mechanism through which ethnic interests and demands can be accommodated. He may hope to promote a coalition between reformers in Moscow and moderates in the non-Russian republics. In the Baltic area, he appears to have gambled that prudence will triumph over passion; that republic party leaders will be able to convince the population that Moscow *will* ultimately resort to force if compelled to do so, and that the republics should not—in a reckless lurch toward secession—risk what they now stand to gain.

However, the radicalization of ethnic demands and expansion of the mass popular base for ethnic assertiveness we see occurring, as well as the entrenchment of communal violence, suggest how tenuous the prospects are for Gorbachev's strategy. Lifting the lid on the nationalities has energized anti-Russian sentiments among the titular nationalities after whom the republics are named, created great anxiety among the Russian settlers who constitute large fractions of the population in major cities in these republics, and opened a path for cross-republic ethnic strife. It has also activated latent conflict between titular and small

2. *(Continued)*

nationalities, produced a flow of more than 340,000 internal refugees since 1987, and set the stage for a potentially sharp Russian backlash against Gorbachev's "permissiveness." In at least one case, Lithuania, it is possible that the republic party organization may proclaim its independence of the CPSU. While security and economic interests probably will constrain some of the titular nationalities from seeking to secede from the USSR, these inhibitions may not apply to Balts, Belorussians, and Ukrainians.

Economic Reform Gambles

In the economic reform area, Gorbachev's vision postulates creation of a self-regulating "socialist market" system in which central physical planning has been largely eliminated and enterprises make decisions essentially by responding to market forces. Decision cues are provided by prices set largely by supply and demand, and inputs are acquired through direct contracts and wholesale trade. In this system the state plays a coordinating role, sets the "overall normative framework," and takes the lead in promoting science and technology, infrastructure development, environmental protection, establishment of a financial-banking-tax system, enactment of antimonopoly measures, and institutionalization of the entire system within a structure of law. Operational control would pass from middle levels of the bureaucracy to the basic production unit, reflected in (a) a breakup of large economic conglomerates and a transfer of control from the economic bureaucracy to production collectives (especially through leasing), and (b) democratization of enterprise management, in which workers' collectives elect their managers and oversee key production decisions. The "socialist" aspect of this postulated system would apparently consist of two features: retention and expansion of a strong welfare state component (Sweden is mentioned as an example to emulate); and continued public ownership of at least most land and capital stock, although leasing and other arrangements would substantially modify the concept of property.

Gorbachev's own policies, however—including the steep reduction of revenues from state alcohol sales, the financing from the budget of the crash machine-building program, wage boosts for some categories of workers, increased spending for social programs, and escalating food subsidies—generated a rapidly rising budgetary deficit and shortage of consumer goods sufficiently ominous to persuade him in 1988-89 to agree to a "stabilization" strategy for the next several years. The main elements of this strategy are (a) postponement of retail and wholesale price reform; (b) the adoption of a crash budget deficit reduction, resource reallocation, and consumption program; and (c) continued pursuit of selected elements of structural reform. This change of course has brought Soviet domestic policy to a fateful crossroads.

Postponement of Price Reform

Gorbachev's statements through mid-1988 strongly favoring price reform make it abundantly clear he understands that full transition to an economy in which financial calculations effectively determine decisionmaking depends on price reform. Nevertheless, he has publicly and repeatedly committed himself since then to postpone retail price reform "two or three years," to discuss it with the public before doing anything, and not to change prices without public consent. In the absence of retail price reform, planned hikes in wholesale prices would require increased state subsidies that would add to the financial imbalance Moscow is fighting to bring under control, and Gorbachev has also delayed these increases indefinitely. There is no mystery why he has agreed to this critical policy position: to proceed with price reform at this point would also have been a difficult gamble. Gorbachev and his advisers were deterred by the prospect of having to cope with a possibly violent popular response to price increases, hoped to buy social peace, and convinced themselves that conditions to move on prices would be more propitious later once financial "stabilization" had been achieved and hyperinflation averted, the monopoly factor dealt with, and other steps taken.

The costs of this gamble are likely to be enormous. By largely postponing the establishment of the indispensable prerequisite for economically rational decisionmaking, the gamble blocks workable decentralization, the introduction of genuine wholesale trade, and reliance on financial levers—thus effectively putting marketization on hold irrespective of other important constraints. Failure to deal with wholesale prices will intensify the problems and costs in the future of currently underpriced nonrenewable resources (especially energy and minerals). It will also build further irrationality into investment and the stock of fixed capital, imposing still higher economic and social costs downstream for corrective actions. Subsidies to agriculture will also have to rise. (C-NF)

On the retail side, Gorbachev's *talk* about price reform has been an invitation to the population to increase hoarding of consumer goods. The longer retail prices are frozen, the more the pattern of consumer demand is distorted, as faulty signals mislead producers and consumers. If food sales increase, so will food subsidies. Most important, delay may make the ultimate problem of dealing with retail prices that much more intractable: prices that might only have had to be doubled, let us say, may—with delay—have to be quadrupled. Meanwhile, the postponement of retail and wholesale price reform will expand corruption throughout the economy, producing an adverse effect on popular morale and public tolerance for *perestroyka*. (C-NF)

The Crash Budget Deficit Reduction, Resource Reallocation, and Consumption Program

In the period 1981-85 the average annual budget deficit was 16.7 billion rubles. This figure rose to 58.7 billion rubles in 1986, 72.9 billion in 1987, 90.2 billion in 1988, and a CIA-projected 126 billion in 1989. Alarmed by the growing financial imbalance in the country, the Soviet leadership has approved an "emergency" program to reduce expenditures on investment,[1] defense, subsidies to unprofitable enterprises, administrative costs, and social programs, and to increase revenues from imports of consumer goods, turnover taxes on increased production of consumer goods, and social insurance payments. There is discussion of financing the deficit, in part at least, through the sale of state securities and bonds bearing an interest rate of 5 percent. The strategy has also

[1] State centralized investment for "productive" uses in 1990 is to be 30 percent less than the target for 1989, and for some sectors of heavy industry the reduction is to be 40 percent. (C)

accelerated conversion of defense industry for civilian production, mandated a crash expansion of consumer goods production by all branches of industry, and reversed signals by accepting the recommendation to initiate increased imports of consumer goods. Gorbachev's hope is that he can "saturate" the consumer market, mop up some of the huge cash savings of the population, eliminate shortages, avert hyperinflation or "barterization" of the economy, head off popular unrest, and create equilibrium conditions under which it will be possible later to initiate full marketization. (C-NF)

Yet it is highly likely that deficit reduction will fall far short of planned targets. It will be hard to impose investment cuts on ministries and republics, and there is pressure—expressed already through the Supreme Soviet—to block delays in the implementation of social programs. Inflation itself will begin feeding back to raise the level of government spending. Moreover, gains in projected revenues from turnover taxes are based on unrealistically high targets for the production of consumer goods, and subsidies for agriculture and other consumer goods will remain a major drain on the budget. (C-NF)

There are other problems with the "stabilization" formula. Without a price-imposed change on the demand side, it is unrealistic to hope that supply can catch up with consumer "needs." The across-the-board campaign approach—implemented through the very "command-edict" methods that Gorbachev says he deplores—is likely to result in inferior products, high costs, and waste. Expansion of consumer-goods imports will impose still greater stress on Soviet hard currency reserves, force acceptance of higher levels of indebtedness, and defer imports for other sectors of the economy. At the same time, fear of the economic and political consequences of a higher hard currency debt, and recognition that imports would have to be far greater to substantially diminish the savings "overhang," are likely to inhibit consumer-goods imports as a central component of financial stabilization. On the investment side, radical, abrupt shifts in proportions historically have—by ignoring the interdependence of different economic sectors—wasted

2. *(Continued)*

resources and thrown the losers into a tailspin. It is not inconceivable that the magnitude of cuts projected in heavy industry could generate a chain reaction of producer-good supply shortages, leading to a spiraling downturn in production in the economy.

Selective Structural Reform
Gorbachev has by no means acknowledged that his decision on prices and macroeconomic "stabilization" puts economic reform on hold. He talks as if he wishes to move ahead. At the September 1989 plenum of the Central Committee he called attention to forthcoming discussion by the Supreme Soviet of draft fundamental laws on ownership, land, leasing, republic economic rights, the local economy, self-management, and taxation. And, in fact, there is momentum to press forward with implementation of the 1987 Law on the State Enterprise and elements of reform that are preconditions of marketization, such as expansion of enterprise rights in setting prices, wages, and output levels; partial derationing of industrial supplies; and reduction in the number of plan indicators. In the absence of rational prices and other essential conditions, however, these steps have the perverse effect of promoting arbitrary or monopolistic price increases rather than cost reduction, wasting "cheap" energy and raw materials, encouraging wage increases not matched by productivity gains, and motivating enterprises to produce the wrong output mix. The devolution of some economic decision making authority from the Center to the republic and regional levels, which is also being conducted under the rubric of economic "reform," can have some beneficial effects, but risks simply transferring "command" methods from the State Planning Committee to local bureaucrats and strengthening autarkic tendencies that weaken overall marketization.

A Gorbachev initiative with serious long-term implications has been the fostering of new forms of "ownership" and management of production units. Gorbachev believes that the establishment of *proprietary* interest is a basic key to economic revitalization and that this condition cannot be achieved under the present depersonalized state ownership of the means of production. Thus he is pushing strongly for acceptance of the proposition that "various" forms of ownership are legitimate under "socialism." Yet, at the same time, he has sharply attacked Western-style private ownership of the means of production, equating this with "exploitation." Although he supports cooperatives, the solution to this ideological dilemma, he emphasizes over and over, is the *leasing* of capital stock and land to production collectives. He has in mind not just agriculture and services, but large chunks of industry. He clearly hopes that leasehold property "ownership" will engender proprietary interest, combat monopoly, and defeat bureaucratic sabotage of *perestroyka*—while avoiding the supposed adverse social consequences of real privatization. In the not too distant future it is quite possible that Gorbachev will unleash a big campaign to shift the economy to leaseholding, despite resistance to it by Yegor Ligachev and perhaps other members of the Politburo.

The difficulty with Gorbachev's calculation is that experience in both Eastern Europe and the West suggests that leaseholding does *not* produce the same positive benefits as private ownership, although in certain limited situations the results may be useful. Leaseholding does not provide the basis for creation of a true capital market, with the sale and purchase of production assets. Thus market prices for capital and land cannot emerge. Prices for these resources would still have to be set by planners and could not reflect particular circumstances or changes in values over time. Nor does leaseholding create the same interest or empowerment of specific individuals to seek to increase the value of enterprise assets. On the contrary, it may well make required investment and structural rationalization decisions more difficult by encouraging leaseholders of state-owned property simply to "mine" their assets—diminishing the economy's production capacity over time.

Possibly Gorbachev recognizes these problems and sees leaseholding as an ideologically defensible "cover" for a longer term transition from collective to private ownership. Reporting suggests, however, that he really does reject *large-scale* private ownership on ideological grounds and believes that leaseholding provides a workable "socialist" alternative. His attacks on private ownership

2. *(Continued)*

have been complemented by hedging in his defense of cooperatives. By making these politically convenient accommodations to the dominant collectivist preferences of Soviet elites and the population, at a time in which the absence of legally regulated markets is spawning growing corruption throughout the decentralized sector of the economy, Gorbachev is reinforcing strong impulses that exist to reassert "administrative" controls over the economy.

The collectivist predicament carries over into the sphere of management. Gorbachev has vigorously supported workplace democratization, including the election of managers, as a means of breaking resistance to *perestroyka* within the bureaucracy and overcoming alienation and apathy among the work force. The principle of electivity of managers was codified in the Law on State Enterprises, adopted in July 1987. In combination with collective leaseholding, however, workplace democratization would appear—potentially at least—to be setting the Soviet Union on the Yugoslav path. It will probably discourage investment by enterprises, encourage unjustified wage increases, make it harder to broaden wage differentials, strengthen pressures to continue subsidizing enterprises operating at a loss, and promote inflation.

Political Reform Gambles

Drawing on the experience of earlier economic reform efforts, Gorbachev has argued that economic reform will fail unless it is underpinned by political reform. Since 1987 he has promoted political reform as the key to *perestroyka*. His aim is to replace the traditional Stalinist system of political power with an entirely new structure that is less centralized, more democratic, more open to the unrestricted flow of political ideas and information, more "constitutionalized" through fundamental law, and more protective of the citizen's civil liberties. The key changes are those affecting the demarcation of functions and power between the party apparatus and the popularly elected soviets.

Transformation of the Communist Party
In the existing Soviet system the Communist Party has provided the central mechanism of political integration. Under its aegis, acting more or less collegially through bureaus selected co-optatively at all levels of the party, representatives of the system's key institutions (the economic hierarchy, the soviets, the security organs, and—especially—the party's own bureaucracy) have decided policy. In this system the party bureaucracy—the "apparatus"—has itself routinely exercised the right to issue binding orders to officials in all other bureaucracies. It has also controlled the process of personnel appointments to all leadership posts in all institutions, whether these posts are appointive or nominally "elective," through the *nomenklatura* system. Below the central level, the key function actually performed by the party apparatus has been to *implement* rather than make or win converts for policy. Its most important role in this respect has been to cope with inconsistencies between enterprise production targets and available inputs caused by incoherent economic plans. (This is why top positions in the party apparatus, at least in the Russian Republic, have generally been staffed with engineers.) The real role of the army of "ideological" functionaries in the party has been not so much to *argue* the party's position and build party "legitimacy," as to communicate what the party leadership's position is on various issues. The problem of party "authority" until recently was not particularly germane, because there was no political competition, few people were prepared to challenge the party line, and those who did were handled by a different bureaucracy—the KGB.

Gorbachev appears to believe that the party should continue to integrate the entire Soviet system ("perform its vanguard role"). He has an altogether different vision, however, of how this function is to be performed. In his view, the party should abandon its de facto executive and legislative activity. It should:
- Cede rulemaking power to the soviets and other state or public organizations.
- Stop issuing binding orders to all other organizations.
- Curtail dictation of personnel appointments through the *nomenklatura* system.
- Remove itself from day-to-day involvement in the implementation of economic plans.

2. (Continued)

At the same time, the party should strengthen its "political" role by:
- Serving as a brain trust at all levels to generate appropriate macropolicies.
- Winning authority for the party and its line by force of persuasion in the emerging competitive political arena.
- Influencing elections and personnel appointments in all institutions by cultivating and presenting the "best" candidates.
- Incorporating the interests of all strata of the population through broad external dialogue and internal party democratization. (C NF)

Gorbachev is, in fact, attempting to implement this model. He has weakened the Central Committee Secretariat and may be reaching policy decisions in an informal group outside the Politburo. He has eliminated the branch economic departments in the apparatus—the organizational base for day-to-day party intervention in the economy. He has ordered party officials to exert influence through persuasion rather than command. He has attacked the *nomenklatura* system as prone to error and the perpetuation of mediocrity. He is urging party leaders at all levels not to wait for instructions from above but to develop their own "action programs." He is demanding that all party officials emulate his own example and carry the case for *perestroyka* to the population through the mass media. He is promoting competitive elections within the party. And he is instigating personnel cuts in the party apparatus and a large-scale turnover of party cadres, to which he attaches great significance. (C NF)

Essentially, Gorbachev's program implies the liquidation of the CPSU as it has existed and the creation of an organization that is new in its functions, structure, personnel, and relationships with other parts of the Soviet system. Through this transformation the party is to regain both the will and the legitimacy to rule. Were such a metamorphosis to succeed, it could in principle create an integrating vehicle compatible with democratized soviets and other elective organizations. It would also clear away resistance in the party apparatus to *perestroyka*. (C NF)

The odds against the desired transformation of the party, nonetheless, are formidable. Exhortation to exert influence through persuasion is unlikely to give the party enough moral authority to compensate for loss of the operational power to issue orders and dictate personnel appointments. It is questionable whether purging the party apparatus will increase its ability to operate in a competitive political environment as much as Gorbachev seems to hope. *Pravda* complained editorially in June that "a considerable part of the party apparatus is in total disarray and is unable to find its bearings in the new situation." And it is difficult to identify, beyond presumed psychic rewards, what the payoffs are to be that will motivate party officials. Rather, the odds seem much higher that Gorbachev's strategy will simply undermine the real-life CPSU, weaken its ability to bring order to a still nonmarketized economy, increase uncertainty as to its role, further demoralize both cadres and rank-and-file members, and intensify the already high level of anger of the apparatus toward Gorbachev. (C NF)

Empowering Democratized Soviets

Gorbachev is banking heavily on the soviets being able in a timely and effective manner to fill the vacuum created by his redefinition of the party's role. What he seeks is a mechanism that enjoys legitimacy, is sensitive to pressures from below, is able to reconcile conflicting popular interests and demands, is capable of controlling officialdom, and is nevertheless responsive at least in general terms to party guidance. With the election of the new Congress of People's Deputies and formation of the Supreme Soviet, the first meeting of the Congress in June and subsequent session of the Supreme Soviet, and the upcoming elections to local soviets in the fall, Gorbachev has launched Soviet politics on a promising but perilous path. (C NF)

We should not exclude the possibility that this venture will eventually succeed. Much of the brief experience of the Congress and new Supreme Soviet—especially

2. (Continued)

the emergence of a new corps of middle-class politicians, the frank discussion of formerly taboo topics, the role of deputies in helping to solve the miners' strikes, and the rejection of some nominees to the Council of Ministers—provides grounds for hope. But the politicization of the Soviet population, the urgency of public needs, and the radicalization of demands made by the rapidly growing number of "informal" groups will impose severe strains on these new institutions. Tolerance and compromise are not yet part of the political culture of either the new Soviet electorate or the new deputies. Political competition in this arena, contrary to Gorbachev's calculations, may work against the establishment of market socialism. Conflicts generated over ethnic issues will be bitter. A "hardhat workers" politics of unpredictable orientation may emerge. The new institutions currently lack most of the operational attributes of functioning democratic parliaments that help them to conduct business and deal with such pressures, and these can develop only with time.

Whether multiparty political competition will emerge as the new soviets evolve is a critical issue. With the formation of the "Interregional Group" of deputies, the collective action of Baltic deputies, and the caucusing of "workers' deputies," organized *opposition* has already arrived in the Supreme Soviet. Some participants in these groups visualize the rapid emergence of multiparty politics. And several groups outside the Supreme Soviet—for example, the Christian Democratic Union, the Social Democratic Association, the Democratic Perestroyka Club, and the various ethnic fronts—are already organizing as political parties, or plan to do so.

It is conceivable that Gorbachev privately welcomes the prospective emergence of multiparty competition as a long-term stabilizer of the USSR's new mass politics. In this scenario, he might hope simply to preserve the Communist Party's de jure monopoly long enough to effect the transfer of real power from the CPSU to the Supreme Soviet, at which point traditionalists in the party would be unable to prevent recognition of a multiparty fait accompli. It is more likely, however, that—as he told Hungarian leaders Nyers and Grosz in July—he is prepared to accept multiparty politics in Hungary but does not want such

a system established in the USSR. Publicly, he has repeatedly criticized advocacy of multipartyism in the Soviet Union—arguing that this would multiply cleavages in an already "complex" society and, most important, would promote ethnic strife. In this scenario, he would be aware that his invitation to informal groups to participate in parliamentary politics could lead to the formation of other parties, as Nikolay Ryzhkov and others have warned, but planned to maintain the CPSU's preponderant role by somehow taming or co-opting the main opposition groups.

In the meantime, as Ryzhkov has also observed, the creation of the new activist Supreme Soviet headed by Gorbachev introduces an element of profound ambiguity in the distribution of power and authority between the CPSU Central Committee and Politburo, the Supreme Soviet, and the Council of Ministers at the very top of the Soviet system. When local elections are held and empowered soviets formed at all lower levels, this ambiguity will spread throughout the system, potentially setting the stage for a generalized "constitutional" crisis. Large numbers of party secretaries are likely to be defeated in these elections. To the extent that election by the populace to the respective soviet is seen to be a necessary validation of a party secretary's tenure of office, political reform will sharply heighten anxiety and promote cleavage within the party apparatus. Gorbachev probably hopes to use the crisis resulting from elections to the soviets to redefine formally, both constitutionally and through revision of the party rules, the division of labor and respective powers of party, state, and government organs.

Implications

Stability

Gorbachev's vision of a liberal Communist future seeks to reconcile satisfaction of ethnic demands with preservation of the Soviet multinational state, piecemeal introduction of marketization with "socialism," and democratization with maintenance of the Communist Party's "vanguard role." Minimizing bloodshed has been central to his tactics. His desire to avoid

2. *(Continued)*

major confrontation with the population and to find "political" solutions to problems is reflected in his encouragement of politicization of the population and tolerance of social turbulence; his readiness to interpret hostility toward the Communist Party and the Soviet system as a product simply of failure by the regime to eradicate past "mistakes"; his propensity to ignore ideological "provocation"; his optimism about reaching the "correct" solutions to problems through rational calculation, dialogue, and compromise; and his disinclination to use force or administrative pressure. (C-NF)

These qualities are reflected in the gambles discussed in this paper, which in turn are generating major problems:

- In the *nationality* arena, *glasnost* and Gorbachev's gamble on defusing ethnic grievances and achieving a more voluntary federative union through dialogue is activating passions on all sides, stimulating a serious secessionist challenge, and fueling an imperial backlash.

- In the *economic* arena, Gorbachev's gamble on postponement of price reform, a crash consumption program, and selective pursuit of certain structural changes has placed real marketization on hold, mortgaged its introduction to a financial stabilization program that is more likely than not to fail, possibly compromised its eventual success with strictures against private economic activity, and set the stage for continued corruption and protracted economic crisis.

- In the *political* arena, Gorbachev's gamble on reconstituting the Communist Party along lines that have no parallel in single-party (or multiparty) systems elsewhere is seriously weakening the central existing mechanism for societal integration in the USSR, while the gamble on instituting guided democracy through the soviets is likely to impose large new strains on the regime sooner than it provides an effective means for dealing with them.

Gorbachev has no easy options, and other gambles would have produced other problems. Wherever those problems might have led, the set of problems Gorbachev has in fact fostered is likely to lead in the foreseeable future to major instability in the USSR. (C-NF)

So far, neither the rioting, nor the communal violence, nor the demonstrations that have occurred in the non-Russian republics have compelled Gorbachev to resort to more than limited doses of armed repression. The most violent conflicts have largely not involved natives versus Russians. However, with the escalation of ethnic assertiveness generally since 1988, the radicalization of Baltic demands, and the growth of Russian nationalist sentiment, the stage is being set for major Russian/non-Russian conflict. Potentially, the most explosive near-term source of such combustion is the backlash of large numbers of Russians living in the borderlands to native attempts to assure priority of the local language, residency requirements for political participation, and progress toward autonomy or even independence. The fears now displayed among Russians in the Baltic republics and Moldavia could lead spontaneously to confrontations that would require large-scale intervention by Moscow. But they also provide fertile soil for provocation by Gorbachev's opponents designed to force broad intervention that would undermine *perestroyka*. At some point, even in the absence of settler-instigated conflict, native assertiveness is likely to precipitate confrontation with the Center, however self-disciplined the non-Russians may be. One factor that could lead to such a clash might be Moscow's determination not to allow relaxation of controls in the Baltic republics to set a precedent for the Ukraine. (C-NF)

Gorbachev has sought to replace Brezhnev's tacit understanding with the population, which essentially provided a guaranteed minimum living standard and social security benefits in return for political passivity, with a new "social contract" that would provide greater economic opportunity and political participation in exchange for harder work and less economic security. But his economic gamble is unlikely to generate the sustained growth in material rewards necessary to support such a transition. At best, the policy will stabilize a deteriorating situation; if it fails, the result could be hyperinflation and the emergence of a barter economy. And the policy still leaves the economy in a state of protracted vulnerability to at least three generators of an economic downturn that

2. (Continued)

would further enhance the likelihood of street politics: the incoherent current blend of "plan" and "market"; the possible chain reaction of producer-good supply shortages noted above; and—not least—major strike activity. (C NF)

Gorbachev was able in July to deflect blame for the miners' strikes and turn them to his own immediate advantage, but only by granting major concessions to the miners that will increase the deficit and may well encourage more groups to use ultimatum politics ▮▮▮▮▮▮▮▮▮▮▮▮▮▮▮▮▮▮▮▮▮▮▮▮ Heady from their success, organized miners are spearheading formation of a mass labor movement, which might develop widespread support among workers who want the security of the old social contract as well as the improved quality of life *perestroyka* promises. (S NF NC OC)

Glasnost, the evaporation of fear of authority, and Gorbachev's attempt to mobilize popular pressure against bureaucratic vested interests have—in combination with consumer dissatisfaction and diffuse public anger toward the Establishment—tapped latent impulses and energized political moods at the base of Soviet society. The old "transmission belts"—especially the trade unions and Komsomol—that integrated the "masses" with the regime have, in the new competitive environment, become increasingly irrelevant. Elections to the Congress of People's Deputies revealed how little confidence the party apparatus itself enjoys among the population at large. Gorbachev's gamble on radically restructuring Soviet political institutions is further weakening the old mechanisms that repressed popular unhappiness. (C NF)

Opinion polls and abundant evidence from other sources suggest that the public's priority concern is improving the standard of living. To the extent that the new Supreme Soviet and local soviets act as vehicles for absorbing mass unrest, they are likely to press for welfare spending, wage increases, subsidies for unprofitable enterprises, delay of price reform, and other measures that will increase the difficulty of moving toward effective marketization. In this sense, the phasing in of political reform before economic reform may have severe long-term costs. (C NF)

But political competition encouraged by reform is giving voice to other concerns as well: about public order, crime, loss of control in the borderlands, environmental destruction, erosion of traditional values, elite corruption, and profiteering by cooperatives. This volatile mixture of grievances could, under conditions of continuing consumer deprivation, lead to outbreaks of anarchic violence or provide a social base for attempts by political elites to reverse Gorbachev's policies. (C NF)

Political Outcomes

Gorbachev's gamble on a protracted transition to marketization, unless modified, is likely to delay serious economic revitalization indefinitely and create conditions of chronic instability irrespective of the destabilizing impact of ethnic conflict. Under these conditions, governing the Soviet Union will become progressively more difficult. Yet the fragmentation of political power currently under way will probably continue. Within the party, divisions now visible pitting natives against Russians within the republics, republic party organizations against other republic party organizations and against the Center, RSFSR oblast party organizations against the Central Committee apparatus, and liberal against traditionalist factions, will expand. And Gorbachev's personal authority within the party and among the population at large will probably continue to decline, despite his political victory at the September plenum of the Central Committee. (C NF)

Some observers have speculated that anarchy will be the end result of these developments. This is a highly unlikely outcome: if "anarchy" does occur, it will simply mark the transition from one set of political arrangements to another. What is likely is that instability will force the Soviet leadership to choose from an array of crackdown measures, ranging from stronger threats, to new restrictions on freedom of speech and assembly, to bans on strikes, to personnel purges, to exertion of economic pressures, to police or military intimidation, to deployment of larger and more aggressive security forces, to declaration of states of emergency, to imposition of martial law. Choices here

2. *(Continued)*

will hinge partly on how threatening to regime survival conditions of instability are judged to be, partly on how effective in suppressing disorder given types of crackdown are predicted to be, and partly on how counterproductive the crackdown measures are held to be in terms of frustrating attainment of other key objectives. (C-NF)

The record suggests that Gorbachev has a high tolerance for disorder, will seek as long as possible to find compromise solutions, and, when decisive action becomes necessary, will attempt to select measures at the lower end of the crackdown scale. He seems to fear that bloodshed resulting from a crackdown would seriously exacerbate conflict situations; he probably has not been impressed by the efficacy of force applied in Central Asia and the Caucasus; and he must fear the consequences for *perestroyka* and his foreign policy of a broad and extended resort to armed might. (C-NF)

A major escalation of repression, especially if it involved the imposition of martial law, could well pose the question of who should lead the USSR. Currently there is much speculation in Moscow about martial law, the acquisition by Gorbachev of unrestrained power, coups, and military takeovers. Gorbachev might be inclined to adopt a broad view of his prerogatives as head of state, and perhaps even exercise limited emergency powers in an effort to advance *perestroyka*. He would be willing to escalate coercion somewhat to maintain order and isolate nationalist or other "extremists." At the September 1989 plenum of the Central Committee he condemned "extremist rallies that provoke interethnic clashes and terrorize and intimidate people of other nationalities," and declared that "where a threat to the safety and life of people arises, we will move decisively using the full force of Soviet laws." He also observed, with respect to Nagorno-Karabakh, that "we stand before the need to take resolute measures; we cannot allow anarchy, let alone bloodshed." (C-NF)

Yet it is highly doubtful that Gorbachev would abandon his reform program and his natural constituency by sanctioning indiscriminate violence, or engage in a bid to seize dictatorial power through an alliance with his political enemies. It is possible, however, that he might choose to resign rather than assume responsibility for a crackdown involving a major imposition of martial law. In his conversation with the Hungarians noted above, Gorbachev seemed to imply that he would have resigned rather than order force to be used against the strikers. And he appeared to be dropping a similar hint in a speech he delivered more recently in Leningrad. Naturally, he could also justify retaining office (if he were indeed inclined to resign) on "lesser evil" grounds. (C-NF)

In the event that Gorbachev remains in power, his resort to force is likely to be limited, and instability will not easily deflect processes that appear to be heading toward further democratization of the political order, some form of multipartyism, and a loosening (or, in the Baltic case, even a breakup) of the Soviet multinational empire—provided Gorbachev can avoid sharp political polarization and achieve some reinstitutionalization of political integration through the soviets. If there is financial stabilization and marketization, there might be high instability in the near term (two to five years) but a course could be set toward long-term (10 to 25 years) social equilibrium. Without financial stabilization and marketization (which are now in serious jeopardy), there would be rising instability in the near-to-medium term, high instability in the long term, and likely movement of the Soviet system toward revolution, a hard-right takeover, or what has been termed "Ottomanization"—a slow process of imperial decline with unplanned piecemeal emancipation of constituent entities in a context of growing relative backwardness of the whole in relation to the capitalist West. (C-NF)

2. (Continued)

The trend toward liberalization and imperial dissolution is perceived as a clear and present danger by some members of the Soviet political elite, who are shocked by what they perceive as a breakdown of social discipline and loss of regime control. Their anxiety, fear, and anger could still crystalize in an attempted coup, legal removal of Gorbachev, or even assassination. Judging by what is being said publicly by Gorbachev's critics in the apparat, as well as in intelligence reporting, a traditionalist restoration would not be simply a throwback to the Brezhnev regime. It would accept the need for significant change, including reductions in defense spending and decentralization of management, but would attempt to "draw the line" in many areas—especially democratization of the party and government, the media, the conduct of "informal" groups, and expression of "nationalist" views—in which Gorbachev's liberalism is seen as outrageous. Although the odds are high that a traditionalist regime would increase restrictions on private entrepreneurial activity and marketization, it is not altogether inconceivable—depending on who was in charge—that such a leadership might take advantage of limits on public expression to move forward vigorously with marketization. Barring this slim possibility, the prognosis for such a regime would be near-term stability but high medium- to long-term instability, leading to Ottomanization or upheaval from below. (C-NF)

The length of Gorbachev's tenure is an important variable. In the event that he is not soon overthrown, his gambles on ethnic and political reform are likely to increase the social forces of resistance to an orthodox reaction. Such a development would correspondingly increase the degree of coercion required to "restore order." Those intent on such a course of action might seek to gain support from the military or KGB, or to mobilize elements of the working-class population to back their cause. Political maneuvering to develop and define a mass "workers'" movement is already under way. Gorbachev is seeking to enlist the "workers" as a force for *perestroyka*. Populist figures such as Boris Yel'tsin may seek to appeal to the welfare-state preferences of the working class. Reactionaries would espouse neofascist slogans designed to tap into the anti-intellectual, anti-Semitic, anticapitalist, xenophobic, Russian nationalist moods that also exist among many "workers." A successful traditionalist or reactionary restoration, however, would solve neither the economic problems nor the nationality problems, and thus would perpetuate instability—repressed if not open. (C-NF)

Implications for the United States

Under any scenario, economic tensions, acute consumer dissatisfaction, labor unrest, and ethnic strife virtually guarantee that the United States will have to deal with a Soviet leadership that faces endemic popular instability. The chances that economic reform will significantly reduce the potential for instability in the foreseeable future are low, and are certainly less than the chances that Gorbachev's own gambles will foster continuing economic stagnation or decline. Gorbachev will maneuver to dampen instability through compromise and to avoid armed confrontation and bloodshed. He may muddle through more successfully than appears likely. But the odds are great nevertheless that labor unrest or ethnic conflict will—perhaps even within the next six months—create strong pressures within the leadership to crack down much harder than it has to date. Gorbachev may well agree to more repression in order to retain power. It is likely, in this context, that an alternative leader would not only initiate more brutal repression than Gorbachev might, but would cite instability as the pretext for a general attack on Gorbachev's political reforms. (C-NF)

Moscow's preoccupation with instability is likely for the foreseeable future—regardless of other factors—to prevent a return to the arsenal state economy that generated the fundamental military threat to the West in the period since World War II. The Soviet leadership's focus on internal order in the USSR will probably accelerate the decay of Communist systems and growth of regional instability in Eastern Europe, pointing to the need for post-Yalta arrangements of some kind and confronting the United States with severe foreign policy and strategic challenges. Instability in the USSR will increase uncertainty in the West about proper policies to pursue toward Moscow, reflecting nervousness about Soviet developments but nonchalance about defense, and will impose stress on domestic and alliance decisionmaking. (C-NF)

2. (Continued)

To cope with the crises that promote instability, Gorbachev needs to transfer more resources from military to consumer needs. From a personal standpoint, he needs to defend himself against charges that he is selling out Soviet security interests and has been seduced by praise from the "class" enemy. Thus, he needs demonstrable results from the arms talks that will permit him to argue that the external "threat" has receded even further. Likewise, he needs trade and technology transfer from the West to overcome bottlenecks in the Soviet economy. Obviously, he does not need Western actions that call into question the efficacy of "New Thinking" in foreign policy, or that could be interpreted as challenging Soviet security interests globally, in Eastern Europe, or internally, or of "taking advantage" of Soviet internal instability. (C-NF)

The chances that Gorbachev will successfully overcome the dilemmas (many of his own making) that confront him are—over the long term—doubtful at best. But the process of pluralistic forces taking root in Soviet society strengthens the rule of law, builds constraints on the exercise of power, and fosters resistance to any turnaround in military spending and to reinvigoration of an expansionist foreign policy—which, as argued above, will be strongly inhibited in any event by the insistent demands of consumption and the civilian sector. This process, and the deterrence of a militantly reactionary restoration that might attempt to bring about a basic shift in the Soviet Union's foreign posture, benefits greatly from each year's prolongation of Gorbachev's rule. (C-NF)

A key weakness in Gorbachev's strategy that will perpetuate instability is its hesitant approach to marketization and its unwillingness to face up to the necessity of real privatization of ownership of capital stock and land. Soviet leaders from Gorbachev down are, at the moment, uniquely open to contact with the West. Serious private Western dialogue with them and their advisers on economic theory could influence their thinking. Reduction of instability over the long term requires the steady extension of a law-based private sector in the Soviet economy. (C-NF)

Harsh repression of labor unrest or of food riots in Russian cities are certainly contingencies that could confront US policymakers with the need to respond. But instability provoked by Gorbachev's gambles is likely to present its severest challenge to US policymaking through a crackdown of some sort in the ethnic arena—probably not in response to communal violence, but in the form of intervention to suppress Russian/native clashes or the drive of non-Russians for greater autonomy. Such a crackdown is most likely in the Baltic region but could also come in the Caucasus, Moldavia, or—down the road—even the Ukraine. (C-NF)

Gorbachev has said he wants to create a constitutionally structured federative union based on the consent of the constituent republics. Movement away from the heretofore existing situation toward such a goal would in general be positive from the US standpoint. However, Gorbachev is not interested in creating a framework for weak confederation or dissolution of the USSR, nor would he be able to marshall political support within the elite for such an outcome; yet this is precisely what acceptance of the more radical Baltic demands would imply. The new draft CPSU platform on nationality policy hints at the acceptability of a regionally differentiated approach to Soviet federalism. It is possible that Gorbachev may be prepared to broker a special status for the Baltic republics, and this could incorporate a potential for evolution toward still greater autonomy. A wide range of configurations of "autonomy" or "independence" is conceivable. In such a context the Soviets might be interested at some point in discussing with Washington their regional security concerns, which would probably bear heavily on such a decision. (C-NF)

3. NIE 11-18-89, November 1989, *The Soviet System in Crisis: Prospects for the Next Two Years*

Director of Central Intelligence

~~Secret~~

The Soviet System in Crisis: Prospects for the Next Two Years

National Intelligence Estimate

This National Intelligence Estimate represents the views of the Director of Central Intelligence with the advice and assistance of the US Intelligence Community.

~~Secret~~

NIE 11-18-89
November 1989

3. *(Continued)*

Directorate of Intelligence

~~Secret~~
~~NOFORN NOCONTRACT~~

NIE 11-18-89

The Soviet System in Crisis: Prospects for the Next Two Years ~~(C NF)~~

Information available as of 21 November 1989 was used in the preparation of this National Intelligence Estimate.

The following intelligence organizations participated in the preparation of this Estimate:
The Central Intelligence Agency
The Defense Intelligence Agency
The National Security Agency
The Bureau of Intelligence and Research, Department of State

also participating:
The Deputy Chief of Staff for Intelligence, Department of the Army
The Director of Naval Intelligence, Department of the Navy
The Assistant Chief of Staff, Intelligence, Department of the Air Force
The Director of Intelligence, Headquarters, Marine Corps

This Estimate was approved for publication by the National Foreign Intelligence Board.

~~Secret~~
November 1989

3. *(Continued)*

~~Secret~~
~~NOFORN-NOCONTRACT~~

The Soviet System in Crisis: Prospects for the Next Two Years (C NF)

- *The Soviet domestic crisis will continue beyond the two years of this Estimate regardless of the policies the regime pursues. The regime will be preoccupied with domestic problems for years to come, will want to keep tensions with the United States low, and will probably still pursue agreements that reduce military competition and make resource trade-offs easier.* (S NF)

- *Despite the enormous problems he faces, Gorbachev's position in the leadership appears relatively secure, and he has increased power and political room to cope with the crisis.* (S NF)

- *There will be greater effort to define the limits of political change, a tougher approach on ethnic issues, and some retrenchment in media policy; but the process of political liberalization will expand with the legislature and independent political groups increasing in power at party expense.* (S NF)

- *The regime will concentrate on stabilizing the economy and, while pulling back on some reforms, will push for others designed to enlarge the role of the market and private enterprise.* (S NF)

- *Despite these efforts, we expect little improvement—and possibly a decline—in economic performance as well as further increase in domestic turmoil. Of several conceivable scenarios:*

    — *Community analysts consider it most likely that the regime will maintain the present course, intensifying reform while making some retreats.*

    — *In a less likely scenario that all analysts believe is a possibility, the political turmoil and economic decline will become unmanageable and lead to a repressive crackdown, effectively ending any serious reform effort. (The CIA's Deputy Director for Intelligence disagrees with both scenarios. See pages vii and 18.)* (S NF)

~~Secret~~

3. *(Continued)*

Figure 1. President Gorbachev: trying to cope with the crisis. (u)

3. *(Continued)*

Key Judgments

The crisis, precipitated by long-simmering problems and Gorbachev's policies to address them, will continue over the next two years and beyond and could threaten the system's viability:
- Ethnic problems are endemic: conflict between the center and regions will increase as will interethnic strife, and the regime can at best hope to manage and cope with these problems, not resolve them.
- Economic ills are deeply rooted in the system, and efforts to reform it will be slowed by the priority given to stabilizing the economy.

At the same time changes in the Soviet leadership during the last year have made Gorbachev's position relatively secure over the next two years and portend a more radical approach to addressing the nation's daunting problems. We believe:

- Gorbachev's power has been significantly enhanced with the weakening of the leadership's orthodox wing and the development of a second power base in the legislature.

- The coming local and republic legislative elections and the party congress next October will probably further undermine the role of the party apparatus, increase the power of the legislature in decisionmaking, and bring a de facto multiparty system to some republics.

- More stringent measures—possibly including some retail price increases and a domestic currency devaluation—are likely to be imposed as part of the current economic stabilization program. Although the need to stabilize the economy has slowed the economic reform effort, we expect to see the introduction of a number of controversial measures—including a redefinition of property rights, a new taxation system, and antitrust legislation—that are designed to enlarge the role of the free market and private enterprise.

- To pursue this course and arrest the growing fear of anarchy in the country, Gorbachev will try to rein in somewhat the now freewheeling Soviet press and be tougher in defining the boundaries of the political and economic autonomy for the country's minority nationalities; he already has and will continue to use repressive measures *if necessary* to control communal violence or prevent secession.

3. *(Continued)*

In view of the continuing turmoil, whether Gorbachev can maintain a reformist course with some tactical retrenchment is uncertain and open to considerable debate. The next two years will undoubtedly be one of the most tumultuous periods in Soviet history.

Tangible benefits from *perestroyka* will be relatively few, although intangibles (greater freedom and religious toleration) will be more apparent. Overly ambitious targets for the production of consumer goods are unlikely to be met. Labor strikes are certain. The enhanced role of the legislature will make needed austerity measures more difficult to pursue and likely compromises will reduce economic effectiveness.

Under these conditions, several scenarios are in the realm of possibility, but two are considered to be much more likely than the others. Most Community analysts hold the view that *a continuation and intensification of the current course is most likely* and believe that, despite the obvious difficulties, the turmoil will be manageable without the need for repressive measures so pervasive that the reform process is derailed:

- The politicization of the populace along with the expanding authority of the legislature are changing the system, giving political reform a broader and deeper base, and making it much more difficult and costly to turn back the clock.

- Although ethnic assertiveness will continue and Baltic peoples will strive for self-determination, the drive for secession will probably be blunted in this period by the regime's more sophisticated use of concessions and warnings and the desire of Baltic leaders to negotiate rather than confront.

- As difficult as the economic situation will be, the regime probably can prevent the supplies of food and consumer goods from declining to the point of provoking large-scale unrest.

In a less likely scenario that all accept as a possibility, the ongoing turmoil will get only worse and lead the regime, with or without Gorbachev, *to use massive force to hold the country together and save the regime*:
- Democratization will accelerate system fragmentation and make it impossible to take necessary austerity and economic reform measures.
- An exacerbation of supply problems—by an upsurge in strike activity, transportation bottlenecks, or severe weather—could increase shortages and lead to social upheaval.

3. *(Continued)*

- While trying to avoid confrontation, the interests of the Baltic peoples and Moscow are bound to clash dramatically, leading to much harsher measures by the center to regain control. (S NF)

Events in Eastern Europe are certain to play a role in determining which scenario the USSR follows in the next two years. As long as the transformations in Eastern Europe do not spiral out of control, they will reinforce the trend toward radical reform in the Soviet Union. In the unlikely event that Moscow deems it necessary to use Soviet troops to restore order and prevent the disintegration of the Warsaw Pact, *perestroyka* in the USSR would be dealt a serious, if not fatal, blow. (S NF)

Either scenario points toward the continuation of current foreign and security policies, at least for the two years of this Estimate. Gorbachev will still push hard for various arms control agreements. Eastern Europe will continue to have heretofore unthinkable leeway to democratize, effectively changing the Warsaw Pact into more of a political alliance than a military one. Even if a crackdown occurred under Gorbachev or another leader, the preoccupation with internal problems would be paramount, the desire to avoid increased tensions high, and the effort to shift resources toward consumption strong. A different regime would not, however, be as inclined to make major concessions to achieve various arms control agreements or be as accommodating to centrifugal trends in Eastern Europe. (S NF)

Alternative View
The CIA's Deputy Director for Intelligence believes that the Estimate does not adequately capture the likely scope of change in the USSR over the next two years. (S NF)

Assuming Gorbachev holds on to power and refrains from repression, the next two years are likely to bring a significant progression toward a pluralist—albeit chaotic—democratic system, accompanied by a higher degree of political instability, social upheaval, and interethnic conflict than this Estimate judges probable. In these circumstances, we believe there is a significant chance that Gorbachev, during the period of this Estimate, will progressively lose control of events. The personal political strength he has accumulated is likely to erode, and his political position will be severely tested. (S NF)

The essence of the Soviet crisis is that neither the political system that Gorbachev is attempting to change nor the emergent system he is fostering is likely to cope effectively with newly mobilized popular demands and the deepening economic crisis. (S NF)

3. *(Continued)*

Contents

	Page
Key Judgments	v
Discussion	1
Leadership Showdown	1
Can the Turmoil Be Managed?	2
Staying the Course	5
Impact of Reform on Soviet Society	14
A Repressive Crackdown: A Less Likely Scenario	16
An Alternative View	18
Implications for the Future of the System	18
Implications for Gorbachev's International Agenda and US Policy	21
Gorbachev Stays the Course	21
Retrenchment	22

3. *(Continued)*

Gorbachev's Politburo Today

Yakovlev. Gorbachev protege . . . strong proponent of radical reform. Frequent target of criticism by party conservatives.

Shevardnadze. One of Gorbachev's strongest supporters on both domestic and foreign policy . . . unorthodox statements challenging ideological underpinnings of foreign policy have aroused objections from Ligachev.

Ryzhkov. Has played a leading role in economic reform . . . more moderate on political and social issues . . . criticized Gorbachev in July for neglecting party duties but appears to be personally close . . . clashes with Ligachev reported.

Medvedev. Ideology secretary in forefront of "new thinking" on foreign policy and radical economic reform . . . more cautious on cultural issues . . . also target of orthodox critics.

Slyun'kov. Economics secretary who has been hedging on radical restructuring . . . some reports suggest not completely in Gorbachev's camp.

Maslyukov. First Deputy Premier and Gosplan chairman—a moderate on reform . . . like his patron Ryzhkov, has better appreciation than Gorbachev of difficulties of translating economic theory into practice.

Zaykov. Secretary and, since 21 November 1989, First Deputy Chairman of the Defense Council . . . takes a traditionalist stand on some key reform issues . . . may have lost clout when failed to derail Yel'tsin election.

Vorotnikov. Only other Politburo member appointed before Gorbachev took power . . . increasingly critical of political pluralism and radical economic measures . . . only other full member in Supreme Soviet.

Kryuchkov. KGB chief who reportedly has close personal ties to Gorbachev . . . echoed perestroyka themes in 1989 Revolution Day speech but urged restraint . . . has publicly called for legislative oversight of KGB.

Ligachev. With "second secretary" powers now removed, less able to hinder Gorbachev's programs . . . views political reform as dangerous, disruptive, unnecessary . . . opponents of reform may look to him as spokesman . . . questions about corruption still alive.

3. (Continued)

Discussion[1]

The Soviet system is in crisis. While noting the potential for turmoil in ▓▓▓▓▓▓▓▓▓ we underestimated how quickly it would develop. The roots of the crisis run deep into the nature of the Soviet state and Russian history and have been nourished by decades of official neglect, corruption, and ineptitude. But the public manifestations—the strikes, demonstrations, and other challenges to authority—are a direct result of Gorbachev's effort to restructure the system. The turmoil that these developments have brought to the fore will continue and probably deepen. (S NF)

This increased popular assertiveness is in one sense a measure of Gorbachev's success in destroying elements of the Stalinist system. The pace and extent of this change have exceeded even our relatively bullish forecast of two years ago; indeed, the new legislature is the beginning of systemic change. His political reforms have brought a reduction in regime repression, an expansion of civil liberties, greater tolerance of religious beliefs, a broader range of permissible public discussion, and an opportunity for previously unrepresented groups to become a part of the system. (S NF)

Gorbachev's policies are breaking the management and control mechanisms of the old regime, however, before new ones are ready to assume these tasks. The effort to create a new political culture and institutions—capable of handling the flood of demands unleashed by Gorbachev—is still in its infancy. (S NF)

His policies, moreover, have yet to alleviate—and in some respects have worsened—many of the social and economic problems he inherited. His efforts to manage the USSR's restive ethnic minorities have not halted their demands for greater independence from Moscow; indeed, the effort to accommodate them has led to a strong push for independence in the Baltic—a step that Moscow will not allow but may not be able to stop without repression. And his economic policies have exacerbated serious shortages of consumer goods and services, guaranteeing a continuation of popular discontent. Not surprisingly, there is widespread pessimism in the country about the ability of the regime to overcome these problems. (S NF)

Leadership Showdown

During the past year this turmoil led to an increasingly open conflict within the Politburo:

- Party secretaries Ligachev and Chebrikov among others seemed convinced that *glasnost* and political reform in general had promoted disorder in the country and were destroying the leadership role of the Communist Party. These leaders made it increasingly clear that significant retrenchment was required to save the party and the country.

- Gorbachev and others rejected reliance on traditional remedies and argued that even more radical changes in the party and its policies were necessary to cope with the crisis and restore the party's authority. (S NF)

That conflict led Gorbachev to move decisively against the Politburo's orthodox wing at the Central Committee plenum in September 1989, removing five full and candidate Politburo members and replacing them with moderate and reformist supporters of *perestroyka*. These changes have significantly altered the balance of power in the Politburo and effectively shattered its orthodox faction (see inset). The plenum's approval of Gorbachev's proposal to convene the 28th Party Congress in October 1990—four months

3. *(Continued)*

earlier than mandated—also allowed him to accelerate his plans to bring new blood into the Central Committee, which has been another source of resistance to his reforms. (S NF)

Gorbachev's success at the plenum was the latest in a series of moves that have significantly strengthened his political position in the leadership, including:

- The Central Committee plenum in September 1988, when he launched a personnel and organizational shakeup of a magnitude not seen since Khrushchev's time.

- The April 1989 plenum, when he succeeded in purging about 20 percent of the Central Committee's members—"dead souls" who no longer held the jobs entitling them to membership—and promoting 24 candidates, mostly of a reformist stripe.

- His acquisition of a newly strengthened presidency in May 1989 followed by a streamlining of the government bureaucracy that had been resisting his economic reforms (see inset).

The cumulative effect of these moves has been to sharply reduce the threat posed by Gorbachev's opponents. As a result, we believe his position in the leadership is relatively secure for the next two years, although an assassination attempt by an individual against him cannot be ruled out. (S NF)

Can the Turmoil Be Managed?

Even with his power and authority enhanced, however, Gorbachev has not yet shown that he has a strategy for dealing with a host of daunting problems his policies have created that defy easy solution and that by his own admission threaten *perestroyka*. On the one hand, he faces powerful pressures for more far-reaching changes:

- The March 1989 elections revealed previously unsuspected grassroots support for political reform and a rejection of the party establishment that came as a shock to entrenched party bureaucrats as well as foreign analysts; an even greater repudiation is likely in the coming legislative elections at the republic and local levels, shifting authority further from party control toward the new legislative system.

An Upgraded Presidency

Gorbachev's clearest personal political gain from the reform of the state system is a strengthened presidency. Under the previous arrangement, the post was largely ceremonial. Gorbachev's scheme makes the president an executive leader of the full Supreme Soviet with constitutional authority in both domestic and foreign affairs and gives him power to:
- *Nominate appointees to top-level government jobs, including the posts of premier, prosecutor general, and Supreme Court chairman.*
- *Recommend appointments to the new Constitutional Oversight Committee.*
- *Chair the Defense Council.*
- *Conduct negotiations and sign international treaties.* (S NF)

The new president is accountable to both the Congress of People's Deputies and the Supreme Soviet, although only the Congress can recall him. There is no legal requirement that the general secretary serve as president, so Gorbachev's removal from the top party spot would not automatically cost him the leading state position. Although the Politburo undoubtedly would try to deprive him of that power base as well, the Supreme Soviet could prevent such a move. (S NF)

As the new legislature has gained authority and become increasingly active in formulating policy, the presidency has taken on added importance and given Gorbachev a substantial advantage over most of his Politburo colleagues who have minimal formal legislative responsibility. Both orthodox party members and reformers fear that this upgrading of the presidency could lead to one-man rule. Party traditionalists fear this will violate the tradition of collective leadership that gives them at least a limited ability to keep Gorbachev's reforms in check, and the reformers are more concerned about what might happen if someone other than Gorbachev held the job. (S NF)

3. *(Continued)*

~~Secret~~

Interlocking Directorate of the Soviet Leadership, November 1989

Party Politburo	Secretariat	Other Post	Government Council of Ministers	Supreme Soviet
Full Member				
Gorbachev (elected October 1980)	General Secretary			Chairman (president)
Ligachev (elected April 1985)	Chairman, Agriculture Commission			
Ryzhkov (elected April 1985)			Chairman (prime minister)	
Maslyukov (elected September 1989)			Gosplan chief	
Shevardnadze (elected July 1985)			Minister of Foreign Affairs	
Medvedev (elected September 1988)	Chairman, Ideological Commission			
Vorotnikov (elected December 1983)		President, RSFSR		Member
Zaykov (elected March 1986)	Member	First Deputy Chairman, Defense Council		
Kryuchkov (elected September 1989)			KGB chief	
Slyunkov (elected June 1989)	Chairman, Socioeconomic Commission			
Yakovlev (elected June 1989)	Chairman, International Commission			
Candidate member				
Lukyanov (elected September 1988)				First Deputy Chairman (vice president)
Vlasov (elected September 1988)		Premier, RSFSR		
Biryukova (elected September 1988)			Deputy Premier	
Primakov (elected September 1989)				Council of Union Chairman
Razumovskiy (elected February 1988)	Chief, Cadres Commission			
Yazov (elected June 1987)			Minister of Defense	
Pugo (elected September 1989)		Party Control Commission		
Secretaries only				
Baklanov (elected February 1988)	Defense Industry			
Stroyev (elected September 1989)	Agriculture			
Manayenkov (elected September 1989)	RSFSR Cadres and Ideology			Member
Usmanov (elected September 1989)	Unknown			
Girenko (elected September 1989)	Unknown			

This table is Unclassified.

3. *(Continued)*

Figure 2. Gorbachev presides over Supreme Soviet—September 1989. (U)

- The level of ethnic mobilization in the Baltic and Caucasus has significantly increased the pressures for independence and promoted articulation of ethnic demands that are often irreconcilable with one another. Managing these centrifugal threats to the state is now much more difficult and the political and social costs of returning to the old ways of maintaining order much greater.

- The worsening economic situation has produced mounting popular dissatisfaction and a wave of strikes, intensifying the pressure on the regime to give workers greater control over their enterprises, to reduce the shortages of necessities and adopt more decisive economic policies. The regime so far has not been able to respond effectively to this pressure.

At the same time, he must deal with a number of strong barriers to change:

- Although reduced in power, an entrenched party and government bureaucracy continues to resist reforms that would lead to increased political accountability, greater "marketization" of the economy, or other changes that would undermine its status and autonomy.

- Many Soviet citizens regard economic reforms that widen differentiations in wages, increase retail prices, and threaten unemployment as violations of the "social contract." This has been an important factor in delaying economic reforms that for all their promise would have such unpopular consequences.

3. *(Continued)*

> ### Gorbachev's Reform Agenda and the KGB
>
> General Secretary Gorbachev needs the KGB in a period of political change to ensure his political survival, to monitor the compliance of local elites, and to control burgeoning societal unrest. During the past year, Gorbachev has strengthened his hold on the security service first by transferring then KGB boss Viktor Chebrikov to the Central Committee Secretariat and a year later retiring him. Current KGB Chairman Vladimir Kryuchkov—recently vaulted to full Politburo membership—is a political ally of the General Secretary and has been an outspoken advocate of reform—including parliamentary oversight of the KGB. Chief of the KGB Border Guard Directorate General Matrosov recently discussed his component's budget at a hearing of the Supreme Soviet Defense and Security Committee, and later this fall Kryuchkov will submit the security service's budget to the Supreme Soviet for the first time.
>
> Some KGB officials are concerned about the effect of *perestroyka* and *glasnost* on KGB prestige and on the organization's ability to carry out its mission at a time of growing unrest.
>
> The KGB on the whole, however, is apparently satisfied that Gorbachev's reforms do not threaten its prominent position. Despite some "KGB bashing" in the Supreme Soviet and the press, Kryuchkov has been successful in defending many of the KGB's vested interests. Thus far, the KGB has taken fewer cuts in its personnel and prerogatives than either the Ministry of Internal Affairs or the Ministry of Defense. For example, although the Fifth (Antidissident) Directorate has been abolished and the Third Chief (Military Counterintelligence) Directorate has been trimmed, many of their personnel have been assigned to a new department formed to fight organized crime. Moreover, KGB departments in the Caucasus and Central Asia remain active in investigating nationalist extremists—reflecting the leadership's continuing need for the KGB's domestic role to maintain control.

- The disorder that accompanies reform—corruption, strikes, civil unrest, inflation, and increased crime—is anathema not only to institutions like the KGB and the military but also to large segments of the general population (see foldout map, figure 10, at the back). An authoritarian and paternalistic culture has instilled in many the belief that the only alternative to a strong hand at the center is anarchy (see inset).

As a result of these pressures and the greater latitude for action he has achieved within the Soviet elite, Community analysts now expect Gorbachev to press ahead with a domestic agenda that combines an intensification of political reform and economic stabilization with a tougher approach to party discipline, ethnic extremism, and media policy. Whether he can maintain such a course given the turmoil and pressures is uncertain and the subject of strong debate in and out of the Intelligence Community. This situation could move in several different directions, but most analysts believe two are much more likely than others: "staying the course" and "a repressive crackdown" (see inset, page 7).

Staying the Course

The most likely scenario in the view of Community analysts is that Gorbachev will be able to keep the reform process going and avoid resorting to draconian measures that would roll back the trend toward greater pluralism and democratization.

3. *(Continued)*

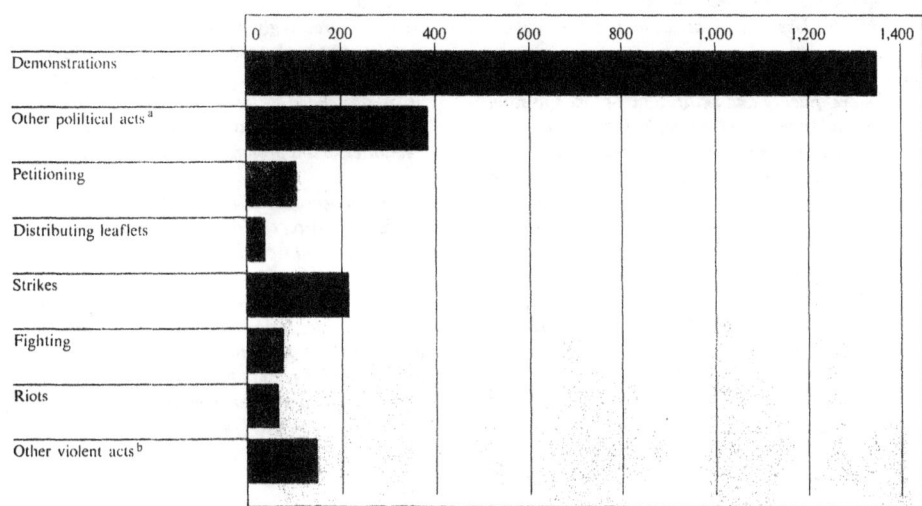

Figure 3
**USSR: Reported Incidents of Unrest by Type,
January 1987–September 1989**

^a Includes mass meetings of informal groups not considered demonstrations, hunger strikes, collection of funds for nonofficial functions, unsanctioned religious activity, such as Hare Krishna meetings and mass meetings of Ukrainian Catholics, and so forth.

^b Includes bombings, assassinations, production of homemade weapons, airline hijackings, and attacks against security forces.

This judgment rests in part on our assessment of Gorbachev, his agenda and his ability. Although lacking a detailed blueprint, he has been enormously successful in using and defining the sense of crisis in the system—in 1985 and now—to drive increasingly radical solutions to Soviet ills. His policies call into question, whether intentionally or not, the role of the Communist Party, its ideology, the Stalinist economic system, and the center's dominance of the regions. As the sense of crisis has mounted, only he in the leadership appears to have the ability to manage the turmoil his own policies have stimulated. At the same time, he is flexible and clever at not getting too far ahead of what his colleagues can tolerate at a given moment; he has made tactical adjustments and occasional retreats to cope with both political and policy consequences of reform.

Our assessment of the likelihood of this scenario also reflects judgments about the manageability of the reform process and the turmoil it has created. Forces have now been unleashed in the USSR that have a life of their own, weakening the regime's control over events. The turmoil will continue under this or any other scenario. Most Community analysts believe the

3. *(Continued)*

> *Other Possible Outcomes*
>
> Although the Intelligence Community considers the two scenarios presented in this Estimate to be the most likely, three other general scenarios—while far less likely—are at least conceivable:
>
> - ***Success story.*** The regime could move much more quickly and skillfully on economic stabilization than we anticipate, be far more accommodating on demands for ethnic autonomy, and more receptive to sharing political power with forces outside the Communist Party. Such a scenario would see the economy revive, the "union" enhanced by genuine devolution of substantial political and economic power to national minorities, and a stable transition toward political democracy that did not threaten—as in Poland, Hungary, and East Germany—the continued viability of the Communist Party.
>
> - ***Social revolution.*** At the opposite end of the spectrum, Gorbachev's concessions to the population, severe weakening of all major regime institutions, and incompetence in managing the economy could lead to his losing control of the situation. Ethnic violence and separatist demands, increasingly potent challenges to Communist Party rule, and catastrophic economic deterioration could lead to large-scale instability and perhaps social revolution. This could include the breakaway of many non-Russian republics and a prolonged period of civil war.
>
> - ***Return to neo-Stalinism.*** The threat of imminent social revolution could prompt a coup against Gorbachev that would not only lead to retrenchment but also to the imposition of political repression more severe than during the Brezhnev years. This scenario would involve the massive use of military force to reimpose order. The effort would certainly be bloody and would only postpone—and over time deepen—the systemic crisis, not resolve it. (S NF)

---

regime can cope with it and press ahead, haltingly and unevenly at times, with the reform process:

- A more open legislative process with real elections, debate, and votes is becoming institutionalized. The population is becoming more involved and interested, enlarging the constituency favoring change and making it much more difficult to alter course.

- Although strikes and shortages will continue, the regime will be able to maintain supplies, particularly food, at a level sufficient to avoid widespread social disruptions; the population, as it has in the past will grudgingly endure the privations, giving the regime more time to get its economic strategy implemented.

- The combination of regime concessions and warnings have blunted somewhat nationalist demands for outright independence, while the Baltic peoples appear disinclined to force a confrontation over the issue any time soon. (S NF)

Political Reform. Analysts expect Gorbachev will intensify his reform of political institutions even further over the next two years, as he attempts to improve their capacity to deal with the demands *perestroyka* has created. The political reforms mapped out in the summer of 1988 will soon be nearing completion in structural terms. A new Congress of People's Deputies and Supreme Soviet already have been elected. Elections to the republic

3. *(Continued)*

Figure 4. Debate in the Supreme Soviet. Left to right: Chairman of the Council of Nationalities, Nishanov; First Deputy Chairman of the Supreme Soviet, Luk'yanov; Chairman of the Supreme Soviet Gorbachev; Chairman of the Council of the Union, Primakov; and Deputy Chairman of the Council of the Union, Iskakova. (U)

congresses of deputies and local soviets are being held late this year and early next, further drawing the populace into the political process and increasing the pressure on the system to respond. The party congress already set for October 1990 will complete the revamping of the party and its Central Committee, shifting the political balance strongly toward a reformist course.

Despite this progress, the reformers recognize that they have far to go to build a political culture and institutions capable of dealing with the demands reforms have unleashed. They are trying to ensure that the new legislative institutions have a genuine measure of power and that the Soviet people have some real influence in selecting their representatives. At the same time they want to achieve these objectives while preserving a national single-party system in which much power remains concentrated at the top. Gorbachev seems prepared to give these new institutions a substantial degree of independence and to permit considerable pluralism within them, however, in order to obtain his larger reform objectives. As is already evident, achieving such a balance will be difficult, requiring consistent effort to make the party more inclusive of diverse opinions while reining in those who exceed the limits.

In addition to strengthening the role of the legislature, we believe Gorbachev will attempt to restore the party's deteriorating position. His speeches and

3. *(Continued)*

actions indicate that he wants the party to shape the reform process rather than be pulled along by it. To do this he intends to use the coming local and republic elections and the party congress to discredit further the opponents of reform and bring more new blood into the apparatus. (S NF)

This reform process will weaken an already beleaguered *nomenklatura* and could destroy it if allowed to continue for much longer. The new blood will align the party more clearly with reform efforts, as it already has in the Baltic, and perhaps give it greater credibility. Such a party would be vastly different from its Leninist predecessor, however, less responsive to Moscow's edicts and more closely tied to its local constituency. Its distinctive claim to rule would be eroded even further as it faced strong competition at the local level from groups (de facto political parties) urging support for their own agendas. Whether intended or not, the reform will, in our view, hasten the ongoing shift of power, legitimacy, and action away from the party to other institutions, particularly the legislatures. (S NF)

We also expect Gorbachev to give new emphasis to his call for a society based on law as part of his effort to strengthen the regime's legitimacy. Actually establishing the rule of law would require steps the regime so far has been reluctant to take: codification and implementation of such ideas as the independence of the judiciary, the subordination of the government to the law, and an emphasis on the freedom of the individual, rather than the individual's obligations to the state. In the "halfway house" Gorbachev is trying to create, we expect coming legal reforms—including new criminal legislation and laws on economic activity and the press—to make steps in those directions but continue to stress the regime's rights over those of its citizens. (S NF)

Nationality Policy. Initially, Gorbachev paid little attention to nationality problems; indeed, he appears to have assumed that reform would not encounter obstacles on this front. As a result, the regime has been struggling ever since to get ahead of the problem. Nationalism has flourished in the more open atmosphere of *glasnost* and public debate. The regime has allowed changes that would have been unthinkable a few years ago, but this accommodation has encouraged more demands rather than limited them (see foldout map, figure 11 at the back). (S NF)

The nationality policy adopted at the September 1989 plenum indicates that Gorbachev's willingness to give the republics greater political and economic autonomy has certain clearly defined limits (see inset). In his speech he affirmed that each nationality had the right of self-determination but noted that this concept was not a "one-time act connected with secession" but the right to develop culturally and economically within the existing state structure. Gorbachev also has ruled out any shifting of borders and rejected the splitting of the Communist Party along ethnic or republic lines. Moreover, his stress on an integrated market and the

---

Gorbachev's Nationalities Policy

To help ease the Soviet Union's nationalities problem, Gorbachev envisions a program that would include:

- *The transition of the USSR from a de facto unitary empire to a union with real federative content.*

- *Constitutional delimitation of the functions of the center and the republics, with a significant increase in the authority allocated to the republics.*

- *Removal of discriminatory and provocative obstacles to the development of non-Russian languages and cultures.*

- *Equalization of the rights of all nationalities.*

- *Integration of the republics within a single unionwide economy, in which the "socialist market" harmonizes the interests of the multiethnic whole with those of its ethnic parts.* (S NF)

3. (Continued)

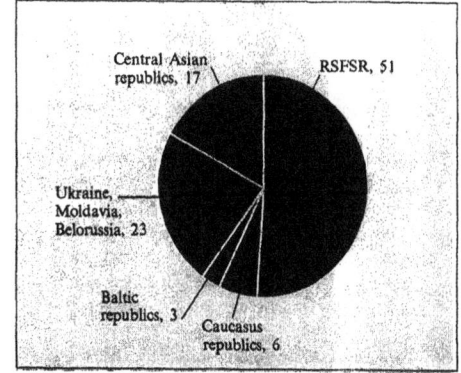

Figure 5
USSR: Distribution of Reported Unrest and of Population by Republics, January 1987 - September 1989

Incidents of Unrest (Percent):
- RSFSR, 37
- Central Asian republics, 6
- Ukraine, Moldavia, Belorussia, 13
- Baltic republics, 19
- Caucasus republics, 25

Population[a] (Percent):
- RSFSR, 51
- Central Asian republics, 17
- Ukraine, Moldavia, Belorussia, 23
- Baltic republics, 3
- Caucasus republics, 6

[a] Figures from 1989 Census.

reality of the economic interdependence of the republics appears to be aimed at reining in the growing zeal among nationalists, especially in the Baltic republics, for virtual economic and political independence from Moscow.

Community analysts believe Gorbachev is fully prepared to use force, if necessary, to control the kind of interethnic violence that broke out over the disputed territory of Nagorno-Karabakh in the Caucasus; the reestablishment of law and order in such cases would not be incompatible with his reform objectives. On the other hand, most expect him to make every effort to avoid the use of force to quell nationalist demands for political independence in the Baltics—a move that would clearly enforce limits on *glasnost*, democratization and other reforms, and cost him some of the international goodwill derived from his liberalization and his diplomatic initiatives.

The political challenge to Soviet rule is the greatest in the Baltics, where actions in support of eventual secession will continue to test Moscow's patience and tolerance. Most analysts believe there is a decent prospect that the regime's willingness to concede a degree of autonomy unthinkable in the past along with warnings of what is not now possible will blunt immediate demands for secession. Some Baltic nationalists are aware of the dangers of going too far, are looking for compromise, and seem inclined to avoid confrontation. This approach could well postpone a pitched battle over independence for some time.

3. *(Continued)*

Even if this fails, we believe the leadership would first exhaust all its political and economic leverage to encourage a nationalist retreat from unacceptable demands before turning to military intervention. For example:

- Central ministries could be directed to exert economic pressure by bargaining over delivery prices or even delaying the delivery of fuel, and blocking foreign financial ventures.

- Moscow might emphasize its disapproval by heightening the visibility of security (MVD and KGB) personnel or military units already present in the Baltics and seal the borders, hoping to cow dissenters and forestall a major bloodletting.

- Advocacy of secession could be criminalized and its advocates prevented from seeking elective office or even arrested.

- The Russian minority in the Baltic could be spurred to use strikes or work stoppages to tie up the local economies.

Gorbachev undoubtedly recognizes that these options carry the risk of provoking demonstrations and escalating into a situation that could ultimately trap the leadership into sending in troops. The risk would be less, however, than that associated with a general crackdown in the Baltic republics, which most believe would be used only as a last resort. Even this latter course would be less risky for him and the system than letting the Baltic republics go. This move would encourage other much larger nationalities, such as Ukrainians, to seek similar goals and make regime survival problematic at best.

The Economy. The USSR's swelling budget deficit, spiraling inflation rate, and continuing shortages of consumer goods threaten not only the country's economic well-being but *perestroyka* itself. Because of this, we expect Gorbachev to give special emphasis to a new economic stabilization program designed to slash the budget deficit, reduce the ruble "overhang," and provide some immediate relief to the consumer. Specifically:

- The plan for 1990 is to cut the budget deficit in half by reducing spending for investment and defense and by increasing revenues through various means.

- Bonds and state housing will be offered to enterprises and individual citizens to soak up excess liquidity.

- Stiff taxes have been imposed on wage hikes of more than 3 percent unless related to increased output of consumer goods.

- Production of consumer goods is programmed to grow by 12 percent in 1990 over the planned level for 1989, and imports of industrial consumer goods are scheduled to rise by 15 percent per year this year and next.

This stabilization program, however, will not achieve the desired objectives. The regime apparently recognizes this and is reportedly considering more stringent measures to help stabilize the economy. This could include a currency reform—the conversion of old rubles into new ones at different rates depending on the size or form of holdings. Price increases on heavily subsidized basic goods and services, which we believe are necessary to get a hold on the monetary imbalance, are apparently not imminent. A draft blueprint for economic reform that is currently under discussion calls for a deregulation of retail prices only on luxury items, most imported goods, and high-quality foods and delicacies beginning in 1991. The rising tide of consumer dissatisfaction, combined with the legislature's increased authority and responsiveness to public opinion, will make it difficult for the leadership to adopt the tougher austerity measures needed to improve the economy's health.

3. *(Continued)*

~~Secret~~

Figure 6
USSR: Summary of Selected Indicators of Consumer Welfare

● Improvement
○ No significant change
● Deterioration

Indicators	Performance measures [a]				Popular perceptions [b]	
	1986	87	88	89 [c]	88	89
Overall consumption per capita	●	○	●	○	●	●
Meat	○	○	○	○	●	●
Vegetables and fruit	●	●	●	●	●	●
Durable goods	○	●	○	○	○	●
Automobiles	●	○	●	●		
Home electronics	○	○	●	●		
Clothing	○	○	●	○	○	●
Personal care and repair services	○	●	●	●	○	○
Housing	○	●	●	●	○	●
Health care	●	●	●	●	○	○
Leisure and recreation	○	●	●	●	●	●
Inflation	○	○	●	●	●	●
Rationing [d]					○	●
Working conditions	●	●	●		●	●
Protection of the environment	○	○	●		●	●

[a] Performance is measured by comparing an indicator's rate of growth with the growth rate achieved during 1981-85, the five-year period that preceded the Gorbachev era.

[b] Based on CIA analysts' judgments of the perception of citizens in the USSR as to how living standards have changed under Gorbachev–through August 1989–in comparison with the first half of the 1980s.

[c] Projections based on data for January-June 1989 compared to the same period in 1988.

[d] No performance measures are included for this indicator because we lack sufficient data on performance during the baseline period, 1981-85.

~~Confidential NOFORN~~ 324197 11-89

3. *(Continued)*

Figure 7
USSR: State Budget Deficit, 1985-90

Note scale change

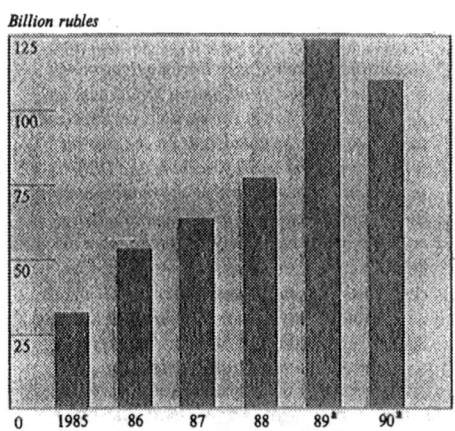
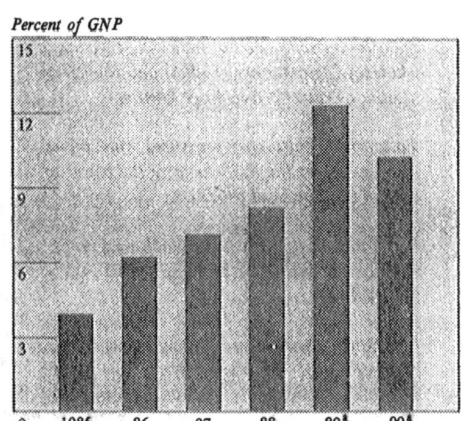

^a The CIA estimates for 1989 and 1990 are based on plan data. The range in the estimates for those years reflects uncertainty about the success of announced Soviet measures to reduce the deficit.

The severity of the economic situation has forced the regime to backtrack on those economic reforms that would exacerbate the fiscal dilemma, hurt the consumer, and undermine popular support for *perestroyka* (see inset, page 14). Gorbachev regards this as a temporary retreat, however, and we expect him to continue his efforts to develop a more coherent plan for enlarging the role of the free market and private enterprise that will lay the groundwork for the introduction of more far-reaching measures when the economy is more stable. These measures include:
- A new corporate and individual income tax system.
- Antitrust legislation designed to break up the country's massive production conglomerates and encourage competition.
- A redefinition of property rights that puts the socialist and cooperative/private sectors on a more equal footing.
- An overhaul of the monetary/financial system to increase the ability of central authorities to employ economic rather than administrative levers. (S NF)

In a move driven more by politics than economics, Gorbachev will continue to provide strong support for efforts to give the republics greater economic autonomy under a system known as regional self-financing. This decentralization of economic authority is designed to assuage some of the republics' demands for

3. (Continued)

> ### Pulling Back on Reform
>
> - Both wholesale and retail price reform, scheduled for implementation in 1990 and 1991, were delayed. At first postponed indefinitely, plans now under discussion would return to the original schedule but make the revision of wholesale prices more gradual and the deregulation of retail prices more limited.
>
> - To control inflationary pressures, enterprises no longer have the right to raise the prices of certain categories of products.
>
> - Mandatory output targets, which were to be sharply reduced, have been reinstated in several sectors.
>
> - Decisions on wage increases, which were to be the preserve of the enterprise, are now to be controlled by centrally imposed taxes on the growth of the enterprise wage fund.

> ### Regional Self-Financing
>
> The Law on Regional Self-Financing, scheduled for nationwide implementation in 1991, will give the republics more authority over and responsibility for the production of food, consumer goods, services, and local construction. According to preliminary Soviet calculations, the overall output of industrial production under the jurisdiction of the republics is expected to increase, on the average, from the current level of 5 percent to 36 percent of the USSR's total production. To involve the republics more directly in the effort to increase productivity, each republic's budget will be made more dependent on the profits of its enterprises. The republics' economic plans, however, will continue to be dominated by state orders and "control figures" established by Moscow, and key sectors of the economy, strategic planning, and control over resources and financial policies will be left in Moscow's hands.

Figure 8. City of the future, Krokodil, *July 1989*
(U)

greater independence while at the same time making them more accountable for their economic performance (see inset).

Impact of Reform on Soviet Society

The Soviet system clearly is changing dramatically. Unlike the leaders in China, Gorbachev appears to believe that the new order must be built on foundations of political and social legitimacy if it is to succeed. But reform is often more difficult than revolution, and the genies he has released will defy the boundaries the system tries to place around them.

Although Gorbachev's economic policies point in the right direction, we believe they are unlikely to bring any substantial improvement in economic performance during the next two years and the situation could get worse, particularly this winter when food supplies will decline and spot fuel shortages may increase:

- The deficit will remain high, there will be little economic growth, and the demand for goods and services will greatly exceed their supply.

3. *(Continued)*

- Overly ambitious targets for the production of consumer goods are unlikely to be met. Some modest improvements are possible, but—even with the cuts in defense spending—any gains will come slowly because of the long leadtimes involved in shifting production capacity toward consumer goods and be restricted to relief in a few areas. Rationing and periodic runs on scarce goods will continue.

- Gorbachev's reforms will put increased financial pressure on the enterprises and should help reduce redundant labor and some waste of materials. But these benefits too will be slow in coming and probably outweighed by dislocations, such as unemployment, and other disruptions resulting from the conflicting signals that piecemeal implementation of reforms will continue to create.

- Increased regional autonomy could eventually make the distribution of food more efficient by reducing Moscow's role as the chief bottleneck in an overly centralized system. Thus far, however, local officials are introducing protectionist measures that are causing even more disruption and disequilibrium in national balances.

- Antimonopoly legislation and other reforms now under consideration hold some promise for the future but will only begin to take root during the period under consideration.

- If Gorbachev adopts a more radical approach on monetary stabilization, the economic and political environment for reforms could improve, allowing him to at least push ahead rather than delay further. (S NF)

Gorbachev's political reforms have more potential to produce results that would make any effort to turn back the clock more difficult and costly:

- His electoral reforms appear to be mobilizing the population, creating channels through which its interests can be expressed, and making officials more accountable to their constituencies.

- The boundaries of intraparty dialogue will probably expand even further, making any return to "democratic centralism" less likely.

- Although the new Supreme Soviet will not achieve the role of a Western legislature in the next two years, it is no longer the rubberstamp organization it once was, and the leadership will have to take it increasingly into account. This will provide a channel for citizen involvement in decisionmaking, give the leadership a more accurate barometer of grassroots opinion, and have an impact on important legislation.

- The challenge of contested elections—whether to party or state posts—also will force the party to engage in a genuine dialogue with other organizations, including informal political groups. Although official opposition to a multiparty system will remain, these new groups are already operating like parties and in many regions could become the governing authority, replacing the Communist Party. (S NF)

The radical transformations under way in *Eastern Europe* are likely to have a major impact on the fate of *perestroyka* in the USSR. As long as widespread domestic violence is avoided, anti-Sovietism held in check, and Warsaw Pact membership maintained, Gorbachev appears willing to tolerate almost any political change in East European countries—including the demise of the Communist parties. A continuation of such fundamental reform in Eastern Europe will reinforce the trend toward the thus far much less radical reform in the Soviet Union. Although the stakes are far greater at home, Gorbachev's willingness to accept multiparty systems in Eastern Europe will over time make it more difficult for him to reject such a course for the USSR. (S NF)

Perestroyka in the Soviet Union and Gorbachev's own political survival would be threatened, however, if events in Eastern Europe were to spiral completely out of control or take on an aggressively anti-Soviet character. Such a scenario—particularly if it occurred in East Germany or Poland and threatened the security of Soviet troops stationed there—would put tremendous pressure on Gorbachev to use Soviet forces to restore order and prevent the breakup of the alliance. An attempt to do so would lead to bloody repression, freeze relations with the West, and halt

3. *(Continued)*

Figure 9
Growth of Rationing in the USSR

Note scale change

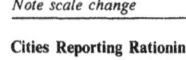
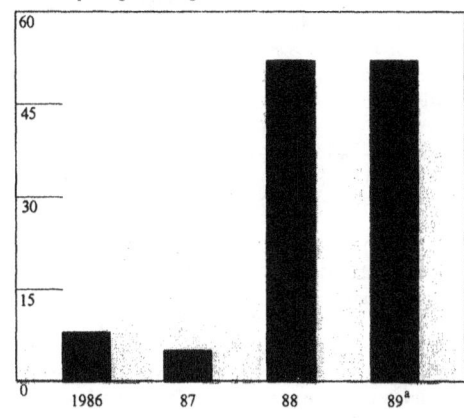

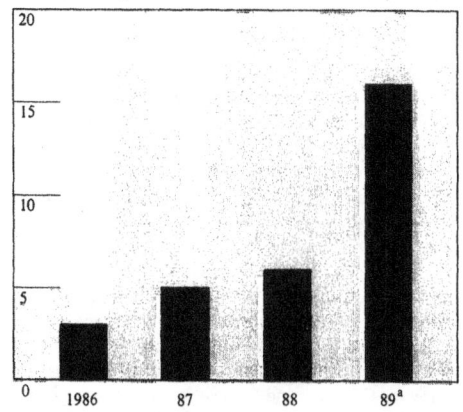

[a] Projected.

liberalization in the USSR. If Gorbachev resisted using Soviet forces in this scenario, orthodox elements in the party, the military, and the security services would almost certainly attempt to oust him. Their success, which would be followed by a violent crackdown on Eastern Europe, would set back *perestroyka* for years, if not kill it entirely.

A Repressive Crackdown: A Less Likely Scenario

There is a less likely scenario for the course of events in the USSR over the next two years that all analysts acknowledge is a possibility. In this scenario the turmoil becomes unmanageable and so threatening to the system that the requirements of survival lead to a massive crackdown, ending reform efforts for some time to come. Several developments could lead to such an outcome:

- The virtual certainty of continuing instability on all fronts could drive the leadership in an ever more orthodox direction that Gorbachev will be unable to resist if he wants to stay in office. Current attempts to rein in the media and draw clearer lines on nationality policy may portend such a course.

- The economy could decline much further over the next two years. Severe shortages of food and fuel this winter would be especially dangerous for the regime. This situation would substantially increase the prospect of regime-threatening labor strife and make the likelihood of a repressive crackdown much greater.

3. *(Continued)*

- Baltic nationalists could push so hard for independence that a confrontation over this issue cannot be avoided and would force the regime to use substantial force to maintain Soviet rule. Less repressive measures may not prevent secession.

Such a crackdown would not be so easy now. The politicization of society has gone quite far. Ethnic minorities will not readily give up their gains and hopes for the future. The longer the current reform process is allowed to continue the more difficult and probably bloody would be any attempt to repress it. The institutional support for repression, nonetheless, remains and would in the view of most analysts still be able to regain some control over society if ordered into action.

Such a repressive regime would retreat to policies that would be less disruptive than the present brand of *perestroyka*. While perhaps pursuing nominally reformist policies, the assault on the fundamentals of the Stalinist system would stop, and the reforms that threaten the party and Moscow's control of the empire would be reversed. This path would increase order at the expense of decentralization, democratization, and human rights. It might in the short run improve government performance by returning to well-known principles of management. It would not address the fundamental economic and social problems now plaguing the Soviet Union. It may be only able to reimpose calm for a relatively short period, making the eventual storm far greater than the one facing the regime now.

In the economic sphere, retrenchment would mean adoption of a more orthodox approach, deviating less markedly from the traditional Soviet model. Such an approach would place less emphasis on market forces, strengthen ministerial controls, and give the enterprises less decisionmaking discretion. It would also impose stricter limitations on private businesses (cooperatives), individual labor, and leasing arrangements by reducing the scope of such activities, introducing stricter eligibility requirements for those engaging in them, and revising the tax structure in ways to make the private sector less attractive. Soviet advocates of this approach still believe economic gains are possible through stricter work discipline, the introduction of high technology, and a crackdown on flagrant official corruption.

There would be an even greater retrenchment on *glasnost* and the liberalization process. Efforts would be made to increase central control over the electoral process and to restrict the Supreme Soviet's newfound authority. This would quite likely require measures now judged to be unconstitutional in the USSR (arrests of Supreme Soviet and Congress deputies, rule by decree, perhaps shutting down the Supreme Soviet) and use of force:

- Within the party, emphasis would be placed on unity rather than a pluralism of views; the formation of unofficial groups would also be prohibited.

- The range of permissible public and media discussion would be significantly narrowed, overt censorship would return, access to information from the West would be reduced, and opportunities for Soviet citizens to travel abroad would become more limited.

- Human rights generally would be much more vulnerable than now; the security services would once again have relatively free rein to deal with dissidents, nationalists, and strikers.

Under such a retrenchment, the regime also over time would become much less willing to make significant concessions to ethnic demands, fearing this would strengthen the hand of those who want nothing less than complete political independence. There would be less reluctance to use draconian measures to put down ethnic strikes and demonstrations that threatened central authority or damaged the national economy. And the planned experiments in regional economic autonomy—designed to assuage the demands for increased political independence—would likely be canceled or sharply curtailed.

3. *(Continued)*

An Alternative View

The CIA's Deputy Director for Intelligence believes that the first of the two main scenarios presented in the Estimate does not adequately capture the likely scope of change in the USSR over the next two years and that the second is not at all the inevitable alternative.

Assuming Gorbachev holds on to power and refrains from repression, the next two years are likely to bring a significant progression toward a pluralist—albeit chaotic—democratic system, accompanied by a higher degree of political instability, social upheaval, and interethnic conflict than this Estimate judges probable. In these circumstances, we believe there is a significant chance that Gorbachev will progressively lose control of the situation. During the period of this Estimate, the personal political strength he has accumulated is likely to erode and his political position will be severely tested.

The essence of the Soviet crisis is that neither the political system that Gorbachev is attempting to change nor the emergent system he is fostering is likely to cope effectively with newly mobilized popular demands and the deepening economic crisis.

Gorbachev and the Soviet regime will increasingly be confronted by the choice of acceding to a substantial loss of political and economic control or attempting to enforce harsh limits—both economic and political. Such limits are not acceptable to nationality groups that want meaningful autonomy, to new political organizations and individuals who want full political freedom, or to the general citizenry who, as workers and consumers, want immediate improvement in what they know to be a deteriorating standard of living. Indeed, a program that could stabilize the economy and prepare the way for serious economic reforms would require reductions in consumer subsidies and other measures painful to the populace. The regime's hopes of producing more consumer goods, including the conversion of defense industries, are unlikely to yield substantial results during the period of this Estimate.

Facing this dilemma, Gorbachev will press for political reforms that propel the process forward, *and* try to keep change within bounds. To do the latter, he will use political and economic pressures and resort to coercion periodically. This approach is unlikely to work. The upshot for Gorbachev personally will be to drive him to either give up his still authoritarian vision in favor of a truly democratic one, or recognize his vision as unreachable and try to backtrack from democratization. Gorbachev is unlikely to choose clearly either of these positions, thereby intensifying the crisis and increasing the prospect of a resort to force and repression.

Massive repression, as the second scenario of the Estimate suggests, is possible. However, this is less likely to be led by Gorbachev than by a political and military coalition that managed to outmaneuver him. Gorbachev is more likely, in CIA's view, to use coercive measures in unsystematic and ad hoc ways that do not stop the ongoing systemic change and destruction of the one-party state.

Implications for the Future of the System

The Intelligence Community believes that Gorbachev's political reforms are designed to strengthen the regime's legitimacy by giving Soviet citizens the ability to improve their lives by *working through the system*. To achieve that legitimacy, however, the system must be able to produce the desired result—namely, real improvement in the quality of Soviet life. The modest improvements we expect in consumer goods and services over the next few years are likely to fall far short of that goal but may be sufficient to buy the regime additional time for its policies to take hold.

The same reforms required to strengthen the system's legitimacy, however, are also *certain to make the next few years some of the most turbulent and destabilizing in Soviet history*. Even though Gorbachev's concern about potential consumer backlash has caused

3. *(Continued)*

him to pull back on some of his economic reforms, his attempt to revitalize the Soviet economy will prove highly disruptive:

- The Stalinist economic mechanism is broken, but the failure to create a new one to do its job has resulted in confusion and contributed to the economic stagnation.

- His effort to improve economic efficiency by reducing the number of excess workers may require many of them to take less attractive positions—at lower pay or in less desirable locations.

- Social tensions also will be exacerbated by his attempt to make wages more dependent on productivity—a move that workers accustomed to the traditional "free lunch" find threatening.

- Resentment of those enriching themselves in the private sector already has led to outbursts of violence and retribution and is likely to increase as the gap in the incomes of productive and unproductive workers widens. (S NF)

We believe Gorbachev's policy of *glasnost* will help to reengage a disaffected populace and provide a vent for the frustrations that built up under Brezhnev. But it will also encourage activities the regime finds undesirable—notably, the mobilization of groups advancing ideas inimical to state interests, such as the separatist movements of minority nationalities. The modest retrenchment on this front will reduce the damage but not eliminate the problem. Gorbachev's electoral reforms are intended to channel this new political activism into official institutions, but under the banner of *glasnost*, groups are issuing demands that challenge central authority and could eventually form the basis of a political opposition. Such a course can ultimately work only if there is at least broad acceptance of the Soviet state. (S NF)

In our view, the growing assertiveness of the Soviet Union's minority nationalities will pose a significant challenge to the stability of the Soviet system during this period. It also is increasing the tensions between the republics' native and Russian populations. As a result, Russian nationalist organizations, including the more hardline groups such as *Pamyat*, are likely to grow bolder and gain increased support. (S NF)

The regime's more repressive approach since last year in the Caucasus—the continued martial law in Armenia and Azerbaijan and harsh suppression of demonstrations in Georgia—will be accompanied by some concessions, including legislation designed to give republics in this region and elsewhere greater economic independence and protect the rights of scattered nationalities. Gorbachev also is attempting to establish new mechanisms to deal with constitutional disputes between Moscow and the republics as a way of keeping such grievances within official channels. (S NF)

The USSR will be plagued by serious labor unrest over the next two years. Strikes will continue as economic conditions fail to meet popular demands. Gorbachev's conciliatory handling of the nationwide coal miners' walkout last summer has legitimized strikes in the minds of Soviet workers, who no longer fear that the regime will use force to break strikes. Moscow is likely to face several strikes at any given time; most will probably be small, but some might involve tens or hundreds of thousands of workers at large enterprises or throughout a city. Although no general strikes over economic problems appear imminent, the possibility cannot be ruled out, especially if distress over rationing spreads and intensifies. (S NF)

We believe Gorbachev will continue to rely on negotiation, rather than violent suppression, to end any strikes that break out. In some cases, he probably will insist on strict enforcement of the new law on labor disputes, which went into effect in late October and requires several weeks of collective bargaining before workers may legally declare a strike. The law bans strikes outright in strategic sectors of the economy, such as energy, transportation, public works and utilities, as well as law and order agencies, and violators may be fined or even fired. Strikers may attempt to thwart application of these sanctions, however, by walking out in large numbers. (S NF)

3. *(Continued)*

> **Whose Perestroyka: The Political Spectrum in the USSR**
>
> *Issues like the creation of a multiparty system, economic reform, preservation of the Soviet federation, and the limits of glasnost have brought the political spectrum in society and the regime into sharp focus. Both have fractured into general groups, from party traditionalists on the right to radical reformers on the left. There are also small factions on the extreme left and right of this spectrum.*
>
> ***Party traditionalists*** *support perestroyka in general terms, but have little tolerance for what they perceive as the step-by-step dismantling of Marxist-Leninist ideology. They believe that political and economic centralization, under the leadership of the Communist Party, is one of the chief reasons that the Soviet Union has achieved superpower status. As a result, they are loath to accept criticism of the Soviet past—the trials and repressions of the Stalin era or the "stagnation" of the Brezhnev years—and prefer to emphasize the positive accomplishments of Soviet power. They strenuously oppose political pluralism and private economic activity. Many in this group have a xenophobic mistrust of foreign influences and institutions, assuming that closer ties to the West will subvert socialist values. Within society at large, groups like the United Workers' Front support these positions; among Politburo members, only Ligachev represents this view.*
>
> ***"Establishment" radicals*** *seek to reform society by transforming society's institutions, beginning with the party. They seek to preserve single-party rule, but through a revamped Communist Party. They support greater republic economic autonomy and some concessions to a free market system, but they insist on the preservation of a strong, united Soviet Union. Glasnost to this group is a means of opening up society to the changes that are necessary to revive political life and awaken economic reform; theirs is a glasnost with distinct, albeit liberal, boundaries. Gorbachev, Yakovlev, Medvedev, and Shevardnadze are the Politburo members most identified with this mindset.*
>
> ***"Antiestablishment" radicals*** *in general draw their inspiration from Western nonsocialist models and support fundamental changes in the political system and the injection of market forces in the economy. They believe strongly in political pluralism, some stressing genuine competition among rival parties. Some, including Yel'tsin, emphasize social justice and the abolition of* nomenklatura *privileges. Many, like Sakharov, believe that the CPSU should be legally responsible to the Supreme Soviet.*

Another potential threat to the stability of the system is the growing openness in questioning the necessity for one-party rule—a development that is likely to escalate with the formation of a non-Communist government in Poland and eventually in Hungary. We believe most of the newly formed groups, with their highly parochial agendas, will find it difficult to coalesce into a countrywide alternative to the Communist Party. If the pressure for political pluralism grows, Gorbachev might eventually have to contemplate a system that allowed nominal organized opposition to the party to build regime credibility. For the near term, however, we believe his strategy of enlarging the scope of intraparty debate and allowing some nonparty criticism of government decisions may obviate the need for such a move (see inset).

These threats will not go away and could lead to Gorbachev's downfall and the demise of reform. His program of allowing greater pluralism of expression and expanded popular participation in the political

3. *(Continued)*

Gorbachev and the Military: Living With Perestroyka

Since becoming General Secretary, Gorbachev has challenged the military's priority status and tightened party control over it. Gorbachev purged the Defense Ministry's senior leadership and tapped a comparative outsider, Gen. Dmitriy Yazov, as Defense Minister, who was mandated to accelerate perestroyka in the armed forces. Since then Gorbachev has kept up the heat on the military. He pushed the General Staff to help him work out the unilateral conventional force cuts announced in December 1988 and to formulate conventional and strategic arms reduction proposals that, if implemented, would mean large reductions in military manpower and capabilities. Simultaneously, Gorbachev has initiated a program converting defense industrial capabilities to support the civil economy. Working through the newly empowered Supreme Soviet, Gorbachev has forced the military to open its books and to submit its budget and some personnel policies to parliamentary oversight.

It has been difficult for the military to assimilate all this. The manpower reductions, for example, are testing the armed forces' ability to efficiently select officers for discharge and resettle their families. Nationalism has become another serious problem as non-Russians refuse to serve outside their home regions and hazing and bullying increasingly take on an ethnic cast. Because the government has frequently used army troops to backstop overextended Interior Ministry assets, the military has become the focus of blame for excesses incurred during police actions against battling ethnic groups. This has added to the surprisingly virulent antimilitarism that has emerged in response to media criticism of military problems. Several Soviet officers have complained to Americans that all these changes have combined to lower the prestige of the military.

Gorbachev has firm control over the military. He has reduced military influence in national security decisionmaking and made cuts to the defense budget. He has created a more malleable high command, led by officers, such as Yazov and General Staff chief Moiseyev, who are more personally beholden to the General Secretary. Various sources indicate that Yazov, who is only a candidate Politburo member, does not play a dominant role in national decisionmaking. The military is continuing to voice its opinion and speak out against reforms that it considers unreasonable—such as the creation of an all-volunteer armed forces—but there is little it can do if the government and parliament insist on the changes.

---

process is predicated on the belief that the Soviet population is fundamentally loyal to the state, that the interests of important social groups can largely be accommodated within the system, and that even non-Russian groups like the Baltic peoples seeking independence can eventually be co-opted into settling for greater autonomy. He is trying to demonstrate that reform can be managed in a way that avoids loss of regime control of the process and heads off pressure for more radical reforms that would truly revolutionize the system. He is, thus, engaged in a gamble of enormous proportions and uncertain consequences.

Implications for Gorbachev's International Agenda and US Policy

Gorbachev Stays the Course

If Gorbachev remains in power and avoids having to retrench significantly, we expect little change in the direction of his foreign policy. He will still have a pressing need for a stable international atmosphere that will allow him to concentrate on *perestroyka* and to shift funds from defense to the domestic economy. Up to a point, the prospect of continuing turmoil at home will reinforce sentiment in favor of a respite from East-West tensions (see inset).

3. *(Continued)*

We expect Gorbachev to:
- Push hard for conclusion of arms control agreements with the West.
- Broaden the base of the improvement in relations with the United States and Western Europe and seek to shape the evolution of the European security order.
- Go further to defuse human rights as a contentious issue in US-Soviet relations.
- Remain tolerant of changes in Eastern Europe that reduce Soviet influence.
- Consolidate the rapprochement with China.
- Seek to reduce military commitments in the Third World and avoid confrontation with the United States.
- Step up efforts to make the USSR into a more credible player in the international economic system. (S NF)

Retrenchment

The retrenchment scenario sketched out above would make Moscow:
- Less likely to make meaningful unilateral arms control concessions or military reductions.
- Less tolerant of liberalization in Eastern Europe, but unwilling to attempt to regain what has been lost.
- More supportive of leftist allies abroad.
- More reluctant to undertake any radical reorganization of the Soviet military and security services. (S NF)

A more orthodox Communist regime's harder line on a range of foreign and domestic issues would certainly increase East-West tensions, but the new regime would try to limit the damage. We see little chance that such a regime would find it in the Soviet interest to revert to an openly confrontational strategy toward the West that would entail a major new military buildup or significant risktaking in the Third World. In fact, its preoccupation with the problems of domestic order and consumer discontent would place some limits on its ability to shift resources back to the defense sector. It would probably implement arms control agreements already reached but be less inclined to make concessions to complete those still being negotiated. (S NF)

3. *(Continued)*

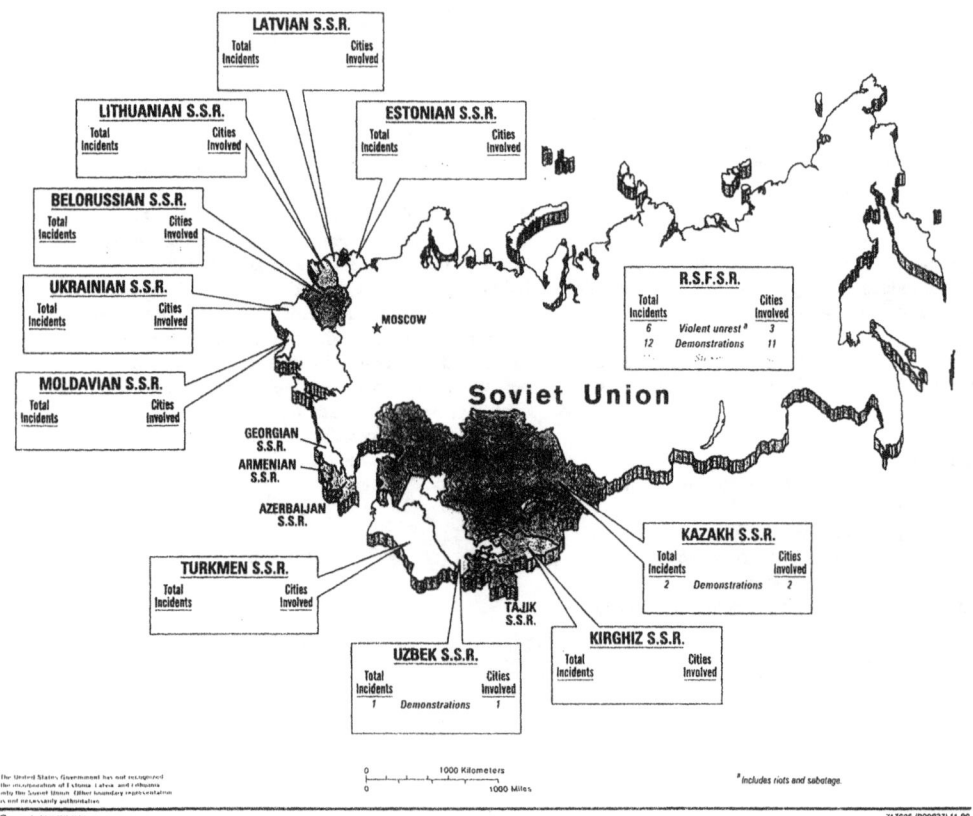

Figure 10
Reported Incidents of Economic Unrest, January 1987–September 1989

3. *(Continued)*

Figure 11
Reported Incidents of Nationalist Unrest, January 1987–September 1989

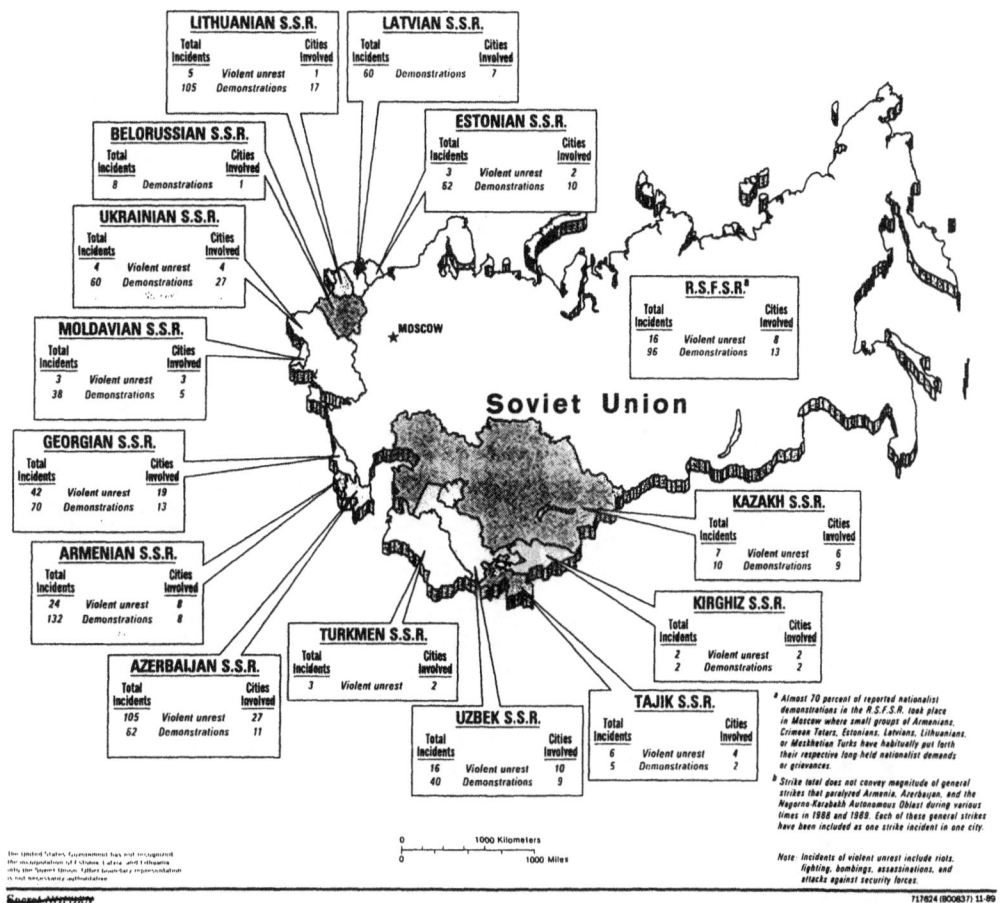

4. NIE 11-18-90, November 1990, *The Deepening Crisis in the USSR: Prospects for the Next Year*

Director of Central Intelligence

~~Secret~~

The Deepening Crisis in the USSR: Prospects for the Next Year

National Intelligence Estimate

This National Intelligence Estimate represents the views of the Director of Central Intelligence with the advice and assistance of the US Intelligence Community.

~~Secret~~

NIE 11-18-90
November 1990
Copy 410

4. *(Continued)*

Director of Central Intelligence

~~Secret~~

NIE 11-18-90

The Deepening Crisis in the USSR: Prospects for the Next Year

Information available as of 1 November 1990 was used in the preparation of this National Intelligence Estimate.

The following intelligence organizations participated in the preparation of this Estimate:
The Central Intelligence Agency
The Defense Intelligence Agency
The National Security Agency
The Bureau of Intelligence and Research, Department of State

also participating:
The Deputy Chief of Staff for Intelligence, Department of the Army
The Director of Naval Intelligence, Department of the Navy
The Assistant Chief of Staff, Intelligence, Department of the Air Force

This Estimate was approved for publication by the National Foreign Intelligence Board.

~~Secret~~
November 1990

4. *(Continued)*

The Deepening Crisis in the USSR: Prospects for the Next Year

- No end to the Soviet domestic crisis is in sight, and there is a strong probability that the situation will get worse—perhaps much worse—during the next year.

- The economy is certain to decline, and an economic breakdown is a possibility. The central government will be weaker, and some republics will be further along the road to political independence.

- The current situation is so fragile that a combination of events—such as the death of Gorbachev or Yel'tsin, a precipitous economic decline, massive consumer unrest, or an outbreak of widespread interethnic violence—could lead to anarchy and/or the intervention of the military into politics.

- The certain continued diffusion of power will make the conduct of Soviet foreign policy more difficult and complicate relations with the West. At a minimum, Western countries will be confronted with more urgent pleas for economic assistance—especially from republic leaders, who will also push for political recognition.

4. *(Continued)*

~~Secret~~
~~NOFORN-NOCONTRACT~~

Figure 1
Scenarios for the Next Year

Scenario [a]	Factors That Could Lead to Scenario	Rough Probability
Deterioration Short of Anarchy	Failure to agree upon and implement effectively a far-reaching marketization plan; or the broad resistance of the population to such a course. Failure of the center and the republics to move to new, mutually acceptable political and economic relations. Inability of political institutions to adapt to changing political realities, and ineffectiveness of new democratically elected leaders in governing. Continued, though diminished, viability of the central government.	Close to even
Anarchy	A precipitous decline of the economy. Massive social protests or labor strikes that proved to be beyond the security services' ability to control. The assassination of Gorbachev or Yel'tsin. The complete breakdown of relations between the center and the republics--especially the Russian Republic.	1 in 5 or less
Military Intervention (ranging from a coup to civilian-directed martial law)	Breakdown of key elements of the national economy, such as the transportation system. Violence against central government institutions. A situation approaching collapse of central authority. Anarchy.	1 in 5 or less overall; much lower for a coup
"Light at the End of the Tunnel"	Substantial progress toward: ☐ Developing a new set of relationships allowing the republics to deal constructively with each other and the center. ☐ The filling of the political power vacuum by new political institutions and parties. ☐ Establishing new economic relations based on the market.	1 in 5 or less

[a] These scenarios are analytical constructs describing overall directions the USSR could take over the next year and are not mutually exclusive.

4. *(Continued)*

Key Judgments

The USSR is in the midst of a historic transformation that threatens to tear the country apart. The old Communist order is in its death throes. But its diehards remain an obstructive force, and new political parties and institutions have yet to prove their effectiveness. The erosion of the center's influence, coupled with the republics' assertion of sovereignty, is creating a power vacuum. Gorbachev has amassed impressive power on paper, but his ability to use it effectively is increasingly in doubt. Meanwhile, economic conditions are steadily deteriorating.

Whether the Soviet Union over the next year can *begin* to find a way out of its crisis will hinge, above all, on two variables:

- *The performance of the economy.* The question is not whether the economy will decline further but how steep that decline will be. A precipitous drop would make crafting a new center-republic relationship next to impossible and markedly increase the likelihood of serious societal unrest and a breakdown of political authority.

- *The Gorbachev-Yel'tsin relationship.* Because of the Russian Republic's disproportionate size and influence in the union and Yel'tsin's role as the most prominent leader of the new political forces emerging throughout the country, the more open the confrontation between the two leaders, the more destabilizing it would be.

In our view, prospects for positive movement in each variable are low. Gorbachev's economic reform plan, while endorsing marketization, falls far short of what is needed to stem the economy's decline. And the Yel'tsin-Gorbachev clash over the plan bodes ill for both economic and center-republic reform.

For these reasons, we believe that over the next year a scenario of "deterioration short of anarchy" is more likely than any of the other three scenarios that we consider possible (see table). There is, however, a significant potential for dramatic departures along the lines of the "anarchy" or "military intervention" scenarios.

In our most likely scenario, *deterioration short of anarchy*, the country's economic, political, ethnic, and societal problems will continue to get worse at an accelerating rate. Gorbachev probably will remain president a year from now, but his authority will continue to decline. His ambivalence

4. *(Continued)*

toward radical transformation of the system probably will continue to delay decisive action and dilute the effectiveness of efforts to implement market reform or negotiate a new union. Yel'tsin's popularity and control over the Russian government will give him significant influence on the country's course over the next year. The different visions the two men have of Russia's and the USSR's future are likely to lead to more damaging political clashes. However, a combination of the remaining powers of the old order and the limited reforms the regime implements would prevent the entire system from disintegrating. (C-NF)

In view of the volatile situation that prevails in the USSR today, however, we believe that three other scenarios—each roughly a 1-in-5 probability—are also possible over the next year.

- An accelerating deterioration is unlikely to continue indefinitely and could during the next year become a free fall that would result in a period of *anarchy*—the breakdown of central political and economic order.

- The chances for *military intervention* in politics would increase markedly in a scenario where the country was on the verge of, or in, a state of anarchy. Military intervention could take several forms: a military coup against the constitutional order, rogue activity by individual commanders, or martial law ordered by Gorbachev to enforce government directives. Of these, Intelligence Community analysts believe a coup to be the least likely variant and a civilian-directed martial law the most likely.

- A *"light at the end of the tunnel"* scenario, where progress over the next year toward the creation of a new system outpaces the breakdown of the old, cannot be ruled out. There would be further progress toward marketization and pluralization in spite of continued economic decline and political turmoil. (C-NF)

Whichever scenario prevails, the USSR during the next year will remain inward looking, with a declining ability to maintain its role as a superpower. The domestic crisis will continue to preoccupy any Soviet leaders and prompt them, at a minimum, to seek to avoid direct confrontation with the West. But the particular foreign policies they pursue could vary significantly depending upon the scenario. Under the "deterioration short of anarchy" or "light at the end of the tunnel" scenarios, Moscow's Western orientation probably would be reflected in continued, possibly greater, Soviet willingness to compromise on a range of international issues. (C-NF)

Special requests to the West for consultations, technical assistance, emergency aid, and trade from the central and republic governments are certain to increase. Unless political conflict over who owns resources and

4. *(Continued)*

controls foreign trade is resolved, which is unlikely, both US governmental and private business relations with the USSR and its republics will be increasingly complicated. (C-NF)

An "anarchy" scenario would create precarious conditions for relations with the West and would present the United States with some difficult choices. If the situation evolved into civil wars, we would face competing claims for recognition and assistance. The prospects for the fighting to spill over into neighboring countries would increase. The West would be inundated with refugees, and there would be enormous uncertainties over who was in control of the Soviet military's nuclear weapons. (C-NF)

In a "military intervention" scenario, a military-dominated regime would take a less concessionary approach than Gorbachev's on foreign policy issues and pursue a tougher line on arms control issues and economic relations with Eastern Europe. A military regime, however, would be unable to restore Soviet influence in Eastern Europe and would be too busy attempting to hold the USSR together to resume a hostile military posture toward the West. (C-NF)

4. *(Continued)*

~~Secret~~
~~NOFORN-NOCONTRACT~~

Contents

	Page
Key Judgments	v
Discussion	1
Toward a New Political Order	1
Political Strategy of the Key Players	2
Impact of Other Players	4
The Crumbling Union	7
What Kind of Union?	10
The Economic Variable	11
Erosion of Central Control	11
Labor and Ethnic Strife	12
Financial Imbalance	13
Market Reform	13
Four Scenarios	14
Deterioration Short of Anarchy	15
Anarchy	16
Military Intervention	17
"Light at the End of the Tunnel"	17
Implications for the United States	18
Annex A: Emerging Democratic Leaders	21
Annex B: Emerging Traditionalist Leaders	23

4. (*Continued*)

Discussion

Since the Intelligence Community's last Estimate of the Soviet domestic situation a year ago,[1] the USSR's internal crisis has deepened considerably:

- The Communist Party is dying but is still obstructive. Gorbachev has tried to shift the locus of power to the new presidency and legislatures, but they have yet to demonstrate their effectiveness.

- New political groups and parties have won power in key republics and cities and are posing a growing challenge to the Communist system.

- The national government is scrambling to control centrifugal trends, but its writ over the republics is fast eroding, and there is growing ethnic turmoil.

- Economic problems have become more intractable. The uncontrolled growth in demand and distribution problems have created increasing consumer discontent. Gorbachev has lost valuable time in stabilizing the economy and beginning the transition to a market economy.

Our previous Estimate, while foreseeing the tumult, overstated the regime's ability to contain the republics' drive for sovereignty and underestimated the challenge to Communist Party rule from new political forces.

In such a volatile atmosphere, events could go in any number of directions. Because of this, the Intelligence Community's uncertainties about the future of the Soviet system are greater today than at any time in the 40 years we have been producing Estimates on the USSR. Accordingly, our projections for the next year will be highly tentative.

[1] NIE 11-18-89, November 1989, *The Soviet System in Crisis: Prospects for the Next Two Years*

Toward a New Political Order

The Communist Party's monopoly of power is history. The party is widely seen as the source of the country's problems, and popular hatred of it is increasingly evident. It lost its constitutional guarantee of political primacy in March, and its 28th Congress in July excluded government leaders (except for Gorbachev) from key party posts. The country's two largest cities and largest republic, as well as the three Baltic republics, Georgia, and Armenia, are now headed or have legislatures dominated by former or non-Communists.

A new pluralistic, decentralized political system is emerging but is not yet capable of running the country. The center and the Communist Party still exercise a considerable, though declining, share of political power. *But the CPSU is too discredited to attract sufficient popular support needed to govern in the current environment.* At the same time, the emerging political groups, while showing strength, are still small and inexperienced in the ways of power and are not competitive on the all-union level (see inset, page 3).

The governmental institutions to which Gorbachev has been attempting to shift power are likewise only in their formative stages. The Congress of People's Deputies (CPD) is foundering. The Supreme Soviet—elected by the CPD—has shown more promise, but is also losing influence because of its lack of popular legitimacy, its inability to act decisively, and the center's difficulty in maintaining control over major sectors of government. Gorbachev has made the presidency the highest organ of executive power, supplanting the CPSU Politburo and the Council of Ministers, but its real authority remains to be proved. This diffusion and confusion of power, coupled with the republics' assertion of sovereignty, is creating a power

4. *(Continued)*

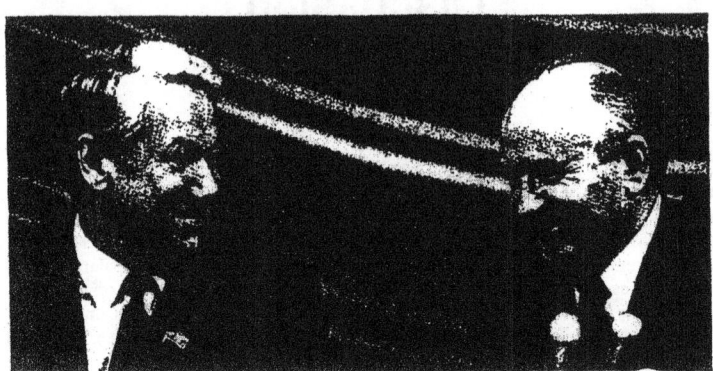

Figure 2. Yel'tsin and Gorbachev: Beyond the smiles, can they cooperate? (U)

vacuum. Gorbachev has amassed impressive power on paper, but his ability to use it effectively is increasingly in question and his popular support— ▬▬▬ —is dwindling ▬▬▬▬▬▬▬▬▬▬. (C NF)

Political Strategy of the Key Players

Gorbachev's defeat of the party's conservative wing at the congress has given him greater room to maneuver. The pressure created by Yel'tsin's growing influence has made Gorbachev realize that he must work with Yel'tsin and other non-Communist forces. He now accepts the inevitability of a weaker central government and a market-oriented economy. Yet Gorbachev, afraid of social upheaval, wants to preserve a significant measure of control over events. This has led him to try to bolster his powers as President, limit the influence of new non-Communist political forces, retain significant powers for the center in a new union, and water down the Shatalin Plan for transformation to a market economy. This course is at odds with Yel'tsin's on some key issues and is slower and not as far reaching as we believe is necessary. (C NF)

The political forces outside the Communist Party are certain to get stronger; there is as yet, however, no coherent strategy among those forces as a whole. Many non-Communist figures are concentrating their efforts on organizing political parties. Others who have already won elections, such as Yel'tsin and Moscow Mayor Gavriil Popov, have shunned involvement—for the time being at least—in any political party and concentrated on the basics of governing (see annexes). If they demonstrate over the next year that they can get things done and make the voices of their constituents heard, the prospects for a more rapid emergence of a non-Communist leadership on the all-union level would increase markedly. (C NF)

Yel'tsin's immediate goal is achieving sovereignty and greater power for the Russian Republic (see p. 7); but the enormous size of that republic and his reputation throughout the USSR as unofficial leader of the non-Communist forces make him a formidable competitor to Gorbachev. Yel'tsin, who quit the CPSU in July, supports a multiparty democracy, rapid movement toward a market economy, and a much looser union in which the republics grant only limited powers to the center. (C NF)

Currently, Yel'tsin appears to have the political advantage over Gorbachev; he is far more popular than Gorbachev in USSR-wide opinion polls. In the six months since Yel'tsin became Russia's President, the two have had periods of cooperation and confrontation. Their willingness and ability to cooperate will play a critical role in the fate of political, economic, and center-republic transformation in the USSR over the next year. Whether they will do so is open to question, given their mutual personal antagonism,

4. *(Continued)*

> **Embryonic National Political Parties**
>
> A wide array of political groups is emerging in the USSR as the country moves toward the development of a multiparty, state-of-law political system. They have the potential to gain significant electoral support but—except for those in the Baltics and the Caucasus—have yet to develop into full-blown political parties. The groups generally lack clear, comprehensive political platforms, and none has a formal membership of more than several thousand. Several groups claim to be parties or will claim that title soon. Although based in the Russian Republic, they have some following in other parts of the country. (C NF)
>
> *Democratic Platform.* This group of democratic reformers from the CPSU is in the process of transforming itself into an independent party. Its leaders predict that 30 percent of the current CPSU membership will eventually join the new party, but the actual figure is likely to be lower. The party's platform supports the market as the prime regulator of the economy, private property, and "independence" for the republics. (C NF)
>
> *Democratic Russia.* This group is currently serving as a legislative coalition and has run proreform candidates for local and Russian Republic elections. It embraces an assortment of political forces opposed to CPSU traditionalists. The group currently has strong majorities in the Moscow and Leningrad city councils and a thin majority in Russian Supreme Soviet. (C NF)
>
> *Social Democratic Party.* Founded in January 1990, this party is trying to associate itself with European Social Democrats. It has generally supported Gorbachev but has charged him with being too cautious and seeking to perpetuate an authoritarian system. (C NF)
>
> *Christian Democratic Union of Russia.* This party openly opposes Gorbachev. It insists that "Russia should become independent of the USSR" by establishing new forms of federation with other democratically inclined republics. The party's economic platform rejects capitalism while supporting a "free market controlled by society" and a progressive tax scale to protect the poor. (C NF)
>
> *Democratic Union.* Radical by Soviet standards, this party believes the Soviet political system should be thoroughly overhauled to establish a voluntary federation of republics based on a Western-style multiparty system and a full market economy. Party leaders have stressed the need to confront government authorities in order to bring attention to the repressive character of the Communist system. (C NF)
>
> *Green Party.* This party is taking shape among approximately 300 ecological organizations. These organizations agree on the need to protect the environment but have not been able to develop a consensus on other political or economic issues. (C NF)

different policy agendas, and political rivalry. Open confrontation would stymie system transformation and lead to greater instability. Cooperation would not guarantee peaceful transformation, but it would help significantly by garnering popular support for painful economic measures linked to marketization and by making it more difficult for the entrenched party machinery in the countryside to be obstructive. If Yel'tsin follows through during the next year on his pledge to stand for popular election to the Russian Republic presidency, a decisive victory would further enhance his political influence. (C NF)

Gorbachev, the Supreme Soviet, and the Congress of People's Deputies, elected before the establishment of independent political parties, lack the popular support

4. *(Continued)*

necessary to push through the difficult and painful measures needed to deal with the country's crises. Accordingly, Gorbachev could decide during the next year to create a "roundtable" between the government and non-Communist leaders a la Poland in 1989 or perhaps even form a grand coalition. This would involve the removal of the increasingly ineffective Nikolay Ryzhkov from the premiership. Elections for the Congress of People's Deputies are not due until 1994 and for the presidency until 1995, but Gorbachev may calculate that holding early legislative elections would allow new parties to gain representation. Submitting himself to the popular will would be risky, and he is unlikely to do so during the coming year.

Impact of Other Players
The Armed Forces and Security Services. Leaders of the military and security services perceive dangerous consequences from Gorbachev's domestic and foreign policies. These concerns reflect alarm over the collapsing authority of the party and the central government, growing domestic disorder, the unchecked spread of separatist movements, and the breakup of the East European security system.

4. (Continued)

These organizations will find their ability to cope with growing internal disorder limited over the next year. The military is averse to using its troops to police the population. Moreover, most Soviet troop units, because they are conscript based, are ill suited to controlling disorder—especially in Slavic areas. The KGB's ability to perform its internal security mission

4. *(Continued)*

will also decline as more light is shed on its activities, independent political movements grow, and more local governments come under control of non-Communist forces. The Ministry of Interior, despite a growth in manpower, is stretched thin and cannot control widespread domestic unrest. (S NF)

4. *(Continued)*

Figure 4. Demonstrations on May Day 1990 in Red Square. Banner reads: "Power to the people and not to the party!" (U)

Despite their apprehension over the current domestic situation and concern about their abilities to perform assigned missions, the military and security services do not pose a serious challenge to Gorbachev's leadership. They view themselves as instruments of the state and are attempting to help Gorbachev in dealing with the turmoil. Even with their many internal problems, they represent the most reliable institutional assets remaining at Gorbachev's disposal. (C-NF)

Society. Popular anger is growing, as is belief in the inability of the central government to lead the country out of the morass it is in. Deep pessimism about the future prevails, especially when it comes to bread and butter issues. People are searching for something to fill the emptiness in Soviet society through such alternatives as religion and nationalism. In particular, Russian nationalism—more likely in an inward-looking, rather than chauvinistic, variant—will play a growing role in the future of the country. (C-NF)

The reforms under way have given the peoples of the USSR greater say in their political and economic lives, and they have expressed their views through the ballot, demonstrations, strikes, and violence. The population's influence is likely to grow even more during the next year as power continues to move away from central institutions. How this influence is exercised and channeled will be critical variables. Separatist groups and new political parties—primarily on the left, but also from the right—will tap much of this popular activism. This will increase their importance but could also embolden them to take steps that lead to greater instability. Outbursts of civil disobedience are almost certain to grow; they are more likely to occur—and be most severe—in non-Russian areas but probably will also take place in the largest cities of the Russian Republic and in energy-producing regions. (C-NF)

The Crumbling Union

The Soviet Union as we have known it is finished. The USSR is, at a minimum, headed toward a smaller and looser union. The republics, led by Yel'tsin and the RSFSR, will intensify efforts to reshape the union independent of the center, further loosening Moscow's

4. *(Continued)*

Figure 5
Soviet Republics

The United States Government has not recognized the incorporation of Estonia, Latvia, and Lithuania into the Soviet Union. Other boundary representation is not necessarily authoritative.

Unclassified

grip over their regions. To date, these efforts are mostly declaratory; actual control over institutions and resources in the republics is still to be tested. (C NF)

In an effort to cope with the nationalist forces straining the fabric of the union, Gorbachev now supports a substantially widened scope for market forces and the conclusion of a new union treaty by early 1991 that would establish new power-sharing relationships between Moscow and each republic. We doubt, however, that a new union treaty can be concluded within the next year. Gorbachev has indicated he will accept a reduction in the center's authority but so far is attempting to hold on to more authority than most republics want to concede. *The initiative now resides mainly with the republics, and any new treaty is likely to be driven more by what powers they are willing to grant the center than by what Gorbachev wants* (see figure 6). (C NF)

Because of the disproportionate size and influence of *Russia*, a new union treaty will not be concluded unless Yel'tsin and Gorbachev work together. How far many of the other republics go in demanding sovereignty will be directly affected by Russia's success in negotiating with the center and with the other republics. (C NF)

4. *(Continued)*

Figure 6
USSR: Soviet Republic Sovereignty Declarations

- ● Yes
- ■ No
- ▲ Unknown

Republic (in order of declaration)

	Estonian SSR	Lithuanian SSR	Latvian SSR	Azerbaijan SSR	Georgian SSR	RSFSR	Uzbek SSR	Moldova	Ukrainian SSR	Belorussian SSR	Turkmen SSR	Armenian SSR	Tajik SSR	Kazakh SSR	Kirghiz SSR
Seeks immediate secession	●	●	●	■	■	■	■	■	■	■	■	■	■	■	■
Supremacy of republic laws	●	●	●	●	●	●	●	●	●	●	●	●	●	●	●
Right to republic military troops	●	●	●	■	■	■	■	■	●	●	■	●	■	●	▲
Independent economic policy	●	●	●	●	●	●	●	●	●	●	●	●	●	▲	▲
Republic banking, tax, currency	●	●	●	■	■	●	■	■	●	●	a	●	a	▲	▲
Independent foreign relations	●	●	●	●	●	●	●	●	●	●	●	●	●	●	▲
Control over natural resources	●	●	●	●	●	●	●	●	●	●	●	●	●	●	▲
Republic citizenship	●	●	●	●	●	●	●	●	●	●	●	●	●	●	▲
Military neutrality	■	■	■	■	■	■	■	b	●	●	■	■	■	▲	▲
Nuclear-free state	■	■	■	■	■	■	■	■	●	●	●	■	■	c	▲
Participant in union treaty talks	■	■	■	●	●	●	●	●	●	●	●	●	●	●	●

[a] Turkmen SSR and Tajik SSR have asserted the right to independent republic banking.

[b] Moldova has declared itself to be a demilitarized zone.

[c] Kazakh SSR, site of principal nuclear test range, has banned all nuclear testing and construction or operation of test sites for weapons of mass destruction.

Unclassified

4. *(Continued)*

~~Secret~~

> *The Range of Republic Demands*
>
> *The two largest and most powerful republics, Russia and the Ukraine, now support a severely limited central government and union as they demand substantial control over their own affairs. The Russian Republic legislature is calling for primacy of its own laws over Soviet ones, control of the republic's land and natural resources, fiscal policy, police and internal security forces, most economic enterprises, foreign trade, and some role in foreign and monetary policy. The Ukraine has gone further, asserting the right to establish its own army, and Belorussia and the Central Asian republics are also making far-reaching demands. The three Baltic republics are flatly rejecting political affiliation with the center before achieving independence. Georgia, Armenia, and Moldova, in which secessionist sentiment is especially strong, appear unwilling to sign a union treaty but are seeking a gradual transition to independence.* (C-NF)

> *The Union Treaty: Areas Over Which the Center Seeks Control*
>
> *Gorbachev apparently wants to maintain the primacy of union laws over republic ones and to preserve substantial central control of:*
> - *Natural resources and land.*
> - *Defense and state security.*
> - *Foreign policy.*
> - *Macroeconomic policy.*
> - *Foreign trade and customs.*
> - *Border control.*
> - *Science and technology policy.*
> - *Power supply.*
> - *Transportation.*
> - *Protection of individual rights.* (C-NF)

What Kind of Union?
The process of reshaping the union will vary according to the republic over the next year; at a minimum, the center will suffer a dramatic reduction in authority. (C-NF)

There is a better than even chance that Moscow and certain republics—*Russia, Belorussia, Azerbaijan, and the Central Asian republics*—will move toward a loosely affiliated union of republics. We believe that Gorbachev will ultimately go a long way to meet Russia's autonomy demands as long as the central government retains a meaningful role in the new union. Considerable difficulties and hard bargaining remain; but so far the demands of Russia and these other republics do not appear irreconcilable with Gorbachev's (see insets). (C-NF)

The *Ukraine*'s future status is more uncertain. Growing radicalization of the nationalist organization *Rukh* and the population generally has pushed the Ukrainian legislature to take increasingly assertive steps in defining the republic's relationship with Moscow. *Rukh* supports a complete break with the central government, but more traditionalist forces in the Russified eastern part of the republic are likely to try to impede any abrupt declaration of independence. (C-NF)

Thus, there is still a significant chance that Moscow will be unable to reach a mutually acceptable division of responsibilities even with the core Slavic republics. Moscow could reject their current demands, or the RSFSR or Ukraine could escalate demands in areas such as defense and monetary policy to the point where Gorbachev would feel he had no choice but to resist. A number of factors could contribute to a breakdown in negotiations, including a continued rise in Ukrainian nationalism, worsening of relations between Gorbachev and Yel'tsin, or rising popular unrest directed against central authority. In these circumstances, struggle for control of key institutions and enterprises in the republics would ensue, leading to sharp—probably violent—confrontation, with the very existence of the union at stake. The advantage in this scenario would belong to the "locals." (C-NF)

The Central Asian republics appear ready to try out a reformed union as a way of addressing their economic

~~Secret~~   10

4. *(Continued)*

difficulties. Market reform will create disproportionate economic pain in the region, however, and could eventually produce disillusion with even a looser union. (C-NF)

Although no republic is likely to become officially independent within the next year, *the Baltic republics are almost certain to hold out for full independence and will be on their way to getting it.* Latvia and Estonia will probably be willing to consider some kind of voluntary economic association with the Soviet Union now, but Lithuania is likely to be willing to do so only after achieving complete independence. *Georgia, Armenia, and Moldova* will probably reject any union treaty but will adopt a more gradual approach to independence than the Balts. As Georgia and Moldova press for independence, ethnic minorities there are likely to intensify calls for autonomy. This probably would not deter republic efforts. But Moscow may yet be able to play on Georgian and Armenian concerns about susceptibility to potential Turkish or other Muslim aggression without the protection of the Soviet security umbrella. And a shift in Romania toward greater authoritarianism would probably make the Moldovans more willing to stay in the union. (C-NF)

The Economic Variable

Last year the Soviet economy slumped badly, and official statistics for the first nine months of 1990 paint a picture of an economy in accelerating decline. Output is down compared with a year ago, inflation is up, and shortages are widespread and increasing. Even though imports and production of some consumer goods are up (such as in agriculture and consumer durables), transportation bottlenecks and systemic inefficiency are denying consumers much of the benefit. Meanwhile, continued rapid growth in personal money incomes and a huge backlog of excess purchasing power have combined to undermine the ruble and cause a vicious circle of shortages and binge buying, enflaming consumer anger and leading to violence. (C-NF)

In the year to come, the economy's performance will depend on how central authorities manage erosion of their control over the economy, the level of labor and ethnic strife, the success of regime efforts to overcome the acute financial imbalance, and the course of marketization. In view of our assessment of the prospects for each of these variables, we believe that the economy will continue declining at an accelerating rate and there is a possibility of an economic breakdown (see inset, page 13). (C-NF)

Erosion of Central Control

The transition from the command economy to a more decentralized market system will ultimately yield major gains in performance. In the short run, however, central controls have begun to wither before an effective new system has been put in place. The Communist Party is no longer able to enforce the state's economic orders; economic reforms have given state enterprises and farms the legal basis to resist the center; and the pursuit of independence and autonomy at the republic and enterprise levels have disrupted old supply and demand relationships. (C-NF)

Over the next year, these trends are almost certain to continue, and the center could be weakened to a point where it would lose control of the allocation of vital goods such as energy, key industrial materials, and grain. Attempts by regional authorities to protect their populations from rampant shortages will worsen the current economic turmoil. At the same time, the interdependence of the republics and localities and the

4. *(Continued)*

Figure 7
Soviet Economic Performance Down

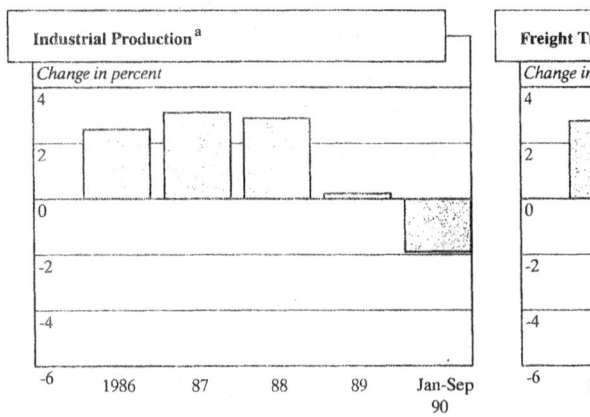
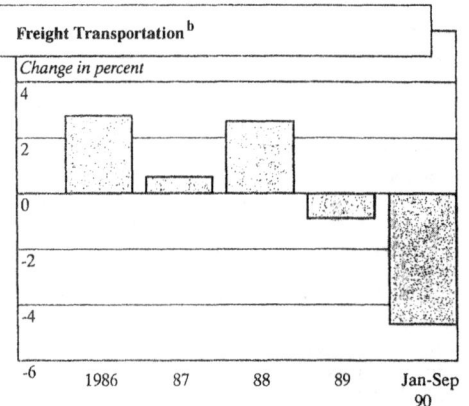

[a] CIA estimates.

[b] CIA estimates except 1990, which is a Soviet official statistic.

NOTE: January-September 1990 is compared with January-September 1989.

interest of the regional authorities in avoiding economic chaos will continue to argue for restraint against severing old relationships.

Labor and Ethnic Strife

Labor and ethnic problems over the past year have been major contributors to the USSR's economic turmoil. Poor living and working conditions, increasing shortages, and greater awareness of the workers of their lot have led to falling worker motivation and fueled labor and ethnic unrest. Because these problems are certain to get worse in the year to come, labor strife will continue, and faith in government solutions to labor problems will remain low.

The economy is most vulnerable to work stoppages in the transportation and energy sectors. The railroad system has virtually no slack capacity or substitutes. Strikes in this sector would immediately damage the already fragile supply network, grinding other sectors to a halt and probably leading to the use of the military to run the railroads. Similarly, an upsurge in unrest in a large republic such as the Ukraine or in the Great Russian heartland would be especially damaging to the economy.

4. *(Continued)*

Economic Breakdown

A severe breakdown in the coordination between supply and demand is rare historically and has been a result of revolution, war, or disastrous economic policies. Under present circumstances, such a breakdown could be precipitated by massive popular unrest, regional autarky that destroys trade flows, a radical economic reform, or prolonged strikes of transport workers or workers in basic industries such as steel and energy. (C NF)

Indicators of such a breakdown would be:
- *A decline in GNP of at least 20 percent.*
- *Hyperinflation, massive bankruptcies and unemployment.*
- *Paralysis of the distribution system for both industrial and consumer goods.*
- *Dramatic flight from the ruble that results in barter trade or payment in hard currency.*

Financial Imbalance

Moscow has struggled unsuccessfully in the past two years to slow or reverse the growth of the excess purchasing power that has destabilized consumer markets. The key to reducing the dangerous backlog of excess purchasing power in the year ahead is to lower the budget deficit and proceed with price reform. Despite the stated intention of the Gorbachev reform program, however, it is doubtful that Moscow will move quickly in either area. Making a dent in this problem will require further cuts in state spending for investment and defense and reductions in social expenditures, particularly the huge subsidies for food. Moscow still fears popular reaction to price increases, however, and a large safety net is an integral part of the Gorbachev program. If the government continues to defer decisive action on these issues, the threat of a real financial crisis will deepen considerably and further complicate reform efforts. (C NF)

Market Reform

The Gorbachev program approved by the Supreme Soviet in October endorses marketization but fails to cut the bureaucracy immediately, thus making it easy for recalcitrants to block progress (see inset). The plan also sets no specific goals or timetables for denationalization of state assets. Although Gorbachev's advisers indicate that this lack of detail is designed to leave the republics free to work out the specifics of denationalization, the program's reliance on state orders and administered prices for at least another year will sharply limit the number of enterprises that could be denationalized. In addition, the plan's measures to stabilize the economy are misconceived—immediate large increases in wholesale prices and continuation of subsidies to consumers through 1992 will spur inflation and undercut deficit reduction. (C NF)

Overall, Gorbachev's program is a heavily political document aimed at garnering republic support while retaining substantial power for the center. It adopts a slower, more cautious approach on moving toward a market than the Shatalin Plan—supported by the Russian and other republics—and thereby probably runs less risk in the short term. The limitations of the Gorbachev program are such, however, that it is unlikely to deliver the promised economic gains and, as a result, over the longer term it will court greater political problems than the Shatalin Plan would have. As the program's deficiencies become apparent in the months ahead, the leadership is likely to consider more radical measures to achieve a transition to a market under even more dire economic conditions. With this program or any other that may be adopted, *it is impossible to overstate how difficult, painful, and contentious it will be for a large multinational state to move from a command to a market economy.* (C NF)

4. *(Continued)*

~~Secret~~

Key Elements of Gorbachev's Market Reform Program

Timing	18- to 24-month conversion to market period in four stages but without a definite schedule for each stage.	*Privatization*	Republics control most assets in their territories and set pace. Republics decide issue of private ownership of land.
Center-republic powers	Both center and republics have budget and tax authority; center taxation requires republic concurrence. Center retains control over key exports for some period, shares hard currency revenues with republics.	*Price reform*	Increase wholesale prices according to government schedule; enterprise contracts to use these prices. State orders and central distribution, not prices, to determine most allocation.
Stabilization	Reduce deficit to 25-30 billion rubles—cut defense, investment, enterprise subsidies. Maintain key consumer subsidies. Finance deficit with bonds. Absorb ruble overhang with bond, consumer warrant sales; sales of some other state assets; and through increases in saving interest rates.	*Foreign economic relations*	Moves gradually toward ruble convertibility. Calls for increased latitude on foreign investment, including 100-percent foreign ownership of firms.

~~Confidential~~

Four Scenarios

I wouldn't hazard a guess.

> Izvestiya *commentator's answer to US Embassy officer's question in July about how he envisioned the USSR in two to three years.* (c)

The interaction of political, ethnic, and economic variables will determine the fate of the country over the next year: major deterioration in any one area would severely strain the current system; breakdowns in all three would mean anarchy. Economic breakdown, in particular, would make crafting a new center-republic relationship next to impossible and markedly increase the likelihood of serious societal unrest. (C-NF)

A further diffusion of power from the center in all three areas—political, economic, and center-republic—is certain. Gorbachev's authority will continue to

~~Secret~~

14

4. (Continued)

decline, although he will probably remain in office a year from now. Even under the most optimistic scenario, the Soviet domestic crisis will be far from resolved in one year's time. The turmoil will continue regardless of the policies pursued. Progress could be made in some areas. But the risk of sudden major discontinuities will remain, and it will take years—at least a decade or more—to find lasting solutions to the country's ills. (C NF)

Given the unpredictable nature of events in the volatile situation that prevails in the USSR today, we believe that four scenarios capture the range of possibilities during the next year: *deterioration short of anarchy; anarchy; military intervention; and "light at the end of the tunnel"* (see figure 1). These scenarios are analytical constructs describing overall directions the country could take over the next year and are not mutually exclusive. Some would be most likely to develop from one of the others. We believe that the "deterioration short of anarchy" scenario, which develops out of current trends, is more likely than any of the other three. There is, however, a significant potential for dramatic departures along the lines of the "anarchy" or "military intervention" scenarios. Conditions are such that the odds *strongly favor* some form of these three "bad news" scenarios during the coming year. (C NF)

Deterioration Short of Anarchy

Current trends in the country and the enormous problems facing it in every sphere make this the most likely scenario over the next year, in our view. Intelligence Community analysts give this scenario a close to even probability. The economic, political, ethnic, and societal problems would continue to get worse at an accelerating rate. This scenario would be characterized by:

- Failure to agree upon and implement effectively a far-reaching marketization program; or the broad resistance of the population to such a course.
- Failure of the center and the republics to move to new mutually acceptable political and economic relations.
- Inability of political institutions to adapt to changing political realities and ineffectiveness of new democratically elected leaders in governing.

However, a combination of the remaining powers of the old order—the party and government machinery and the security services—and the limited reforms the regime implements would prevent the entire system from collapsing. (C NF)

Some positive trends could also occur under this scenario but would not be likely to develop sufficiently to stem the country's rapidly declining fortunes during the next year. Gorbachev's ambivalence toward radical transformation of the system would end up delaying decisive action and diluting the effectiveness of steps his government takes. The non-Communist forces both in and out of government would not be able to form coalitions on a nationwide scale to give clear-cut direction. The complexities and social pain associated with putting a market reform plan in place would not even begin to restore confidence in the currency, reverse autarkic trends, or revitalize commerce, not to mention improve economic performance. The growing autonomy and self-confidence of non-Russians throughout the country would lead to escalating demands and make the achievement of a voluntary union much more complicated. (C NF)

This diffusion of power would lead during the next year to an increasing power vacuum. With the accelerating deterioration of central control and organizational weaknesses of the opposition, more power would be likely to move into the streets. Strikes and consumer unrest would almost certainly grow, the more so the more rapidly the economy declines. Ethnic unrest and violence would also increase. The security services and the military would be able to manage as long as protests remain scattered and uncoordinated. (C NF)

The key determinant of how long this scenario would persist is how long the economy can keep from collapsing under these conditions. *The longer this scenario prevailed, the greater the prospects would be for anarchy or military intervention.* (C NF)

4. (Continued)

Anarchy

An accelerating deterioration is unlikely to continue indefinitely and could, during the next year, become a free fall that would result in a period of anarchy. Community analysts generally believe that the likelihood of this scenario is roughly 1 in 5 or less. Anarchy would be characterized by a breakdown of the economic system, collapse of central political authority, and widespread social upheaval. (C-NF)

Such an outcome could result from the interaction of a number of developments. In fact, any one development could trigger a cascade that eventually leads to a collapse of the system:
- A sharp acceleration of negative economic trends already in evidence—local autarky, severe food shortages this winter, numerous plant closings due to lack of fuel and supplies.
- Massive social protests or labor strikes that proved to be beyond the security and armed services' ability to control or resulted in large-scale civilian casualties.
- The assassination of a key leader, such as Gorbachev or Yel'tsin.
- The complete breakdown of relations between the center and the republics—particularly the Russian Republic.
- The outbreak of sustained, widespread interethnic violence—especially if directed against Russians. (C-NF)

There are several likely consequences of such a scenario:
- Gorbachev would not politically survive such an upheaval.
- The potential for severe food shortages and malnutrition would be high.
- The union would disintegrate. Most republics would break away from the center, potentially setting off civil wars and massive migrations.
- There probably would be various political outcomes (authoritarian, military dominated, democratic) in different regions of what is now the USSR. (C-NF)

The Departure of Gorbachev or Yel'tsin

The impact of their sudden departure from the scene would vary according to whether it occurred via assassination, death by natural causes, or political pressure—with assassination undoubtedly being the most destabilizing. But leaving aside the circumstances, what would their absence mean? (C-NF)

Gorbachev's departure two years—or even one year—ago, while the traditionalists still retained considerable strength in the leadership and the democratic reforms had barely begun to get off the ground, probably would have set back those reforms many years. His demise in the next year would be certain to throw the country into flux. The CPSU has no obvious successor who could wield the influence Gorbachev has, and the presidency would not be as influential a post without such a strong leader. At the same time, traditionalists could see an opportunity to make a comeback. The democratic and market reforms have now taken on a life of their own, however, beyond the control of even as formidable a figure as Gorbachev. The transformation of the Soviet system would take place in a more uncertain atmosphere in the immediate aftermath of Gorbachev's departure, but he is no longer "the indispensable man." (C-NF)

Yel'tsin has become the unofficial head of the democratic reform movement, and no one else in the movement currently has the stature to challenge Gorbachev. His departure would be a major setback to the movement over the next year but probably not a fatal one over the longer term. There are a number of other emerging democratic leaders who lack Yel'tsin's popular appeal but have other strengths that over time might enable them to play a national role. (C-NF)

4. *(Continued)*

Military Intervention

Community analysts believe that the prospects for military intervention in politics are roughly the same as those for "anarchy"—1 in 5 or less. Besides Gorbachev's apparent extreme reluctance to use military force to deal with the country's problems, most Soviet leaders probably believe there is a strong danger that military intervention could accelerate the trend toward chaos and lead to the outbreak of virtual civil war. Problems in society, moreover, have had a debilitating effect upon the military, making it increasingly less suitable and reliable for use in putting down social unrest or enforcing unpopular government directives.

Even so, under conditions of continuing deterioration, the likelihood of the military's becoming more involved in internal politics will grow as the leadership becomes more dependent on the Armed Forces and security services to maintain control. The traditional Russian desire for order could even foster a perception of the military among elements of the population as the key to national salvation in a time of growing chaos. Many senior military leaders share this view of the Armed Forces as the conservator of the Soviet state. *The chances for military intervention would increase markedly in a scenario where the country was on the verge of, or in, a state of anarchy.*

Military intervention could take several forms: a military coup against the constitutional order, rogue activity by individual commanders, or martial law ordered by Gorbachev. Of these, Community analysts believe a coup—either the military acting alone or in conjunction with the security services and CPSU traditionalists—to be the least likely variant. Such an attempt would have to overcome numerous obstacles, including the difficulty of secretly coordinating the activities of the *many* units required for a successful putsch, the increasing political polarization of the Armed Forces, the military leadership's professional inhibitions against such a drastic step, and the fear of large-scale resistance by Soviet society.

Only slightly more probable, in our view, would be independent action by local military units in the face of widespread violence that threatens or causes the collapse of civil government. In such an event, a military district commander—operating independently of Moscow and possibly at the request of besieged regional authorities—could order his forces to restore control locally. Whether troops would obey under these conditions would depend greatly on local circumstances. Lacking clear direction and coordination, such independent military actions probably would not succeed for very long, except perhaps in a situation of countrywide anarchy.

We believe that the most likely variant of military intervention would be one in which the central government in Moscow, believing it was losing all control of events and wanting to stabilize the situation, called on the military to impose martial law in selected areas and enforce government directives in the name of salvaging reform. Such an effort probably would be limited to Russia and a few other key republics. The High Command would try to execute such orders, seeing this as its duty to the state. If the conditions are severe enough, such military intervention might be welcomed by the local population and could stabilize the situation temporarily. Unless accompanied by a program offering solutions to the country's political, ethnic, and economic crises, however, the benefits from such a step would be transitory and probably counterproductive in the long run.

"Light at the End of the Tunnel"

The prospects that progress toward the creation of a new system over the next year could outpace the breakdown of the old are also about 1 in 5 or less, in our view. This scenario would develop out of current pressure toward a pluralistic political system, self-determination, and marketization. Such trends, while not ending the societal turmoil, might gather sufficient steam to improve prospects for long-term social stability. Economic hardship would increase as movement toward a market economy began and enormous difficulties in creating a new politcal order would lay ahead, but a psychological corner would be turned to give the population some hope for a brighter future.

4. *(Continued)*

Secret

In order for this scenario to play out, there would have to be substantial progress toward:

- Developing a new set of relationships that would allow the republics to deal constructively with each other, the center, and the outside world.

- The filling of the political power vacuum by new political institutions and parties. Key political leaders would need to work together constructively.

- Establishing new economic relations based on the market.

- Changing the mood of the Soviet population from one of fear of impending disaster to one of hope. Without such a change in the psychology of the population, a successful transition to the market and democracy would be almost impossible.

The economy would also have to avoid a decline so precipitous as to cause unmanageable social unrest. Progress toward market reform and republic autonomy will be difficult enough to achieve with the certain dropoff in economic performance. A dramatically shrinking economic pie would make unilateral steps by the republics to assert their economic independence more likely. It would also increase the prospects for widespread consumer and labor unrest. If not effectively managed, such developments could break any government.

Implications for the United States

Whichever scenario prevails, the USSR during the next year will remain an inward-looking, weakened giant with a declining ability to maintain its role as a superpower. The domestic crisis will continue to preoccupy any Soviet leaders and prompt them to seek, at a minimum, to avoid confrontation with the West. But the particular foreign policies they pursue could vary significantly depending on the scenario.

Under the "deterioration short of collapse" or "light at the end of the tunnel" scenarios, Moscow's Western orientation probably would be reflected in continued, possibly greater, Soviet willingness to compromise on a range of international issues. The Soviets would be *very likely* to continue:

- Deepening the growing economic and political relationships with the United States, Western Europe, and, to a lesser extent, Japan.
- Negotiating ongoing and new arms control agreements.
- Cooperating in crafting a new European security order.
- Reducing military and economic commitments in the Third World and expanding cooperation with the United States there.[2]

In these scenarios, Soviet as well as republic interest in Western economic involvement would continue to expand rapidly. The liberalization of laws on joint ventures, property ownership, and personal entrepeneurship create improved conditions for Western investment. However, uncertainties over prospects for market reform, the role of the central versus the republic governments in such areas as banking and foreign trade, and the ongoing turmoil in Soviet society will make significant investment a risky venture for Western firms and make it unlikely that many will commit much to the effort.

The central and republic leaders also appear not to have thought through what forms of Western aid or investment they would like, the scale of assistance, or the timing. Proposals range from a "modern Marshall Plan," to Soviet inclusion in international financial organizations, to technical assistance for marketization. The USSR faces serious structural and societal obstacles, however, that would dilute the impact of most forms of foreign aid except for technical assistance. Recent experience has shown that the country's transportation and distribution networks are ill equipped to move large quantities of imports efficiently. Wide-scale corruption and black-marketeering further diminish the system's capabilities to get goods to their destinations. If Moscow moves decisively toward

---

[2] These issues will be addressed more fully in the forthcoming NIE 11-4-91, *Soviet National Security Strategy in the Post-Cold-War Era.*

4. *(Continued)*

a market economy, Soviet leaders will press the West and Japan even harder for assistance to cushion the transition.

Internal *political* developments may also push Gorbachev to conclude agreements with the West as quickly as possible. Assertions of autonomy by republics in the areas of economics and defense will increasingly challenge his authority to speak on behalf of the USSR. The diffusion of power is bringing new actors to the scene who will attempt to develop their own relations with Western states, especially in the economic sphere. Special requests for consultations, technical assistance, emergency aid, and trade from republic governments are likely to increase. Unless political conflict over who owns resources and controls foreign trade is resolved, both US governmental and private business relations with the USSR and its republics will be complicated. Those direct Western contacts with the republics disapproved of by Moscow would be perceived as interference and could result in steps by the central government to block Western assistance to republics and localities.

An "anarchy" scenario would create precarious conditions for relations with the West and would present the United States with some difficult choices. Various factions would declare independence or claim legitimacy as a central government and push for Western recognition and assistance—including military aid. Each Western government would be faced with the dilemma of which factions to deal with and support. If the situation evolved into civil wars, the fighting could spill over into neighboring countries. Eastern Europe and Western countries would be inundated with refugees, and there would be enormous uncertainties over who was in control of the Soviet military's nuclear weapons.

Under conditions of anarchy, a coherent Soviet foreign policy would be highly unlikely, and Soviet ability to conclude ongoing arms control negotiations, implement accords already reached, and carry out troop withdrawals from Eastern Europe would be undercut. Troop withdrawals from Germany, for example, could be delayed or stymied by transport disruptions or by wholesale defections of Soviet troops eager to escape the turmoil awaiting them in the USSR.

In a "military intervention" scenario, a military-dominated regime would take a less concessionary approach than Gorbachev's on foreign policy issues and pursue a tougher line on arms control issues because of the military's current misgivings about CFE, START, and the changes in Eastern Europe. Moreover, such a regime probably would diverge significantly from current policy on Jewish emigration and be less inclined to support the presence of US military forces in the Persian Gulf region. Such policy shifts could undermine the entire panoply of Soviet political, economic, and military ties to the West. A military regime, however, would be too busy attempting to hold the USSR together to resume a hostile military posture toward the West, although further shifts in resources away from the defense sector could be halted. Such a regime would be unable to restore Soviet influence in Eastern Europe but would be likely to take a tougher line on economic issues and would make East-West cooperaton in the region more difficult.

5. Central Intelligence Agency, Office of Soviet Analysis, April 1991, "The Soviet Cauldron"

CIA SOV 91-20177 M

The Soviet Cauldron

25 April 1991

1. Economic crisis, independence aspirations, and anti-Communist forces are breaking down the Soviet empire and system of governance:

- -- Boris Yel'tsin has become the archfoe of the old order and has a good prospect of becoming the first popularly elected leader of Russia in history, acquiring the legitimacy that comes with such a mandate.

- -- In the Ukraine, the union's second largest republic with 50 million inhabitants, the drive for sovereignty is picking up speed.

- -- Belorussian authorities have recognized and begun negotiations with the strike committee that is opposed to continued rule by the republic's own Communist Party as well as the Kremlin.

- -- The Baltic republics are using the uneasy calm between themselves and the Kremlin to solidify new institutions and the support of nonnative populations, primarily Russians, for independence.

- -- Georgia has declared its independence, and all the other republics are insisting on much greater local power.

- -- The striking miners are persisting in their demand not just for economic benefits, but for structural economic and political change as well. Their call is now resonating in other industrial sectors.

- -- The centrally-planned economy has broken down irretrievably and is being replaced by a mixture of republic and local barter arrangements, some of whose aspects resemble a market, but which do not constitute a coherent system.

This document was prepared by the Central Intelligence Agency, Directorate of Intelligence, Office of Soviet Analysis.
This document was prepared for NSC, Ed Hewett.

SOV M 91-20177

5. *(Continued)*

~~SECRET~~
~~NOFORN NOCONTRACT ORCON~~

The Soviet Cauldron

   -- The center's reassertion of control over central
      television has not stifled the birth of new radio
      and TV companies and of some 800 new independent
      newspapers that are filling the news breach.

   -- The Communist Party of the Soviet Union (CPSU) is
      breaking up along regional and ideological lines.
      A still inchoate but growing system of new parties
      is arising. ~~(S-NF)~~

   2. In the midst of this chaos, Gorbachev has gone from
ardent reformer to consolidator. A stream of intelligence
reporting and his public declarations indicate that
Gorbachev has chosen this course both because of his own
political credo and because of pressures on him by other
traditionalists, who would like him to use much tougher
repressive measures. His attempts to preserve the essence
of a center-dominated union, Communist Party rule, and a
centrally-planned economy without the broad use of force,
however, have driven him to tactical expedients that are not
solving basic problems and are hindering but not preventing
the development of a new system:

   -- The union referendum with its vaguely worded
      question is turning out to be a glittering nonevent
      and is having no impact on the talks for a new
      union treaty.

   -- The newly unveiled anticrisis program contains
      the government's umpteenth economic plan and, like
      its predecessors, holds out the promise of reform
      following a stabilization program that will not
      work.

   -- In a successful effort to dominate its
      proceedings, Gorbachev has expanded the Federal
      Council into a massive group of varying membership.
      This stratagem has undermined the one institution
      that, under its original design of membership for
      the presidents of the union and the republics,
      could have become a forum for airing out and
      settling disputes.

   -- As a result of his political meandering and
      policy failures, Gorbachev's credibility has sunk
      to near zero. Even some of his closest, newly
      found, traditionalist colleagues are distancing
      themselves from him. In a recent poll, a majority
      of respondents--52 percent--selected hypocrisy as
      the trait that best describes him. ~~(S NF NC OC)~~

~~NOFORN NOCONTRACT ORCON~~
~~SECRET~~

5. *(Continued)*

~~SECRET~~
NOFORN ~~NOCONTRACT ORCON~~

The Soviet Cauldron

    3. Gorbachev has truly been faced with terrible choices in his effort to move the USSR away from the failed, rigid old system. His expedients have so far kept him in office and changed that system irretrievably, but have also prolonged and complicated the agony of transition to a new system and meant a political stalemate in the overall power equation.

- The economy is in a downward spiral with no end in sight, and only luck can prevent the decline in GNP from going into double digits this year.

- Inflation was about 20 percent at the end of last year and will be at least double that this year.

- The continued preference given to reliance on a top-down approach to problems, particularly in regard to republics, has generated a war of laws between various levels of power and created a legal mess to match the economic mess. ~~(C-NF)~~

    4. In this situation of growing chaos, explosive events have become increasingly possible.

- Public anger over deteriorating economic conditions could produce riots or massive strikes, particularly in the newly disadvantaged industrial center of the Slavic republics with their large labor populations.

- A failed maneuver by the central government, such as the violence in Vilnius in January, could give new impulses to antigovernment forces that would attract Western sympathy.

- Gorbachev, Yel'tsin, and other lesser but nevertheless important leaders could die under the incredible strains in which they work or be assassinated with incalculable consequences.

- Some potent new leader could arise in one or more places, much as Walesa in Poland or Landsbergis in Lithuania, and begin to make history.

- Reactionary leaders, with or without Gorbachev, could judge that the last chance to act had come and move under the banner of law-and-order. ~~(C-NF)~~

NOFORN ~~NOCONTRACT ORCON~~
~~SECRET~~

5. *(Continued)*

SECRET
NOFORN NOCONTRACT ORCON

The Soviet Cauldron

5. Of all these possible explosions, a premeditated, organized attempt to restore a full-fledged dictatorship would be the most fateful in that it would try to roll back newly acquired freedoms and be inherently destabilizing in the long term. Unfortunately, preparations for dictatorial rule have begun in two ways:

--- Gorbachev may not want this turn of events but is increasing the chances of it through his personnel appointments; through his estrangement from the reformers and consequent reliance on the traditionalists whom he thereby strengthens; and through his attempted rule by decree, which does not work but invites dictatorship to make it work.

--- More ominously, military, MVD, and KGB leaders are making preparations for a broad use of force in the political process:

- Through speeches, articles, and declarations, various leaders have laid the psychological groundwork. Kryuchkov has denounced foreign interference and argued that the military's help is sometimes necessary in restoring internal order. Akhromeyev has called for a strong hand. Yazov has issued public orders permitting the use of firearms allegedly to defend military installations and monuments; although admitting that the Vilnius garrison commander should not have acted the way he did, he failed to discipline him for the killing of innocent civilians. Ground Forces Commander Varennikov called for a tougher policy in the Baltic republics at a Federation Council meeting, and a number of commanders have either petitioned Gorbachev for tough measures or called for them in large meetings.

- The Communist Party is doing its utmost, with Gorbachev's approval, to retain its leading role in the military by retaining the structure of the Main Political Administration while modifying its external appearance--in essence a change in name only. Party conferences have been held at the all-Army level and below to institutionalize the new structure. They have almost certainly been used as well to propagandize the need to retain a center-dominated union at all cost.

--- A campaign to retire democratically inclined officers or at least move them out of key positions has been going on for some time. More recently a sensitive source reported that Yazov had ordered

4
NOFORN NOCONTRACT ORCON
SECRET

5. *(Continued)*

SECRET
NOFORN NOCONTRACT ORCON

The Soviet Cauldron

    the Western Group of Forces (based in Germany) to form units of particularly reliable troops to do whatever was necessary to preserve the union. Although we lack direct evidence, it is highly likely that similar activity is going on in the military districts within the USSR.

-- The deployment into Moscow on 28 March of some 50,000 troops from the Army and the MVD, with KGB participation, went smoothly, indicating that a command structure for such an operation has been set up.

It is probably the totality of these psychological and actual preparations for the use of force that moved Shevardnadze to reiterate his warning that "dictatorship is coming." (C NF)

    6. Should the reactionaries make their move, with or without Gorbachev, their first target this time would be Boris Yel'tsin and the Russian democrats.

-- Yel'tsin is the only leader with mass appeal and with support outside his own republic, most importantly in the Ukraine.

-- He is gradually and with much difficulty maintaining Russia's drive for autonomy.

-- Those who would preserve a center-dominated union know they cannot do so if Russia escapes their control. (C NF)

    7. Any attempt to restore full-fledged dictatorship would start in Moscow with the arrest or assassination of Yel'tsin and other democratic leaders such as Mayor Popov and Deputy Mayor Stankevich; the seizure of all media and restoration of full censorship; and the banning of all gatherings enforced by an intimidating display of force. A committee of national salvation--probably under a less sullied name--would be set up and proclaim its intent to save the fatherland through tough but temporary measures that would pave the way for democracy and economic reform.

    8. The long-term prospects of such an enterprise are poor, and even short-term success is far from assured:

5
NOFORN NOCONTRACT ORCON
SECRET

5. *(Continued)*

SECRET
NOFORN NOCONTRACT ORCON

The Soviet Cauldron

- -- The number of troops that can be counted on to enforce repression is limited.

- -- The cohesion of the participating forces would be hard to sustain if, as is likely, the democrats refused to fade away.

- -- Any action against Yel'tsin would spark activity in other places, and security and military forces would be spread thin in any attempt to establish control over other Russian cities. (C NF)

9. Even if the putsch works in Russia, a number of other republics would make use of the turmoil for their own ends. If it did not collapse rapidly, the attempted authoritarian restoration would fail over the next few years. Its putative leaders lack any constructive program and would not have the economic resources, nor most likely the political savvy, necessary to make dictatorship stick. It would probably run its course much as martial law did in Poland, with the added element of secessions, but would almost certainly entail more bloodshed and economic damage along the way. (C NF)

10. Even a putsch is not likely to prevent the pluralistic forces from emerging in a dominant position before the end of this decade. They are blunting the center's drive against them and consolidating their own regional holds on power, while the traditionalist forces, which still control the government and other central institutions, increasingly discredit themselves because they lack a viable, forward-looking program. (C NF)

11. Such slow progress by the pluralist forces, however, leaves them at risk for several years to a putsch and to popular disenchantment with them for failing to produce rapid improvements. Knowing this, they are likely to intensify their push for a breakthrough involving most importantly a union treaty that gives the republics considerable say over the policies of the central government. They might succeed. Even Gorbachev himself is not yet totally lost to their cause. Faced with the choice of throwing in irrevocably with the traditionalists, who hate him and do not share his aversion to the use of outright force, or tacking back toward the reformers, he might still choose the latter course. Despite this policy of repressive retrenchment, after all, the central government is also condoning or even initiating some actions that could lay the groundwork for the restart of a reformist effort:

- -- A number of laws necessary for the establishment of a market system have been passed.

6
NOFORN NOCONTRACT ORCON
SECRET

5. *(Continued)*

SECRET
~~NOFORN NOCONTRACT ORCON~~

The Soviet Cauldron

-- Gorbachev's advisor Shakhnazarov and Yel'tsin have both talked about the desirability of a national roundtable, although with very different declared purposes.

-- The central and Russian governments are at least establishing, albeit extremely slowly, the mechanisms for settling differences and responsibility about military and KGB issues, primarily through Col. General Kobets' Russian Committee on Defense and Security.

-- Similarly a collegium of republic foreign ministers under the chairmanship of the USSR foreign minister has been created.

-- Talks with the Baltic Republics have started, although again with much difficulty and with the two sides totally at odds over their ultimate purpose.

So far, these various actions have not had any operational significance. Nor will they if the central government persists with its current policy objectives. But if it were willing to change its policy direction, these actions have the potential for creating a way out of the current stalemate. (C NF)

12. The reformers would most likely seize upon any such effort to retard the chances of intensified repression and then try to turn it into a strategic breakthrough. With or without Gorbachev, with or without a putsch, the most likely prospect for the end of this decade, if not earlier, is a Soviet Union transformed into some independent states and a confederation of the remaining republics, including Russia. This confederation will have the size, economic resources, and accumulated hardware to remain a major military power, but its decentralized nature will prevent it from replicating the militaristic, aggressive policies of yesteryear. (C NF)

13. The current Soviet situation and the various directions in which it could develop over the short term present us with three possible Soviet Unions over the next year:

~~SECRET~~
~~NOFORN NOCONTRACT~~ ORCON

The Soviet Cauldron

-- Continuation of the current political stalemate would maintain the current Western dilemma of developing the proper mix of relationships with contending forces. The dilemma would probably sharpen because the struggle is likely to intensify and the economy to spiral downward at an ever faster rate. Social explosions such as the current miners' strike and the Belorussian flareup would occur and could transform the situation into major violence or martial law at any time. Short of this, the USSR would be more and more of an economic basket case and Gorbachev a spent force who would multiply his appeals for Western assistance. Although the USSR might still try to take some new initiative on the international scene, such as in the Middle East and in the arms control sphere, its growing instability would greatly diminish its diplomatic clout and probably prevent it from effectively advancing its agenda. Its growing instability will have a negative effect on Eastern Europe in the form of lost economic interaction and inability to develop a new basis for Soviet-East European relations.

-- An attempt at the restoration of dictatorship would face the West with a repetition of Poland 1981, but almost certainly with more brutality and bloodshed. The country would still be an economic basket case. The new regime would pledge to maintain a cooperative policy toward the world and most likely continue troop withdrawals from Eastern Europe, probably with even greater attempts at extortion. In reality there would be greater foreign policy truculence, but this USSR could not regain its previous influence in the world nor its position in the Third World. It would, however, attempt greatly to step up arms sales for cash; look for gains in the Middle East at US expense; and may well work with fifth columns in Eastern Europe in an attempt to subvert those developing democracies. Some in Western Europe would argue that this domestic retrenchment might be regrettable but that Gorbachev, or whoever was in charge, really had no choice but to restore order and that the best way to influence the situation toward the better (and save whatever Western investments and credits that had been advanced) was through continued cooperation coupled with symbolic

5. *(Continued)*

~~SECRET~~
~~NOFORN~~ ~~NOCONTRACT~~ ~~ORCON~~

The Soviet Cauldron

    gestures of disapproval. Unless brutality reached a level much higher than it did at Tiananmen Square, a Western consensus on either interpretation of events or policy would be highly unlikely.

-- An accelerated breakthrough by the pluralists would create the best prospects for internal and external stability based on cooperative arrangements. But this pluralist victory would also bring problems of another sort. The ability of pluralist forces to rule effectively is unproven and might not be assured for quite some time, probably a generation. The nationality problem could not be settled overnight, and there would be tensions within and between republics over the most desirable politicoeconomic system. Some of the republics would not be governed by democrats, but all republics would lay claim to US assistance. New leaders who would have prevailed because of their domestic appeal and single-minded determination would not have much experience in foreign affairs and would probably make exaggerated demands, much as is already happening with some of them. Despite these difficulties and the likely lengthy process of internal and external adaptation to new rules of behavior, this breakthrough, particularly if it occurred in the Slavic core, would present the best prospects for an East-West reconciliation analogous to that which has brought Franco-German relations to what they are today. ~~(S NF)~~

~~NOFORN~~ ~~NOCONTRACT~~ ~~ORCON~~
~~SECRET~~

6. NIE 11-18-91, June 1991, *Implications of Alternative Soviet Futures*

Director of Central Intelligence

~~Secret~~

Implications of Alternative Soviet Futures

National Intelligence Estimate

This National Intelligence Estimate represents the views of the Director of Central Intelligence with the advice and assistance of the US Intelligence Community.

~~Secret~~

NIE 11-18-91
June 1991
Copy 415

6. *(Continued)*

 Director of Central Intelligence

~~Secret~~
~~NOFORN NOCONTRACT~~

NIE 11-18-91

Implications of Alternative Soviet Futures (s)

*Information available as of 27 June 1991 was used
in the preparation of this National Intelligence Estimate.*

*The following intelligence organizations participated
in the preparation of this Estimate:*
The Central Intelligence Agency
The Defense Intelligence Agency
The National Security Agency
The Bureau of Intelligence and Research,
Department of State
The Office of Intelligence Support,
Department of the Treasury
The Intelligence Division, Federal Bureau of Investigation

also participating:
The Office of the Deputy Chief of Staff for Intelligence,
Department of the Army
The Office of the Director of Naval Intelligence,
Department of the Navy
The Office of the Assistant Chief of Staff, Intelligence,
Department of the Air Force
The Director of Intelligence, Headquarters, Marine Corps

*This Estimate was approved for publication by the
National Foreign Intelligence Board.*

~~Secret~~
June 1991

6. *(Continued)*

**Figure 1
Scenarios for the USSR
Over the Next Five Years**

Chronic Crisis	Continuation of current situation
	Neither entire collapse of system nor substantial progress toward resolution of country's problems
	Continued devolution of power below but unable to govern
	Political gridlock
	Economy would verge on breakdown but somehow manage to limp along
	Scenario unlikely to last next five years
System Change	System replaced with relatively little violence
	Slavic and Central Asian core state: smaller, less militarily powerful, more pluralistic than USSR
	Baltic states, Georgia, Armenia, and Moldova become independent
	Economies of all troubled, but moving rapidly toward market
	Government increasingly reflects popular will, but may not survive economic disarray
Regression	Hardliners in military, security services, and CPSU impose martial law type regime
	Democratic reform and republic independence drives halted
	Strong nationalist and reformist pressures remain
	Economy's downward spiral accelerates
	Scenario unlikely to last long
Fragmentation	Violent, chaotic collapse of system
	Republics become independent
	Some governments reflect popular will, others more authoritarian
	Warfare within and between many republics
	Economic conditions deteriorate dramatically; barter main form of economic interaction; famine widespread

6. *(Continued)*

Key Judgments
Implications of Alternative Soviet Futures

The USSR is in the midst of a revolution that probably will sweep the Communist Party from power and reshape the country within the five-year time frame of this Estimate. The outcome of this revolution will be affected by a number of factors, including the following:
- A sharply declining economy and standard of living that will get worse for the next few years no matter what economic program is adopted.
- The difficulties in implementing a market reform program and sustaining it against a likely popular backlash.
- Continued devolution of power to republic and local governments at the expense of the central government.
- The rising claim of nationalism on defining the state and legitimizing its policies.
- The increasing importance of popular expectations and aspirations, and the government's abilities to meet them, on a wide range of issues—including living standards and personal freedom.

No one can know what the duration or the ultimate outcome of the revolution will be—particularly in a society where repression and centralized control have been the rule, and the culture has been resistant to change, but where recently, democratic aspirations appear to have become widespread. (C NF)

Of the many conceivable outcomes, we believe four scenarios span the range of possibilities: a continuation of the current "chronic crisis" with no political resolution; a relatively peaceful "system change" into a smaller, more pluralistic and voluntary union in which the central government relinquishes substantial power; a chaotic and violent "fragmentation" of the country resulting in many new states with widely varying political and economic systems; and a "regression" through renewed repression into an authoritarian state run by a combination of hardliners in the military, security services, and Communist Party (see figure 1).[1]

---

[1] The approach taken by the Intelligence Community in this Estimate is intended to be more speculative, and less predictive, than in previous estimates on political developments in the USSR. We focus on a range of possible outcomes and their implications for both the USSR and the West, rather than on current developments. Although the scenarios we use to describe these outcomes are very similar to the four used in NIE 11-18-90, November 1990, *The Deepening Crisis in the USSR: Prospects for the Next Year*, they are meant to be "ideal cases" in order to make the distinctions between them clear. The reality is certain to be much more complicated.

6. *(Continued)*

Figure 2
Implications of Scenarios for Key Issues

Issues	Scenarios			
	Chronic Crisis	System Change	Regression	Fragmentation
Policy toward the West	Accommodation, but increasingly erratic policy Will seek economic assistance/engagement and accept some conditionality	Would seek full-scale accommodation, inclusion in European security structures Would seek economic assistance/engagement and accept conditionality	Wary, but would seek to avoid confrontation Would not expect economic assistance	No coherent policy Many governments in republics and regions that break away would seek close ties, military and economic assistance
Military posture	Continued gradual reduction in military capabilities Deteriorating economy could lead to deeper cuts "Defensive" doctrine maintained	Slavic and Central Asian core: significantly reduced military; would remain nuclear superpower; increased emphasis on "defensive" doctrine Independent 6: Small militaries; a threat only to small neighbors	Would seek to maintain Soviet military strength, within constraints of deteriorating economy Increased emphasis on counteroffensive capabilities	No coherent military doctrine or threat to West But possible loss of control over nuclear weapons would lead to dangerous, unpredictable situation Most military power vested in Russia
Arms control	Continued pursuit of new agreements, but within old frameworks Increasing disarray and periodic ascendancy of hardliners would complicate progress Adherence to agreements likely	Slavic and Central Asian core: vigorous pursuit of wide-ranging arms reduction treaties Independent 6: Would seek to join CSCE arms control and confidence-building process Adherence to agreements not an issue	Might enter negotiations, but only on Soviet terms Willingness to adhere to existing agreements increasingly doubtful	No coherent policy Unable to ensure compliance with existing agreements
Policy toward Eastern Europe	No military threat, but would continue to push for neutral Eastern Europe	No military threat Basis for new cooperative relationships between various new states and Eastern Europe Would not oppose East European entry into European security structures	Unlikely to threaten militarily But could stall on withdrawal from Poland Would push hard for neutral Eastern Europe Might use energy deliveries as leverage	Massive numbers of refugees Potential spillover of civil war Potential clashes over Moldova, Kaliningrad, western Ukraine and Belorussia
Forces in Germany	Potential point of instability Would offer to remove them earlier in return for German economic sweetener	Would be willing to bring them home more quickly Issue not likely to be troublesome	Internal political situation would have destabilizing effect on WGF Increase in defections Hardline leadership could threaten to delay withdrawal	Breakdown of discipline, unit cohesion Thousands of defectors

125

6. *(Continued)*

Secret
NOFORN-NOCONTRACT

This Estimate's focus is on the content and implications rather than on the relative probabilities of such scenarios. The USSR could pass through any or all of these scenarios during the next five years. Nevertheless, we believe that, on the basis of current trends and our assessment of the critical variables—particularly the bleak prospects for the economy—the country is much more likely to be in a "system change" or "fragmentation" scenario five years from now than to remain where it is today in "chronic crisis." In our view, an attempt to impose the hardline regime of the "regression" scenario becomes more likely as the country verges on "system change" or "fragmentation," but, of the four scenarios, this is the least likely to be a lasting outcome. In any event, we believe that the USSR in its present form will not exist five years from now. (C-NF)

There will be profound effects on the geopolitical balance in Eurasia whatever the outcome. "System change," the most favorable scenario for the USSR and the West, would leave the USSR somewhat smaller than it is today and still a nuclear superpower, but this Slavic–Central Asian state would have adopted a political and economic system much more conducive to close ties to the West. Even so, the difficulties associated with such a transformation over the longer term may be too heavy a burden for the government and population to bear. (C-NF)

The geopolitical shift would be most drastic in a "fragmentation" scenario, where the country broke apart in a chaotic fashion. Some form of a Russian or Russian-dominated state would eventually emerge out of the chaos, but for a good many years it would be a far less influential actor on the world scene than today's Soviet Union, and it would be bordered by many new countries of varying stability and military strength. (C-NF)

The ability of Western governments to influence the course of events inside the USSR is likely to grow in the "chronic crisis" and "system change" scenarios and in the *aftermath* of a "fragmentation" scenario:

- The country's crumbling economy will increase the likelihood that any government, except one led by hardliners, will turn to the West for aid and accept some degree of economic and political conditionality in return. The need for such aid would give most national and republic leaders an incentive to avoid repressive measures.

- Even though the upper limits of what the West might realistically offer would fall far short of the country's total capital needs, such aid could play an important role in moving the country toward "system change"; that is, the transition toward a market economy and a more pluralistic political system.

6. *(Continued)*

- Western assistance could play an important role in the newly independent Baltic republics, simply because of their much smaller size. On the other hand, local and regional instabilities in the Transcaucasus and Central Asia are likely to limit Western inclination to provide assistance to these republics. (S-NF)

With the exception of the "system change" scenario, the West would face major obstacles in actually exerting influence. In a "chronic crisis" scenario, which the USSR is in today, aid for political and economic reform would be hard to channel into projects that would benefit long-term growth and could get caught in a struggle for power between the center and the republics. In this, and particularly in the "fragmentation" scenario, the gathering political and economic disarray would make it more difficult to determine whom to aid, how to get it to them, and how to follow up to ensure the aid had its intended effect. (S-NF)

The aftereffects of increased instability or repression would also pose challenges to the West:

- The East Europeans, the Turks, and the Nordic countries would turn to the United States and other major Western powers for assistance in coping with refugees, instability on their borders, or a military-led government in Moscow.

- In a "fragmentation" scenario, various factions or republics could gain access to and control of nuclear weapons and threaten to use them against internal rivals or other countries. Although any Western involvement would depend on a number of variables, timely Western offers of assistance in securing and/or disposing of such weapons could have pivotal effect.

- Seizure of control by hardliners in a "regression" scenario would lead to an increase in East-West tensions, a greatly diminished interest in arms control and other negotiations, and a slowing in the reduction in the capabilities of the Soviet military.

- Violence at home could spread to the Soviet troops that are due to remain in Germany until the end of 1994. (S-NF)

6. *(Continued)*

Secret
NOFORN-NOCONTRACT

Contents

	Page
Key Judgments	iii
Discussion	1
Chronic Crisis	1
Implications for the USSR	1
Implications for the West	2
System Change	3
Implications for the USSR	3
Implications for the West	5
Regression	6
Implications for the USSR	7
Implications for the West	7
Fragmentation	8
Implications for the USSR	8
Implications for the West	10

6. *(Continued)*

Discussion

Chronic Crisis

This scenario assumes a continuation of the current crisis with neither an entire collapse of the system nor substantial progress toward resolution of the country's problems. Gorbachev might manage to hang on to power in a weakened central government because neither the left nor the right would have enough strength to oust him, but, even if he left the scene, neither side would gain the upper hand. The country goes from one system-threatening crisis to another. Despite the turmoil, much backtracking, and political stalemate at the top, the trend is toward more autonomy for the republics and a market-based economy but in a bottom-up and relatively chaotic way. The command economy verges on breakdown but somehow manages to limp along.

Implications for the USSR

The current situation in the USSR is best described by this scenario. This is a highly unstable scenario. Although there would be some continued movement toward a pluralistic system, a voluntary union, and a market economy, governmental authority would weaken, and the potential for major popular upheavals would grow. It is unlikely this scenario could prevail for the five years of this Estimate. Indeed, a transition to one of the other three scenarios of "system change," "fragmentation," or "regression" is likely earlier rather than later in this period.

If Gorbachev remained in office, he would become less and less powerful. Neither the left nor the right would prevail, but both would remain strong enough to pose a serious threat to Gorbachev and to each other. The potential for large-scale intervention into politics by the security services and the military would continue to hang over the country. Although less likely, this scenario could still exist if Gorbachev is removed constitutionally, decides on his own to step down, or dies a natural death. Whoever is in charge, the central government would continue to lose authority, although without Gorbachev this would occur more quickly.

> *Indicators of "Chronic Crisis"*
>
> - *Economy continues to deteriorate, but command economy does not collapse.*
>
> - *Center/republics discussions on economic stabilization/reform plan drag out without resolution (or they agree and the plan fails); center pursues ineffective ad hoc policies; republics try to implement individual economic programs.*
>
> - *Central government remains viable but power steadily erodes.*
>
> - *Center/republics unable to resolve key differences concerning powers of national and republic governments.*
>
> - *Political polarization grows, but neither right nor left are strong enough to become dominant.*
>
> - *Violence continues but at relatively low levels; periodic incidents of regional repression occur.*
>
> - *Military and security services act more independently but shrink from a coup.*

The republics would gather a good deal of the authority the center lost but still would not be able to govern effectively. None would be fully independent, but many—the Baltic states, Georgia, Armenia, and Moldova—would remain tethered to the union only by the continued presence of Soviet troops and the vestiges of the central command economy. Russia would gain greater control over its own affairs

6. (Continued)

and increased influence with other republics, but it would not yet be strong enough to transform the center to its liking or assume all of the central government's former authority within the RSFSR. Yel'tsin's strength in Russia and the USSR would grow, at least initially, but he would be hamstrung by the center's continuing ability to limit the RSFSR's economic sovereignty, by infighting within his own camp (abetted by the KGB), and by demands of non-Russians in the republic for greater autonomy or independence.

With no resolution of the center-republic relationship, there would be no hope of stabilizing or reversing the economic slide. GNP would drop dramatically, and the country would face worsening shortages of industrial materials, consumer goods, and food. Inflation and unemployment would skyrocket; strikes would proliferate. Significant human suffering would develop in some areas. Foreign credits would dry up as the country failed to meet debt service payments; Western companies—scared off by the growing political and economic chaos—would take their business elsewhere. Nevertheless, the economy would avoid collapse through a major expansion of independent arrangements and barter deals that republics, enterprises, and individuals made with each other.

The economic disarray and growing republic autonomy would accelerate the trend toward reduced military capabilities. The military leadership would try to ensure that the drop in allocations to the military was not dramatic, but the trend would still be decidedly downward because the military economy would not be insulated from the accelerating decline. The republics' quest for greater autonomy or independence would exacerbate the Soviet armed forces' manpower and morale problems. Modernization of Moscow's strategic forces would continue within the limits of a START treaty, but even these forces would increasingly be affected by the economy's dismal performance.

Implications for the West

In this scenario, the ability to conduct foreign policy by whoever leads the central Soviet government would be constrained by the turmoil at home. Western governments would find Gorbachev or a successor not only preoccupied by the domestic crisis but also less and less able to ensure that the USSR is capable of fulfilling the foreign commitments it makes. Nevertheless, any Soviet regime in this scenario probably would still seek accommodation on a range of international issues and almost certainly would want to avoid confrontation. The Soviets would be likely to continue:

- Deepening the growing economic and political relationships with the United States, Western Europe, and, to a lesser extent, Japan.
- Negotiating ongoing and new arms control agreements.
- Cooperating in crafting a new European security order.
- Reducing military and economic commitments, while expanding cooperation with the United States, in the Third World.

Whatever the Soviet Government's *intentions*, the economy's rapidly decreasing ability to support a massive military, the likely increased involvement of the Soviet army in quelling domestic unrest, and the general lack of cohesion within the country would seriously limit the USSR's *capability* to threaten its neighbors or the West. The Soviet Union would almost certainly complete its withdrawal of forces from Eastern Europe, possibly more quickly than scheduled. The leadership would have every incentive to adhere to the terms of the CFE and START treaties and probably would seek further arms reductions to lighten the military burden on the economy.

In this scenario, Soviet as well as republic interest in Western economic involvement would continue to expand rapidly. The deteriorating economy would ensure that the central government would continue to seek access to Western economic institutions and be on the West's doorstep for loans, credits, and general economic assistance, although it would not be able to repay such assistance.

6. (*Continued*)

as interference and could result in attempts by the central government to block Western assistance to republics and localities. (C-NF)

System Change

This scenario assumes that the existing political system is replaced with relatively little violence. This occurs with the old regime's dissolution as a result of republic or popular pressure—as in Czechoslovakia in 1989—or through agreement between the center and the republics. In either case, a loose federation or confederation of the Slavic and Central Asian republics emerges, and independence is granted to those republics seeking it. The political and economic systems that emerge in the core Slavic–Central Asian state and the independent states vary widely. (C-NF)

Implications for the USSR

The level of instability in this scenario would depend on the manner in which the system was changed. If it collapsed due to internal pressure, the instability initially would be greater: new governing mechanisms would have to be created in the midst of revolution, and many elements of the old system—while defeated—would remain capable and desirous of complicating the transition to a new system. A voluntary sharing of power by the center would be more stable, although, even in this variant, the new systems that emerged from what was the USSR would encounter problems much more serious than those now being experienced by post-Communist regimes in Eastern Europe. (C-NF)

Special requests for consultations, technical assistance, emergency aid, and trade from republic and local governments are likely to increase. Without political resolution of the conflict over who owns resources and controls foreign trade, both US governmental and private business relations with the USSR and its republics will be complicated and harder to sustain. Those direct Western contacts with the republics disapproved of by Moscow would be perceived

The newly transformed core state that emerges in this scenario would reflect the political and economic trends in Russia and, to a lesser extent, in the Ukraine. As such, it—particularly its Slavic portion—would have, at least initially, a much more pluralistic political and economic system than ever before. It would have a popularly elected parliamentary government with numerous political parties. While the role of the state would remain large, its authority would depend much more than heretofore on popular acceptance. The government's respect for human rights

6. *(Continued)*

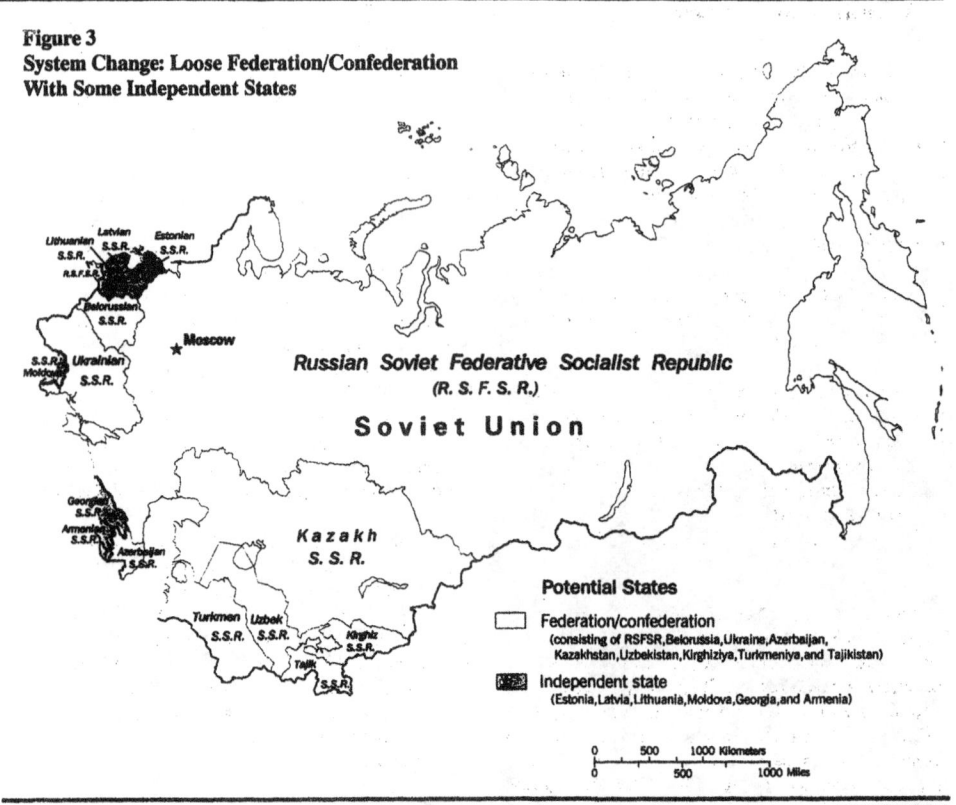

Figure 3
System Change: Loose Federation/Confederation With Some Independent States

Potential States
- Federation/confederation (consisting of RSFSR, Belorussia, Ukraine, Azerbaijan, Kazakhstan, Uzbekistan, Kirghiziya, Turkmeniya, and Tajikistan)
- Independent state (Estonia, Latvia, Lithuania, Moldova, Georgia, and Armenia)

would start to resemble that of Western governments. The Central Asian regions, on the other hand, would remain basically authoritarian and have poor human rights records.

The republics would have substantial autonomy, with the center playing the leading—though even here not exclusive—role in foreign, defense, fiscal/monetary, and communications/transportation policies. The presidency of the new union would have less scope and be a less powerful office than it is today. There would be a strong push toward a market economy, although the central and republic governments would continue to run a large portion of major industry, and reforms would be implemented unevenly in the republics. Progress would be much more gradual and the social pain much greater than has been the case in Poland.

Russia's influence in the new union could become a source of tension. Its leadership, most likely under Yel'tsin, would have played the leading role in creating the new system giving greater power to the

6. *(Continued)*

> *Indicators of "System Change"*
>
> - *Center/republics sign and begin implementation of union treaty and new constitution devolving significant power to republics.*
> - *Republics assume control of their economic and political lives; undertake substantial steps toward market reform.* (C NF)
>
> *Or, alternatively:*
>
> - *Large-scale public protests, labor unrest, and republic pressure cause the central government to collapse.*
> - *Reformers/republics give up hope of reaching negotiated settlement with the center and conclude bilateral and multilateral agreements reserving most powers to themselves and defining areas of the center's limited authority.* (C NF)

individual republics. Yet Russia would be an even more powerful primus inter pares than it is today because of Yel'tsin's prestige and because of the resources it would control. Its growing sense of national identity and the possible emergence of a "Russia first" attitude could also undermine the new union. Ukrainian nationalism could also lead this republic to go its own way with similar effect. (C NF)

A Slavic–Central Asian state would have most of the military potential that the USSR has today, although it probably would choose to field smaller and more Slavic armed forces. It would continue to be a nuclear superpower, but its conventional forces would be much reduced and their posture largely defensive. The market reforms that such a state would undertake, however, would over time (but not in the five-year time frame of this Estimate) give it a more reliable economic base for developing military technologies and modernizing the military, should its leadership and people decide on such a course. (C NF)

The biggest problem for the six republics that would form independent states would be economic because of their meager industrial and resource bases and their small populations. Most would move quickly toward market economies, but how well their economies functioned would also depend heavily on the degree to which they cooperated with the Slavic–Central Asian state, each other, and their other neighbors. The Baltic states would be parliamentary democracies; the other three—while democratic in form—probably would tend more toward authoritarian states. (C NF)

The internal growing pains that the Slavic–Central Asian state and the others experience would complicate relations among them. Demarcating the new borders alone would be enough to generate tensions. The most serious problems—which would entail some violence—would most likely be between Armenia and Azerbaijan, and between the new union, on the one hand, and Georgia and Moldova, on the other. (C NF)

Such problems among and inside the new regimes that emerged in "system change" could over the longer run become serious enough to cause such a regime to fail. Reestablishment of the old Communist order would not occur, but the military and security services might be able to resume control (as in the "regression" scenario) or chaos and wide-scale violence could ensue (as in the "fragmentation" scenario) due to the failure of political and economic reform. (C NF)

Implications for the West
Despite the uncertainties such tensions among the former components of the USSR would create for the West, this would be far and away the most favorable outcome for Western countries. The Slavic–Central Asian core state would be smaller, less militarily powerful, much more pluralistic, and almost certainly more desirous of close relations with the West than was the USSR. Especially in the period following its creation, it would seek extensive Western involvement in developing its political and, particularly, economic

6. *(Continued)*

structures. This probably would give the West unprecedented opportunities to shape development of the new state, but it would also bring with it requests for far more substantial economic aid than Western countries would be willing to provide. The West would face very hard choices in apportioning limited economic assistance among the Slavic–Central Asian state, the other newly independent states, and the democracies of Eastern Europe. (C NF)

The Slavic–Central Asian state, while heavily focused during the time frame of this Estimate on creating a new system at home, would still be an important player on the world scene. It would seek admission to European economic and security structures, posing dilemmas for Western governments. East European states already seek membership in these institutions, and some would worry that the new Soviet Union's acceptance into these clubs would dilute the meaningfulness of their membership. On the other hand, East European fears of a resurgent, militaristic USSR or of massive instability there would be substantially reduced in such a scenario. (C NF)

The Slavic–Central Asian core state probably would seek a major expansion of arms control agreements with the West. It would have an economic interest in cutting its military, and—perceiving the United States as a vital source of assistance—probably would seek significant reductions in strategic arms. This state would not forgo nuclear weapons, since they would continue to be important to its security and superpower status, but it probably would be willing to make reciprocal, and perhaps even radical, cuts in numbers of weapons. (C NF)

The Allies probably would see less justification for maintaining NATO and a US troop presence on the Continent if the Soviet Union disintegrated as depicted in this scenario. The Europeans would almost certainly invite the new states to join CSCE. The Allies, however, would resist any efforts by these new states to join NATO. (C NF)

Regression

This scenario assumes traditionalist forces seize control in order to break the back of the democratic reform movement and halt the republics' move toward sovereignty and independence. Although Gorbachev could lead such a move, it is more likely he would be compelled to go along or be forced from office. The security services and the military, who spearhead this course, use force on a large scale to reassert central control. Widespread arrests of leading opponents, including Yel'tsin, occur. The new leaders attempt to

6. *(Continued)*

reinstitute centralized control over the economy. Although this averts collapse of the command economy for awhile, it does little to halt the economy's continuing sharp decline. (C NF)

Implications for the USSR
This scenario would involve a series of harsh measures that succeed in reestablishing a measure of central control. The use of force could produce political "stability" for a few years, given the organizational weakness of the democratic forces and the lack of unity among the republics bent on secession. This course might also appeal to a significant portion of the Slavic–Central Asian publics tired of political debate and seeking political order and economic stability. Such popular support would prove short-lived, however, if the new government failed to deliver. Eventually, renewed political opposition and civil disorder would probably develop. (C NF)

The new leaders would find it difficult to gain popular legitimacy for their rule. The draconian step of reintroducing the command-administrative economic system, largely discarded under Gorbachev, would not be able to rebuild the center-republic economic ties disrupted by the independence movement. As workers saw their economic status continuing to deteriorate, they would become less reluctant to engage in passive and active resistance to the center's power. (C NF)

The new government would also lack an ideological basis to justify its actions, since Marxism-Leninism has been totally discredited, along with the Communist Party. An appeal to Russian nationalism by the conservative leadership would be possible—and could take the form of a national salvation committee—but such a step would further antagonize the restive republics. It could provide the basis for an authoritarian regime in Russia, however, that follows a "Russia first" policy at the expense of the rest of the union. (C NF)

The biggest problem for the leadership would be maintaining unionwide control. The use of force to hold the union together would almost certainly lead to open civil conflict within several republics, particularly those having their own paramilitary forces, such as Georgia and Armenia. Controlling such unrest

---

Indicators of "Regression"

- *Gorbachev, or successors, use whatever force necessary to maintain the union.*
- *Traditionalists gain dominance, begin setting political and economic agenda.*
- *Regime censors media, suppresses individual freedoms; harasses/arrests opposition groups.*
- *Regime reasserts central control over the economy.* (C NF)

---

would severely tax security and military forces; prolonged conflict would threaten the internal cohesion and discipline of the troops, particularly if they had to be used against Slavic groups. (C NF)

This scenario could unravel quickly if the center were unable to quash the democratic resistance, if Yel'tsin or another popular leader were able to escape the center's dragnet and rally popular resistance, or if the military proved unreliable. Even so, reform and republic leaders might not survive even a short-lived repression, leaving a political vacuum at the center and in many republics. Such widespread unrest would also exacerbate the ethnic, political, and generational splits within the armed forces and security services. (C NF)

If repression failed, the result probably would be anarchy and a chaotic disintegration of the union; that is, the "fragmentation" scenario. In that event, most republics would break away from the center. This breakup of the union would most likely be accompanied by civil wars. (C NF)

Implications for the West
This scenario, while less volatile than "fragmentation," would create conditions least responsive to Western influence. The immediate outcome would be a more combative posture toward the West, which the new leadership would see as opposed to its seizure of power and its harsh internal measures. Western criticism would fuel a "hunker down" attitude among the

6. *(Continued)*

leadership, further straining relations. The regime's probable political, economic, and military policies would generate renewed concern in the West over the USSR's intentions and would frighten the Soviet Union's neighbors, particularly in Eastern Europe. Such a regime, however, probably would seek to avoid confrontation with the West because of the fragility of the situation within the USSR. (C-NF)

The hardline leadership would place arms control negotiations on the back burner, and its willingness to adhere to existing arms control agreements—particularly CFE—would be increasingly doubtful as political tensions with the West rose. There probably would be a greatly reduced willingness to cooperate with the West in reducing regional tensions, although for economic reasons the new leadership would be reluctant to be drawn into foreign adventures. Nevertheless, the regime would take an aggressive approach to arms sales to the Third World, complicating Western efforts at promoting regional security. (C-NF)

Such a regime would adopt a more assertive attitude toward the countries of Eastern Europe and might threaten to hold up any remaining troop withdrawals unless Germany and Poland acceded to Soviet security and economic demands. Given its weakened condition and preoccupation with maintaining internal control, however, a traditionalist regime would almost certainly remove these forces in the end rather than precipitate an East-West crisis. (C-NF)

Although more confrontational, the regime would be unable, due to the changed social environment and the weakened economy, to conduct an arms buildup similar to the Brezhnev era, even though it might place greater priority on heavy and defense industry. It would assert its rights as a military power, but its main focus would be on the USSR's internal problems. (C-NF)

Fragmentation

This scenario assumes there is no effective central government. Power resides in the republics and, in some cases, even in localities. Republics, along with many of the ethnically based regions, secede en masse from the union. Ethnic and social tensions explode in many areas; the security services and military are unable to maintain order. The result is widespread anarchy and local civil wars made worse by the proliferation of paramilitary forces and the defection of units from the military. Attempts to establish ties among republics prove difficult due to differences in political and economic agendas and the ineffective control of most governments. Many regional and local governments quickly rise and fall. The collapse of the national command economy and its supporting infrastructure leads to local systems of exchange, largely based on barter. (C-NF)

Implications for the USSR

This scenario not only would spell the end of the USSR as a unitary state, it would also make it unlikely that the union could reconstitute itself as a federation, or even a confederation, during the time frame of this Estimate. The country's fragmentation into a number of individual political units, many overtly or potentially hostile toward one another, would increase the likelihood of prolonged civil wars, which would further sap the strength of already besieged local economies. The economic chaos would lead to severe food shortages or even famine in parts of the country. (C-NF)

The power vacuum in Moscow would heighten prospects for a military seizure of power and a succession of coups, as senior military commanders tried to hold

6. *(Continued)*

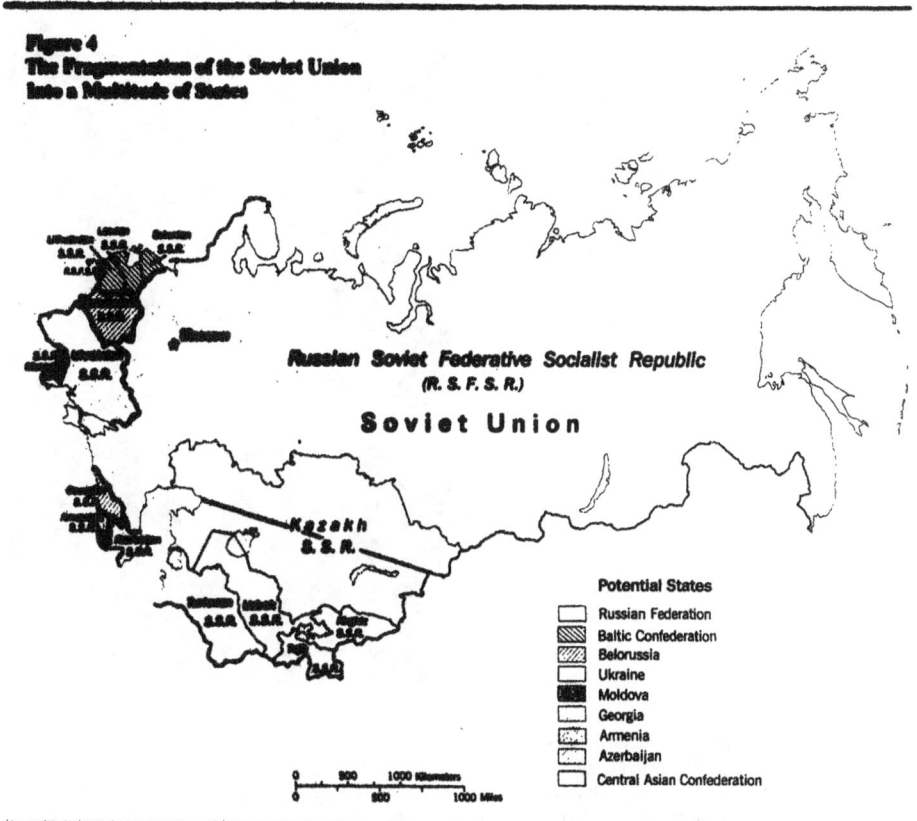

Figure 4
The Fragmentation of the Soviet Union
Into a Multitude of States

Potential States
- Russian Federation
- Baltic Confederation
- Belorussia
- Ukraine
- Moldova
- Georgia
- Armenia
- Azerbaijan
- Central Asian Confederation

together the rapidly collapsing union. Even if elements in the military and security services were inclined to intervene in an effort to rescue the union, they would not be able to ensure the loyalty of many of the individual units. Widespread defections and mutinies would make large-scale use of force to stabilize the situation impossible. There would be a very real danger that military and security force units would defect to the leadership of the republics, providing a ready pool of men and arms with which to prosecute conflict against other republics or disaffected elements within the republics. Some of these forces could also pose a threat to the leadership of the now independent republics.

"Fragmentation" is not likely to last indefinitely. As with "system change," there would be no possibility of putting the old system back together again, but new

Indicators of "Fragmentation"

- Cooperation between center and most republics ceases; republics ignore center's directives, including laws on military conscription.

- Central and republic governments increasingly unable to control violent protests over deteriorating economic and political conditions; but opposition unable to unite, coordinate actions.

- Interrepublic ties dwindle sharply; republics make political, economic, and territorial demands on one another.

- Command economy collapses; attempts by republics and localities to establish alternative economic systems fail; economic conditions deteriorate sharply.

- Military discipline begins to unravel.

- Ethnic and labor disturbances spread rapidly.

attempts at forging cooperation among some of the peoples of the former Soviet Union would be made. Russia would be the key. The establishment of strong and effective leadership in the Russian Republic could stabilize the political and economic situation in a relatively short period (perhaps several years) depending on the policies it adopted and its abilities to establish economic ties to other republics and countries. Such a development would also depend on the Russian leadership's ability to exercise control over its own disaffected ethnic groups, as well as its ability to gain command of what remains of the armed forces. An economically and politically viable Russia would exercise a strong influence on neighboring peoples still wrestling with the effects of the collapse of the USSR.

Implications for the West

This scenario is potentially the most dangerous for the West because of the chaos and unpredictability of events. Although the USSR would disappear as a cohesive military power, the prospects of nuclear and other weapons of mass destruction falling into the hands of some republics, mutinous troops, or radical groups would pose a new set of risks. There would be a heightened risk of threatened or accidental use of such weapons inside—and much less likely, outside—the Soviet Union. There would also be a greater chance for nuclear materials and expertise finding their way to foreign states seeking to develop nuclear weapons.

6. (*Continued*)

Widespread civil conflict or war within and between republics would also pose major dangers for the West. Conflict within the former territory of the USSR would have the potential for spilling across borders, particularly in central and southern Europe and Southwest Asia. Western countries would have to weigh the merits of recognizing new governments in breakaway republics or in Russia itself. One or another of the contending factions would be likely to appeal to the West for economic and military assistance, if not outright security guarantees. (C-NF)

Beyond the dangers posed to the West by the internecine strife would be the very real challenge of dealing with the extreme economic hardship, including famine, likely to affect the bulk of the former USSR. Massive infusions of assistance and capital would almost certainly be required to alleviate suffering, but the lack of a central government, or perhaps even republic governments, capable of directing the inflow of economic aid—as well as ongoing violence—would undermine the effectiveness of any effort. The West would also be confronted with the problem of massive numbers of refugees fleeing the disorder, which could destabilize countries bordering the USSR. Despite these problems, Western assistance probably would be critical to the ability of the various republics and regions to move beyond the difficulties associated with this scenario to more stable political and economic systems. (C-NF)

This scenario would also make any coherent Soviet foreign policy extremely unlikely. There would be no central authority in Moscow to conclude arms control negotiations, implement accords already reached, or to ensure the completion of troop withdrawals from Central Europe. Moreover, in a situation of anarchy and civil wars in the USSR, Soviet forces remaining in the region would not be a military threat but would present serious problems for their hosts should they refuse repatriation; widespread disorder among these troops would be likely. (C-NF)

7. NIE 11-18.3-91, November 1991, *Civil Disorder in the Former USSR: Can It Be Managed This Winter?*

Director of Central Intelligence

~~Secret~~

Civil Disorder in the Former USSR: Can It Be Managed This Winter?

National Intelligence Estimate

This National Intelligence Estimate represents the views of the Director of Central Intelligence with the advice and assistance of the US Intelligence Community.

~~Secret~~

NIE 11-18.3-91
November 1991

Copy 484

7. *(Continued)*

 **Director of Central Intelligence**

~~Secret~~
~~NOFORN NOCONTRACT~~

NIE 11-18.3-91

Civil Disorder in the Former USSR: Can It Be Managed This Winter? (C NF)

Information available as of 29 November 1991 was used in the preparation of this Estimate.

The following intelligence organizations participated in the preparation of this Estimate:
The Central Intelligence Agency
The Defense Intelligence Agency
The National Security Agency
The Assistant Secretary for Intelligence and Research, Department of State
The Office of Intelligence Support, Department of the Treasury
The Director for Intelligence, Department of Energy

also participating:
The Deputy Chief of Staff for Intelligence, Department of the Army
The Director of Naval Intelligence, Department of the Navy
The Assistant Chief of Staff, Intelligence, Department of the Air Force
The Director of Intelligence, Headquarters, Marine Corps

This Estimate was approved for publication by the National Foreign Intelligence Board.

~~Secret~~
November 1991

7. *(Continued)*

~~Secret~~
~~NOFORN-NOCONTRACT~~

> This Estimate is one of a series to be published in the coming weeks on various crises facing the former USSR. ▓▓▓▓▓▓▓▓▓▓▓▓▓▓▓▓▓▓▓▓▓▓▓▓▓▓▓▓▓▓▓▓ The multiplicity of problems facing the new governments and their limited ability to cope with them make it likely that one or more of these problems will take on "worst case" proportions. (C NF)

7. *(Continued)*

Key Judgments

Civil Disorder in the Former USSR: Can It Be Managed This Winter? (C-NF)

- Severe economic conditions, the fragmentation of the armed forces, and ongoing interethnic conflict this winter will combine to produce the most significant civil disorder in the former USSR since the Bolsheviks consolidated power. (C-NF)

- Directly targeted and administered Western assistance would improve Russia's chances of maintaining stability through the winter, but the odds of preventing a social explosion that would overwhelm or topple the goverment depend most critically on Yel'tsin's ability to manage painful reforms effectively. (C-NF)

- Yel'tsin's performance thus far is mildly encouraging: he apparently will not restrict credit and spending so rapidly as to result immediately in massive unemployment and bankruptcies. But his mishandling of price liberalization—causing panic buying by announcing it in advance—demonstrates the potential for further mismanagement that could lead to the collapse of his government and, with it, prospects for reform. (C-NF)

- Because of less severe food shortages, Ukraine's prospects of remaining stable through the winter are good as long as it continues to avoid significant friction with Russia. The impact of civil disorder in other republics will vary, but all would eventually be seriously affected by instability in Russia. (C-NF)

- All republics will resort to some authoritarian measures to cope with unrest, but Russia and Ukraine at least will avoid a heavy reliance on coercive force that would generate intense opposition and hasten political destabilization. (C-NF)

7. *(Continued)*

Figure 1
Potential Areas of Unrest in the Former Soviet Union

1 Checheno-Ingushskaya Autonomous Soviet Socialist Republic (ASSR)
2 Kabardino-Balkarskaya ASSR
3 Karachayevo-Cherkesskaya Autonomous Oblast (AO)
4 Nagorno-Karabakhskaya AO
5 Severo Osetinskaya ASSR (North Ossetia)
6 Yugo-Osetinskaya AO (South Ossetia)

7. *(Continued)*

Discussion

During the winter months, the likelihood that civil disorder will be sufficient to destabilize governments at all levels will be higher than at any time since the 1920s. Mass demonstrations, strikes, violent protests, and even acts of terrorism are probable, given the severe problems that each republic, especially Russia, must grapple with over the next four to five months.

Likely Flashpoints

Where?
Over the next few months, differing degrees of unrest will occur in virtually every republic of the former USSR. Of these, civil disorder in Russia represents the greatest danger to stability in the region by virtue of Russia's size, influence, and resources.

Those areas of Russia most likely to experience serious unrest include the two largest cities, Moscow and St. Petersburg; industrial cities of the Urals, such as Ekaterinburg (formerly Sverdlovsk), Perm', and Chelyabinsk; and rebellious regions, such as the Tatar, Checheno-Ingush, and Yakut Autonomous Republics.

Yel'tsin's performance in managing the economic reform process will be critical. Liberalizing prices, cutting defense expenditures, and shutting down loss-making firms are all essential to restoring stability to the economy and laying the groundwork for its recovery. Moving too rapidly to curtail government spending and commercial credit, however, could cause bankruptcies to skyrocket and unemployment to soar by winter's end. Yel'tsin, therefore, has strong incentives to avoid so hasty an approach. He must also avoid the kinds of counterproductive actions and

7. (Continued)

statements he has made occasionally in the past. By announcing in advance that price controls would be removed, for example, Yel'tsin sparked panic buying that emptied store shelves and increased social tension. (C-NF)

Lingering "independence euphoria" and less severe food shortages will give Ukraine a better chance than Russia of remaining stable through the winter months. Serious energy shortages, however, will probably cause some social unrest. In addition, tensions between ethnic Ukrainians and minority Russians are likely to increase to some degree as the Ukrainian government acts to consolidate independence. Interethnic frictions would intensify significantly if Kiev—contrary to its current policies—tried to impose discriminatory language and citizenship laws on Russian-populated areas, or if regions with large Russian populations attempt to assert their autonomy. Areas that face the greatest potential of unrest include Crimea, where 67 percent of the population is Russian, and the Donbass mining region, where difficult economic conditions will aggravate relations between Ukrainians and the large minority of Russians living there. (C-NF)

Perceived mistreatment of ethnic Russians in Ukraine would worsen relations between the governments of Ukraine and Russia. Such a development might rally a majority of each republic's population to support its government, but, over time, any breakdown in bilateral cooperation would have an even more destabilizing economic and social impact on both republics. (C-NF)

Outside of Russia and Ukraine, the extent of civil disorder will vary, depending on economic conditions, ethnic rivalries, and political traditions. Food shortages and unemployment will generate some unrest in parts of Central Asia, although authoritarian governments and the relative lack of organized political opposition or economic pressure groups are likely to inhibit protest efforts, at least in Kazakhstan and Kyrgyzstan. (C-NF)

Interethnic conflict is a more likely source of destabilizing civil disorder in Central Asia, especially if sizable and relatively privileged ethnic Russian populations become the targets of discrimination, protest, or even violence by resentful Central Asians. Such actions would accelerate and make more destabilizing an exodus of Russians that has already begun.

Ethnic tensions elsewhere will also trigger civil disorders this winter. The Transcaucasus region is already on the verge of civil war. The simmering conflicts between the government of Moldova and Russian and Turkic minorities in the breakaway Dnestr and Gagauz regions also are likely to flare up. (C-NF)

Who?

Besides dissaffected ethnic minorities, civil disorder is most likely to involve the groups most affected by economic hardships. (C-NF)

Military Personnel. While central control of the military remains largely intact, servicemen are growing increasingly intolerant of abysmal housing conditions, food shortages, and insufficient incomes. Some individual officers, groups of soldiers, or even regimental units already have threatened to disobey central command structures. They could look for governmental allies at the republic or local level, in some cases begin foraging for food and supplies, and possibly become powers unto themselves. (C-NF)

Ferment in the military is already creating extraordinary situations. On 15 November, for example, the first "strike committee" in the armed forces was established in Ukraine, threatening protest actions in support of economic demands. (C-NF)

Perhaps the greatest potential for unrest will be among military personnel scheduled to be withdrawn from Eastern Europe and the Baltic states, where conditions are relatively comfortable. *Representatives of officers' assemblies of military units stationed in the Baltic states have already threatened not to leave until better conditions are created for them at the new places they will be stationed.* (C-NF)

7. *(Continued)*

Workers. Increased labor unrest is certain. Striking workers in the energy and transportation sectors would have the greatest impact. Coal miners demonstrated their power last spring when they staged strikes that forced major economic concessions from the central government. If anything, worker disgruntlement is even more widespread now:

- Labor organizations, many of which are opposed to marketizing reforms, staged a "week of united trade union actions" this fall aimed at pressing Russian Republic authorities to increase wages and improve living conditions.

- Medical workers held demonstrations and "warning strikes" throughout the Russian Republic on 13 November to protest miserably low wages, unbearable working conditions, and shortages of critical medicines.

- A Moscow students' trade union committee recently appealed to Yel'tsin to increase funding for higher education, warning that the "slightest delay" could be "the catalyst that sparks off a social explosion among students."

The Unemployed. As unemployment grows substantially, it will hit industries across the board. At least half of those thrown out of work will probably come from defense plants in Russia and Ukraine. Other heavy industries, such as ferrous metals, will also be hit. Republic governments probably will be unable to cope with an avalanche of demands for help from unemployed workers. Under such circumstances, protest actions are inevitable. Although the unemployed lack organization at present, they are a likely target of mobilization by organized political or economic groups.

Consumers. Consumers are long accustomed to scarce and shoddy goods, but food and fuel shortages combined with skyrocketing prices of many essential goods could finally push them over the edge. Like the unemployed, consumers lack organization. Moreover, those who will suffer the most economic pain—pensioners, the disabled, and children—are least likely to engage in direct protest action.

Figure 2. Cartoon published in Izvestiya *depicts man with sign: "Hunger strike against starvation." He is leaning against the door of a produce store with a sign affixed that says "no goods."* (U)

Nevertheless, spontaneous protests, riots, and violence are probable in shopping places as tempers reach the boiling point. *For example, police were recently called in to restore order at one St. Petersburg store when customers trying to buy low-priced eggs went on a rampage after finding that the shelves had been emptied.* Many such frustrated consumers will join mass rallies and demonstrations organized by other protesting groups. Adept handling by the authorities will be critical in determining whether such protests remain just a letting-off of steam or become truly destabilizing.

Impact on Stability

No one knows whether the Yel'tsin government can survive the winter. We believe that there is some possibility that it will be overthrown or simply lose its authority, due mainly to government mismanagement of the economic reform process.

7. *(Continued)*

Secret

On balance, however, Yel'tsin's statements and actions give grounds for modest optimism that the Russian government will not be destabilized. Faced with the prospect of growing unrest, we believe Yel'tsin will take steps to defuse or inhibit it:

- He has already boosted the wages of state-funded workers in an effort to ease the pain of the transition to a market economy. Although he will proceed with the liberalization of prices on most commodities, he probably will not curtail credit and spending so rapidly as to cause widespread bankruptcies and massive unemployment in early 1992. Such steps might preserve short-term stability at the expense of long-term economic health, however.

- Yel'tsin is willing to curb democratic practices in order to maintain stability. He will most likely make selective use of executive rule to deal with local unrest. He is less likely to adopt more sweeping strong-arm measures in an effort to buy time to administer harsh economic medicine. *As the recent "state of emergency" debacle in Checheno-Ingushetiya illustrated, Yel'tsin would encounter serious difficulties in carrying out emergency decrees.* Moreover, it would alienate his most important political constituencies and jeopardize his political position. (C NF)

The reaction of the military to requests from civilian authorities to suppress civil disorder in the Russian Republic will depend greatly on the circumstances of each case. On balance, however, we have serious doubts that Russian-dominated military forces would be reliable instruments in using deadly force against fellow Russians. (C NF)

Besides economic factors, stability in Ukraine depends in large measure on the zeal with which the government moves to affirm its independence. Ukrainian government policies probably will strain relations with minority Russians and further the disintegration of the Soviet armed forces. Military units and officers stationed in Ukraine will face increasing pressure to decide whether their loyalties extend to Moscow or to Kiev. Combined with deteriorating socioeconomic conditions, such pressures will almost certainly deepen turmoil within the military and increase the danger that renegade units will appear. (C NF)

Outside of Russia and Ukraine, the prospects for destabilization vary:

- Byelorussia's ex-Communist leadership has at least a 50-percent chance of surviving the winter, despite deteriorating economic conditions that will probably produce widespread unrest. Over time, it will be undercut by radical economic reforms in Russia, and labor unrest similar to that which hit the republic last April would follow.

- Georgian President Gamsakhurdia faces intense political opposition, as well as resistance to Georgian rule in South Ossetia and the Abkhaz Autonomous Republic. But his continued popular support—he was elected overwhelming by direct popular vote earlier this year—and his dictatorial methods probably will keep him in power, at least over the next few months.

- The bloody dispute between Armenians and Azeris over the status of Nagorno-Karabakh already is threatening to escalate into a civil war. That outcome would be ensured if the USSR Interior Ministry Troops are removed, a likely prospect if efforts to form a political union languish.

- Central Asian republics—especially Kazakhstan and, to some extent, Kyrgyzstan—probably will be relatively quiet this winter. Tajikistan and Uzbekistan are more likely to experience instability in the near term. (C NF)

All republics would eventually be affected by the destabilization of Russia. Most republic governments would seek to protect themselves by turning inward and imposing authoritarian rule. In most cases, these responses would fail to stem internal unrest. (C NF)

Directly distributed Western assistance this winter, especially emergency food and medical aid targeted to major cities, would probably help increase the prospects for stability. Such aid, delivered by airlift and administered by Westerners on the ground, would have the greatest chance of circumventing distributional roadblocks—the most likely cause of severe food shortages. Aid programs that rely on internal

7. *(Continued)*

> *A Better Winter?*
>
> *There is some chance that conditions will not be as bad as this Estimate depicts and that civil disorder will not be as widespread. Several factors could inhibit massive political protests:*
>
> - *A reservoir of support for Yel'tsin exists that transcends the immediate performance of his government. This could inhibit civil unrest—at least among ethnic Russians within Russia—so long as he is seen as playing straight with them.*
>
> - *Russians, as well as other ethnic groups, have a long history of enduring conditions almost unthinkable in the West. While there is a breaking point, our analysis may err in assuming that the population is closer to it than it actually is.*
>
> - *Winter conditions in most of the former USSR are hardly ideal for massive outdoor rallies and demonstrations.* (C NF)
>
> *In addition, the black, gray, and new legal markets may be more effective than we expect in taking up the slack:*
>
> - *We are uncertain how much has been diverted into these channels as well as how much individual citizens are hoarding; the amount undoubtedly is more than official statistics suggest.*
>
> - *As prices are liberalized, more goods could become available throughout the country than we now anticipate.*
>
> - *We may not account sufficiently for the deal making—barter, theft, selling of services, and so forth—that citizens have historically used to survive amid shortages.* (C NF)

distribution systems will have little immediate impact on shortages and run the risk of increasing the level of public unrest, as news would spread of clogged storage and transportation facilities, spoilage, black-market diversions, and theft. (C NF)

Going From Bad to Worse

Several developments are possible that would increase the chances of destabilization of governments beyond the level already discussed, especially if they occurred in combination. While some are more likely than others, we believe that none is probable in the next four to five months:

- Yel'tsin's death, especially by assassination, would probably throw the Russian government into chaos, strengthen centrifugal forces within the Russian Republic, reduce the prospects for successful interrepublic cooperation, and lower the odds that economic reform and democratization—long-term guarantors of stability—would be successfully implemented.

- Russian economic "shock therapy" could be so poorly conceived and unevenly implemented that it produces hyperinflation and unemployment far higher than we now anticipate and seriously aggravates interrepublic trade problems.

- An attempt by individual republics, especially Ukraine, to seize control over military assets on its territory would accelerate the disintegration of the armed forces and create the potential for a dangerous conflict.

- A large number of refugees crossing republic borders to escape interethnic strife or economic conditions would place new demands on the already insufficient resources of republic goverments. (C NF)

Widespread civil disorder in the next few months would deal a deathblow to current efforts to cobble together interrepublic institutions. At best, republic governments will be too preoccupied with their internal difficulties to devote time or energy to interrepublic negotiations. At worst, economic stringencies and ethnic feuding will bring to power xenophobic nationalist groups advocating "go-it-alone" policies. (C NF)

The End of Empire I
Eastern Europe

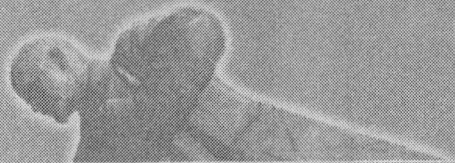

8. NIE 11/12-9-88, May 1988, *Soviet Policy Toward Eastern Europe Under Gorbachev*

Director of Central Intelligence

~~Secret~~

Soviet Policy Toward Eastern Europe Under Gorbachev

National Intelligence Estimate

~~Secret~~

NIE 11/12-9-88
May 1988

Copy 355

8. *(Continued)*

~~SECRET~~
~~NOFORN/NOCONTRACT~~

NIE 11/12-9-88

SOVIET POLICY TOWARD EASTERN EUROPE UNDER GORBACHEV ~~(C NF)~~

Information available as of 26 May 1988 was used in the preparation of this Estimate, which was approved by the National Foreign Intelligence Board on that date.

~~SECRET~~

8. *(Continued)*

~~SECRET~~
~~NOFORN/NOCONTRACT~~

CONTENTS

	Page
KEY JUDGMENTS	1
DISCUSSION	5
Eastern Europe in the Mid-1980s	5
Economies in Decline	5
Aging Leaderships	6
Challenges to Soviet Authority	6
Gorbachev's Policies Toward Eastern Europe	6
Foreign and Security Policy Coordination	7
Economic Pressures	8
Succession Dilemmas	8
Outlook: Growing Diversity, Sharper Conflict	11
Growing Diversity	11
Strained Economic Relations	13
Succession Scenarios	14
Sharper Conflict	15
Potential Challenges to Soviet Control	15
Popular Upheaval	15
Sweeping Reform	17
Conservative Backlash	17
Prospects and Variations	18
Implications for the United States	18
ANNEX: KEY SOVIET OFFICIALS RESPONSIBLE FOR EASTERN EUROPE	23

8. *(Continued)*

KEY JUDGMENTS

General Secretary Gorbachev's policies have increased the potential for instability in Eastern Europe. But they have also expanded the scope for diversity and experimentation, affording new possibilities for evolutionary reform in the region.

Gorbachev has set an ambitious agenda for Eastern Europe. His aims are to secure East European support for the Soviet modernization drive, promote broader Soviet foreign policy objectives through closer Warsaw Pact coordination, and stimulate a deeper process of economic and political regeneration in the region. Aware of the region's diversity, he has set general guidelines for reform rather than detailed plans. But he faces East European realities—severe economic problems, aging leaderships, and mounting social discontent—that conflict with Soviet objectives.

Soviet policy under Gorbachev has sought to balance the competing objectives of encouraging change and promoting stability. Although Gorbachev has avoided a high-risk strategy of forcing change on these fragile political systems, continuing Soviet pressure, as well as the example of the Soviet reform program, has introduced new tensions into the region.

Growing Diversity, Sharper Conflict

For the next three to five years, Eastern Europe's outlook is for growing diversity—in responding to reform pressures, crafting approaches to the West, and managing relations with Moscow:

— Economically, Eastern Europe cannot deliver what Gorbachev wants. As the gap between goals and results grows more acute, Gorbachev is likely to exert stronger pressure on his allies to forge closer economic ties, upgrade performance, and implement domestic economic reforms.

— While the recent leadership change in Hungary probably comes close to Gorbachev's preferences for Eastern Europe, prospective successions elsewhere are not likely to yield the dynamic, innovative leaders Gorbachev needs to achieve his more ambitious goals in the region. Consequently, his pressures for change will continue to be aimed at regimes ill-equipped and, in some cases, unwilling to respond.

8. *(Continued)*

Thus, at best, Gorbachev's approach can achieve only evolutionary progress toward political rejuvenation and improved economic performance in Eastern Europe. Continued, and probably heightened, Soviet pressure will lead to sharper conflicts, both within East European societies and between Moscow and its allies.

Potential Challenges to Soviet Control

Cross-pressures emanating from Moscow, coupled with severe economic and political dilemmas in Eastern Europe, could yield more serious challenges to Soviet interests. Three extreme scenarios are possible:

— *Popular upheaval* in Poland, Romania, or Hungary, involving a broad-based challenge to party supremacy and ultimately to Soviet control.

— *Sweeping reform* in Hungary or Poland, going well beyond Gorbachev's agenda and eventually threatening to erode party control.

— *Conservative backlash*, involving open repudiation of Soviet policies by orthodox leaders in East Germany, Romania, or elsewhere.

Of these, popular upheaval is the most likely contingency. Gorbachev will expect his allies to act decisively to end any political violence or major unrest. Indeed, East European leaders are at least as aware of the need for vigilance as Gorbachev is, and they have at their disposal powerful security forces that have proved effective in containing unrest. Should events spin out of their control and beyond the limits of Soviet tolerance, the ultimate controlling factor on change in Eastern Europe will be Soviet force:

— Gorbachev faces greater constraints than did his predecessors against intervening militarily in Eastern Europe; his foreign policy and arms control agenda, and much of his domestic program as well, would be threatened.

— A Dubcek-like regime would have much greater latitude to pursue reforms now than in 1968, and Soviet intervention to stop it would be more problematic.

— In extremis, however, there is no reason to doubt his willingness to intervene to preserve party rule and decisive Soviet influence in the region.

8. *(Continued)*

Implications for the United States

Gorbachev's sanctioning of diversity and experimentation have expanded the limits of the thinkable in Eastern Europe, presenting new opportunities for US and Western policies:

— Economic dilemmas and high-technology requirements will lend strength to US calls for internal reforms of the kind already legitimized by Moscow.

— Gorbachev's active European policy and the generally more dynamic period of East-West relations will offer new opportunities for the West to engage even the more conservative East European regimes.

At the same time, Gorbachev's policies will complicate the coordination of Western policies toward European security. Differing Western approaches will make it harder for Western governments to reach a political consensus on dealing with Moscow and its allies, and harder for NATO to maintain a security consensus.

Gorbachev's policies also call into question some of the assumptions upon which the US policy of differentiation is based, in that the twin US goals of diversity and liberalization increasingly collide. Those regimes most at odds with Gorbachev's approach also tend to be the most orthodox and repressive, and the reform-minded Hungarians and Poles are now closely attuned to the Soviet line. In practice, however, our ability to influence the grand alternatives—reform or retrenchment, crisis or stability—will remain limited; we can at best encourage evolutionary movement toward internal liberalization and greater independence from Soviet tutelage.

This information is Secret Noforn.

8. *(Continued)*

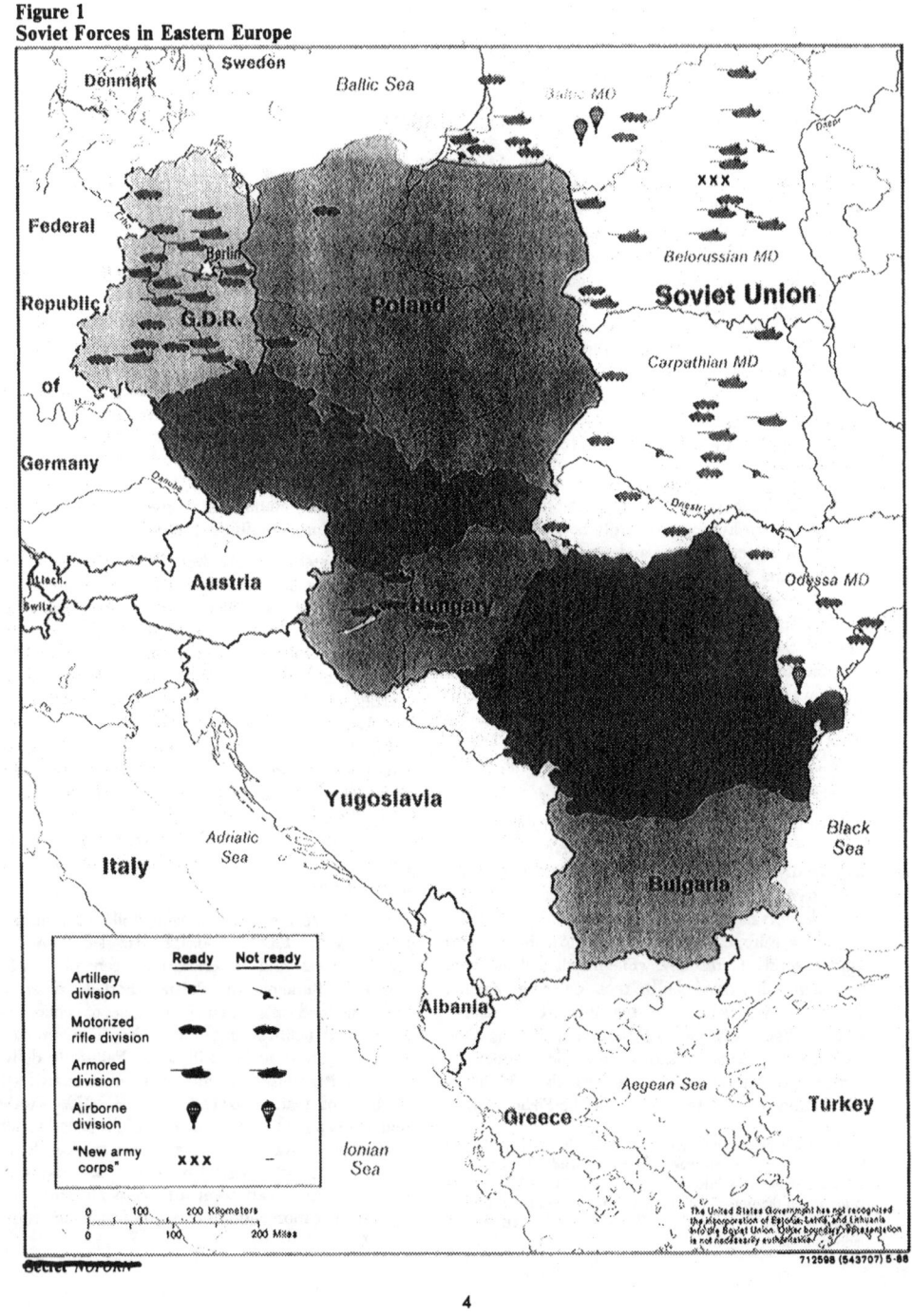

Figure 1
Soviet Forces in Eastern Europe

8. (Continued)

DISCUSSION

1. Not since the early Khrushchev years have policy changes in the USSR had so profound an impact on Eastern Europe as those now being pushed by General Secretary Mikhail Gorbachev. These new winds blowing from Moscow, as well as serious internal economic and political dilemmas, have ushered in an era of considerable uncertainty—and potentially of significant change—in Eastern Europe. With the impending passing of an entire generation of leaders in the region, Soviet policy over the next three to five years is likely to be decisive in determining the scope and direction of change and, ultimately, the stability of the Soviet empire.[1]

2. For Gorbachev as for his predecessors, the importance of Eastern Europe can hardly be exaggerated: it serves as a buffer, military and ideological, between the USSR and the West, a base for projecting Soviet power and influence throughout Europe, a conduit of Western trade and technology, and a key external pillar of the Soviet system itself. The Soviet Union continues to exercise decisive influence over the region through a complex web of political, economic, and military and security ties, and there is no reason to doubt ultimate Soviet willingness to employ armed force to maintain party rule and preserve the Soviet position in the region.

3. At the same time, however, Eastern Europe is a region of chronic instability, recurrent crisis, and growing diversity; the tasks of Soviet alliance management have grown progressively greater. Successive Soviet leaders have sought both cohesion and viability in Eastern Europe; they have failed to achieve them simultaneously. Gorbachev, while mindful of the need for stability, has tilted the balance toward an agenda of change and reform in the interest of regime viability. Some veteran East European officials liken the current situation to Khrushchev's de-Stalinization campaign and the subsequent upheavals in Hungary and Poland in 1956; they fear that the Soviet reform drive will unleash potentially uncontrollable pressures for change in Eastern Europe.

Eastern Europe in the Mid-1980s

4. The new Soviet leadership under Gorbachev inherited an Eastern Europe whose seeming quiescence was belied by serious problems just beneath the surface. To be sure, the challenge posed by Solidarity in Poland had been successfully contained with the imposition of martial law in December 1981, and the Jaruzelski regime had made some progress toward restoring party control and neutralizing its domestic opposition. Yet, throughout Eastern Europe, severe economic problems, rising social discontent, and political stagnation among the aging party leaderships created an unstable situation.

5. *Economies in Decline.* When Gorbachev assumed power in 1985, Eastern Europe had endured nearly a decade of economic decline and stagnation. Most obviously, the region-wide financial crisis of the early 1980s contributed to the end of an era of East-West economic detente: trade with the West declined sharply, new credits were scarce, and several of the East European regimes were compelled to enter into extensive refinancing negotiations with Western creditors. Trade relations with the USSR fared little better, as Soviet oil prices reached a new peak in 1982-83, belatedly reflecting the full brunt of the 1978-79 increases in the world market (as the five-year averaging mechanism for Soviet oil deliveries caught up with prevailing world rates).

6. These reversals took a heavy toll on standards of living, as the East Europeans struggled with large foreign debts and deteriorating economic performance. In Romania and Poland, shortages of energy and basic foodstuffs raised the prospect of economically induced political instability; elsewhere, problems were less disastrous but still acute. Failure to deliver the promised improvements in living standards—the linchpin of regime strategies in the 1970s—further undermined political legitimacy and deepened societal alienation. Reduced investments and growing lags in the scientific-technological revolution had also weakened East European competitiveness on world markets, further mortgaging the region's economic future.

---

[1] This Estimate examines relations between the Soviet Union and its six Warsaw Pact allies—East Germany, Poland, Czechoslovakia, Hungary, Romania, and Bulgaria—over the next three to five years. It focuses on the impact and implications of Soviet policies in the region as a whole rather than offering detailed assessments of individual countries.

7. *Aging Leaderships.* Adding to Eastern Europe's decline was the stagnation and immobility of its aging party leaderships. By 1987, the average age of the six top party leaders was well over 70, their average tenure in office more than two decades. Only Poland's General Jaruzelski, a relative youngster at 64, and East German party leader Erich Honecker, still spry at 75, seemed capable of energetic leadership; most of the others were in poor health, presiding over leaderships bereft of new ideas. These were hardly the men to grapple with the difficult policy issues of the 1980s.

8. Political malaise in Eastern Europe had been accentuated by a long period of enfeeblement in Moscow, stretching from the latter years of the Brezhnev era through the interregna of Yuri Andropov and Konstantin Chernenko. Three Soviet successions in the space of as many years, coupled with mixed policy signals, heightened uncertainties and complicated succession dilemmas in Eastern Europe. The absence of clear and decisive Soviet leadership also contributed to a period of drift in Eastern Europe, as each regime began to ad-lib its own approaches, even on some sensitive foreign policy issues.

9. *Challenges to Soviet Authority.* Ideological erosion in Eastern Europe—accelerated by the crushing of Solidarity in Poland—gave rise to new independent social groups and, above all, to a resurgence of national consciousness throughout the region. In some cases, the regimes responded by attempting to co-opt nationalist sentiments, as in the Honecker regime's appropriation of Martin Luther, Frederick the Great, and others as precursors of the East German state. In others, official policy played on exclusivist, chauvinistic nationalism: the Bulgarian regime mounted a brutal assimilation campaign against its Turkish minority, and Romania's President Ceausescu increased repression against the Hungarian minority in Transylvania.

10. More worrisome from Moscow's perspective were new signs of national self-assertiveness among its allies, particularly in the aftermath of INF (intermediate-range nuclear force) deployments in Western Europe in late 1983 and 1984. East European concern about the Soviet walkout from the Geneva disarmament talks in late 1983 betrayed deeper anxieties over the erosion of European detente. During the fall of 1984, there was an unprecedented, semipublic display of Warsaw Pact disunity—the Soviet and Czechoslovak regimes called for a tougher line and closed ranks, while the East Germans, Hungarians, and Romanians pressed for improved East-West relations and stressed the special role of small states in promoting detente.

11. For most of the East European regimes, the preservation of European detente was no longer just desirable; it had become an essential ingredient of their economic and political strategies. It also corresponded to rising pressures from below for national self-expression and self-assertion and for affirming the "Europeanness" of the East European states. Unlike the upheavals of 1956, 1968, and 1980-81, these trends did not directly threaten Soviet primacy in the region but were aimed at achieving greater scope for diversity in the interest of economic and political stability. Together with mounting internal problems, they added up to considerable disarray in Moscow's East European empire.

Gorbachev's Policies Toward Eastern Europe

12. In Eastern Europe as elsewhere, Gorbachev's initial approaches were extensions of his broader domestic and arms control agenda:

— Domestically, Gorbachev was seeking to revitalize Soviet power and prestige through economic "restructuring" (*perestroika*) and a carefully regulated campaign of "openness" (*glasnost*), designed to strengthen a lagging economy, overcome bureaucratic resistance, and breathe new life into society at large.

— Externally, Gorbachev needed a respite from East-West tension and the debilitating arms race with the United States. He also sought to replace the rigid, ideological world view of his predecessors with a more sophisticated pursuit of Soviet regional interests, particularly in Western Europe and East Asia.

13. As for Eastern Europe, Gorbachev probably did not have a fully developed conception of its problems and, as at home, lacked a clear and detailed plan of action. Improved economic performance was a high priority—to transform Eastern Europe from a drain on Soviet resources to an asset in the Soviet modernization drive and to promote economic and political viability. Gorbachev viewed with obvious disdain the hidebound leaderships in Prague, Sofia, and Bucharest, which reflected the corruption, inefficiency, and dogmatism of Brezhnev's latter years. Given his ambitious foreign policy program, he also required renewed discipline and greater coordination among the East Europeans:

— In pursuit of these objectives, Gorbachev needed to press change on the East Europeans, particularly in economic policy. But he also needed

8. *(Continued)*

SECRET
NOFORN/NOCONTRACT

stability in the region, so as not to jeopardize his more urgent priorities at home.

— Although Gorbachev was not inclined to embark on a high-risk strategy, he also saw dangers in continued stagnation and hence was more ready than any Soviet leader since Khrushchev to encourage diversity and experimentation as the keys to long-term viability in the region.

— And, of course, Soviet approaches to Eastern Europe were not Gorbachev's alone. As on domestic policy, Gorbachev also had to take into account the views of other key Soviet officials. (See annex.) (S NF)

14. *Foreign and Security Policy Coordination.* Gorbachev's first task was to reassert firm leadership over Warsaw Pact foreign policy and improve coordination to support his far-reaching arms control agenda. This he achieved through a series of Warsaw Pact summits—six in his first two years—and the adoption of something approaching a conciliar system, whereby the East Europeans were briefed before and after major Soviet foreign policy initiatives. More important, the Soviet shift from confrontation to dialogue on arms control issues helped allay East European concerns of being caught in the middle of rising tensions, facilitating a natural convergence of Soviet and East European approaches on East-West issues. (S NF)

15. Gorbachev's ambitious foreign agenda also entailed a much greater role for the East Europeans. Jaruzelski and Honecker paid early visits to China aimed at restoring normal interstate and interparty ties, and several East European governments began exploring the prospects for normalizing relations with Israel. Some—notably the Poles and East Germans—floated new arms control and other security proposals. And Honecker's visit to Bonn exemplified a more active Western policy by the GDR. (S NF)

16. In light of growing East European diplomatic activity, it should not be surprising that Gorbachev laid great stress on coordination and discipline in Warsaw Pact councils. The renewal of the Pact itself was instructive. With its initial term due to expire in May 1985, the Romanians and others hinted that they favored certain changes to the text—a watering down of mutual defense obligations and more precise provisions for the Pact's eventual dissolution—and that they wanted only a 10-year extension. In the event, the Pact was renewed without a single change; and Gorbachev, then only two months on the job, had achieved an

Multilateral Summit Meetings of Soviet and East European Party Leaders, 1985-87

Date	Location	Event	Agenda
March 1985	Moscow	Chernenko funeral	
May 1985	Warsaw	Warsaw Pact 30th anniversary	Renewal of Warsaw Pact
October 1985	Sofia	Warsaw Pact Political Consultative Committee (PCC) meeting	Pre-Geneva arms control proposals
November 1985	Prague	Ad hoc	Informal debriefing on US-Soviet summit at Geneva
June 1986	Budapest	PCC	"Budapest appeal" for conventional and tactical nuclear force reductions
November 1986	Moscow	Ad hoc meeting of CEMA (Council for Economic Mutual Assistance) party leaders	"CEMA 2000" program for scientific-technological cooperation
May 1987	East Berlin	PCC	Conventional force reductions; military doctrine; "new international economic order"
December 1987	East Berlin	Ad hoc	Debriefing on US-Soviet summit in Washington

Unclassified

impressive show of unity. (Gorbachev reportedly hammered out this agreement at the time of Chernenko's funeral—literally his first day in office—but only at the price of offering new Soviet energy deliveries in return for Ceausescu's agreement.) Gorbachev also has moved to expand the infrastructure of the Warsaw Pact. In May 1987, two new Pact bodies were created to facilitate ongoing coordination of Soviet and East

8. *(Continued)*

European arms control positions and supervision of East European foreign visits and contacts.[2]

17. At the same time, however, Gorbachev has used the Bloc's consultative bodies for substantive policy discussions rather than ritualistic endorsement of pre-cooked resolutions. Soviet influence remains paramount, but Gorbachev's new stress on consultation and consensus-building reflects his understanding that the East Europeans have extensive and useful foreign ties of their own and that an effective Soviet approach to the West must take these realities into account. Once a common position is reached, Gorbachev has insisted on closed ranks and alliance discipline, and even the loyal Bulgarians have been called to task for failing to endorse Soviet arms control initiatives with sufficient enthusiasm. Gorbachev also instructed the Poles to redraft the "Jaruzelski Plan" for arms reductions in Central Europe, and he played a key role in controlling the pace and timing of inter-German relations.

18. *Economic Pressures*. The second major item on Gorbachev's agenda was to link the East European economies to the Soviet modernization drive. Both bilaterally and through CEMA (the Council for Economic Mutual Assistance), Gorbachev moved to redress the trade deficits the East Europeans ran up in the 1970s, maintaining a freeze on Soviet oil deliveries at their early 1980s level and demanding increased imports of higher quality East European goods, particularly consumer items and high-technology machinery and equipment. The heavily indebted Poles, Romanians, and Hungarians were enjoined to reduce their economic dependence on the West; the Bulgarian and Czechoslovak regimes were exhorted to revive their stagnant economies and upgrade performance. And all were pressed to join the Soviet-led "Comprehensive Program" for scientific-technical cooperation through the year 2000—"CEMA 2000," for short—through joint ventures and coordinated production in key high-technology areas:

— To enforce these strictures, Gorbachev created new quality-control inspections and delivered blunt messages to several East European leaders.

— Gorbachev lobbied personally for the swift implementation of the CEMA 2000 program in late 1985 and, in doing so, moved CEMA toward a new agenda.

— He also pushed through new bilateral agreements on scientific-technological cooperation and secured new legislation in the East European countries to facilitate coproduction and joint ventures.

19. The actual conduct of Soviet–East European economic relations in Gorbachev's first two years revealed less change than the early rhetoric seemed to promise. Indeed, the East European trade deficit with Moscow rose sharply in 1986 to 2.6 billion rubles—the largest annual trade gap since 1981. Although trade for 1987 was nearly balanced, the favorable trends were due chiefly to a decline in the value of Soviet oil rather than increased East European deliveries. In export performance, as well as domestic "restructuring," the veteran East European leaders temporized with the familiar foot-dragging that has frustrated Soviet leaders from Khrushchev on.

20. The East Europeans were particularly wary of being drawn into Soviet-sponsored (and Soviet-dominated) joint ventures in high-technology areas, and resistance was evident in the elaboration of the CEMA 2000 program. Owing to its industrial power and unique access to Western technology via "inner-German" trade, the GDR was the key East European participant; but the East Germans, like the Hungarians and Romanians, were reluctant to jeopardize their own carefully cultivated trade relations with the West in support of Gorbachev's domestic agenda. Soviet–East European differences were evident at the hastily convened November 1986 Moscow summit on CEMA integration, which yielded only minimal consensus on the next stage of scientific-technological cooperation. Even Soviet planners now concede CEMA 2000 goals are too optimistic.

21. *Succession Dilemmas*. These frustrations pointed to Gorbachev's more basic dilemma: how to impart some of his own dynamism to Eastern Europe without a wholesale shakeup of the ossified party leaderships in Prague, Sofia, and elsewhere. Gorbachev evidently recognized, however, that any direct attempt to instigate an East European succession would entail great risks. Consequently, Soviet efforts have been largely indirect, aimed at shaking up the ruling establishments by projecting reformist ideas and the example of Moscow's own domestic innovations. These efforts also aimed at shifting the internal party debates in those countries toward the preferred Gorbachev agenda, and in so doing altering the context and accelerating the pace of presuccession maneuvering.

---

[2] These are the Multilateral Group for Current Information Exchange and the Special Commission on Disarmament Questions.

8. *(Continued)*

22. Such pressure was evident in May 1987, when Soviet Foreign Minister Shevardnadze visited Budapest to convey Gorbachev's dissatisfaction with the Hungarian leadership's procrastination on further economic reform. A month later, Karoly Grosz, reputed to be an able and energetic administrator, was named Hungarian Prime Minister. And in July, after a quick visit to Moscow by Grosz, the Hungarian leadership unveiled a long-discussed, long-postponed set of economic reform (and austerity) measures. A year later, the succession process took a much more decisive turn:

— At a special party conference in May 1988, Grosz was named party General Secretary, forcing out Janos Kadar, who had served in the top party post since 1956.

— Most of Kadar's proteges were also dramatically removed from the top leadership, replaced by a strongly reformist group of younger officials.

Although the initiative for these decisions was probably Hungarian, Soviet pressure clearly forced the pace and direction of change. (s nf)

23. Even without direct Soviet calls for change in Eastern Europe, the demonstration effect of Gorbachev's domestic departures was unsettling. The very existence of a reform-minded Soviet leader, coupled with his critique of Brezhnev-era mismanagement, served to undermine the authority and cohesion of the more orthodox East European regimes. And the new legitimacy accorded to economic "restructuring" and political "openness" threatened to unleash widespread public expectations for rapid change. Nowhere were these trends more evident than in Czechoslovakia, where the seeming vindication of reformist and even dissident ideas sent shock waves through the divided party leadership. These pressures, combined with the declining health of party leader Gustav Husak, led to his abrupt resignation in December 1987. (See inset, page 10.) (s nf)

24. The Czechoslovak succession confirmed Gorbachev's determination to promote change without threatening stability. Through strong, if largely indirect, pressure on the divided Prague leadership, Gorbachev helped secure the removal of Husak, the personification of Brezhnev-era conservatism—only to accept a safe, almost Chernenko-like successor in Milos Jakes. Indeed, Soviet pressure for change probably could not have succeeded had Gorbachev attempted to push a reformist successor on a still-conservative Czechoslovak leadership. Jakes, then, was probably a compromise choice for Moscow as well as Prague; the

The Hungarian Succession

Karoly Grosz

Age 57... General Secretary of the Hungarian Socialist Workers' Party (HSWP) since 22 May 1988; Premier since June 1987; Politburo member since 1985... May party conference gave a mandate to institute both economic and political changes... commitment to economic reform untested, accomplishments as Premier limited... respected by business leaders as dynamic, vigorous executive willing to make tough decisions... Budapest party secretary, 1984-87.

Janos Kadar

Age 76... HSWP President since 22 May 1988; removed as party leader, Politburo member at that time... after 1956 revolution, forged social consensus based on consumerism and relaxed relations between party and people... ability to convince Soviets of Hungarian loyalty and stability contributed to long reign... recently seen as impediment to economic and political progress because of unwillingness to expand reforms of 1970s, also declining energy level, progressive health problems.

8. *(Continued)*

The Czechoslovak Succession

Gustav Husak's December 1987 resignation as Czechoslovak party leader (while retaining the largely honorific state presidency) came in the wake of a long Soviet campaign to push the Gorbachev agenda in Prague; the resulting pressures undoubtedly encouraged the Czechoslovak leadership to move against Husak. His successor, Milos Jakes, brought to the party leadership a mixed bag of credentials:

— Jakes carried the baggage of post-1968 "normalization," having been among the anti-Dubcek conspirators and having directed the 1969-70 purge of party members associated with the Prague Spring.

— He had served since 1981 as party secretary for economic affairs and recently seemed to have sided with pragmatic elements in the party favoring cautious economic reform—stressing, however, that economic change must take place under strict party control. (S NF)

Though hardly a green light for reform, Jakes's elevation will help move the regime toward long overdue economic change and political rejuvenation, already hinted at by the April 1988 changes to the Central Committee secretariat. And Jakes, a firm Moscow loyalist, will be more receptive to Soviet calls for improved economic performance, closer cooperation in Soviet-sponsored joint ventures in high-technology areas, and domestic "restructuring." He is also likely to oversee further changes in the party leadership, still dominated by holdovers from the 1969-70 "normalization" period and now thrown into ethnic imbalance by the overrepresentation of Czechs in top regime positions. (S NF)

These changes are not likely to spark social upheaval, nor will they lead to significant liberalizing reform in Czechoslovakia. But they may herald a long-awaited change in economic policy and encourage opposition groups to become more active, if only to test the limits of tolerance under the Jakes regime. (S NF)

Milos Jakes (U)

Age 66 . . . party leader since 17 December 1987 . . . party Central Committee secretary, 1977-87, responsible for agriculture until 1981, for economy until April 1988 . . . Presidium member since 1981 . . . attended CPSU Higher Party School in Moscow (1955-58), presumably speaks fluent Russian . . . Czech. (C NF)

Gustav Husak (U)

Age 75 . . . President since 1975 . . . party leader, 1969-87 . . . resigned as party chief but remains a member of policymaking Presidium . . . has had cataract surgery, suffers continuing vision problems, declining general health . . . reportedly drinks excessively . . . Slovak. (C NF)

Czechoslovak succession underscored the limits of the achievable in Soviet policy in dealing with the more conservative regimes in Eastern Europe. (S NF)

25. The gap between Gorbachev's ultimate objectives, as outlined in numerous speeches and documents, and the actual policies he has pursued reflects the fundamental contradiction between his desire for change and the imperatives of party control in Eastern Europe:

— Gorbachev has set an ambitious agenda for Eastern Europe that addresses many of the region's problems, but it is neither broad nor deep enough to remedy underlying systemic weaknesses.

— He has expanded the scope of permissible experimentation for reformist regimes, such as Hungary, and has succeeded in pushing some of the more conservative East European regimes toward long overdue, though still timid, reforms.

— In the process, he has accentuated divisions within the East European leaderships and awakened a combination of popular hopes and anxieties about impending change. These trends, coupled with severe economic problems, have heightened uncertainties in the region and increased the potential for crisis. (S NF)

8. *(Continued)*

Outlook: Growing Diversity, Sharper Conflict

26. Soviet policy toward Eastern Europe is likely to continue along the lines already established under Gorbachev. Its key elements will be:

— Within the framework of firm party control, *sanctioning of diversity and experimentation* as the keys to economic and political viability.

— Continued *pressure for reform* without dictating specific measures or demanding slavish emulation of Soviet practices.

— Insistence on *foreign policy coordination*, whereby the East Europeans are afforded greater room for tactical maneuver but are expected to hew closely to the broad lines set in Moscow.

— Mounting pressure for *improved East European economic performance* and increased cooperation in high-technology areas.

— Longer term efforts toward *strengthened institutional ties*, coupled with alliance management techniques that facilitate Soviet control and influence through a more participatory system of give-and-take.

27. These broad contours of Soviet policy will remain in place so long as Gorbachev's domestic position is secure and Eastern Europe remains quiescent. A major change in Moscow would obviously alter the equation:

— *Gorbachev's ouster* would curtail the Soviet reform drive and heighten uncertainties in Eastern Europe as the new regime sorted itself out. His removal on political grounds would send another new signal to the divided East European regimes—this time a sharply antireformist one—and undercut Soviet authority, at least temporarily.

— *Retrenchment in Moscow* (with Gorbachev still in office) would strengthen the existing orthodox leaders in Eastern Europe without fully arresting the pressures for change. Perceived lack of unity in the Kremlin would further polarize Eastern Europe, with conservatives seeking to restore the status quo ante and reformists continuing to push for change.

— *More daring Soviet reforms*—a result, perhaps, of Gorbachev's need to overcome bureaucratic resistance through radical policy and personnel changes—would further destabilize Eastern Europe and strain relations with Moscow. Rising pressures within the East European regimes might prompt some of them to implement sweeping reforms or force out existing leaders.

28. Gorbachev has played a skillful political game so far, pulling back when necessary while gathering support for the next push forward. Although the chances of a domestic showdown have increased, Gorbachev seems to have the upper hand and appears inclined to push his reform agenda further and more forcefully.

29. **Growing Diversity.** For the next three to five years, the outlook in Eastern Europe is for growing diversity—in responding to reform pressures, crafting approaches to the West, and managing relations with Moscow. Diverse East European arms control proposals and economic approaches to the West will facilitate some Soviet objectives, but they will also complicate the tasks of alliance management and run counter to the joint action needed for scientific-technological cooperation. In Gorbachev's broader view, moreover, diversity is no end in itself but rather a vehicle for economic and political regeneration. These goals are nowhere in sight in Eastern Europe. Except perhaps in Hungary, they are not likely even to be seriously pursued.

30. *Glasnost* and *perestroika* will continue to yield mixed results. Barring leadership changes, Romania and East Germany will continue to resist reform pressures; Bulgaria will continue to experiment at the margins but will proceed only haltingly toward real "restructuring." The new Czechoslovak leadership under Jakes will push more forcefully for economic change, but serious movement toward economic and political reform remains a distant prospect. Hungary and Poland could be more interesting:

— The appointment of Karoly Grosz—a tough, self-confident risk taker in the Gorbachev mold—as General Secretary of the Hungarian party and the promotion into the leadership of outspoken reform advocates marks an important turning point. The new leadership is likely to be much more aggressive in pressing economic and political reforms, but it faces severe problems—including workers unhappy with austerity, intellectuals demanding more freedom, and an economy that is stagnating and burdened with a heavy foreign debt. Failure to develop a more radical

8. (Continued)

and effective reform program would further contribute to a rise in tensions.

— Evidently with Soviet blessings, General Jaruzelski has already consolidated a rather unorthodox pattern of party-military rule, moved toward granting the Catholic Church new legal status, and proposed economic reforms that, on paper at least, go well beyond Moscow's. The disastrous economic situation and social discontent—as shown by the recent wave of strikes—make successful realization of the reforms unlikely, but the urgency of domestic problems may also push the regime toward the social dialogue it has rejected up to now. (S-NF)

31. In foreign policy, the East European regimes have reason to be satisfied with Gorbachev's skillful engagement of the West and their own increased room for maneuver. So long as Moscow maintains a conciliatory approach to the West, Soviet and East European policies will remain generally congruent. At the same time, Gorbachev's encouragement of a more active role for the East Europeans will increase the chances for open conflicts of interest at CSCE (Conference on Security and Cooperation in Europe) talks and in other Pan-European forums. There will also be increased risk of further embarrassments to Moscow arising from Hungarian-Romanian polemics or public airing of East European human rights violations. Hence, foreign policy coordination will require more skillful management, and Gorbachev will need to prod the Czechoslovak and Bulgarian regimes toward more active diplomacy while restraining the occasional independent-mindedness of the Romanians, Hungarians, Poles, and East Germans. (S-NF)

32. At the same time, East European realities will limit the parameters of possible Soviet initiatives. Not only must Gorbachev weigh the consequences of Soviet policies on political stability in Eastern Europe, but he must also take into account the perceptions and likely reactions of East European leaders. Their views are not likely to deter him from policies he considers vital to Soviet interests; but, on matters as potentially destabilizing as inter-German relations, his options are limited. Indeed, Gorbachev's campaign for a common "European house" of growing intra-European cooperation implies a degree of national autonomy in Eastern Europe far beyond what he or any other Soviet leader would countenance. Moscow will find it increasingly difficult to promote this line in the West without introducing new divisions into Eastern Europe as well. (The Berlin Wall will stay, whatever tactical advantages Gorbachev might see in its removal.) (S-NF)

Table 1
Eastern Europe: Projected Debt Figures, 1987-90 [a]

Million US $

	1987	1988	1989	1990
Bulgaria				
Gross debt	4,954	5,121	5,375	5,730
Net debt [b]	3,531	3,598	3,745	3,986
Debt service ratio [c] (*percent*)	36.7	36.4	37.1	38.4
Czechoslovakia				
Gross debt	4,714	4,940	5,150	5,335
Net debt	3,497	3,723	3,933	4,118
Debt service ratio (*percent*)	15.3	15.8	16.4	16.7
East Germany				
Gross debt	16,775	16,573	16,447	16,423
Net debt	8,862	8,660	8,534	8,510
Debt service ratio (*percent*)	41.0	38.7	36.1	33.8
Hungary				
Gross debt	15,314	16,684	18,084	19,502
Net debt	13,414	14,784	16,184	17,602
Debt service ratio (*percent*)	54.1	53.4	54.9	57.1
Poland				
Gross debt	34,570	35,937	37,417	38,908
Net debt	32,850	34,117	35,497	36,888
Debt service ratio (*percent*)	73.9	74.0	64.2	74.5
Romania				
Gross debt	4,214	3,324	2,679	2,053
Net debt	3,632	2,490	1,593	967
Debt service ratio (*percent*)	34.5	21.5	16.3	14.5

[a] Last updated: 14 January 1988.
[b] Reserve figures used in calculating net debt exclude gold reserves.
[c] The debt service ratio is calculated using the following formula: Interest payments + medium- and long-term principal repayments/total exports + invisible receipts. The debt service ratio for Poland is calculated using the amount of interest owed, not the amount paid.

This table is Confidential Noforn.

8. *(Continued)*

SECRET
NOFORN/NOCONTRACT

Table 2
Eastern Europe's Economic Outlook: Average Annual
Growth by Five-Year Plan Period [a]

Percent

	1971-75	1976-80	1981-85	1986-90 [b]
Bulgaria				
Total GNP	4.7	1.0	0.8	1.0
Gross fixed investment	6.4	−9.1	−1.1	2.5
Personal consumption	3.9	1.6	2.1	1.0
Czechoslovakia				
Total GNP	3.4	2.2	1.1	1.0
Gross fixed investment	6.5	−0.3	−1.2	1.0
Personal consumption	2.7	1.5	1.1	1.0
East Germany				
Total GNP	3.5	2.3	1.7	2.0
Gross fixed investment	1.5	1.7	−10.0	2.0
Personal consumption	3.8	2.0	1.2	1.5
Hungary				
Total GNP	3.3	2.0	0.7	1.0
Gross fixed investment	2.3	0.3	−5.2	1.0
Personal consumption	3.2	2.2	0.4	0.5
Poland				
Total GNP	6.5	0.7	0.6	2.0
Gross fixed investment	14.4	−2.9	−4.9	1.5
Personal consumption	5.6	2.4	−0.2	1.5
Romania				
Total GNP	6.7	3.9	1.8	2.0
Gross fixed investment	10.4	6.9	−2.2	2.0
Personal consumption	5.1	4.7	0.2	1.0

[a] Last updated: 12 January 1988.
[b] Projections for 1986-90 were based on analysis of current trends, results of econometric models, and consultations with country experts.

This table is Confidential-Noforn.

33. *Strained Economic Relations*. Eastern Europe cannot deliver what Gorbachev wants: significant improvements in trade performance, particularly in high-technology areas. Poland and Hungary will remain saddled with enormous debts for the foreseeable future, with East Germany and Bulgaria also facing debt problems. The Romanian economy, drained to repay Western creditors, will remain devastated for years to come, and Czechoslovakia's industrial and technological base has been rendered obsolete by years of neglect. Throughout the region, projected growth rates and shares devoted to investment will remain suppressed, leaving the East European economies with only limited capacity to assist in the Soviet modernization drive. Nor are the East Europeans likely to jeopardize economic relations with the West or risk further reductions in domestic living standards for the sake of Gorbachev's economic agenda. (s NF)

34. So far, Gorbachev's economic pressures—like those of Soviet leaders before him—have yielded few tangible results aside from improved deliveries in some areas like machine tools. Foreign trade plans for 1986-90 are inconsistent with Gorbachev's main goals, calling for an average annual growth of only 5 percent in Soviet-East European trade—the slowest growth in planned trade in the last 15 years. Similarly, most of the CEMA 2000 technical goals appear unattainable—only a handful of joint ventures have been created, and the push for "direct links" between enterprises remains hamstrung by economic and bureaucratic

8. *(Continued)*

impediments that have frustrated Soviet planners from the beginning. Moreover, Soviet–East European terms of trade have begun to shift against Moscow, as the five-year averaging mechanism for Soviet oil prices has caught up with declining prices on the world market. If world oil prices hold roughly steady for the next few years—or even if they increase somewhat—the East European ruble debt will begin to disappear, further weakening Moscow's economic bargaining power.

35. Gorbachev will face a growing gap between his economic goals and results over the next three to five years, at the very time that his domestic modernization plans call for a significant increase in East European inputs and tangible progress in the CEMA 2000 program. Following the pattern of his domestic policies, Gorbachev has come to realize that his goals in Soviet–East European economic relations cannot be met without systemic economic and institutional reform. At the October 1987 meeting of the CEMA prime ministers, the Soviets reopened some of the fundamental problems raised earlier by the East Europeans themselves: lack of convertible currency, inadequacy of direct links among firms, and absence of a rational pricing mechanism. And Gorbachev will soon learn, if he has not learned already, that reforming intra-CEMA trading procedures is futile without deep structural reforms in the domestic economic systems.

36. Thus, the dilemma of promoting change without provoking instability in Eastern Europe will grow more acute. Faced with an almost certain need to increase the pace of reform at home, Gorbachev is likely to step up pressure on the East Europeans to introduce *perestroika* and economic reform, albeit not with the same intensity or impact as in the USSR.

37. *Succession Scenarios.* Leadership changes in Eastern Europe present both risks and opportunities for Gorbachev. On the one hand, it is increasingly clear that change of the kind Gorbachev wants will not take place under the current crop of leaders. The prospective departure of several veteran leaders gives Gorbachev an unparalleled opportunity to influence the selection of more energetic and innovative party leaderships. On the other hand, several East European successions—some already under way—pose risks for political stability and hence for Gorbachev's broader agenda.

38. The Hungarian succession of May 1988 dramatically altered the top leadership and raised popular expectations for reform, but the attendant austerity measures are likely to heighten domestic tensions. Nor is the succession process complete: further leadership changes, including the naming of a new prime minister, are still ahead. In Czechoslovakia as well, Husak's replacement by Jakes is just the beginning of a turnover of the entire post-1968 leadership, with the need for Czech-Slovak proportionality adding to the disruption. Elsewhere, impending successions promise to be similarly unsettling:

— Zhivkov has been in power for more than three decades; his departure will reverberate throughout the Bulgarian apparat.

— With seven Politburo members over 70, the East German party faces a major turnover of the remaining leaders of the wartime generation.

— The post-Ceausescu succession in Romania will introduce considerable uncertainties into that highly personalized leadership and may invite East-West rivalry as Moscow attempts to reassert influence with a successor regime.

39. Gorbachev's task will be to manage several leadership transitions, perhaps simultaneously, to assure that preferred, or at least acceptable, successors are named and that regime authority is preserved in the process. His ability to do so will depend on his success in defeating conservative forces in his own leadership. The options and constraints confronting him in Eastern Europe are fairly clear:

— He will need to work with the existing top leaderships; Soviet preferences will be important but not decisive.

— There will be a short list of three to five figures in each party whose seniority gives them some claim to the job.

— Excluding the Ceausescu clan, nearly all these figures meet the minimum qualifications of experience and reliability.

— Except in Hungary, none has demonstrated the kind of dynamism Gorbachev wants, though a few have reformist credentials.

While the Hungarian succession probably comes close to Gorbachev's preferences for Eastern Europe, prospective leadership changes elsewhere are not likely to yield the dynamic, innovative leaders Gorbachev needs to achieve his more ambitious goals in the region as a whole. He will probably have to settle for a series of transitional leaderships and then work to ensure that a new generation of reform-minded leaders is groomed.

8. *(Continued)*

40. This cautious and gradualist approach has the advantage of minimizing the disruption inherent in East European successions. If carefully managed, it may also facilitate the eventual transfer of power to a new and more forward-looking generation of leaders. But it will not soon yield the dynamic, innovative leaderships Gorbachev needs to achieve his more ambitious economic and political goals in Eastern Europe. It also means that Gorbachev's reform pressures will continue to be aimed at leaderships ill equipped and, in some cases, unwilling to respond.

41. *Sharper Conflict.* Thus, at best, Gorbachev can achieve only evolutionary progress toward political rejuvenation and improved economic performance in Eastern Europe. And currently contemplated reforms will not solve deep-seated political and economic problems. As the gap between objectives and results becomes more evident, Gorbachev will be inclined to push more aggressively for deeper changes as the necessary precondition to economic and political revitalization. To do so will require a careful calibration of Soviet policy: he will need to push hard enough to achieve tangible results but not so hard as to provoke system-threatening instability. The danger of miscalculation will increase.

42. Already Gorbachev has introduced new destabilizing tendencies into Eastern Europe through his open critique of past failures of socialism, heightened economic pressure on his allies, and, above all, the demonstration effect of his domestic reform program. Sharper conflict is likely even if Gorbachev does not increase the pressure on his allies. The longer the Soviet reform dynamic continues, the stronger will be the internal pressures for change on the East European regimes.

43. These cross-pressures, coupled with severe economic problems and leadership uncertainties, will heighten popular unrest in Eastern Europe. In Poland, newly implemented austerity measures have led already to widespread strikes, protests, and demonstrations; Hungary and Romania also face growing unrest. There will be a general increase of antiregime activism, owing to the climate of "openness" and greater willingness to test the limits of regime tolerance. Human rights, religious, pacifist, environmentalist, and other groups—already active in most of Eastern Europe—will grow more assertive. The pattern of cooperation among Hungarian, Czech, and Polish dissidents is also likely to expand.

44. These developments alone will not threaten party rule, but collectively they will:

— Weaken regime authority.

— Undermine economic recovery prospects.

— Lay the groundwork for more serious challenges.

Potential Challenges to Soviet Control

45. There are at least three more extreme scenarios that could lead to serious challenges to Soviet control over Eastern Europe.

46. The Hungarian Revolution of 1956, the 1968 Prague Spring, and the Polish social revolution of 1980-81 (along with numerous lesser upheavals) provide ample evidence of the inherent instability of Moscow's East European empire. Each of these had its own dynamic, but each led ultimately to a broad-based challenge to party supremacy and Soviet control in the region. And each led to crisis—meaning in the East European context the actuality or imminent likelihood of Soviet military intervention.

47. However, Gorbachev's sanctioning of reform and experimentation implies a more liberal Soviet definition of "crisis." Liberalizing reform (of the kind espoused by the 1968 Czechoslovak leadership) may no longer lead so swiftly and automatically to a "crisis situation" in Moscow's eyes.

48. *Popular Upheaval.* Several of the usual instability indicators—discontent over living standards, weak and divided leadership, social unrest—are evident in several countries, and all face pressures emanating from Moscow. New shocks—severe austerity measures, the death or ouster of a top party leader, or the emergence of an organized and emboldened opposition—could bring about serious instability almost anywhere, with Poland, Romania, and Hungary the most likely candidates for trouble:

— The likelihood of multiple, simultaneous upheavals is higher than it has been in more than 30 years. In the late 1980s and into the early 1990s, virtually all the East European countries face

8. *(Continued)*

Romania: Impending Crisis?

The potential for regime-threatening crisis is growing in Romania, the country least affected by Gorbachev's policies and most defiant of Soviet strictures. Romania's problems are homegrown, owing to the Ceausescu regime's severe austerity measures and draconian domestic policies.

A major riot involving an estimated 5,000 to 10,000 protesters in Brasov in November 1987 was the most visible manifestation of growing public unrest, which has given rise to scattered strikes, demonstrations, and acts of sabotage. So far, unrest has remained isolated and localized: there is no organized opposition, and security forces are well equipped to quell protests—with stocks of foodstuffs as well as truncheons.

Evidence is also growing of ferment within the party hierarchy itself. Disenchantment within the rank and file, fueled by popular protests and Ceausescu's scapegoating of the party for his economic failures, has left him isolated. Gorbachev's public criticism of Ceausescu's ruling style and widespread knowledge of Ceausescu's medical problems are accelerating this trend, as officials throughout the system try to distance themselves from him to avoid being caught up in a post-Ceausescu housecleaning. Discontent within the party has been diffuse up to now, and Ceausescu's reshuffling of key leaders has precluded the emergence of an oppositionist faction.

These economic and political pressures add up to an increasingly volatile internal situation, however, and several possible scenarios could bring about a full-scale upheaval:

— *Ceausescu's death or incapacitation.* Ceausescu suffers from prostate cancer and has visibly weakened in the past year (although he maintains a vigorous schedule). If he were to die in office, he would probably be replaced by a collective including his wife Elena and other loyalists; such a regime would probably be embroiled quickly in a broader succession struggle.

— *A palace coup.* The most likely crisis scenario would have growing popular unrest, stimulating still more dissatisfaction within the party and setting the stage for Ceausescu's ouster. He would probably be succeeded by a collective of figures currently within the party leadership; Elena and the rest of the clan would be swept away along with Ceausescu himself.

— *A brushfire of popular unrest.* Simultaneous outbreaks of protest could spark a more widespread uprising, overwhelming Securitate resources and leading to a breakdown of public order. The resulting near-anarchy could lead to a seizure of power by the military.

Soviet Attitudes

So long as Romania did not descend into complete disorder, Moscow would probably have more to gain than lose in a crisis scenario. A post-Ceausescu leadership would offer opportunities for restoring lost influence; and Romania's geopolitical and economic realities would remain severe constraints on any successor regime in Bucharest.

Military intervention would not even be a plausible contingency unless there were incipient anarchy in Romania or the advent of a successor leadership that threatened to remove Romania from the Warsaw Pact. Neither is likely.

Spillover in Eastern Europe

Short of a Soviet invasion, events in Romania would not have wide repercussions elsewhere. Nor would they impinge on Gorbachev's broader agenda, in that a Romanian crisis would not be linked to Soviet policies or pressure tactics; indeed, a crisis provoked by Ceausescu's misrule would strengthen Gorbachev's argument that stability demands economic and political rejuvenation. However:

— Hungarian-Romanian relations would be severely strained if domestic violence in Romania were to turn into ethnic violence directed at the Hungarian minority in Transylvania.

— And Yugoslavia would be involved if bloodshed or chaos in Romania precipitated an exodus of Romanians seeking refuge abroad via Yugoslavia.

---

analogous sets of problems: stagnant economies, leadership successions, and reformist pressures from Moscow.

— As in the past, however, possible scenarios would be highly country-specific. Only in Romania is there a significant possibility of widespread violence; elsewhere, the greater likelihood would be a broad-based, organized challenge to regime authority. (In Poland, however, this latter scenario could also lead to a cycle of repression and violence.)

49. For Gorbachev, a possible upheaval in Eastern Europe constitutes the greatest external threat to the Soviet reform program and his own continued tenure.

8. *(Continued)*

Despite the greater tolerance he has shown for experimentation, he will expect his allies to take swift, decisive action to end any political violence or major unrest. Indeed, the East European leaderships are at least as aware as Gorbachev is of the need for vigilance, and they have at their disposal large security forces that have been effective thus far in containing disturbances. Should events overwhelm the capacity of local leaders, there is no reason to doubt that he would take whatever action was required, including military intervention, to preserve party rule and Soviet authority in the region. Like his predecessors, Gorbachev would exhaust all other options before undertaking Soviet military intervention. Indeed, he faces even greater constraints:

— A Soviet invasion of an allied country would do irreparable damage to his image in the West and undermine the entire edifice of his foreign policy.

— An upheaval in Eastern Europe, particularly one attributable to Gorbachev's reform pressures, could also threaten his domestic standing. It would add to domestic political pressures for his removal from power and the curtailment of his reform program.

50. *Sweeping Reform*. Gorbachev has expanded the limits of acceptable reform. In Hungary and Poland particularly, reform blueprints are being circulated that go well beyond anything now on the agenda in Moscow. And now the Hungarians have put in place a leadership team containing radical reformers, such as Imre Pozsgay, head of Hungary's Patriotic People's Front. Although Grosz has more conservative leanings than the newcomers, he is action-oriented and willing to take some chances to get the party out in front of the reform process. In light of the looming economic decline and coalescence of dissident and establishment pressures around a reform package, he could be pulled by his new Politburo toward more radical solutions to Hungary's problems. Given the fate of previous reform movements, there would be strong elite and popular inhibitions against direct challenges to party supremacy and the Soviet alliance system. If Eastern Europe's past is any guide, however, a genuine reform movement in Hungary or elsewhere would tend inevitably toward national self-determination and autonomy.

51. Such a scenario would be the most hopeful for Eastern Europe and the most problematic for Moscow, particularly if public discipline were maintained. There would be no incipient anarchy to facilitate Soviet suppression, few pro-Soviet collaborators to call on, and no cataclysmic event to spur Moscow to take early and decisive action. By the time Gorbachev had decided that the course of events had gone too far, he could be faced with a relatively unified reform leadership and a disciplined and determined population; the costs of intervention would be much higher than under a scenario of serious internal instability. Gorbachev would have to choose between suppressing a genuine reform movement—inspired by his own calls for *glasnost* and *perestroika*—or countenancing at least a partial erosion of Soviet control. His choice—by no means a foregone conclusion—would hinge on the scope of change and the perceived challenge to Soviet influence in the region.

52. *Conservative Backlash*. Gorbachev's pressure for reform also could lead to stronger and more open defiance on the part of orthodox leaders in East Berlin, Bucharest, or elsewhere. Prague's chief ideologist Vasil Bilak has publicly rejected the applicability of Gorbachev's reforms to Czechoslovakia, and the East German official press regularly, if indirectly, dismisses the Soviet reform program. If further Soviet pressures create new cleavages that impinge more directly on the job security of the conservative East European leaderships, and if future Yeltsin affairs strengthen perceptions in Eastern Europe that Gorbachev is faltering, hardliners there might become much more openly confrontational.

53. If, for example, perceived divisions in the Kremlin emboldened some East European leaders to adopt stridently antireformist platforms, the damage to Gorbachev's authority would be magnified. He would probably have the clout to silence Zhivkov and Jakes, but his capacity to ward off a conservative backlash led by Honecker or Ceausescu would be less certain, particularly if they and other recalcitrants joined forces in an informal rejectionist front (indeed, Gorbachev is already reported to have criticized Ceausescu for trying to form an "antireform alliance" with Honecker):

— Such a scenario would be interactive—it would require the tacit approval of Gorbachev's domestic opponents, who in turn would be strengthened by an East European backlash.

— While a less threatening—and less likely—contingency, it would nonetheless represent a major challenge to Gorbachev's authority and policies in the Bloc. To avert irretrievable damage to

8. *(Continued)*

Figure 2
Potential Challenges to Soviet Control, Probabilities Over the Next Five Years

Percent

Popular Upheaval
Internal instability leading to serious challenge to party control.

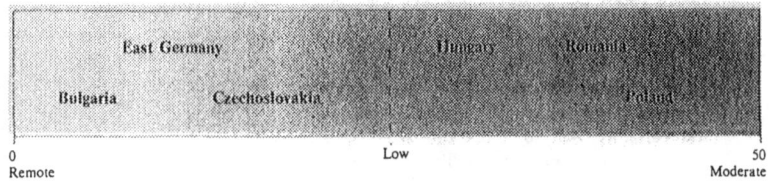

Sweeping Reform
Regime-led economic and political reforms going well beyond anything acceptable to Moscow.

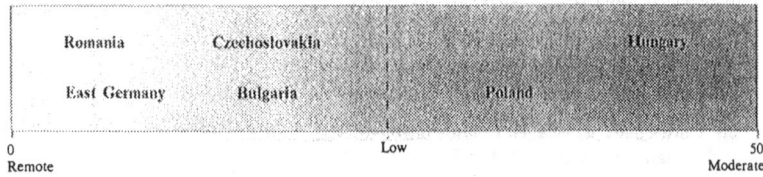

Conservative Backlash
Strong and open repudiation of Soviet reforms and policies by East European leaders.

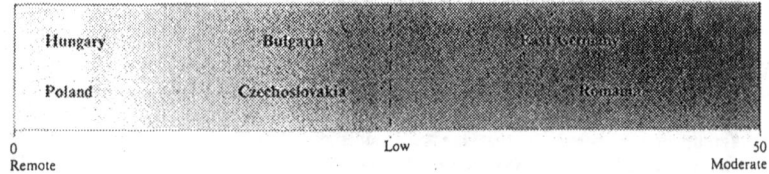

both, he might have to force a showdown in Eastern Europe—perhaps by demanding the resignation of his most strident critics. (S NF)

54. *Prospects and Variations.* None of these more extreme scenarios is likely to be played out in the near future, but their probability will increase over the next three to five years. Moreover, these evolutions need not be manifest in their pure forms, nor are they mutually exclusive. Short of these extreme scenarios, it is a virtual certainty that somewhere in Eastern Europe there will be new movement toward more daring reform, a new outburst of public unrest, or more open resistance to Moscow's reform agenda. We could see all three at once. (S NF)

Implications for the United States

55. Eastern Europe is entering a period of flux. Change is facing more countries—and across more

8. *(Continued)*

dimensions—than at any time since the immediate post-Stalin period. Developments over the next three to five years are likely to determine the key contours of political life in the region for a generation to come:

- Within the time frame of this Estimate, these developments will not lead to the unraveling of Moscow's East European empire, nor will they by themselves diminish the military threat posed by the Warsaw Pact.

- A crisis in Eastern Europe would undermine Pact cohesion, at least temporarily, but it would almost certainly lead to a crackdown (with or without Soviet intervention), rolling back whatever concessions had been wrested from the regime.

- Short of such an extreme evolution, however, the scope of conceivable change in the region has expanded considerably. And the likelihood of growing diversity and sharper conflict will create new opportunities for Western engagement of Eastern Europe.

56. Gorbachev's agenda of reform, openness, and experimentation is congruent with US goals of promoting pluralism in Eastern Europe and greater independence from Moscow. This endgame is not what Gorbachev has in mind, of course; but, in encouraging change as the key to dynamism and ultimately to greater viability, he has sanctioned diversity and expanded the limits of the thinkable in Eastern Europe.

57. Gorbachev's policies also call into question some of the assumptions upon which the US policy of differentiation is based, in that the twin aims of liberalization and independence from Moscow increasingly collide in Eastern Europe. Those regimes most at odds with Gorbachev's approach also tend to be the most conservative and repressive. Conversely, relatively open countries like Poland and Hungary, which have received favored US treatment, are now closely attuned with Moscow.

58. These contradictions in US policy will grow more acute the longer Gorbachev remains in power and the Soviet reform dynamic continues. However, our ability to influence the grand alternatives—reform or retrenchment, crisis or stability—will remain limited indeed; we can at best promote favorable change on the margins:

- Gorbachev's policies have created new opportunities for Western encouragement of liberalizing

---

US Policy Toward Eastern Europe

Excerpts From NSDD 54, 2 September 1982:

"The primary long-term U.S. goal in Eastern Europe is to ▓▓▓▓▓ facilitate its eventual reintegration into the European community of nations.... The United States... can have an important impact on the region, provided it continues to differentiate in its policies toward the Soviet Union and the Warsaw Pact countries of Eastern Europe, so as to encourage diversity through political and economic policies tailored to individual countries....

"Differentiation will aim at:

— Encouraging more liberal trends in the region.

— Furthering human and civil rights in East European countries.

— Reinforcing the pro-Western orientation of their peoples.

— Lessening their economic and political dependence on the USSR and facilitating their association with the free nations of Western Europe.

▓▓▓▓▓▓▓▓▓▓▓▓▓▓▓▓▓▓▓▓▓▓▓▓▓▓

— Encouraging more private market-oriented development of their economies, free trade union activity, etc. ...

"In implementing its policy, the U.S. will calibrate its policies to discriminate carefully in favor of governments which:

— Show relative independence from the Soviet Union in the conduct of foreign policy as manifested by the degree to which they resist associating themselves with Soviet foreign policy objectives and support or refrain from obstructing Western objectives; or

— Show relatively greater internal liberalization as manifested in a willingness to observe internationally recognized human rights and to pursue a degree of pluralism and decentralization, including a more market-oriented economy...."

---

reform on the part of regimes so inclined, like the Hungarian and the Polish. For the others, the United States also may have new leverage to promote diversity, even if reform prospects are remote.

8. *(Continued)*

— US policy faces the dilemma that large segments of the East European societies are not willing to accept the austerity that implementation of economic reforms would entail. And the regimes are loath to risk the political reforms needed to win public acceptance of painful economic measures.

59. Gorbachev's policies will complicate the coordination of Western approaches to European security. For Bonn, the prospect of closer relations with its eastern neighbors has revived old ambitions for a greater central European role. The French, worried about Bonn's eastward drift and suspicious of Gorbachev's ultimate aims, have taken the lead in resisting a new wave of European detente:

— These differences will make it harder for Western governments to reach a political consensus on dealing with Moscow and its allies, and harder for NATO to maintain a security consensus.

— However, differing Western policies toward Eastern Europe create cross-pressures that promote diversity, inhibit CEMA integration, and erode Warsaw Pact foreign policy discipline.

60. *Influencing Eastern Europe.* The United States has always pursued a two-track policy in Eastern Europe, communicating directly with East European populaces as well as with their governments. These direct channels of communication will be particularly important as new ideas circulate and new opportunities emerge:

— International broadcasting—particularly via Radio Free Europe, but also from other Western radios—will be an important vehicle for informing East European publics on Soviet reforms and exerting indirect pressure on the East European regimes.

— There will be greater opportunity for developing East-West contacts: those regimes that already pursue relatively open policies will have greater latitude to expand them; the others will come under pressure from both Moscow and their own populaces to do likewise. Such contacts—ranging from scientific exchanges to scholarly dialogues and people-to-people programs—will serve to push forward the limits of diversity, strengthen public and elite pressure for internal reform, and help cultivate second-level officials who may play key roles in successor regimes.

61. There also will be new opportunities for Western engagement of the East European regimes, owing to:

— Economic dilemmas that virtually compel several East European governments to accept previously unpalatable conditions in exchange for Western credits.

— High-technology requirements, pushing the East Europeans to facilitate direct contacts with Western firms and international economic organizations.

— Gorbachev's campaign for a "European house," which impels the East Europeans toward more active diplomacy and also heightens their sensitivity to charges of human rights violations.

— The general climate of reform and "openness," which offers opportunities for engaging Eastern Europe on formerly taboo subjects and pressing more directly for internal reforms of the kind already legitimized by Moscow.

62. The East European regimes will continue to be wary of any Western proposals that impinge on regime control or Soviet prerogatives on foreign and security policy. They are likely, however, to be more receptive than in the past to US proposals for counterterrorism and counternarcotics cooperation, expanded East-West contacts, and even improvements in the area of human rights:

— The CSCE process offers new forums for separate, if not fully independent, East European diplomatic activity—as in Hungary's cosponsorship with Canada of a proposal on national minorities. Such developments suggest there is greater scope for Western engagement of Eastern Europe on key East-West issues, and in so doing for promoting greater diversity and independence in the region.

— A prospective umbrella agreement between the European Community and CEMA, along with a possible CSCE follow-on conference on East-West economic relations, would complicate US efforts to control technology transfer, but they would also offer new venues for engaging Eastern Europe on foreign trade policy and domestic reform.

— New opportunities also may develop for a more genuine security dialogue, particularly if a new round of talks on conventional force reductions affords greater scope for East European diplomacy.

8. *(Continued)*

— On matters of internal liberalization, the ironic convergence of US and Soviet calls for economic and political reform will lend strength to the conditions the United States attaches to expanded economic cooperation. (S NF)

63. *Influencing Soviet Behavior.* Should the trends Gorbachev himself has set in motion lead to upheaval or sweeping reform in Eastern Europe, the ultimate controlling factor will be the limits of Soviet tolerance. Gorbachev has strong disincentives to intervening in Eastern Europe, particularly for the purpose of suppressing a genuine reform movement. He and his Politburo are not likely to be deterred from actions they deem vital to Soviet interests, but the United States and its allies may be able to alter at the margin the Soviet risk calculus by maximizing the price Moscow would have to pay. The extent of direct, heavyhanded Soviet interference would be influenced marginally by the ability of the United States to convey clearly how such Soviet behavior would affect the broader US-Soviet agenda. (S NF)

8. *(Continued)*

ANNEX

KEY SOVIET OFFICIALS RESPONSIBLE FOR EASTERN EUROPE

Interparty Relations

Mikhail Gorbachev
CPSU General Secretary (since March 1985)

By the time he became General Secretary in March 1985, Gorbachev had already met all East European party leaders and had spoken with some of their principal lieutenants as well. In November 1969 he was part of a low-level delegation to Czechoslovakia. After becoming CPSU secretary for agriculture in 1978, he returned to Czechoslovakia (April 1979). Gorbachev visited Hungary in October 1983 and Bulgaria in September 1984, and he almost certainly met in Moscow with these leaders and others during the annual CEMA gathering each June, as well as at other summits. He also was involved in hosting visits of each of the East European party leaders in the early 1980s.

At Chernenko's funeral in March 1985, the party leaders of the Warsaw Pact states were the first foreign dignitaries with whom Gorbachev met. Since that time, he has visited every East European country (except Albania) at least once. He has also met in Moscow with East European officials on 39 occasions.

Yegor Ligachev
Politburo member and secretary, Central Committee (since 1985)

As unofficial "second secretary," Ligachev, 67, is involved in general oversight of foreign policy; he currently chairs the Supreme Soviet Commission on Foreign Affairs. He has not frequently visited East European countries, but, in 1987, he traveled twice to Hungary. He also visited Poland in 1984. Despite his reputation as the leading conservative in the Soviet Politburo, Ligachev has praised Hungary's economic reforms, strongly suggesting that Budapest need not imitate Soviet economic policies and structures. His cautious approach to domestic reform in the Soviet Union, however, suggests he would be similarly cautious about major change in Eastern Europe.

Aleksandr Yakovlev
Politburo member (since June 1987) and secretary, Central Committee (since March 1986)

Yakovlev, 64, is one of Gorbachev's closest advisers on foreign affairs and an influential figure in Soviet policymaking toward Eastern Europe. He led the Soviet delegation to the January 1987 Socialist Bloc Ideological/International Secretaries meeting in Warsaw, where he advocated new media techniques to aggressively promote a socialist concept of democratization and human rights. A leading reform proponent, Yakovlev has also pushed for a more sophisticated European policy and has stressed the need for more flexibility in socialist development, which suggests that he is relatively open to internal diversity in the Bloc countries. He has met frequently in Moscow with visiting East European delegations and in 1987 traveled to Poland and East Germany.

8. *(Continued)*

Vadim Medvedev
Chief, Liaison With Communist and Workers' Parties of Socialist Countries ("Bloc Relations") Department; and secretary, Central Committee (since March 1986)

Although Medvedev, a proponent of economic reform, has not worked on East European matters, his writings have stressed that socialist economic theory should draw both on the Soviet model and on the experiences of other Bloc countries. Medvedev, 59, has headed several delegations to Soviet Bloc countries and accompanied Gorbachev on a trip to Hungary in June 1986. He advocates diversity for the economic and political policies of East European regimes, with the caveat that Soviet tolerance will depend on their ability to contribute to Soviet economic modernization.

Diplomatic Relations

Eduard Shevardnadze
Foreign Minister

Since becoming Foreign Minister in June 1985, Shevardnadze, 60, has frequently traveled to Eastern Europe, visiting all East European foreign ministers in their capitals and attending regular Warsaw Pact foreign minister meetings. The past year has clearly been Shevardnadze's most active, with nearly half of his 20 trips abroad made to Eastern Europe. During a June 1987 visit to Budapest, he reportedly pressed the Hungarians to move economic reform forward, expressing dissatisfaction with bilateral economic, scientific, and technical relations. In 1986, Shevardnadze visited Romania in October and Poland in March. He has been an increasingly outspoken advocate of reform and foreign policy "new thinking."

Economic Relations

Nikolay Ryzhkov
Chairman, USSR Council of Ministers; Politburo member (since 1985)

Premier Ryzhkov, 58, coordinates government-to-government economic ties between the Soviet Union and Eastern Europe. A strong supporter of domestic economic reform, he has also encouraged CEMA premiers to endorse changes in CEMA operations and trade. During a meeting with his East European counterparts in 1987, Ryzhkov recommended intra-CEMA currency reforms, direct enterprise contacts, joint ventures, and a new CEMA organizational structure. In response to the opposition of several East European leaders to this limited decentralization of planned management, Ryzhkov warned that those countries unwilling to participate in these changes should not hinder those who do.

8. *(Continued)*

Military Relations

Viktor Kulikov
First Deputy Minister of Defense (since 1971); Commander in Chief of the Warsaw Pact Forces (since January 1977)

An able field commander, Marshal Kulikov, 67, is the third-ranking official in the Soviet military hierarchy. He wields considerable political clout throughout Eastern Europe and, through a combination of persuasion and bullying, has reportedly won compliance with Moscow's policies, especially in operational matters and in planning for the imposition of martial law in Poland in 1981. Although US officials have consistently been impressed by Kulikov, ▮▮▮▮▮▮▮▮▮▮ has indicated that he will soon be retired. Kremlin leaders may view Kulikov, who only cautiously supports Gorbachev's program of sufficiency and doctrinal revision, as an impediment to significant change in the defense sector.

This annex is Confidential Noforn.

9. NIE 12-90, April 1990, *The Future of Eastern Europe* **(Key Judgments only)**

Director of
Central
Intelligence

~~Confidential~~
~~NOFORN NOCONTRACT~~

The Future of Eastern Europe (C NF)

National Intelligence Estimate

*This Estimate represents the views
of the Director of Central Intelligence
with the advice and assistance of the
US Intelligence Community.*

~~Confidential~~

NIE 12-90
April 1990

Copy 857

9. *(Continued)*

 **Director of Central Intelligence**

~~Confidential~~
~~NOFORN-NOCONTRACT~~

NIE 12-90

The Future of Eastern Europe (C NF)

Information available as of 26 April 1990 was used in the preparation of this National Intelligence Estimate.

The following intelligence organizations participated in the preparation of this Estimate:
The Central Intelligence Agency
The Defense Intelligence Agency
The National Security Agency
The Federal Bureau of Investigation
The Bureau of Intelligence and Research, Department of State
The Office of Intelligence Support, Department of the Treasury

also participating:
The Office of the Deputy Chief of Staff for Intelligence, Department of the Army
The Office of the Director of Naval Intelligence, Department of the Navy
The Assistant Chief of Staff, Intelligence, Department of the Air Force
The Director of Intelligence, Headquarters, Marine Corps

This Estimate was approved for publication by the National Foreign Intelligence Board.

~~Confidential~~
April 1990

9. (*Continued*)

The Future of Eastern Europe (C NF)

- The revolutions in Eastern Europe provide the basis for developing democracy and market economies. But this will not be a linear process, and a number of countries will continue to face political instability, ethnic turmoil, and economic backwardness.

- Even with Western help, East European economies—excluding that of East Germany—are likely to make only modest progress during the next five years.

- The possibility remains of a relapse to authoritarianism, particularly in the Balkans, where the lifting of Communist hegemony threatens to revive old ethnic animosities, civil strife, and interstate tensions. The environmental nightmare will also persist.

- West Europeans are better positioned to lead in shaping the East European future, but the United States has important advantages, among them the desire of East Europeans for a counterweight to Soviet and German influence. (C NF)

9. *(Continued)*

~~Confidential~~
~~NOFORN-NOCONTRACT~~

Key Judgments

Communist party rule in Eastern Europe is finished, and it will not be revived. This and the lifting of Soviet hegemony create new opportunities for establishing representative democracies and self-sustaining market economies. The way will also open for new modes of regional political and economic cooperation. The greatest impetus is the resolve of East Europeans and their leaders to achieve reforms by emulating Western economic and political models. (C NF)

The evolution of the region will make the designation "Eastern Europe" increasingly imprecise, as East-Central European countries—Poland, Czechoslovakia, Hungary, and East Germany—move ahead in closer association with the West, and the Balkans—Bulgaria, Romania, and Albania—settle into a more separate role. Yugoslavia, if it holds together, will continue close ties to the West.[1] (C NF)

In some East European countries, however, we will see political instability and perhaps even a revival of authoritarianism, amidst lingering economic backwardness and reemerging ethnic animosities. Despite Western aid and investment, the East European economies—excluding that of East Germany—are likely to make only uneven progress during the five-year timespan of this Estimate. (C NF)

Ultimately, prospects for healthy democracy will be closely tied to the way in which East Europeans resolve their systemic economic crisis:
- Western aid will be essential, especially in the early stages, to make up the "capital deficit" required to cushion any transition to market economies.
- Such aid will have to be linked to private investment, access to Western markets, and long-term programs designed to develop the skills and institutions necessary for a modern economy, as well as to full mobilization of indigenous resources for investment. (C NF)

The outlook is more promising for the countries in East-Central Europe—particularly East Germany, which will rapidly merge into West Germany's economy. Elsewhere, several countries have good potential as sites for

---

[1] *The Assistant Secretary of State for Intelligence and Research, Department of State, believes that broad regional subgroupings adopted for analytical convenience—such as East-Central Europe and the Balkans—at times obscure the differences between countries.* (C NF)

9. *(Continued)*

Western-owned manufacturing plants with preferential entree to the European Community. The agricultural sector has the capability for quick turnaround. (C-NF)

But the strains of even successful economic reform that is accompanied by inflation and unemployment will test the patience of people fed up with economic hardship and traditionally cynical about political promises. Lingering economic crises and resurgent ethnic divisions may fuel chronic political instability and interstate tensions, notably in the Balkans:

- The major near-term danger to democratization in East-Central Europe is that the whole process will run out of steam as popular euphoria wanes and little substantial economic improvement has occurred. The result would be a paralyzing political impasse or prolonged "muddling through," as in the Third World.

- The worst case scenario—most likely in Romania and Yugoslavia—will not be a return to Communist regimes but a turn to authoritarianism, growing repression of ethnic minorities, civil strife, and even the onset of greater interstate frictions. (C-NF)

Meanwhile, despite the Albanian regime's readiness to use brutal repressive measures to suppress dissent, it is likely that revolution and reform will come to Albania within five years. (C-NF)

The Soviet Union's size, geographical proximity, security concerns, raw materials, and market will continue to make it a major factor in Eastern Europe. But even an aggressive, post-Gorbachev Kremlin leadership would not—or could not—substantially alter the course of events there. Moscow will seek to replace its lost domination of Eastern Europe with the advantages of a broader engagement with Europe as a whole. (C-NF)

A united Germany, however, will move even more assertively into Eastern Europe as an economic and political influence in the vanguard of the European Community. This will be a source of worry for most East Europeans, particularly the Poles. This concern, however, will be cushioned, because Germany will be democratic and integrated into the European Community. German influence will be somewhat diluted as other Western countries also build economic and political ties to the region. Even so, Germany's weight and occasional insensitivity will raise hackles. (C-NF)

East European events will continue to take place against a backdrop of declining relevance for the Warsaw Pact and NATO. The Warsaw Pact as a military alliance is essentially dead, and Soviet efforts to convert it into a

9. *(Continued)*

political alliance will ultimately fail. Most East European states will aspire to build links to Western Europe and will hope that the CSCE process can provide a basis for such broader security arrangements. (C-NF)

East Europeans will continue to seek substantial US participation in their development as a counterweight to the Soviets and Germans. In the region where both world wars and the Cold War began, a democratic, prosperous, and independent Eastern Europe would be an element of stability rather than an object of great power rivalry in the borderlands between East and West. (C-NF)

The End of Empire II
National Secession and Ethnic Conflict in the USSR

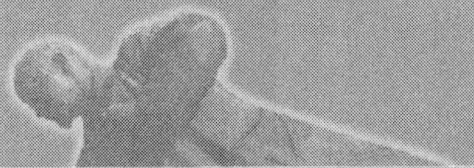

10. 11-18.2-91, September 1991, *The Republics of the Former USSR: The Outlook for the Next Year*

Director of Central Intelligence

~~Secret~~

The Republics of the Former USSR: The Outlook for the Next Year

Special National Intelligence Estimate

This Special National Intelligence Estimate represents the views of the Director of Central Intelligence with the advice and assistance of the US Intelligence Community.

~~Secret~~

SNIE 11-18.2-91
September 1991
Copy 458

10. *(Continued)*

Director of
Central
Intelligence

~~Secret~~
~~NOFORN NOCONTRACT~~

SNIE 11-18.2-91

The Republics of the Former USSR: The Outlook for the Next Year ~~(C-NF)~~

Information available as of 23 September 1991 was used in the preparation of this Estimate.

The following intelligence organizations participated in the preparation of this Estimate:
The Central Intelligence Agency
The Defense Intelligence Agency
The National Security Agency
The Bureau of Intelligence and Research, Department of State
The Office of Intelligence Support, Department of the Treasury

also participating:
The Deputy Chief of Staff for Intelligence, Department of the Army
The Director of Naval Intelligence, Department of the Navy
The Assistant Chief of Staff, Intelligence, Department of the Air Force
The Director of Intelligence, Headquarters, Marine Corps

This Estimate was approved for publication by the National Foreign Intelligence Board.

~~Secret~~
September 1991

10. *(Continued)*

Scope Note

The Republics of the Former USSR: The Outlook for the Next Year (C NF)

This Estimate examines the key factors that will determine developments in the USSR (excluding the Baltic states) over the next year and the possible alternative outcomes. It focuses primarily on the question of interrepublic relations within and outside a union. Although many internal factors will be important determinants of the long-term course of political and economic development of the republics, this Estimate does not attempt to assess internal republic issues in any detail. Such issues will become more important and will be the focus of much of our future estimative work.

10. *(Continued)*

~~Secret~~
~~NOFORN-NOCONTRACT~~

Figure 1
Scenarios for the Republics of the Former USSR Over the Next Year

Confederation	Republics agree on economic union and political confederation. Republics coordinate economic, defense, and foreign policies. Republic governments remain stable despite economic problems. Efforts at market reforms accelerate.
Loose Association	Political/economic reform process continues. Several republics, including Ukraine, go their own way. Loose common market formed. Russia forms limited political association with several republics. Economic problems intensify, threaten legitimacy of some republic leaders.
Disintegration	Minimal economic and political cooperation; confederation collapses. Relations between republics become increasingly hostile. Separatist sentiment grows sharply in Russia. Economic distress deepens sharply, causing large-scale social unrest. Nationalism in republics grows, authoritarian movements gain strength.

~~Secret NOFORN~~ 332463 9-91

10. *(Continued)*

Key Judgments

The USSR and its Communist system are dead. What *ultimately* replaces them will not be known within the next year, but several trends are evident:

- Overall, there will be a high level of instability.

- The economy will get much worse, making a bold approach toward economic reform more necessary but politically riskier and harder to do.

- Russia and Ukraine will make credible attempts at applying democratic political principles at all levels of government and shifting to market economics; most other republics probably will not.

- Ethnic turmoil will increase as nationalism grows and ethnic minorities resist the authority of newly dominant ethnic majorities.

- Defense spending and military forces will be reduced, and republics will participate in collective defense decisions and exercise greater authority over defense matters within their own borders.

- Foreign policy will be increasingly fragmented, with the republics conducting their own bilateral relations and to some extent their own diplomacy in multilateral forums.

- Yel'tsin will be the most powerful national leader; Gorbachev will have only limited power to act independently and could not win an election without Yel'tsin's support.

- The West will face increased pleas for economic assistance from individual republics as well as from the central government, giving Western countries increased opportunity to promote economic and political reform, but increasing requirements for close coordination of Western aid efforts.

Over the next 12 months, the interplay of several variables will be critical to determining whether the new system evolves in a relatively peaceful manner and in a democratic direction. Three variables are especially important:

- The *economy* will be the most critical variable. We do not believe that economic conditions this winter will lead to widespread starvation or massive social unrest. If economic hardships are significantly worse than we expect, however, governments at all levels would lose popular support and authoritarian alternatives would become more attractive.

10. *(Continued)*

Secret

- *Russia* is of paramount importance not only to the fate of the fragile confederal structures that are being built but also to the prospects for democracy and for the transformation to a market economy. Continued progress by Russia in these areas or a relapse into authoritarianism, which is less likely during the next year, will decisively affect the course of reform in the other republics.

- If *Ukraine* chooses the path of independence without participating in a confederation—a strong possibility at this point—the viability of a confederation of other republics would be diminished significantly. This development would increase the risk of ethnic conflict between Ukrainians and the Russian minority in the republic and of disputes with Russia over borders and control of military forces on Ukrainian territory.

Over the next year, we believe that three basic scenarios capture the likely evolution of republic relationships:

- *Confederation:* This scenario is the preferred outcome of Gorbachev and Yel'tsin. There would be a weak central authority but close cooperation among the republics in the political, economic, and military spheres. Russia and Ukraine, at least, would lay the groundwork for democratization and a market economy. Nuclear weapons would be controlled operationally by the center. Lines of authority would be relatively clear, and foreign governments could identify and deal with the appropriate levels of government on different policy questions. This scenario would provide the West the advantage of greater predictability. It would also provide increased confidence that nuclear weapons would remain under centralized control, arms control would remain on track, economic assistance to the republics could be more effectively managed, and the democratization process would advance.

- *Loose Association:* The process of political and economic reform continues, but several republics, including Ukraine, establish independence and participate in a loose common market. Although Russia and many of the associated states try to coordinate foreign and military policy, the republics basically pursue independent policies in these areas. Ukraine and other non-Russian republics probably would agree to removal or elimination of strategic nuclear weapons on their territory. Some republics would try to obtain some control over the tactical nuclear weapons on their territories. The potential for divergent foreign and national security policies would increase, but all the key republics would pursue pro-Western foreign policies, and armed forces would be scaled back significantly. Follow-on arms control negotiations for even deeper cuts in nuclear and conventional forces would go forward, although perhaps

Secret

10. *(Continued)*

more slowly than in a confederation scenario. Implementation and verification of the START and CFE treaties would be complicated. The West would face competing demands for massive assistance, although some mechanism for coordination would exist. (C NF)

- *Disintegration:* Cooperation among the republics breaks down at all levels, and the last remnants of a political center disappear. Nationalism becomes more virulent, and economic conditions become increasingly chaotic. As a result, political stability erodes, and conditions are ripe for rightwing coups and authoritarian government in many republics, including Russia and Ukraine. The disposition of nuclear weapons would be contentious, as some republics seek to assert operational control over nuclear weapons on their territory. There would be an increased risk of such weapons falling into terrorist hands and even of their use within the borders of the former USSR. The West probably would be unable to implement and verify arms control agreements. Republics would attempt to involve the West in interrepublic disputes, while demands for Western aid would continue. (C NF)

Reality is likely to be more complex than any of these scenarios, and elements of all three are likely to be encountered. In our view, it is likely that conditions 12 months from now will most closely resemble the "loose association" scenario. Although the economic situation is grave and the republics are having serious problems in reaching agreement on key economic issues, most understand that they cannot survive on their own. This awareness argues strongly for some kind of economic association that will move, however haltingly, toward a common-market-type system. (C NF)

We believe the "confederation" scenario is less likely because of the unwillingness of many republics to cede some of their political sovereignty and power to a confederal government. Ukraine will be the key: forces supporting independence with some form of cooperation are currently favored to win the December elections, but their strength is eroding and a vote for those favoring separatism is possible. Even if Ukraine is willing to work toward a new union, difficulties over political and economic approaches and burgeoning nationalism will make it difficult for the republics to agree on a confederal political structure. Potentially the most explosive of these forces is unrest among Russian minorities in non-Russian republics. (C NF)

The least likely scenario within the time frame of this Estimate is "disintegration." Beyond the year, however, this scenario becomes more likely if elected governments fail to stem the deterioration of economic conditions. (C NF)

10. (Continued)

**Table 1
Implications of the Scenarios
for Key National Security Issues**

Issues	Scenarios		
	Confederation	Loose Association	Disintegration
Foreign economic relations	Center would coordinate/facilitate assistance. Most aid channeled to republics.	Multiple requests for aid. Republics more eager for aid to overcome economic plight.	Western aid vital, but republics lack means to pay. Internal strife complicates aid efforts.
Military policy	Continued sharp cuts in defense spending. Unified military command. Most republics establish small "national guards."	Ukraine begins setting up republic army. Unitary command retained; increasingly under Russian control. Defense spending cut sharply.	No unified military command. Most republics begin setting up own armies. Defense spending still limited by economic realities.
Foreign policy	Foreign policies proliferate, but generally coordinated. Central leaders remain primary interlocutors with West. Center frames broad issues, but flexibility limited because of need for consensus.	Republics insist on right to conduct own affairs. Most seek to expand contacts with West, integration into regional/international forums. Russia dominates policy.	Numerous foreign policies. Little if any coordination. Ability, desire to enter into good faith agreements doubtful.
Arms control	Prospects for ratifying START, CFE good. Verification unlikely to be disrupted. Readiness to negotiate mutual deep reductions in forces; unilateral cuts likely.	Ukrainian independence poses risks to START, CFE. Negotiations more complicated; verification uncertain. Most republics remain committed to deep force cuts; Russia likely to reduce strategic forces unilaterally.	Renegotiation of START, CFE required. Ability to reach future agreements in doubt. Willingness to make deep force cuts uncertain because of tensions between republics.
Control of nuclear weapons	Unified control system remains, but republics exercise joint control over weapons stationed on their territory.	Confederation members agree to keep centralized control. Ukraine attempts to retain control of some weapons.	Centralized control imperiled. Ukraine, other republics insist on retaining some weapons.

10. *(Continued)*

The United States and other Western countries would have influence on developments across the former USSR in either the "confederation" or "loose association" scenario. Russia and most other republic governments will be highly receptive to Western advice on and technical assistance for internal and external reform in exchange for economic assistance. Western influence would be the most effective in those republics, especially Russia, pushing for democratization and marketization.

If the situation moved toward a "disintegration" scenario, Western opportunities to influence the direction of change would diminish significantly with the growth of xenophobic nationalism and would be limited to those republics, if any, resisting the trend toward authoritarianism. (C NF)

10. *(Continued)*

Secret
NOFORN-NOCONTRACT

Contents

	Page
Scope Note	iii
Key Judgments	v
Discussion	1
Aftermath of the Coup	1
Key Variables	1
Continuing Economic Disarray	1
Popular Mood	4
Republic Cooperation	5
Diminishing Role of the Center	6
Russia's Preeminence	7
Ukraine Heads Toward Independence	8
Three Alternative Scenarios	9
Confederation	9
Loose Association	12
Disintegration	14
Prospects for Scenarios	17
	17

10. *(Continued)*

Discussion

Aftermath of the Coup

The failed coup has created the most favorable opportunity for political democracy and a market economy in the history of the former USSR. The main institutional obstacles to fundamental changes in the system have been severely weakened, and the preconditions for self-determination of republics have been established. (C-NF)

Russia has eclipsed the central government as the most powerful entity in the system, and Yel'tsin is now the country's most influential leader. At the same time, the abortive coup has accelerated the breakup of the union. Republic governments are attempting to assert supreme authority on their territories, but their political legitimacy and their ability to fill the power vacuum left by the weakened center varies widely. Most republics are participating in ongoing negotiations toward political, economic, and military cooperation. (C-NF)

Key Variables

The failure of the coup has not guaranteed the success of democratic change and marketization. Democratic norms and market relations will take many years, if not decades, to develop. In the short term, continued progress toward these goals will depend on developments in several key areas. (C-NF)

Continuing Economic Disarray

Over the course of this Estimate, the accelerated deterioration of economic performance will result in further sharp declines in output, greater financial instability, increasing unemployment, and growing problems in the distribution of food and fuel. Negative economic trends now in train will not permit early reversal of the economic slide, regardless of the economic policies that are undertaken. (C-NF)

Table 2 — *Percent change*
Soviet Official Indicators of Economic Performance in First Half of 1991, as Compared With 1990 [a]

	First Quarter	Second Quarter
GNP	−8	−12
Industrial output	−5	−7
Oil	−9	−10
Natural gas	0.3	0.2
Coal	−11	−11
Agricultural output	−13	−9
Personal incomes [b]	24	63
Retail prices [c]	25	96
Retail sales	0.2	−25

[a] Except as noted, rates of change are calculated from ruble values in prices Soviets claim are constant.
[b] Calculated from ruble values in current prices.
[c] Calculated by dividing retail sales in current prices by sales in prices Soviets claim are constant.

This table is Unclassified.

In the first six months of 1991:
- GNP dropped 10 percent as output fell in most sectors of the economy, in some cases at a very rapid rate. We believe it could decline by approximately 20 percent by the end of the year.
- Widespread shortages affected not only such consumer goods as food and medicine but also vital industrial inputs.
- Projections for the combined central and republic budget deficit for the year climbed to 10 to 15 percent of GNP.
- The inflation rate rapidly approached triple digits.
- Foreign trade contracted sharply; imports dropped 50 percent. (C-NF)

10. *(Continued)*

> **The Private Sector: Bright Spot on the Horizon**
>
> *In contrast to the rest of the economy, the private sector continues to exhibit encouraging signs of growth. During the first half of 1991 the number of industrial enterprises leased from the state grew by over 50 percent to 3,700, and the number of small-scale peasant farms climbed by more than 70 percent to 70,000. New restrictions took a slight toll on cooperatives, but they still numbered 255,000. Nonstate sources providing services to these fledgling enterprises also grew during the first six months, with independent commodity exchanges reaching 300 and commercial banks totaling 1,500. The Soviets report that they have concluded more than 3,000 joint ventures that employ more than 100,000 Soviet citizens, although probably less than one-third are actually operating.* (C NF)

Table 3 — Billion US $
Estimated Soviet Hard Currency Financing Requirements

	1990	First Half 1991	Second Half 1991	1991
Revenues	38.4	17.8	15.8	33.6
Exports	35.6	14.6	13.7	28.3
Other [a]	2.8	3.2	2.1	5.3
Expenditures	63.6	27.8	26.3	54.1
Imports	35.2	12.5	17.7	30.2
Debt service	10.0	7.0	5.2	12.2
Repayment of short-term debt	10.1	5.2	1.3	6.5
Other	8.3	3.1	2.1	5.2
Financing requirement	25.1	10.0	10.5	20.5
Financing sources	25.1	10.0	10.5	20.5
Borrowing	10.5	6.1	8.2	14.3
Official [b]	8.1	6.0	8.0	14.0
Commercial	2.4	0.1	0.2	0.3
Gold sales	4.5	2.0	2.0	4.0
Drawdown of reserves	6.0	1.6	0.3	1.9
Payment arrears	4.1	0.3	0.0	0.3

[a] Includes net inflows from former soft currency partners, invisibles, and asset earnings.
[b] Assuming for 1991 that the Soviets will be able to draw on existing official credit lines to meet general, balance-of-payment financing. This may not be the case, given that most credits are tied to export purchases, some credit lines are tied up with other bureaucratic redtape, and many banks are unwilling to extend loans even with extensive official guarantees.

This table is Noforn.

While the emergence of market-oriented institutions—new cooperatives, commodity exchanges, commercial banks, joint ventures, and a growing entrepreneurial class—is encouraging, they are still too weak and limited to compensate for the negative effects on everyday life of the breakdown of the command economy. (C NF)

The Problems of Divisiveness. The coup has brought even greater disarray to policymaking, thus hindering restoration of macroeconomic stability and rapid implementation of structural reform. Political turmoil at the center and inside the individual republics makes it unlikely that a strong consensus on economic policy will be reached. (C NF)

Maintaining Interrepublic Trade. Declining output places a premium on reducing chokepoints in distribution. Economic linkages are numerous—11 of the 12 republics plus the Baltic states rely on imports from each other for at least 50 percent of their national income. In addition, the IMF estimates that 30 to 40 percent of industrial output consists of products for which there is only one manufacturer. Even foreign trade flows depend on cooperation because key ports and pipelines are concentrated in a few republics. (C NF)

Worsening Hard Currency Woes. The continuing contraction of imports will further diminish vital supplies. Large-scale debt restructuring or rescheduling, if not debt default, appears imminent. The USSR has yet to service about $5 billion in debt over the remainder of the year and already is more than $4 billion in arrears. (C NF)

10. *(Continued)*

Continuing Monetary and Fiscal Instability. The collapse of the center will not neccessarily lead to lower expenditures or a reduction in the deficit. Indeed, budget deficits of both the central and republic governments, lack of constraints on new lending internally, and republican drives for their own currencies will make it difficult to rein in the growth of the money supply. (C NF)

Uncertain Pace of Reforms. A Polish-style shock approach is unlikely anywhere in the short run because of its high costs in terms of unemployment and inflation. Moreover, pressures to reverse the economic decline will push many republic policymakers toward the use of administrative decrees rather than marketizing reforms. (C NF)

Stepped-Up Demilitarization. Military reductions will accelerate, although most political leaders and the High Command wish to avoid a chaotic reduction. Defense industry procurement and production will be hit hard by budget cutbacks and the rising prices of inputs. (C NF)

Differing Impacts on Republics. Russia, thanks to its vast resources, is best positioned to cope with economic crises. It has leverage with the other republics in trading for food and manufactured goods and in seeking foreign goods and financing. On the downside, Russia faces serious distribution problems, especially in getting food to cities in the north, Far East, and the Urals. Despite Russia's vast energy resources, fuel shortages are likely as a result of distribution and labor problems. (C NF)

Elsewhere, the problems will vary:

- Only Kazakhstan, Azerbaijan, and Turkmeniya are net energy exporters among the remaining republics. Moldova, Armenia, Byelorussia, and Georgia would be particularly hard hit by supply disruptions and/or price hikes.

- All republics face reductions in food supplies and other consumer goods as cross-border trade and foreign imports decline. Uzbekistan and Tajikistan are likely to suffer the most. At greatest risk in all republics are pensioners, the poor, and large families, who must rely on poorly stocked state stores because they cannot afford to buy food through higher priced alternative channels.

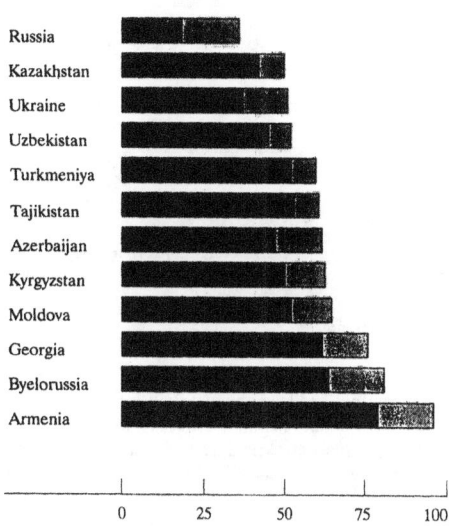

Figure 2
Republic Imports as Percentage of Net Material Product, 1988 [a]

Percent

■ Imports from other republics   ▨ Imports from abroad

[a] These figures are calculated from official Soviet data in domestic administered prices; the value of each republic's imports is divided by the value of its net material product (national income used), a measure that differs from GNP in excluding depreciation and most consumer services.

10. *(Continued)*

Table 4
Oil, Gas, and Coal Balances of the Republics

	Crude Oil	Petroleum Products	Natural Gas	Coal
Russia	X	X	X	O
Ukraine	O	O	O	X
Byelorussia	O	X	O	O
Kazakhstan	X	O	O	X
Moldova	—	O	O	O
Armenia	—	O	O	O
Azerbaijan	O	X	O	O
Georgia	O	O	O	=
Kyrgyzstan	—	O	O	O
Tajikistan	—	O	O	O
Turkmeniya	X	=	X	O
Uzbekistan	O	O	X	O

Note: X = net exporter
O = net importer
— Neither imports nor exports because it has no refining capacity
= production equals consumption.

This table is Unclassified.

Table 5
Soviet Food Situation: Surplus or Deficit of Selected Foods [a]

	Meat	Milk [b]	Grain [c]	Potatoes [c]	Vegetables
Russia	—	—	—	—	—
Ukraine	+	+	+	+	+
Byelorussia	+	+	—	+	+
Kazakhstan	+	+	+	Even	—
Moldova	+	+	—	—	+
Armenia	—	—	—	+	+
Azerbaijan	—	—	—	—	+
Georgia	—	—	—	—	+
Kyrgyzstan	Even	—	—	—	+
Tajikistan	—	—	—	Even	—
Turkmeniya	—	—	—	—	—
Uzbekistan	—	—	—	—	+

[a] Based on official Soviet statistics for production and consumption of major food products for 1988. Pluses indicate that area produces more than sufficient quantities based on historical consumption levels. Minuses indicate an area produces less.
[b] Includes butter.
[c] Adjusted for feed use.

This table is Unclassified.

- Declining output and lower budgets will cause unemployment in all republics. Ukraine—like Russia—has extensive defense industries vulnerable to cuts in defense spending.

While the economic news is mostly gloomy and many observers in and out of the former USSR fear catastrophe, in our view, conditions are not likely to lead to widespread famine, epidemics, or numerous deaths from freezing. While pockets of extreme economic distress—including malnutrition—could emerge, distribution will be more of a problem than production. Absent development of adversarial relations among the republics, however, the food and fuel crises this winter should be manageable.

Popular Mood
Public euphoria over the collapse of the centralized Communist state has lent legitimacy to some republic governments and bought them some time to grapple with economic problems. Others, most notably Georgia and Azerbaijan, have been thrown into disarray because of public displeasure with their leaders' posture during the coup. Legitimacy of some governments will increase as elections are held in several republics and localities this fall. This will probably be sufficient to sustain these governments politically over the next year.

How long popular support for elected governments and democratic principles will endure under harsh economic conditions is highly uncertain. Voter support for Yel'tsin and other democrats, as well as popular opposition to the attempted coup, were based largely on antipathy toward Communism. Now that democratically elected leaders are being held accountable for the economy, their public support will erode as conditions worsen. Political forces arguing for authoritarian solutions will gain increased support in Russia during the year, but not political power.

10. *(Continued)*

> *Soviet Food Supplies: Between Feast and Famine*
>
> *The decline in Soviet food production this year is aggravating food shortages, and food supplies will diminish in the months ahead. Widespread famine appears unlikely, however, barring a much more serious breakdown in the economic system. On the supply side:*
>
> - *This year's estimated grain crop of 185 million tons is down 50 million tons from last year but is only about 10 million tons below the average harvest for the last decade.*
>
> - *Soviet data show that overall food production was down about 8 percent in the first six months of the year, as compared with the same period in 1990. Output of potatoes and vegetables will be higher than last year, but the production of meat and milk will be down for the second consecutive year.*
>
> - *Imports of substantial quantities of foodstuffs and feed continue despite the hard currency crunch.*
>
> - *Republics, cities, and enterprises have been lining up bilateral barter agreements for food in exchange for consumer goods, energy, and raw materials. (C NF)*
>
> *Nevertheless, severe food shortages probably will develop in some localities, due largely to distribution problems:*
>
> - *The disintegration of authority and increasing republic autarky have left officials preoccupied with political solutions and requests for Western food assistance at the expense of the harvesting and handling of this year's farm production.*
>
> - *Widespread panic buying and hoarding the last two years have left wholesale and retail inventories of food at their lowest levels in several years. Although this implies private stocks are up, they are unevenly distributed.*
>
> - *Hoarding is also occurring in the countryside and by various republics. Farms and local officials are refusing to sell grain because they think prices may soon be raised or decontrolled.*
>
> - *Ukraine and several other republics have banned the export of harvested grain and other foodstuffs, at least until internal needs are met. Many republics have erected border customs posts to control the movement of goods. (C NF)*

Public readiness for a market economy is even less certain. Although opinion polls show rising support for marketization, popular understanding of this concept and willingness to endure the pain remain in doubt. It is very likely that large-scale public demonstrations and work stoppages will occur if major market reform measures are pursued vigorously. (C NF)

The public's disdain for Communism has seriously weakened the party, but it has not yet destroyed it. In parts of Central Asia and the Transcaucasus, where democratic movements are weak, Communist Party structures are being transformed into instruments of control under the banner of nationalism. At the center and in the Slavic republics, Communists will continue to lose their influence over policymaking, although in the short term they may retain considerable influence over policy implementation. (C NF)

Republic Cooperation

Despite the "independence fever" that has swept the USSR, the "10 + 1" process recognizes the need to maintain some links and a mechanism to facilitate continuing cooperation.[1] Interrepublic cooperation

---
[1] 10 + 1 refers to the agreement among 10 republics plus Gorbachev, ratified at the recent Congress of People's Deputies, to accept the interim governmental structures and to move toward cooperation on political, economic, and military issues. (U)

10. *(Continued)*

Table 6
Possible Ethnic Flashpoints
Over the Next Year

	Potential for Significant Violence		
	High	Medium	Low
Moldova			
Ethnic Ukrainian and Russian minorities	X		
Turkic Gagauz minority	X		
Central Asia			
Ethnic Russian minorities in Uzbekistan, Tajikistan, and Kyrgyzstan		X	
Ethnic Russians in Kazakhstan			X
Islamic fundamentalism			X
Transcaucasus			
Armenian enclave of Nagorno-Karabakh	X		
Azeri exclave of Nakhichivan'			X
Nationalist opposition to Azerbaijan government	X		
Opposition to Georgian President Gamsakhurdia	X		
Ukraine			
Ethnic Russians in Crimea, eastern Ukraine			X
Ethnic Poles in western Ukraine			X
Uniate-Orthodox religious tensions			X
Russia			
Separatists in Tataria		X	
Chechen-Ingush nationalists		X	
Ossetian unification movement	X		
Access to Kaliningrad through Lithuania			X

This table is Confidential Noforn.

also is required to contain such explosive social and political issues as the status and rights of ethnic minorities and the permanence of republic borders. Interethnic conflict is on the rise and will be aggravated significantly if the republics accelerate their unilateral moves toward independence. The sorting out of relations between the republics will take most of the decade, however. (C NF)

Diminishing Role of the Center

Whatever cooperative arrangements emerge, the republics do not want to re-create a central government with independent power. *Central institutions will be vehicles for coordinating interrepublic cooperation and for reaching and carrying out collective decisions.* Over the next year:

- A central government will probably play a coordinating role in the area of defense, with republics acting collectively through a state-council-like structure to determine defense policy. Republics will attempt to oversee the activities of central forces within their borders. Some republics such as Ukraine will establish territorial defense forces of their own.

- A central government will probably continue to take the lead on broad foreign policy and national security issues. The republics, especially Russia, will exert greater influence on all matters, and they will conduct their own policies toward countries and regions. They will also take increasing responsibility for foreign economic relations. Mixed signals and contradictory policies are sure to result.

- The center's economic role will depend on the outcome of debate over the proposed economic union. Most decisions on monetary policy, debt repayment, and other key questions probably will be coordinated, but there are strong differences between and within republics over the powers of the center on these questions. The center will be able to issue directives or impose an economic reform blueprint, but only as the agent of the larger republics. However, enforcement of republic compliance with these directives will be problematical, given the compromise nature of the central structures. (C NF)

Gorbachev's power has diminished greatly along with that of the center. He will probably play an important role during the next year as facilitator of the coordination process and mediator of disputes between republics. His international stature also makes it likely he will remain a conduit to the West. As long as

10. *(Continued)*

Secret

**Table 7
Competing Visions of Economic Union**

	Yavlinskiy	Saburov	Shatalin
Degree of unity	Federation of most former republics. Full members agree to all treaty provisions. Associate members accept coordinated monetary, budget, and tax policy.	Federation of core former republics. Others may participate as partial members in a customs union.	Economic community of former republics and some East European states. Members choose full, associate, or observer status.
Provisions for union market	One external customs. Goal is free movement of goods, capital, and labor. Economic laws harmonized.	Goal is one external customs, free movement of goods. Economic laws harmonized.	Goal is one external customs, free movement of goods, and perhaps labor. Economic laws harmonized.
Monetary policy	Ruble is common currency. Members may introduce own currency by special agreement.	Ruble is common currency for core states. Other members may have own by special agreement.	Members may have own currencies.
Fiscal policy	One tax system for all members. Limited budget for center formed from members' dues.	Members coordinate independent tax policies. Fund some national programs.	Members encouraged to coordinate independent tax policies. Fund few activities for center.
Price policy	Gradual, coordinated liberalization. Interim maintenance of state orders.	Phased transition to world prices.	Not specified.
Foreign economic relations	Foreign debt serviced jointly, new debt incurred individually or jointly.	Republics service foreign debt and receive new assistance. Republics conduct trade.	Republics may service debt alone or jointly. Each conducts trade.

This table is Confidential Noforn.

he stays aligned with Yel'tsin and the republics remain committed to working within a common institutional framework, he will be viewed as a valuable player and will continue to have some influence on the course of events. Non-Russian republics may also consider Gorbachev a potential counterweight to Yel'tsin, but a serious split between the two would be likely to spell the end of what remains of Gorbachev's power. Gorbachev could not win an election for the presidency once a new constitution is written without strong support from Yel'tsin and other key republic leaders. (C NF)

Russia's Preeminence
Russia is critical to the outcome of the ongoing transformation. There can be no confederation without Russia, and, without progress toward democracy in Russia, the prospects for its development in the remaining republics are significantly diminished. Without a healthy Russian economy, the prospects for economic recovery elsewhere are bleak. (C NF)

Political trends in Russia favor fundamental change. Yel'tsin has done more than other republic leaders to strengthen democratic institutions, and his advisers and allies have a record of support for democracy and economic reform. Moreover, his popularity and dynamic style of leadership make bold action to propel the republic forward more likely in the next year. (C NF)

The depth and durability of the Russian leadership's commitment to democracy and market principles has yet to be tested, however, and some important uncertainties remain:
- Yel'tsin's propensity to rule by decree has raised concerns among fellow democrats over his commitment to constitutional order and due process.
- Although Yel'tsin and most other leaders of the republic have broken with the Communist Party, their centralizing instincts could die hard. (C NF)

10. *(Continued)*

> ### What if Yel'tsin Leaves the Scene?
>
> **In Russia**
> Yel'tsin's absence from the Russian leadership would result in factional infighting among democrats and a slowing of reform measures that require a strong leader to keep the public on board. Russian institutions have had time to sink some roots, however, and the coup deepened the democratic direction of Russian policies. Any successor would probably not change course but would almost certainly have greater difficulty reaching a consensus and implementing reform throughout Russia.
>
> Vice President Rutskoy would assume the presidency until new elections are held. Who would win an election is not clear. St. Petersburg Mayor Sobchak ranks a distant second in most recent public opinion polls, but his popularity would probably rise with Yel'tsin gone because of name recognition. Other officials such as Rutskoy, former Russian Prime Minister Silayev, KGB Chief Bakatin, Moscow Mayor Popov and Movement for Democratic Reform leader Aleksandr Yakovlev have registered in polls, but all lack Yel'tsin's grassroots support.
>
> **In the Economy**
> The loss of Yel'tsin's guiding hand would slow current negotiations to preserve an economic union as well as Russia's own progress toward economic reform. It would also make implementing austerity measures much more politically risky. Without Yel'tsin's commitment to maintaining interrepublic economic relations—including a single currency and common tariffs and monetary policy—forceful advocates of autonomy within Russia would push for the republic's independence.
>
> **At the Center**
> Yel'tsin's absence from the political scene would probably raise Gorbachev's standing—as the only other leader with significant national recognition—but without Yel'tsin behind him, he may have a more difficult time working out agreements with other republic leaders. Yel'tsin's cooperation with Gorbachev has been a driving force behind progress on the union treaty. Without Yel'tsin, voices in the Russian government advocating a "go it alone" strategy may gain prominence and Russia may not have the same ability to jawbone other republic leaders into supporting some union structures.

The growing assertiveness of "autonomous" regions, particularly Tatarskaya, threatens the governability and cohesiveness of the Russian Republic. Their status has been problematic for Yel'tsin since the beginning of the union treaty process. When local elections occur in Russia, the leaders of these regions are likely to grow even more assertive as they seek to satisfy their constituents. Some conflict with Yel'tsin's appointed plenipotentiaries is certain. Local leaders will almost certainly try to exploit a weakening of Yel'tsin's political position or that of Russia vis-a-vis other republics.

Russian nationalism, already a formidable force in republic politics, will grow over the next year and would be fanned by mistreatment of Russian minorities in other republics. Nationalist extremists are currently a small element on the Russian political spectrum, but their influence may grow markedly if public support for the current government erodes more than we anticipate. An increase in the political influence of antidemocratic Russian nationalism would heighten the fear in the other republics of resurgent Russian imperialism.

Ukraine Heads Toward Independence
The durability and effectiveness of a new union depends heavily on the role of Ukraine. Kravchuk and other Ukrainian leaders seem inclined toward participating in a confederation agreement, but they are

10. *(Continued)*

under strong pressure from nationalist forces to pursue independence. As the 1 December presidential election and referendum on independence approach, Kravchuk will look for opportunities to demonstrate his commitment to protecting Ukrainian sovereignty, even if it means publicly supporting withdrawal from the "10 + 1" process and going for complete independence.

Ukraine is almost certain to approve the independence resolution in December. We do not know how complete the break with Russia and other republics will be. If Kravchuk wins the presidential election, Ukraine will probably agree to at least associate status in a confederation and continue a measure of cooperation on economic and military issues. A sharper break would probably occur if his opponent wins and would have serious consequences:

- A disruption of trade links between Ukraine and other republics would have a major impact. Ukraine depends on Russia for imports of crude oil and other energy supplies. Russia and other republics depend heavily on Ukraine for food.

- Opposition to total independence by Russians, Russified Ukrainians, and other ethnic groups living in Ukraine would pose a serious threat to political stability, raise border issues with Russia, spark violent incidents, and at a minimum make bilateral cooperation more difficult.

- Disagreement over control of military assets on Ukrainian territory probably would intensify. Ukraine would probably reverse its position on removing nuclear weapons from the republic and demand that they be put under command and control of the Ukrainian military. It would also take steps toward creating a large republic standing army, and demand that all union forces withdraw from the republic.

Three Alternative Scenarios

The large number of variables could eventually lead to widely differing political, economic, and military outcomes in the former USSR. We believe three scenarios—*confederation, loose association,* and *dis-*

The Heated Presidential Race in Ukraine

The presidential election scheduled for 1 December in Ukraine has spawned a heated race between parliamentary chairman Leonid Kravchuk and his nationalist opponents. Kravchuk is currently the frontrunner. Although tainted by his Communist past and his perceived indecisiveness during the coup attempt, his strengths as a consensus builder and astute politician have kept his position strong. Moreover, his vision of an independent Ukraine as part of a loose economic association and a collective security arrangement probably appeals to the majority of the voters. Kravchuk wants to bridge regional differences between the Russified east and the nationalistic west. He could fall behind the nationalist momentum, however, and become vulnerable to a more charismatic, nationalist opponent.

The leading challenger, endorsed by the nationalist organization Rukh, is Vyacheslav Chornovil. He and other nationalist candidates support the goal of complete independence within 18 months. Chornovil has expressed reluctance to hand over to Russia nuclear weapons situated on Ukrainian territory. The increasing strength of anti-Communist, separatist sentiment since the coup has bolstered Chornovil's prospects, but he and other nationalist candidates, such as Lev Lukyanenko, do not have as much support in the populous eastern and southern Ukraine.

---

integration—capture the range of possibilities over the next year or so. Elements of all three are likely to be encountered.

Confederation

This scenario is the preferred outcome of Gorbachev and Yel'tsin. The leading republics agree on and implement a workable framework for close cooperation. The framework allows each republic to set its

10. *(Continued)*

> **Indicators of Confederation**
>
> - Agreements between 10 republic leaders and Gorbachev on economic union and economic reform.
> - Rapid movement toward/agreement on constitution establishing confederation's political structures and power-sharing arrangements.
> - Nationalist elements in republics fail to press demands for independence, agree to abide by terms of confederation.
> - Yel'tsin and Gorbachev continue to cooperate.
> - Economic problems do not intensify dramatically; no large-scale labor unrest.
>
> *Confidential Noforn*

own basic political and economic course, but it provides for a coordinated approach to monetary and financial policy, interrepublic trade, debt repayment, foreign affairs, and defense. Lines of authority are clarified, and foreign governments can identify and deal with the appropriate levels of government on different policy questions. Republic governments remain stable through the food and fuel crises this winter, and democratic institutions and practices in Slavic areas at least gain strength.

Internal Implications. Economic. While the republics would suffer the consequences of economic trends evident before the abortive coup, the damage would be contained and the longer-term prospects for stabilizing and reforming the economy would improve:

- The republics would not enact disruptive measures, such as tariffs, exorbitant energy and commodity price hikes, and cancellation of contracts.

- Some control over the money supply would be ensured, with a single currency remaining the means of interrepublic exchange. If republic currencies were allowed, a union banking agreement would restrain the printing of money.

- Coordination of fiscal policies could begin to arrest the growth of budget deficits. Agreement on republic and local tax contributions to the center would facilitate narrowing the central budgetary gap.

- Some republics—particularly Russia—would press ahead more vigorously toward a market economy, although Polish-style "shock therapy" would not be tried in the next year.

- Some old-style administrative approaches aimed at stabilization, including state orders and wage and price controls, would remain, but the overall environment for foreign investment and membership in international economic organizations would be improved.

Political. This scenario would provide the best prospects for political stability and, therefore, democratic change throughout the confederation. Interrepublic cooperation would help prevent interethnic tensions from escalating into violent conflicts within or between republics.

An agreement to establish a confederal political structure would enable a central government to continue to exist and do business with foreign governments, but the center would not dominate the republics. The sphere of central responsiblities would be greatly reduced, as would the central bureaucracy and the power of the presidency. The authority of these institutions would be enhanced by popular elections.

Russia would be the most powerful state in the confederation. All major policies of the center would require Russia's concurrence, but the other republic members would try to use central structures to check Russian dominance.

Gorbachev, in alliance with Yel'tsin, would be a key player in the negotiations on the economic and political framework for interrepublic cooperation, at least until elections are held. As head of the interim government, he and his foreign ministry would remain the chief interlocutors with foreign governments, but he would not have the power to make major foreign policy decisions without the republics' concurrence.

Military. Military reform would accelerate. Under this scenario, a common decisionmaking structure would allow for a reasonably coherent and controlled

10. *(Continued)*

Figure 3
System Confederation: "The Union of Sovereign States"

force reduction as well as restructuring. A unified command over strategic and general purpose forces would be retained, preserving the stability of the armed forces and providing the strongest guarantees for the security of nuclear weapons. The center would also retain operational control of smaller air and naval forces and rapid reaction ground forces, backed up by republic-controlled reserves.

The republics probably would spend less of their own money in establishing their own military forces. Although the military under a unified command would have some influence in government circles, they would not be able to protect the armed forces from drastic reductions.

Implications for the West. This scenario would provide a more predictable path to the future. A new confederal union would remain a major military power, but would be strongly committed to reducing the defense burden through negotiations and unilateral cuts. The prospects would be good for ratifying the

CFE and START agreements, as would the chances that implementation and verification of arms control agreements would not be disrupted. (C-NF)

The West inevitably would have to deal with a proliferation of foreign policies as republics seek representation in international forums. Under this scenario, however, it is less likely that these foreign policies would work at cross-purposes. (C-NF)

The smaller threat of political instability and interrepublic conflict under this scenario would reduce but not eliminate the risks to Western engagement. As economic performance continued to decline, at least in the short term, the outlook for Western trade and investment would remain poor. Debt default might be averted, but large-scale debt restructuring would be likely. (C-NF)

With demands for aid increasing from all republics, Western governments would have to channel most assistance directly to them. A union agreement, however, would facilitate interrepublic coordination in the allocation and distribution of assistance and make the economic and political climate more favorable for foreign investment. (C-NF)

Under this scenario, the republics would exert their independence in bilateral relations but would allow the central foreign ministry to represent their interests in arms control and other multilateral republic matters. They would retain responsibility for framing the discussion of foreign policy questions in interrepublic bodies, for communicating Western proposals to those bodies, and for negotiating with Western partners. While Gorbachev remains president, his experience, international stature, and skills at persuasion would give him considerable influence in determining the outcome of collective decisions. (C-NF)

Loose Association

In this scenario, the process of political and economic reform continues, but several republics—most important, Ukraine—go their own way. The republics—including some that have opted for independence—form a loose common market, but implementation of common economic policies is hindered by the absence of strong political ties among all the republics. Varying degrees of political cooperation exist, however: several republics, most likely those of central Asia and possibly Byelorussia, agree to association with Russia. Although Russia and the associated states try to coordinate foreign and military policy, the republics basically pursue independent policies in these areas. (C-NF)

Indicators of Loose Association:

- *Agreement is reached on forming a loose economic union.*
- *Russia, other republics, conclude series of bilateral agreements on economic and political cooperation.*
- *Strong vote for Ukrainian independence in 1 December referendum leads to severing of ties to confederation.*
- *Chornovil defeats Kravchuk in presidential election.*

Confidential Noforn

Internal Implications. Economic. The republics would reach broad agreements covering fiscal and monetary targets, a common currency, and foreign debt repayment. The republics are unlikely, however, to reach consensus on the details needed to effectively carry out all of the provisions of the common market. Trade disruptions and shortages would intensify because of the lack of strong enforcement mechanisms, the differing pace of economic reforms within each republic, and growing republic protectionism. Under these circumstances, republic administrative decrees aimed at stabilization would increase; necessary, but unpopular, steps toward marketization would slow. (C-NF)

Political. Russian dominance of any political association would heighten fears among other republic leaders of Russian hegemonism. Even if Russia did not behave toward these republics in a heavy-handed fashion, fears of Russian domination would jeopardize the long-term survival of this association. The legitimacy of some republic leaders would become more

10. *(Continued)*

Figure 4
Republic Distribution of Soviet Strategic Offensive Forces

fragile as they failed to halt their republics' economic slide. This would lead to increased popular discontent and pressures to adopt more authoritarian measures. Gorbachev's political role would be minimal. (C NF)

Military. Russia and the associated republics could agree to smaller centrally commanded strategic and general purpose forces, but the non-Russian republics would expand the "national guard" units under their control to counterbalance a Russian-dominated army. Ukraine would press ahead with forming its own armed forces and would seek removal of central forces remaining in the republic. Ukrainian and other non-Russian republic leaders probably would agree to removal or destruction of strategic weapons on their territory. Some republic leaders might insist on obtaining control of the tactical nuclear arsenal on their territories as a hedge against Russian imperialism. (C NF)

Implications for the West. Western governments would be dealing mostly with Russia and Ukraine as those republics tried to develop democratic governments and market economies. The other republics, however, would be sensitive to Western, Russian, or Ukrainian conduct that suggested their interests could be ignored. Because the republics would insist on

10. *(Continued)*

conducting a significant portion of their own foreign affairs, there would be greater difficulty in negotiating and ensuring compliance with international agreements. At the same time, most republics would be eager to expand their contacts and cooperation with the West, primarily for economic reasons. The individual republics would be even more eager for economic assistance given the difficulty of negotiating effective mechanisms for interrepublic economic cooperation. They would also seek membership in regional and international organizations and pursue collective security agreements. (C-NF)

Russia and its associates would adhere to arms control agreements and pursue follow-on negotiations aimed at ensuring even deeper force cuts. Ukraine's decision to build up its own forces would endanger the implementation and verification of existing treaties. (C-NF)

Disintegration

Efforts to form a new confederation and an economic community fail. Interrepublic cooperation is modest and bilateral. Animosities between republics rise sharply, and, as nationalism becomes a more virulent force, threats and counterthreats crop up over border disputes. Separatist movements in the republics gain popular strength, and the integrity of the Russian Republic is undermined as some ethnic minorities pursue their independence. Republics assume control over economic resources and establish strict border and tariff controls, but leaders cannot cope with mounting economic and political problems. Nationalist, authoritarian politicians and political parties gain strength. The potential for rightwing coups in key republics increases. (C-NF)

Internal Implications. Economic. The republics would be left to their own devices. For a short time, Russian leaders would have the popular support and political will to attempt economic reforms, but serious food shortages exacerbated by barriers to interrepublic trade would soon erode their legitimacy. Other republic leaders would be overwhelmed by economic problems and look outward for assistance. Central Asian republics would look toward the Middle East for help. The success of efforts in Russia and the other democratically oriented republics would depend largely on the conclusion of trade agreements with the West

---

Indicators of Disintegration:

- *Negotiations on political and economic cooperation collapse.*
- *Economic conditions deteriorate sharply; numerous incidents of food shortages, perhaps famine, provoke large-scale strikes.*
- *Rivalries between republic leaders intensify sharply; threats and counterthreats exchanged over treatment of national minorities within republics.*
- *Sharp growth in popularity of authoritarian political parties/movements calling for establishment of authoritarian regimes within republics.*

---

and the other breakaway republics, but negotiations probably would be prolonged. The pressure of time would be intense, however, because of mounting economic chaos. (C-NF)

Political. The inability of the Russian leadership to hold the confederation together would encourage national groups within its borders to assert their sovereignty in a scramble to seize control of critical economic resources. At the same time, Russian minorities in other republics, fearing hostile treatment, would attempt to migrate or seek unification with Russia, thereby increasing the prospects for civil strife. (C-NF)

Xenophobic Russian nationalism would gain in strength as economic conditions worsened and as societal tensions increased. Leaders in the less democratically oriented republics of Central Asia, confronted by popular unrest and economic disorder, would quickly institute even more authoritarian measures. Over time, the fragmentation of the former USSR into a number of independent republics, some

10. *(Continued)*

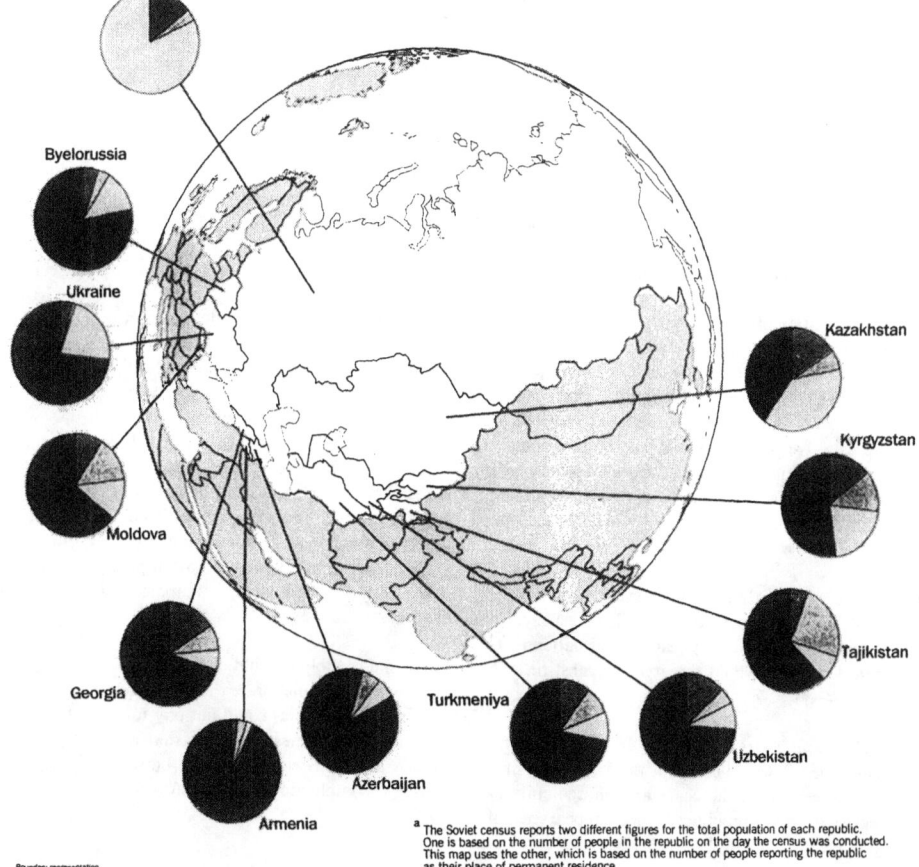

Figure 5
Comparative Nationalities, by Republic

Republic	Russian (percent)	Minor Nationality (percent)			Total Republic Population (thousands)[a]
Russia	-	82	Tatar	4	15	147,002
Byelorussia	78	13	Polish	4	5	10,149
Ukraine	73	22	Jewish	1	4	51,449
Moldova	64	13	Ukrainian	14	9	4,332
Georgia	70	6	Armenian	8	16	5,396
Armenia	93	2	Azeri	3	2	3,304
Azerbaijan	83	6	Armenian	6	5	7,020
Kazakhstan	40	38	German	6	16	16,463
Turkmeniya	72	9	Uzbek	9	10	3,512
Tajikistan	62	8	Uzbek	24	6	5,090
Uzbekistan	71	8	Tajik	5	16	19,808
Kyrgyzstan	52	21	Uzbek	13	14	4,258

[a] The Soviet census reports two different figures for the total population of each republic. One is based on the number of people in the republic on the day the census was conducted. This map uses the other, which is based on the number of people reporting the republic as their place of permanent residence.

10. *(Continued)*

of them politically unstable and hostile toward one another, would increase the likelihood of serious civil conflict.

Military. Russia would assume immediate control of the conventional and nuclear forces on its territory and probably would try to do so over some assets in other republics. Non-Russian republics would move quickly to establish their own armed forces for protection against Russia, against one another, or against other states along their borders. Economic difficulties would limit their size and capabilities, however. Russia would still be under strong pressure to continue to cut military spending in an effort to overcome its economic problems.

The risk of serious civil conflict would rise as the republics attempted to assert authority over military installations and units within their territory. Many commanders and soldiers would have to decide to whom they owed their allegiance; their willingness to submit to a new authority or lay down their arms would be an open question.

The disposition of nuclear weapons would be a much more contentious issue in this scenario. As each republic looked to its own security, some republics with nuclear weapons would seek to assert operational control over them, rather than turning them all over to Russia. Authoritarian political leaders, unconstrained by central authority or even a loose confederation, would view nuclear weapons as a means of enhancing the status of their republic in the eyes of the world.

The probability of military intervention in politics would increase as political instability deepened. An alliance between military leaders and nationalists would form that would threaten the constitutional order.

Implications for the West. The fragmentation of the former USSR would confront the West with grave dangers because of the chaos and unpredictability of events within the republics. The disappearance of reliable central control over nuclear weapons in some republics, as well as uncertainty over their disposition, would increase the prospect of nuclear weapons falling into terrorist hands. The risk would mount of an accident involving such weapons within the former boundaries of the USSR or even their use in interrepublic conflict. Use against the outside world would be much less likely. The danger that nuclear materials and expertise would find their way to other states seeking to develop nuclear weapons would become greater.

Conflict within or between republics would pose serious risks for the West because violence could easily spill across international boundaries. Long-quiescent border disputes probably would reappear, and the proliferation of republic armies would increase the likelihood that states would seek to resolve such disputes by force. Western countries and international organizations, such as the UN and CSCE, would be drawn into efforts to end such disputes given the possible stakes involved.

This scenario would make implementing and verifying arms control agreements, particularly CFE, virtually impossible. The West would confront numerous uncoordinated foreign policies rather than one, and the willingness of many of the new states to enter into agreements in good faith would be questionable. Agreements on conventional forces in Europe probably would have to be renegotiated. It is doubtful, moreover, that the former members of the USSR could reach an agreement on reallocation of forces to comply with the CFE force ceilings. The START agreement would also be endangered if Ukraine, Byelorussia, or Kazakhstan attempted to retain control over strategic nuclear weapons on their territory.

All the republics would call on the West to provide assistance to ameliorate the great economic hardships, but most republics could not pay for it and many would have domestic policies that would discourage providing it. Strife within and between republics would complicate aid efforts.

10. *(Continued)*

Prospects for Scenarios

Reality is likely to be more complex than any of three scenarios we have discussed in this Estimate. We believe, however, that they capture the broad range of possibilities. In our view, it is likely that conditions 12 months from now will most closely resemble the "loose association" scenario. Although the economic situation is grave and the republics are having serious problems in reaching agreement on key economic issues, most understand that they cannot survive on their own. This awareness argues strongly for some kind of economic association that will move, however haltingly, toward a common market-type system.

We believe the "confederation" scenario is less likely. Ukraine will be the key: forces supporting confederation are currently favored to win the December elections, but their strength may be eroding and an upset is possible. Even if Ukraine is willing to work toward a new union, centrifugal forces may overwhelm the republics. Potentially the most explosive of these forces is unrest among the Russian minorities living outside the Russian Republic. A new center could offer little in the way of incentives to gain republic support. Although many republics would like to see a counterweight to Russia, they have no interest in buying into a strengthened center to get it.

The least likely scenario within the time frame of this Estimate is "disintegration." Most republic governments have sufficient public support to sustain themselves through the difficult months ahead, and they understand the need for continued cooperation with other republics. Forces of reaction are too weak at present and their political prospects over the next year are poor unless an economic catastrophe occurs. Beyond the next year, however, this scenario becomes more likely if elected governments fail to stem the deterioration of economic conditions.

Receptivity to Western influence is greater than ever before. Central, republic, and even local leaders are eager for emergency economic assistance, and for Western help and expertise in laying the foundations of a market economy, building democratic political institutions, and reducing the burden of defense.

Over the next year, the possibility of a catastrophic winter poses the most serious threat to the successful transformation of the old system. Western food assistance, targeted at key population centers and effectively distributed, would reduce the danger that popular anger over food shortages would destabilize democratic governments. If widely visible, such assistance could promote goodwill toward the West.

Getting the aid to where it is most needed, however, will not be an easy undertaking. Potentially serious shortages this winter of food, fuel, and medicines are scattered over large geographic areas. Well-documented problems with communications, transportation, and storage, as well as bureaucratic inefficiencies and black-marketeering, will hamper assistance efforts.

Western policies that would alleviate economic hardship and increase hope for better times ahead could help stave off further political fragmentation and instability. These include: a coordinated debt restructuring package, new credits, accelerated steps toward IMF membership, and a ruble stabilization fund.

10. *(Continued)*

~~Secret~~

Figure 6
The Republics on the Issues

● Yes
▲ No
■ Unknown

	Armenia	Azerbaijan	Byelorussia	Georgia	Kazakhstan	Kyrgyzstan	Moldova	Russia	Tajikistan	Turkmeniya	Ukraine	Uzbekistan
Political Issues												
Democratic reformers in control	●	▲	▲	▲	▲	●	●	●	▲	▲	●	▲
Commitment to free elections	●	▲	▲	●	■	●	●	●	■	▲	●	▲
Independence declared	▲	●	●	●	▲	●	●	▲	●	▲	●	●
Commitment to human rights for all republic residents	▲	▲	●	▲	●	●	●	●	■	▲	●	▲
Economic Issues												
Commitment to market reforms	●	■	▲	▲	●	●	●	●	▲	▲	▲	▲
Independent reform program emerging	●	▲	●	▲	●	●	●	● [a]	▲	▲	●	▲
Commitment to independent monetary system	▲	▲	▲	●	▲	▲	▲	▲	▲	▲	●	▲
Independent foreign economic relations	●	●	●	●	●	●	●	●	●	●	●	●
Foreign Policy/Security Issues												
Independent foreign policy	●	●	●	●	▲	■	●	●	▲	▲	●	■
Declaration of nuclear free status	▲	▲	●	●	▲	▲	●	▲	▲	●	●	▲
Declaration of military neutrality	▲	▲	●	▲	▲	▲	▲	▲	▲	▲	●	▲
Seeking membership in regional/ international bodies	●	●	●	●	▲	▲	●	▲	▲	●	●	▲
Stability Factors												
Serious ethnic unrest	●	●	▲	●	▲	●	●	▲	▲ [b]	▲	▲	●
Strong local separatist movements	▲	●	▲	●	■	▲	●	●	▲	▲	▲	▲
Current conflict with other republics	●	●	▲	▲	▲	●	▲	▲	▲ [c]	▲	▲	■
Millitary Issues												
Independent defense ministry	●	●	▲	●	▲	▲	●	●	▲	▲	●	●
Forming own military	●	●	d	●	●	▲	●	● [e]	▲	▲	●	●
Claims to military installations on territory	■	■	▲	●	▲	▲	■	▲	▲	▲	●	▲

[a] Russia's precoup reform program is "on hold" pending discussions on new center-republic institutions but important reform elements, for example, land reform, are already in place.

[b] Several areas of serious unrest, but these are localized and do not threaten Russia as a whole.

[c] Ethnic and territorial tensions exist, but so far no direct clashes or conflicts.

[d] Internal troops only.

[e] At this point, only a small national guard.

~~Confidential NOFORN~~

332465 9-91

10. *(Continued)*

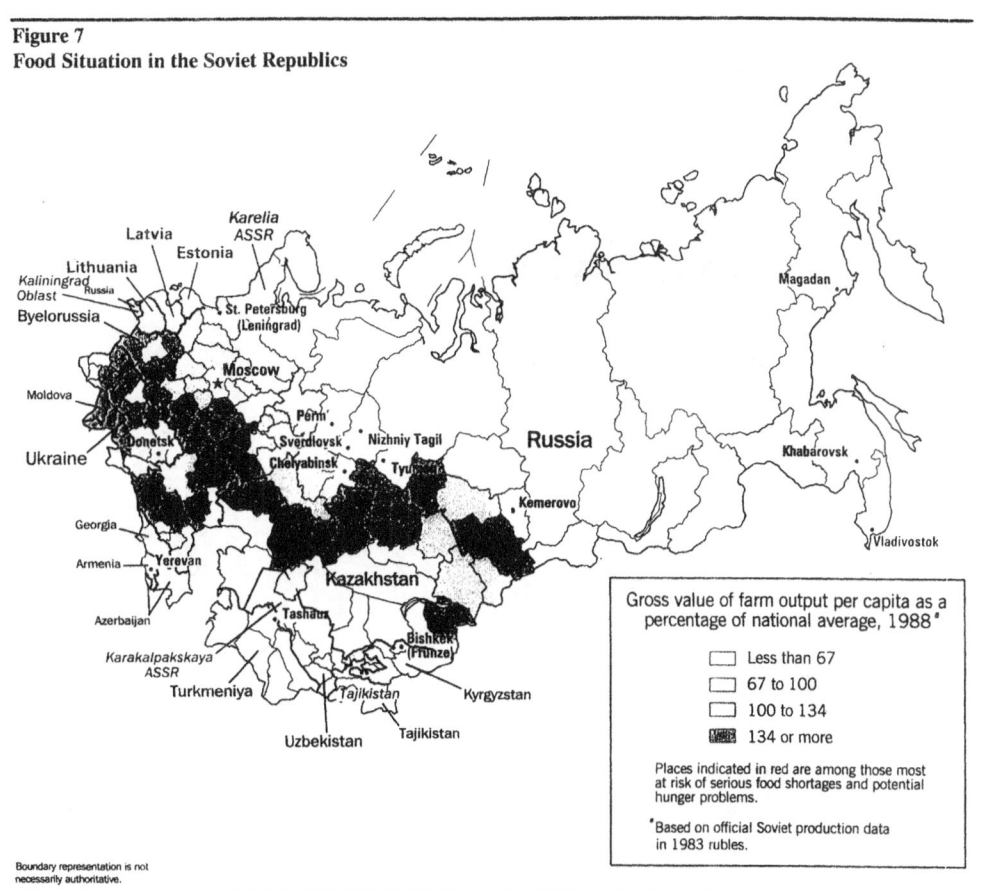

Figure 7
Food Situation in the Soviet Republics

In either the "confederation" or the "loose association" scenarios, the West would have influence on subsequent developments by focusing primarily on Russia and Ukraine. Russia would be the principal player in decisionmaking for defense policy and arms control. It would have the best chance among the republics of carrying out economic reform and political democratization. The West could coax, but not compel, Ukraine toward a more cooperative approach with Russia and other republics as well as toward more democratic processes in internal policies. Tensions over such issues as borders, minority rights,

10. *(Continued)*

economic relations, and military forces could be reduced with the help of Western "good offices" ▬▬▬▬▬▬▬▬▬▬▬▬ Thus, to the extent that Western involvement facilitated cooperation, it could affect developments elsewhere. (C NF)

Western influence would be most limited under the "disintegration" scenario. If authoritarian regimes came to power in the republics, they would want Western economic assistance and cooperation, but they would resist ▬▬▬▬▬▬▬ demanding respect for human rights and democratic freedoms. It would be especially difficult to promote republic cooperation in working out common problems. As nationalist sentiment grew stronger, anti-Western feelings would become more pronounced. (C NF)

"New Thinking"
Soviet Foreign Relations

11. SNIE 11/37-88, March 1988, *USSR: Withdrawal From Afghanistan* (Key Judgments only)

 Director of Central Intelligence

~~Secret~~

USSR: Withdrawal From Afghanistan

Special National Intelligence Estimate

~~Secret~~

SNIE 11/37-88
March 1988

Copy 425

11. *(Continued)*

THIS ESTIMATE IS ISSUED BY THE DIRECTOR OF CENTRAL INTELLIGENCE.

THE NATIONAL FOREIGN INTELLIGENCE BOARD CONCURS.

The following intelligence organizations participated in the preparation of the Estimate:

> The Central Intelligence Agency, the Defense Intelligence Agency, the National Security Agency, and the intelligence organization of the Department of State.

Also Participating:

> The Deputy Chief of Staff for Intelligence, Department of the Army
>
> The Director of Naval Intelligence, Department of the Navy
>
> The Assistant Chief of Staff, Intelligence, Department of the Air Force

Warning Notice
Intelligence Sources or Methods Involved
(WNINTEL)

NATIONAL SECURITY INFORMATION
Unauthorized Disclosure Subject to Criminal Sanctions

DISSEMINATION CONTROL ABBREVIATIONS

NOFORN–	Not Releasable to Foreign Nationals
NOCONTRACT–	Not Releasable to Contractors or Contractor/Consultants
PROPIN–	Caution—Proprietary Information Involved
ORCON–	Dissemination and Extraction of Information Controlled by Originator
REL . . .–	This Information Has Been Authorized for Release to . . .

DERIVATIVE CL BY 0384892
REVIEW ON   OADR
DERIVED FROM   Multiple

A microfiche copy of this document is available from OIR/DLB (482-7177); printed copies from CPAS/IMC (482-5203; or AIM request to userid CPASIMC).

11. *(Continued)*

~~SECRET~~
~~NOFORN/NOCONTRACT~~

SNIE 11/37-88

USSR: WITHDRAWAL FROM AFGHANISTAN (U)

Information available as of 24 March 1988 was used in the preparation of this Estimate, which was approved by the National Foreign Intelligence Board on that date.

~~SECRET~~

11. *(Continued)*

~~SECRET~~
~~NOFORN/NOCONTRACT~~

CONTENTS

	Page
KEY JUDGMENTS	1
DISCUSSION	3
The Soviet Withdrawal Calculus and Conditions	3
Aftermath of Withdrawal Inside Afghanistan	5
The Impact of Withdrawal Inside the USSR	8
Impact on Soviet Allies and Clients	9
Impact on Moscow's Global Position	10
Implications for the United States	11

11. *(Continued)*

KEY JUDGMENTS

We believe Moscow has made a firm decision to withdraw from Afghanistan. The decision stems from the war's effect on the Soviet regime's ability to carry out its agenda at home and abroad and its pessimism about the military and political prospects for creating a viable client regime:

— Although Afghanistan has been a controversial issue, we believe General Secretary Gorbachev has built a leadership consensus for withdrawal. The regime is aware that its client's chances of surviving without Soviet troops are poor. We do not believe that Moscow will attempt a partition of Afghanistan or start withdrawal and then renege.

— The Soviets want to withdraw under the cover of the Geneva accords. We believe they would prefer to withdraw without an agreement, however, rather than sign one that formally restricts their right to provide aid and further undermines the legitimacy of the Kabul regime.

— In our view, the Soviets will begin withdrawal this year even if the Geneva talks are deadlocked. Under such conditions, however, the Soviet leadership would not feel constrained by the provisions of the draft accords, and withdrawal would more likely be accompanied by heavy fighting. Although the Soviets in this case would have the option of delaying or prolonging the withdrawal process, we believe that—once begun in earnest—geographic, political, and military factors would lead them to opt for a relatively rapid exit.

— There is an alternative scenario. A more chaotic situation accompanying withdrawal than the Soviets expect or a political crisis in Moscow could fracture the Politburo consensus for withdrawal and lead them to delay or even reverse course. We believe the odds of this scenario are small—perhaps less than one in five.

We judge that the Najibullah regime will not long survive the completion of Soviet withdrawal even with continued Soviet assistance. The regime may fall before withdrawal is complete.

Despite infighting, we believe the resistance will retain sufficient supplies and military strength to ensure the demise of the Communist government. We cannot confidently predict the composition of the new regime, but we believe it initially will be an unstable coalition of traditionalist and fundamentalist groups whose writ will not extend far beyond Kabul and the leaders' home areas. It will be Islamic—possibly strongly fundamentalist, but not as extreme as Iran. While anti-Soviet, it

11. *(Continued)*

will eventually establish "correct"—not friendly—ties to the USSR. We cannot be confident of the new government's orientation toward the West; at best it will be ambivalent and at worst it may be actively hostile, especially toward the United States.

There are two alternative scenarios. There is some chance—less than 1 in 3 in our view—that fighting among resistance groups will produce so much chaos that no stable government will take hold for an extended period after the Afghan Communist regime collapses. We also cannot rule out a scenario in which the Kabul regime manages to survive for a protracted period after withdrawal, due to an increasingly divided resistance. The odds of this outcome, in our view, are very small. Both scenarios would complicate relief efforts, reduce the prospects that refugees would return, and increase opportunities for Soviet maneuvering.

The impact of the Soviet withdrawal will depend on how it proceeds and what kind of situation the Soviets leave behind. At home, we believe that ending the war will be a net plus for Gorbachev, boosting his popularity and his reform agenda. Nonetheless, withdrawal will not be universally popular and is sure to cause recriminations. There is some chance—if it proves to have a more damaging impact on Soviet interests over the long term than either we or Gorbachev anticipate—that the decision could eventually form part of a "bill of attainder" used by his opponents in an effort to oust him.

Moscow's defeat in Afghanistan will have significant international costs. It is an implicit admission that Soviet-supported revolutions can be reversed. It will demonstrate that there are limits on Moscow's willingness and ability to use its power abroad, tarnish its prestige among some elements of the Communist movement, and lead other beleaguered Soviet clients to question Soviet resolve.

Nevertheless, we—as well as the Soviets—believe the withdrawal will yield important benefits for Moscow. The move will be popular even among some Soviet allies. Moscow will net substantial public relations gains in the rest of the world—particularly in Western Europe—that could ultimately translate into more concrete diplomatic benefits. Gorbachev expects the withdrawal to have a positive impact on US-Soviet relations.

By enhancing the Soviet Union's image as a responsible superpower, withdrawal will present new challenges to Western diplomacy. In South Asia, US relations with Pakistan will be complicated. But Soviet withdrawal under the conditions we anticipate will also produce substantial benefits for the West:

— It will be seen as a triumph for Western policy.

— If it produces the benefits that Gorbachev expects, withdrawal will probably add impetus to the ongoing rethinking in Moscow about the utility of military power in Third World conflicts and accelerate efforts to reach negotiated solutions on other issues.

12. SNIE 11-16-88 CX, November 1988, *Soviet Policy During the Next Phase of Arms Control in Europe* **(Key Judgments only)**

Director of Central Intelligence

~~Top Secret~~

Soviet Policy During the Next Phase of Arms Control in Europe

Special National Intelligence Estimate

This Special National Intelligence Estimate represents the views of the Director of Central Intelligence with the advice and assistance of the US Intelligence Community.

~~Top Secret~~

SNIE 11-16-88CX
~~SC 03771-88~~
November 1988

Copy 193

12. *(Continued)*

 Director of Central Intelligence

~~Top Secret~~
~~UMBRA~~
~~NOFORN NOCONTRACT~~
~~ORCON~~

~~GAMMA item~~

SNIE 11-16-88

Soviet Policy During the Next Phase of Arms Control in Europe (U)

Information available as of 17 November 1988 was used in the preparation of this Special National Intelligence Estimate.

The following intelligence organizations participated in the preparation of this Estimate:
The Central Intelligence Agency
The Defense Intelligence Agency
The National Security Agency
The Bureau of Intelligence and Research, Department of State

also participating:
The Office of the Deputy Chief of Staff for Intelligence, Department of the Army
The Office of the Director of Naval Intelligence, Department of the Navy
The Office of the Assistant Chief of Staff, Intelligence, Department of the Air Force
The Director of Intelligence, Headquarters, Marine Corps

This Estimate was approved for publication by the National Foreign Intelligence Board.

Handle via COMINT Channels

~~Top Secret~~
SC 03771-88
November 1988

12. *(Continued)*

Figure 1
NATO and Warsaw Pact Forces Within the Atlantic-to-the-Urals Zone

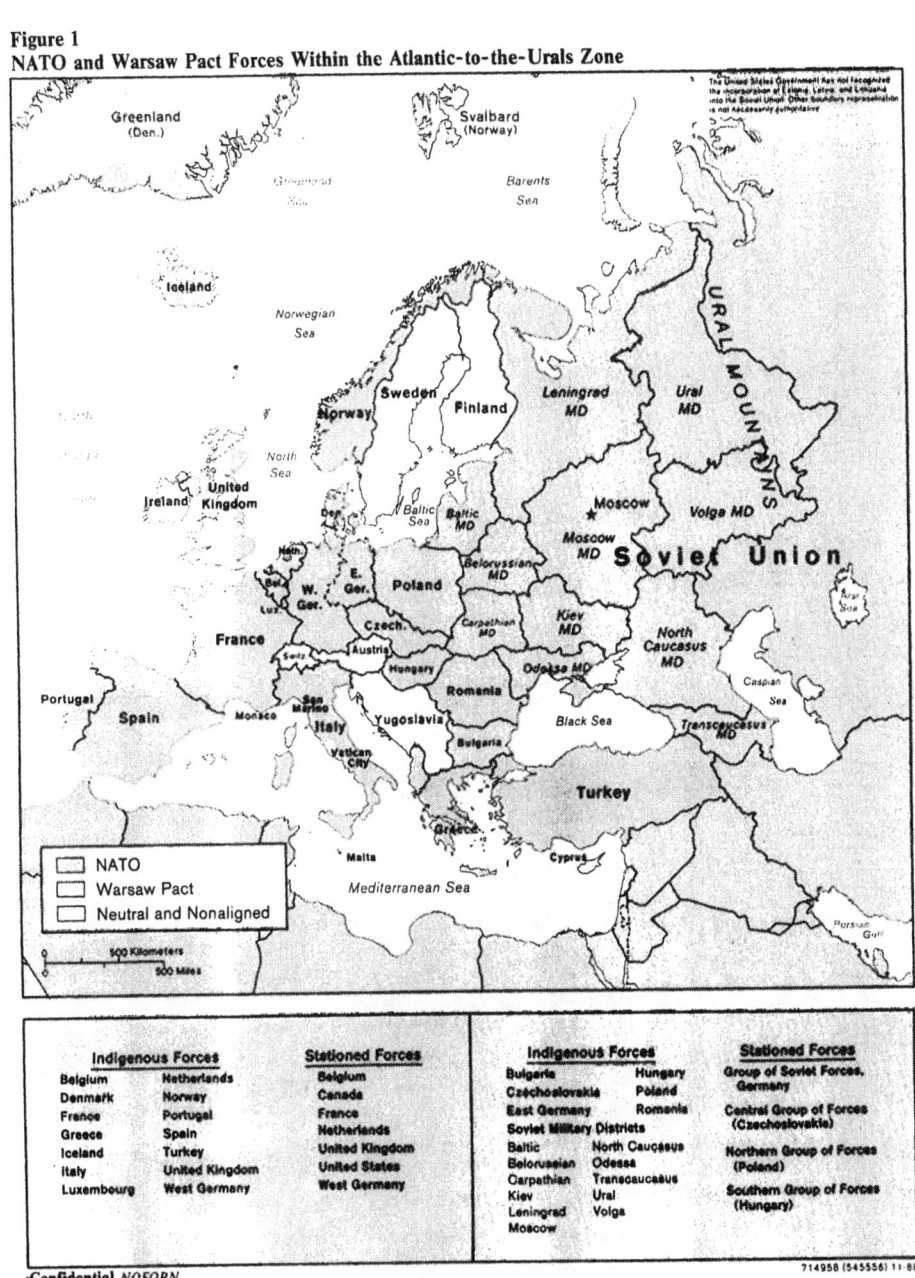

12. *(Continued)*

~~Top Secret~~
~~UMBRA~~
~~NOFORN-NOCONTRACT-~~
~~ORCON~~

~~GAMMA~~ Item

Key Judgments

We judge that the Soviets and their allies have a number of interrelated military, political, and economic reasons to engage the West in conventional arms control:

- Military:
    - To improve the correlation of forces and to reduce what they perceive as NATO's capability to launch a surprise attack.
    - To impede NATO's force modernization plans and to prevent or impede NATO's deployment of advanced technology weapons.

- Political:
    - To demonstrate the "new thinking" in Soviet foreign and domestic policy.
    - To appeal to foreign and domestic public opinion in a generalized way, while adding to Moscow's overall arms control posture and enhancing the USSR's image as a trustworthy, rational player in the international arena.

- Economic:
    - To reduce the threat from NATO and thereby reduce the urgency on the part of the Soviet Union to match or better NATO's high-technology modernization programs.
    - To make it politically easier to allocate economic resources within the Soviet Union from the defense sector to the civilian sector to carry out *perestroyka*.

We believe the Soviets and their allies *prefer* to negotiate with NATO to achieve *mutual* reductions of conventional forces. Militarily, it makes more sense to trade force reductions, thereby retaining a balance in the correlation of forces. However, the Warsaw Pact probably realizes that negotiating an agreement with NATO that is acceptable to the Soviets could take years—and might not even be possible.

In the short term (up to two years), we believe the Pact will pursue a strategy aimed at reducing the West's perception of the Soviet threat in the expectation that this course will make it difficult for NATO governments to maintain or increase defense spending. The Pact will engage NATO in the Conventional Stability Talks and probably will introduce sweeping proposals for asymmetric reductions.

12. *(Continued)*

We predict that, when formal negotiations concerning conventional forces in the Atlantic-to-the-Urals zone begin, the Warsaw Pact will quickly present a formal version of its public diplomacy position—and might even table a draft treaty very early in the negotiations. It will probably insist on an initial discussion of data regarding asymmetries between the two sides' forces and will probably suggest establishing a working group on data.

The Warsaw Pact states will *not* accept the current NATO proposal, which in effect calls on the Pact to take gigantic cuts in tanks and artillery for minor cuts on the NATO side so that there is parity between the Pact and NATO. For example, this would mean the Pact would have to withdraw or destroy about 25,000 tanks while NATO would withdraw or destroy about 900 tanks.

Outside of the negotiating process itself, for political effect, the Soviets may also take unilateral initiatives:

- We judge the Soviets could garner significant political gains in Western Europe at tolerable risks by unilaterally removing some of their forces from Eastern Europe, especially all from Hungary. The evidence on Soviet timing and conditions is insufficient to predict with confidence when and whether a withdrawal announcement might be made.

- Given the West German concern about short-range nuclear-capable forces, it is possible that the Soviets might make a gesture by unilaterally withdrawing some short-range ballistic missile launchers from Eastern Europe; however, we judge the likelihood of such a move to be low for the period of this Estimate.

- The Soviets may attempt to portray force restructuring as a unilateral force reduction; however, we judge that the ongoing restructuring of the Soviet ground forces is intended primarily to make units more effective for prolonged conventional combat operations against NATO.

We judge that, among our NATO Allies, France will be the most resistant to potential Soviet gambits, with the United Kingdom a strong second. Of the major partners, the Federal Republic of Germany will be the most responsive to such ploys, because of its strong desire to reduce defense spending and to reduce the chance of the country becoming Europe's nuclear battleground. The challenge for the United States and the rest of NATO will be to continue the ongoing NATO modernization, while at the same time negotiating on a possible agreement with a more sophisticated adversary in an environment where the public perception of the Warsaw Pact threat has been softened significantly.

13. NIE 11-4-89, April 1989, *Soviet Policy Toward the West: The Gorbachev Challenge*

 **Director of Central Intelligence**

Soviet Policy Toward the West: The Gorbachev Challenge

National Intelligence Estimate

This Estimate represents the views of the Director of Central Intelligence with the advice and assistance of the US Intelligence Community.

NIE 11-4-89
April 1989

13. *(Continued)*

Director of Central Intelligence

~~Secret~~
~~NOFORN NOCONTRACT~~
~~ORCON~~

NIE 11-4-89

Soviet Policy Toward the West: The Gorbachev Challenge (U)

Information available as of 17 April 1989 was used in the preparation of this Estimate.

The following intelligence organizations participated in the preparation of this Estimate:
The Central Intelligence Agency
The Defense Intelligence Agency
The National Security Agency
The Bureau of Intelligence and Research, Department of State
The Intelligence Division, Federal Bureau of Investigation

also participating:
The Deputy Chief of Staff for Intelligence, Department of the Army
The Director of Naval Intelligence, Department of the Navy
The Assistant Chief of Staff, Intelligence, Department of the Air Force
The Director of Intelligence, Headquarters, Marine Corps

This Estimate was approved for publication by the National Foreign Intelligence Board.

~~Secret~~
April 1989

13. *(Continued)*

Key Judgments

Dramatic changes in approach to the West under Soviet leader Gorbachev are driven by economic and social decay at home, a widening technological gap with the West, and a growing realism about trends in the outside world. For the foreseeable future, the USSR will remain the West's principal adversary. But the process Gorbachev has set in motion is likely to change the nature of the Soviet challenge over the next five years or so:
- New Soviet policies will threaten the security consensus developed in the West to combat Soviet expansionism.
- The Soviets are likely to succeed to a degree in undercutting support abroad for defense programs and in reducing political barriers to Western participation in their economic development.
- At the same time new policies will make Moscow more flexible on regional issues and human rights and pave the way for a potentially significant reduction of the military threat.
- Alliance cohesion will decline faster in the Warsaw Pact than in NATO, giving the East Europeans much greater scope for change.

We believe Moscow wants to shift competition with the West to a largely political and economic plane. In order to prepare the ground for such a shift, Soviet leaders are making major policy changes and promoting a broad reassessment of the West.

These new policies serve domestic as well as foreign policy needs:
- They aim to create an international environment more conducive to domestic reform and to undermine the rationale for high defense budgets and repressive political controls.
- They are seen as more effective than past policies in advancing Soviet foreign interests.

There are limits on how far the new Soviet leadership wants to go in the direction of a less confrontational East-West relationship:
- Vigorous efforts to protect and advance Soviet geopolitical interests and selective support for Communist regimes and revolutionary movements will continue.
- Moscow will continue to employ active measures and covert efforts to advance its objectives. Foreign intelligence activity is likely to increase.

13. *(Continued)*

~~Secret~~
~~NOFORN NOCONTRACT~~
~~ORCON~~

Given the turmoil unleashed by the reform process, we cannot predict policy trends during the period of the Estimate with high confidence. Nevertheless, we believe that Gorbachev is likely to stay in power and that the reform effort is more likely than not to continue. If so, we believe the following developments are probable:

- *Military power.* While increasing so far under Gorbachev, Soviet defense spending will decline significantly in real terms. Moscow will maintain vigorous force modernization programs and a strong R&D effort in key areas, but production and procurement of many major weapons will decline. Gorbachev is likely to make further concessions to achieve a START agreement, show flexibility on chemical weapons, and take further steps to trim and redeploy Soviet conventional forces—moving unilaterally if necessary.

- *The Western Alliance.* Moscow will attempt to translate its more benign image into expanded credits, trade, and technology sales and reduced support for defense spending and force modernization in Western Europe. While trying to reduce US influence and military presence, Moscow does not see an abrupt unraveling of current Alliance arrangements as serving Soviet interests.

- *Third World competition.* The Soviets will seek to expand their influence and continue support to leftist causes deemed to have some future. But they will be more careful to consider how such moves affect broader Soviet interests, including relations with the West. They will encourage their clients to make economic and political reforms and seek Western aid. It is highly unlikely that Moscow will become directly involved in military support to another leftist seizure of power in the Third World as it did in the 1970s. ~~(C NF)~~

Alternative Scenarios
We see a number of developments that—while unlikely—could disrupt current trends and push Gorbachev onto a different course:

- A widespread crackdown on unrest at home or in Eastern Europe would probably trigger a reescalation of East-West tensions, causing Gorbachev to tack in a conservative direction. A shift of this sort would limit Gorbachev's freedom of maneuver in negotiations and his ability to transfer resources away from defense.

- Were nationality unrest to threaten central control or the territorial integrity of the country, we see a risk that the leadership would revert to more hostile rhetoric and policies toward the West in an attempt to reunify the country. ~~(C NF)~~

13. *(Continued)*

Gorbachev's removal—unlikely but not to be ruled out—would have a significant impact:
- A more orthodox regime would slow the pace of change, be more supportive of military interests and leftist allies abroad, and eschew unilateral arms control concessions.
- We see little chance that a successor leadership would completely roll back Gorbachev's policies or revert to a major military buildup and aggressive policies in the Third World. (C NF)

Disagreements
There is general agreement in the Intelligence Community over the outlook for the next five to seven years, but differing views over the *longer term* prospects for fundamental and enduring change toward less competitive Soviet behavior:

- Some analysts see current policy changes as largely tactical, driven by the need for breathing space from the competition. They believe the ideological imperatives of Marxism-Leninism and its hostility toward capitalist countries are enduring. They point to previous failures of reform and the transient nature of past "detentes." They judge that there is a serious risk of Moscow returning to traditionally combative behavior when the hoped for gains in economic performance are achieved.

- Other analysts believe Gorbachev's policies reflect a fundamental rethinking of national interests and ideology as well as more tactical considerations. They argue that ideological tenets of Marxism-Leninism such as class conflict and capitalist-socialist enmity are being revised. They consider the withdrawal from Afghanistan and the shift toward tolerance of power sharing in Eastern Europe to be historic shifts in the Soviet definition of national interest. They judge that Gorbachev's changes are likely to have sufficient momentum to produce lasting shifts in Soviet behavior. (C NF)

Indicators
As evidence of Moscow's progress over the next two to three years toward fulfilling the promise of more responsible behavior, we will be watching for:
- Soviet acceptance of real liberalization in Eastern Europe.
- Full implementation of announced force reductions.
- A substantial conversion in the defense industry to production for the civilian economy. (C NF)

13. *(Continued)*

> *The Soviet World View in Flux*
>
> *From the days of Lenin, Soviet policy toward the West has been shaped by a body of ideological dogma centered around negative images of the West and the necessity of a long-term struggle by the "socialist camp" against the West. These tenets have pictured the West as in an inevitable state of decline and forced relentlessly toward militarization to shore up its position. They have depicted East-West relations as based on unremitting class struggle, leaving little or no common ground for cooperation.*
>
> *Tensions in Moscow over how far to go in seeking accommodation with the West have been reflected in disputes over how much change is called for in this traditional world view:*
>
> - *Gorbachev and his reform-minded allies believe that significant revisions are required to provide a long-term basis for a less conflictual relationship with the West—a shift they believe is essential to their efforts to modernize the country. They argue that capitalism remains in a robust state of health, that it is not inherently militaristic, and that the West can rise above a narrow class-based approach to relations with the Communist Bloc. While reaffirming the continuing relevance of class analysis, they are seeking to diminish the centrality of class conflict to East-West relations and assert the overriding importance of "universal human values."*
>
> - *More orthodox leaders, such as senior party secretary Ligachev, accept the need for reduced tensions with the West and for some ideological adjustments. But they are skeptical about the feasibility of seeking a fundamentally less conflictual relationship and believe a more limited accommodation will suffice. They believe the reformers are going too far in tampering with fundamental tenets of socialism and are resisting the effort to revise traditional notions about class struggle, capitalism and the threat it poses, and the nature of the East-West relationship.*

We believe that, over the longer term, the most reliable guarantees of enduring change will be in the institutionalization of a more open society and relationship with the outside world:
- The establishment of a more pluralistic and open decisionmaking process on foreign policy and defense issues.
- Progress toward the rule of law and a significant relaxation of barriers to free travel and emigration.

13. *(Continued)*

Contents

	Page
Key Judgments	iii
Discussion	1
Soviet Objectives Under Gorbachev	1
How Moscow Views Its Current Predicament	2
Changing Strategy Toward the West	4
Military Power and Arms Control	6
Policy Toward the Western Alliance	11
Competition in the Third World	12
Prospects for Gains and Losses	15
Implications for Western Policy	18
Indicators of Enduring Change	20

13. *(Continued)*

Discussion

Soviet Objectives Under Gorbachev

The dramatic changes in approach to the West under General Secretary Gorbachev are driven by reinforcing domestic and foreign objectives:

- Domestically, Soviet leaders appreciate that, for decades if not generations, the main goal will be reforming and modernizing the Soviet political and economic system. They want to create an era of reduced tensions and expanded relations with the Western powers that will facilitate this task.

- Equally important, these changes are viewed as essential in their own right for strengthening Moscow's international position, advancing its claim to a global superpower role, and—ultimately—reviving the credibility of socialism as a model of development.

Traditional objectives continue to influence Soviet policy toward the West. Moscow remains committed to:

- Eroding NATO cohesion and US influence in Western Europe.

- Undermining support for the US military presence overseas.

- Selectively backing Communist and other leftwing causes around the globe.

But under Gorbachev, more clearly than before, Soviet leaders recognize that in pursuing such objectives they have often done more harm than good for broader Soviet interests by antagonizing adversaries and drawing them closer together, by encouraging military buildup, and, in some respects, by reducing Soviet security. Moreover, the Soviets appreciate that, in the current situation, maintaining good relations with the West assumes an even higher priority:

- Reduced tensions will promote trends abroad that diminish Western defense efforts and reduce the cohesion of opposing alliances.

- Formal or informal limitations on the arms competition will enable Moscow to maintain an acceptable military balance while reducing defense spending and diverting resources to the civilian economy.

- Expanded trade and economic ties, in the long run at least, will be important to the success of economic revival.

We believe there is a broad consensus in the Soviet leadership in support of these objectives that will persist through the time frame of this Estimate. Nevertheless, the relaxed constraints on political expression under Gorbachev have revealed even more clearly than before the sharp divisions and wide-ranging debate that persist over the extent of the accommodation with the West that Moscow should seek:

- At one end of the spectrum, reformers appear to believe that only a decisive break with the confrontational mentality of the past and a much more extensive engagement on arms control, economics, and global political issues will avert impending crisis and ensure the renewed competitiveness of the country.

- At the other end, many orthodox members of the elite agree that the USSR needs "breathing space" but believe that a more limited and tactical accommodation would suffice. These officials represent a coalition of Russian nationalists, old-line Marxist-Leninist internationalists, and conservative bureaucrats alarmed by Gorbachev's rejection of traditional principles.

The extent to which Moscow shifts toward an accommodation with the West will depend in part on how this debate is resolved. Nevertheless, most analysts believe that the process Gorbachev has set in motion—if it continues—is likely to lead to lasting changes in Soviet international behavior whether or not that is the current leadership's intention.

13. *(Continued)*

Is Gorbachev's "Detente" Different?

This is not the first time that a Soviet leader has attempted to introduce liberalizing reforms at home or move toward detente abroad. The limited impact of these previous attempts at reform and the strong cultural barriers to change in the USSR suggest caution in predicting success for the current round of reforms. But we believe Gorbachev's efforts are far more comprehensive than those attempted by Khrushchev or Brezhnev. At the same time, the domestic and international factors compelling the process forward are now more substantial:

- Khrushchev ended mass terror, exposed Stalin's excesses, and periodically reorganized the Soviet bureaucracy. But—with the economy growing at the fastest rate in Soviet history—he saw no need to alter the fundamentals of the command economy or the political system. Gorbachev and his allies—faced with domestic crisis—are challenging the ideology and institutions of the Stalinist system itself and groping toward something radically different to replace them.

- Khrushchev made some dramatic initiatives in foreign and defense policy (agreeing to a peace treaty with Austria and slashing Soviet ground forces by over 2 million men) and modified traditional doctrine in some areas (discarding Stalinist dogma on the inevitability of war). But with optimism on the rise about the USSR's ability to overtake the United States and the advance of Communism in the Third World, the pressures for change were limited. Khrushchev introduced a new competitiveness in East-West relations and directly challenged US security interests in West Berlin and Cuba. Gorbachev's ideological revisions—by questioning traditional notions about the West's inherently militaristic nature and the centrality of class struggle to East-West relations—go well beyond those of Khrushchev.

- Efforts to reform the economy under Brezhnev were more shallow and narrower in scope, lacking in particular any serious effort to address necessary political and social reforms. In the 1970s, Brezhnev saw detente as permitting a more assertive thrust in the Third World while easing pressure for fundamental domestic reform. Gorbachev, on the other hand, seeks reduced tensions to facilitate thoroughgoing and probably wrenching changes at home.

- Gorbachev faces very different pressures from Soviet society than his predecessors—a population better educated, more demanding, and more knowledgeable about the outside world. Global trends—the information and technological revolution—are also impelling the leadership toward change more strongly now than in the 1950s and 1960s. Gorbachev's reforms have accentuated these trends by reducing the barriers that have inhibited political expression and sealed Soviet society off from Western influence.

How Moscow Views Its Current Predicament

Moscow's willingness to undertake potentially wrenching changes derives from a growing appreciation that the USSR faces a looming systemic crisis and the prospect of falling further behind the major Western powers economically and technologically:

- Gorbachev himself has consistently underscored the gravity of the problem the USSR faces and used it to justify his increasingly radical reforms. ▓▓▓ in May 1986, Gorbachev asserted that the USSR needed *perestroyka* simply to survive—if it failed, the USSR would become a third-rate power and the cause of socialism would be imperiled.

- Economic stagnation has frayed the social fabric at home and undermined Moscow's claims to superpower status abroad.

13. *(Continued)*

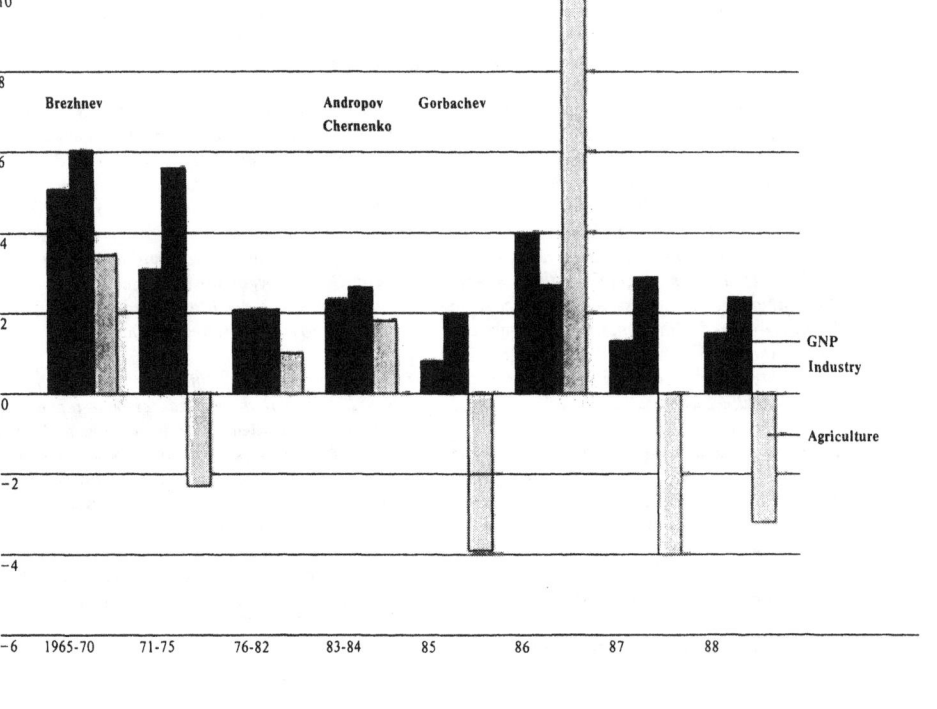

Figure 1
Soviet Economic Performance Under Gorbachev and His Predecessors

Unclassified

- The Soviet leadership is increasingly doubtful about the military's ability over the long run to keep pace with Western technological advances, in particular the long-term impact that the US SDI program and its spinoffs could have on Soviet military strategy.

- The technological dilemma also inhibits the USSR's ability to become a global economic player at a time when the Soviet Bloc is less able to sustain itself with its own resources and Soviet industry is finding it increasingly difficult to provide goods in sufficient quantities and of competitive quality.

13. *(Continued)*

New approaches to the West are also fueled by international factors quite independent of the USSR's internal weakness:

- Recognition of Moscow's responsibility for a series of foreign policy failures and a growing realism about trends in the outside world.

- The irrelevance of traditional Marxist dogma to current global trends.

- The continuing vitality of the Western economies, the hollow ring of Moscow's former talk about the "growing crisis of capitalism," and the need to borrow from the Western experience.

- China's growing ties to the capitalist world and increased use of market principles in its economy.

- The burden of empire; states that have emulated the Soviet model (Cuba, Vietnam, East European countries) are expensive to support and suffer from endemic economic malaise similar to the USSR.

- The declining appeal of Communist ideology in the West as well as the Third World. (C-NF)

Changing Strategy Toward the West

The USSR's growing domestic and foreign troubles have served to discredit the lingering legacy of isolation and autarky and have led to major changes in foreign and national security strategy. Reformers who believe a much broader-based engagement of the West is necessary to turn things around have been given authority to reshape the Soviet approach:

- Gorbachev and his allies have concluded that only a significant shift away from past thinking about East-West relations and toward less confrontational international behavior will produce the decisive improvement in relations with the West that they need. (C-NF)

Soviet leaders have launched a wide-ranging reassessment of the West and the prospects for improving East-West relations:

- They are redefining the USSR's national security calculus, linking security with long-term modernization of the Soviet industrial base and playing down the perceived military threat from the West.

- They have substituted new doctrinal precepts to govern Soviet foreign and defense policy, diminishing the centrality of class conflict to East-West relations, abjuring the notion that Moscow could win a nuclear war, and challenging the high-priority claim that the military has had on resources.

- In order to justify such an approach to the domestic audience, reformers in the foreign policy establishment have launched a systematic attack in the Soviet media on stereotypical thinking that has exaggerated the military threat, ignored the nonmilitary dimensions of national security, and obscured Soviet backwardness by minimizing economic and social progress in the West. (C-NF)

Although this shift in strategy toward the West is borne in large measure out of weakness, it also has an offensive intent:

- It is seen in Moscow as an effective means to eliminate the USSR's "enemy image" that has cemented Western unity, fueled support for defense programs, and sustained resistance to expanded cooperation with the East.

- Given the likelihood that solving the USSR's domestic problems will take decades if not generations, Soviet leaders appreciate that they can score gains far more quickly on the foreign policy front. In effect, new strategies toward the West are a means for Moscow to improve its competitive position in the short run through political means while waiting for domestic reforms to take effect. (C-NF)

13. *(Continued)*

Attitude Toward International Organizations

Moscow's new international strategy has led it to attach growing political importance to the United Nations and other international organizations beyond the traditional emphasis on propaganda and intelligence collection:

- The Soviets have adopted a more businesslike, less polemical stance toward participation in UN bodies; for example, accepting compulsory jurisdiction of the International Court of Justice in implementing international human rights agreements.

- Moscow has adopted a philosophy toward the United Nations that places more emphasis on substantive proposals. Where it formerly sought to keep the United Nations at arm's length on serious questions, Moscow is now advocating an increased role for the world body in resolving regional conflicts and monitoring international agreements.

- Soviet leaders calculate that, through a more extensive UN role, they can expand their global involvement and constrain US unilateral actions, thus compensating in part for inherent political and economic weaknesses that continue to limit their ability to play a global superpower role.

International Economic Strategy

The far-reaching campaign to reorganize the foreign trade and financial sectors and increase the USSR's role in world economic affairs is an integral part of Moscow's changing global strategy.[1] Gorbachev sees this campaign as important to the success of *perestroyka* over the longer term. Nonetheless, he is aware of the risks of overindebtedness and exposing the Soviet economy to the vagaries of the international market. He remains determined to find indigenous solutions to Moscow's problems:

- We expect Moscow to continue taking incremental steps to create conditions for more extensive involvement in the global economy and to open the Soviet economy to some foreign participation and competition.

[1] For a fuller treatment of Soviet economic prospects, see NIE 11-23-88, *Gorbachev's Economic Programs: The Challenges Ahead,* December 1988. (U)

- We believe Soviet leaders want eventually to make the ruble convertible with Western currencies and are beginning to take some steps in this direction. They see full convertibility as the culmination of the reform process, however, and are unlikely to complete the process until at least the late 1990s.

Soviet interest in international organizations such as the General Agreement on Tariffs and Trade (GATT) and the International Monetary Fund (IMF) signals Moscow's hope to become fully involved in the international economic and financial community:

- Moscow is probably most interested in becoming a party to GATT rules and negotiations as part of its long-term effort to expand foreign trade and reduce barriers to the export of Soviet products.

- Discussions with the IMF and the World Bank will remain more exploratory in nature.

Continuing Traditional Behavior

Soviet leaders want to move away from strategies that led to and fueled the Cold War. But there are limits on how far Soviet policy is likely to evolve toward a less confrontational relationship. Even the reformers in the leadership continue to see the East-West relationship as adversarial:

- Despite the changes in Soviet thinking, ideological and geopolitical differences will remain a major obstacle to improved East-West relations. Moscow remains committed to supporting Communist and "socialist-oriented" regimes, still actively seeks to enhance its involvement in Europe, Asia, and the Third World, and continues to back selected revolutionary movements.

Moscow still employs unsavory practices to advance its objectives. Active measures campaigns against US interests continue. There is no evidence that even the reformers in the leadership would reject these practices altogether, although the Gorbachev leadership is likely to take steps to constrain excesses and will be more responsive to Western pressure on these issues:

- Moscow has during the last year reduced the amount of blatant disinformation in its own press and has begun to participate in bilateral talks in which US complaints about disinformation are conveyed directly to Soviet political leaders. Nonetheless, stories accusing the United States of developing ethnic weapons, inventing the AIDS virus, and trafficking in body organs have continued overseas via covert press placements. We have seen no evidence that Moscow is prepared to exert influence on its allies and clients abroad—especially in the Third World—to curtail such activities.

- In an effort to bring its network of front groups—led by the World Peace Council—in line with new policies, Moscow has replaced individuals in senior leadership positions and pushed for measures that would allow diverse opinions to be voiced. While Soviet leaders are giving less priority to front groups, they and their Bloc allies continue to finance an agenda of front activities designed to promote Soviet positions on key issues such as arms control and human rights.

- Intelligence operations against the West are undiminished. Some key areas, such as illegal acquisition of technology, are receiving increased emphasis. Intelligence activities are likely to increase further as the Soviet presence abroad grows.

Military Power and Arms Control

Moscow's strategic reassessment extends to the core of its national security posture—the way it calculates its military requirements vis-a-vis the West and the optimum size and configuration of its armed forces. In the past, Moscow worked hard to build offensively oriented strategic and conventional forces that would give it a preponderance of power. The Soviet Union now appears to believe such efforts were often too costly, politically counterproductive, and militarily ineffective—and that Soviet national security can be ensured with smaller, less threatening military forces.

Changes in this sphere are driven by a variety of factors:

- Growing concern about the costs of maintaining, equipping, and modernizing a large standing army and the need to divert scarce resources to rebuild the civilian economy.

- A recognition that the military buildup in the past was excessive and enhanced NATO cohesion, triggered a Western buildup, increased tensions on Soviet borders, and in some respects eroded Soviet security.

- A growing awareness of the role of economic power and international diplomacy in national security calculations.

Evidence that the leadership is serious about taking steps to act on this reassessment and reduce resources devoted to defense has been accumulating steadily:

- Gorbachev's pronouncement of "reasonable sufficiency" as the guiding concept for the future size and structure of Soviet forces has opened a wide-ranging debate over military policy. While still ill defined, the concept has been used by reform spokesmen to argue that more modest force levels than Moscow has maintained in the past are sufficient for Soviet security. The unilateral cuts in conventional forces Gorbachev announced at the United Nations in December 1988 suggest that the reformers' arguments have prevailed.

- Since last summer political and military leaders have begun to speak with increasing frankness about Moscow's determination to base future improvements in military capability on qualitative rather than quantitative factors, to prepare for an era in which ground and naval forces will be receiving less arms and equipment, and to shift a growing proportion of defense industry production to civilian needs.

- The political leadership has taken steps to reassert its control of decisionmaking on national security issues in order to implement "new thinking." Gorbachev has challenged the privileged status enjoyed by the military under Brezhnev. Competing centers of defense and security analysis and more civilian involvement are being encouraged. The foreign ministry and the Central Committee apparatus are playing a more assertive role.

Not all Soviet officials share the new national security calculus on which Gorbachev's initiatives are based. Most military leaders probably support *perestroyka* in

13. *(Continued)*

Figure 2
Soviet Defense Expenditures, 1970-88

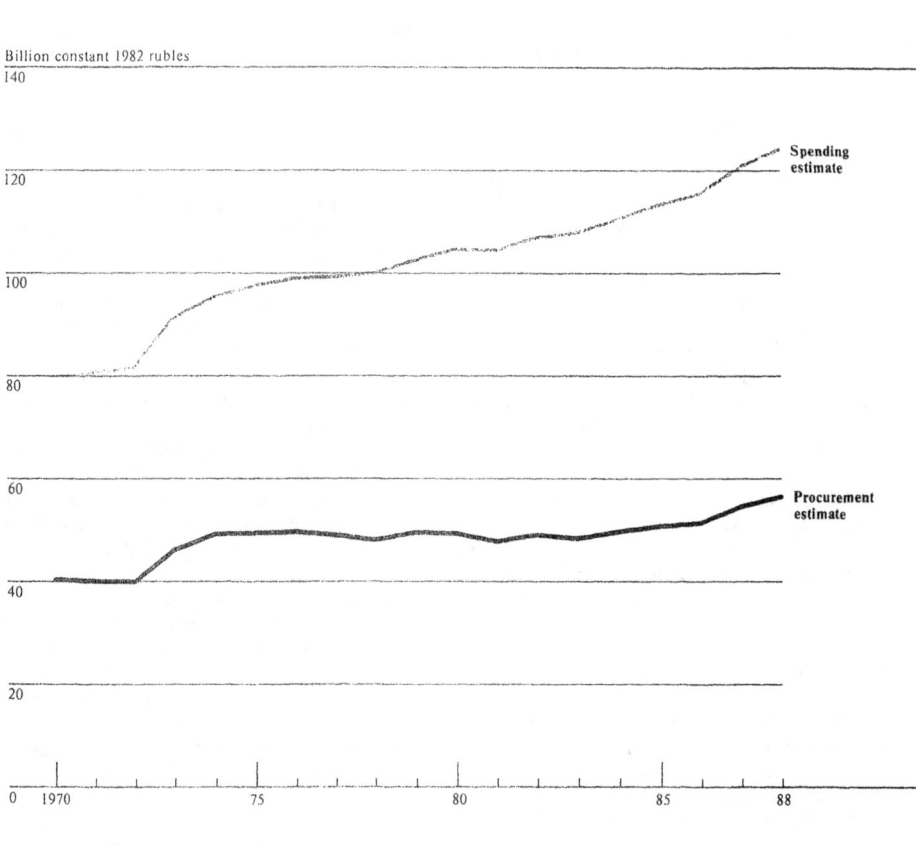

principle, but many are troubled by Gorbachev's dramatic unilateral gestures and shifts in negotiating posture and probably question his more benign depiction of the Western threat. We have little direct evidence, but we believe some political leaders share concerns about what they see as Gorbachev's excessively conciliatory posture. These concerns are likely to play a role if Gorbachev's critics ever mount a political challenge. We believe, however, that Gorbachev is likely to retain the initiative on national security issues for the foreseeable future.

13. *(Continued)*

~~Secret~~

Arms Control

To create a propitious political climate for such reductions in defense spending, Gorbachev is taking steps to ensure that Western arms programs are similarly constrained, making arms control central to his policy and agenda. (C NF)

Arms control has been vital to the Soviets' efforts to shape the arms competition in their favor since the 1950s, but we believe it plays a more important role in Gorbachev's national security calculus:

- Gorbachev's innovations in doctrine and ideology, and his willingness to open the USSR to intrusive on-site inspections, remove key barriers that have traditionally limited Moscow's flexibility. At the same time, a looming domestic crisis gives him a far stronger economic incentive than his predecessors.

- Like other Soviet leaders before him, Gorbachev sees arms control as a means of limiting Western arms programs, but to achieve that objective he is willing to negotiate reductions in Soviet forces that go far beyond what his predecessors were prepared to contemplate. (C NF)

Unilateral reductions are both a sign of Gorbachev's determination not to have his program held hostage by the negotiation process and a way of pressuring the West to be more forthcoming. Unilateral initiatives in a variety of areas are likely as a means to undermine support in the West for defense programs, "kick-start" arms control negotiations, and save resources at home. We believe Moscow prefers to achieve reductions primarily through negotiated agreements or reciprocal measures that maintain at least a rough parity with the West. (C NF)

The Soviet approach to arms control also retains propagandistic elements. Many Gorbachev proposals are obviously self-serving or quixotic (nuclear-weapons-free zones, reductions in naval exercises, withdrawal from foreign bases, abolition of nuclear weapons). Nevertheless, Moscow is more willing than in the past to translate vague arms control concepts into specific negotiating proposals. (C NF)

Outlook

There is agreement in the Intelligence Community that this reassessment of military requirements is only now beginning to have an effect on Soviet forces.

The Soviet Defense Modernization Program

Despite changes in military doctrine under Gorbachev and the promise of significant reductions in the Soviet defense effort, the USSR has continued to field and modernize a potent military force:

- *Since 1987, the Soviet Union has begun to deploy:*
    — *Two improved variants of silo-based ICBMs.*
    — *A rail-mobile ICBM.*
    — *The Blackjack supersonic strategic bomber.*

- *The Soviets also continue to deploy:*
    — *Road-mobile ICBMs.*
    — *Two new classes of submarines carrying ballistic missiles.*
    — *More modern air defense weapons.*

- *Tank production levels in 1988 reached their highest level in the postwar period.*

- *The Soviets will:*
    — *Probably deploy a Stealth bomber by the year 2000.*
    — *Extensively modernize their strategic nuclear forces so that by the late 1990s about half of their ICBMs will be mobile.*
    — *Field a variety of new high-technology conventional weapons.* (S NF)

Modernization has proceeded apace under Gorbachev, and new highs in spending on military R&D as well as on hardware have been reached in his first four years. Our preliminary estimates suggest that the value of military procurement grew in real terms by about 3 to 4 percent per year during this period. But, despite these initial trends, we believe—on the basis of private and public comments and the regime's recent initiatives—that the leadership now intends to take steps over the next several years that will affect virtually all areas of the Soviet defense effort. (C NF)

13. *(Continued)*

Gorbachev's success in consolidating power in a leadership shakeup last fall and the reduction in East-West tensions have improved his ability to move ahead forcefully with his defense agenda. Given the current ferment and flux in Soviet policy, we cannot predict the future with high confidence. But, if current policy trends in Moscow continue—and, in our view, they are likely to for at least the next few years—we believe the following developments are likely.

Defense Spending. In light of Gorbachev's recent actions and the public commitment of the defense industries to step up drastically their support for consumer programs, we now judge it likely that—barring a dramatic escalation of East-West tensions—Soviet defense spending in real terms will decline over the next couple of years, while efforts to reduce the defense burden will continue during the 1991-95 Five-Year Plan:

- The unilateral reductions Gorbachev announced at the United Nations in December, the withdrawal from Afghanistan, and the elimination of missiles and equipment under the INF Treaty could yield annual savings equivalent to about 6 percent of estimated Soviet defense spending in 1988 (7.5 billion rubles).

- Gorbachev's recent assertion that defense spending will be trimmed by 14.2 percent over the next two years—we estimate a 124-billion-ruble 1988 defense budget—implies that further cuts beyond those already announced are in the offing.

- To implement this pledge, we believe the Soviets are likely to reduce procurement in most areas. R&D may also be reduced, but we believe they are likely to sustain a strong R&D effort in the areas of space- and ground-based strategic defense systems, directed-energy and radiofrequency weapons, and advanced conventional munitions.

- To implement Gorbachev's companion promise to cut procurement by 19.5 percent, the Soviets are likely to stretch out procurement rates, phase out older weapons more rapidly, cancel some programs, and use greater selectivity in choosing weapon programs to develop. We believe this will especially affect tank and military aircraft production, where the potential savings are substantial and the resources readily convertible to civilian needs.[2]

Strategic Arms. Achieving reductions in strategic arms—for military and political more than economic reasons—will remain high on the Gorbachev regime's agenda.[3] Completing work on a START agreement and constraining SDI will be top priorities in 1989. We believe the Soviets are likely to show further flexibility:

- They will continue to insist on a simultaneous reaffirmation of the ABM Treaty, but will settle for language that establishes a less explicit link to START reductions than does their current position.

- They may agree to defer the sea-launched cruise missile issue or accept a simple declaratory statement of limits.

- Gorbachev will dismantle the Krasnoyarsk radar if necessary to achieve a START agreement.

- The Soviets will not let verification become an obstacle.

- Should negotiations stall, Gorbachev may take unilateral steps—implementing some of the prospective START agreement's provisions—to generate additional pressure on US negotiators and capture the economic savings in the near term.

Follow-on strategic arms talks will raise additional complications, such as the need to factor other nations' forces into the equation. Moscow may well

---

[2] A successful diversion of resources from the defense sector to the civilian economy could do much to increase worker incentives and ease inflationary pressures, thereby paving the way for the eventual implementation of key economic reforms. Effecting such a diversion, however, will be no easy task given the inefficiencies that plague the Soviet economy.

[3] The outlook for Soviet strategic forces is discussed in greater detail in NIE 11-3/8-88, *Soviet Forces and Capabilities for Strategic Nuclear Conflict Through the Late 1990s*, December 1988.

13. *(Continued)*

Secret

pursue further reductions in strategic systems, but will insist on maintaining at least a rough parity with the West. Despite Gorbachev's call for the elimination of nuclear weapons by the end of the century, the Soviets will want to retain sufficient strategic forces for deterrent purposes and to buttress their superpower status, and we do not believe they see a total ban on nuclear weapons as a realistic objective.

Conventional Arms. The impact of new thinking on conventional forces is likely to be greater than on strategic arms:[4]

- Conventional forces are large and expensive to maintain and modernize. Without cuts here, the increased allocation of resources toward civilian use that Gorbachev wants would be impossible.

- Initiatives to reduce the USSR's conventional force preponderance have the greatest potential to undercut support in NATO for increases in defense spending and weapon modernization programs.

The reductions Gorbachev announced at the United Nations in December 1988—when implemented— will cut substantially into Soviet force structure in Central Europe and will significantly reduce the prospect of a short warning theater offensive. Moscow will retain the capability to conduct a major offensive into NATO territory after a period of mobilization. As Moscow implements these cuts over the next two years, it seems likely that the Soviets will argue the ball is now in NATO's court. Any new unilateral initiatives in the time frame of this Estimate may be addressed to other defense sector elements.

Over the longer term, we believe the leadership's recent statements and the ongoing ferment in military doctrine indicate Moscow will go much further:

- A majority of analysts believe that, over the next few years, Moscow will take additional steps to address remaining asymmetries that favor the Warsaw Pact and restructure and redeploy its forces into a more defensive posture. Moscow will prefer that any steps on this scale be part of negotiated arrangements with the West that also limit perceived Western advantages in air and naval forces. But, given the prospects for protracted negotiations, the potential for further unilateral initiatives remains high.

- By pointing approvingly to Khrushchev's announced demobilization of 1.2 million troops in January 1960, some Soviet officials are clearly arguing for substantial cuts beyond what Gorbachev promised at the United Nations.

- There has been some discussion at lower levels in the USSR of truly radical initiatives, including an abolition of universal service and a shift to a much smaller professional army manned by volunteers and supported by a large territorial reserve army structure. Such a force could reduce the costs associated with a large standing force and allow diversion of significant resources to the civilian economy and to high-technology conventional weapons. This discussion has provoked sharp rejoinders from senior military officials. We believe initiatives on this scale are unlikely during the time frame of this Estimate but we do not rule them out.

Chemical Weapons. The Soviet leadership will give a high priority during this period to reaching some kind of global CW convention that would stop the United States from modernizing its CW stockpile. How far to go in putting the Soviet arsenal on the negotiating table has probably been a subject of some controversy within the senior military and political leadership:

- On the one hand, Soviet Foreign Minister Shevardnadze has spoken out forcefully against chemical weapons to Soviet audiences, arguing that geographic considerations make chemical weapons a much greater threat to the USSR than to NATO; that Soviet CW stockpiles are "barbaric" and harm the USSR's reputation abroad; and that they represent a colossal waste of resources.

---

[4] The outlook for Soviet conventional forces is discussed in greater detail in NIE 11-14-89, *Trends and Developments in Warsaw Pact Theater Forces and Doctrine Through the 1990s*, February 1989. (U)

13. *(Continued)*

- On the other hand, on the basis of our own estimates, we believe official Soviet statements continue to obscure the scope of Moscow's CW stockpile.

President Bush's strong statements of his own interest in a chemical accord probably add to Moscow's interest in exploring the prospects, despite the difficult verification issues remaining. Further initiatives from Moscow are certain, and—given the uncertain prospects for a negotiated agreement—unilateral steps are likely. We believe Moscow will probably:

- Seek to undercut Western skepticism about Soviet sincerity by agreeing to intrusive on-site monitoring of some Soviet facilities, putting pressure on the United States to reciprocate.

- Clarify its willingness to go beyond the destruction of old CW stockpiles and address the issues of research and development of new CW agents and of CW proliferation in the developing countries.

Despite the changes in size and posture we believe are possible over the next five years or so, Soviet military forces will remain large, diverse, and increasingly modern, and will continue to pose a formidable threat to the West. Moscow will retain forces sufficient to launch large-scale offensive operations should war occur. The specific dimensions of the military threat that Soviet forces will present to the West over time remain to be determined and are beyond the scope of this Estimate.[5]

Policy Toward the Western Alliance

Moscow is giving greater priority than in the past to relations with Western Europe. Moscow's increased interest in the region reflects domestic as well as foreign policy considerations:

- The Soviets expect that Western Europe's global clout will grow and that non-US members of NATO will acquire greater influence within the Alliance. Gorbachev protege Aleksandr Yakovlev, now in charge of the Central Committee Foreign Policy Commission, has underscored these trends in his writings and public remarks and argued that Moscow should take the potentially divergent interests of the United States and Western Europe into account as it pursues its national security agenda in the region.

- Moscow does not want to be left out as the European Community (EC) heads toward closer economic integration and growing economic power.

- Western Europe is a critical source of the foreign technology, investment, and trade that over the long run will be important to the success of *perestroyka*. The West Europeans are seen in Moscow as more willing and reliable suppliers than the United States.

A series of new initiatives aimed at the West Europeans have shifted from heavyhanded military intimidation toward more sophisticated political approaches. Gorbachev is scheduled to visit the key West European capitals in the first half of 1989:

- Soviet leaders acknowledge that past policies toward the Alliance—such as the deployment of SS-20s and withdrawal from the INF talks in December 1983—triggered counterproductive Western responses.

- After years of criticizing the EC, the Soviets have decided that the potential benefits of relations—symbolized by the signing of an EC-CEMA cooperation agreement in June 1988—outweigh any risks to Warsaw Pact cohesion.

- Moscow's emphasis on the theme of a "common European home" symbolizes its shift from the stick to the carrot as it seeks to expand its influence while limiting that of the United States.

- Moscow's credentials in Western Europe will be enhanced by its willingness to give its East European allies substantial new room for maneuver. The Soviets will allow the East Europeans wide latitude

---

[5] These issues are discussed in NIE 11-14-89, NIE 11-3/8-88, and the forthcoming NIE 11-15-89, *Soviet Naval Strategy and Programs Toward the 21st Century*. (U)

13. *(Continued)*

for expanded economic ties to Western Europe short of leaving the CEMA framework or taking steps that leave them excessively vulnerable to Western leverage.

While Gorbachev has spoken of a united Europe free of alliances and divisions and wants to reduce US presence and influence on the Continent, Moscow almost certainly accepts current alignments as a reality for the foreseeable future. Although concerned about NATO's military capabilities, the Soviet leadership sees NATO as providing certain benefits: helping to preserve European stability, managing the German question, inhibiting the development of an independent European military organization, and influencing and even restraining the United States. Taking steps to end the political division of Europe for the foreseeable future would also run serious risks in Eastern Europe. Soviet accounts of an important foreign ministry conference in Moscow last summer reported a consensus view that attempting to decouple the United States from Western Europe would at least for now be counterproductive.

Outlook

While Moscow's ultimate goal is a Western Europe closer to the USSR and more distant from the United States, we believe that, for the time frame of this Estimate and indeed well beyond, Soviet objectives are more modest:

- Moscow will attempt to translate its more benign image under Gorbachev into tangible gains—expanding economic ties and technology sales, slowing modernization of NATO's conventional forces, and undercutting support for defense spending in Western Europe—and more generally into an expansion of Soviet influence on the Continent.

- Blocking modernization of NATO's short-range nuclear weapons will be a top priority. Gorbachev is likely to announce some unilateral reductions in Moscow's arsenal of short-range nuclear forces as early as this year as NATO approaches a decision on modernization of the Lance missile.

- Moscow's interest in maintaining stability on the Continent will limit its initiatives on West Germany and Berlin. The Soviets hope that West German concerns about becoming the battlefield in a future war can assist them in impeding NATO's plans to modernize its nuclear and conventional arsenal. Gorbachev will attempt to cultivate a separate relationship with West Germany that covers security as well as economic issues. Soviet initiatives that play to Bonn's interest in improving relations with East Germany are likely; there are even hints of flexibility concerning the Berlin Wall. Soviet and East European sensitivities about a resurgent Germany, however, will, in our view, prevent Moscow from condoning any serious steps toward reunification or from launching any other initiatives that would raise questions about the basic postwar framework.

Competition in the Third World

The Soviets are engaged in a broad-range review of their objectives and strategy in the Third World that directly affects their relations with the West. They now believe that their past policies failed to achieve what they had hoped in terms of lasting gain and redressing the East-West balance. At the same time, they incurred some significant economic and diplomatic costs:

- Soviet leaders have ceased to see the Third World as ripe for leftist revolution or adding to the socialist camp.

- Current Soviet policy is more pragmatic and less encumbered by ideological blinders.

- Given the importance of reduced East-West tensions to Gorbachev's agenda, Moscow is more careful to consider how its actions affect broader Soviet interests, including relations with the West.

Under Gorbachev the accent is on political rather than military competition and on finding political solutions to regional conflicts. Moreover, the Soviets emphasize there are limits to Soviet largess and that leftist Third World regimes must bear greater responsibility for their own revolutions.

13. *(Continued)*

The Soviets, nevertheless, continue to see the Third World as a region of rivalry with the West:

- They continue attempts to reduce US influence and especially the US military presence. Moscow expects that its initiatives to assume a less threatening and more cooperative image will create an international atmosphere less tolerant of a major US military presence.

- Moscow continues to back Communist allies and to selectively support client states and some revolutionary movements (notably the African National Congress, the South-West African People's Organization, and the Farabundo Marti National Liberation Front in El Salvador).

Under Gorbachev, Moscow is assigning a much more important role in carrying out its strategy in the Third World to international organizations, and particularly to the United Nations. Moscow is probing for ways to exploit UN peacekeeping mechanisms as a means to constrain unilateral US initiatives and enlarge its own role.

Looking Ahead
Moscow will continue low-profile support when feasible to leftist insurgencies and groups that are deemed to have some future, mainly those that will not require massive Soviet assistance. The Soviets will press their allies and clients to be sensitive to broader Soviet interests and to eschew behavior that could excessively antagonize the Western powers:

- Soviet clients in the Third World will also be encouraged to undertake economic and political reforms and to accept and even seek Western economic assistance.

- Soviet economic and military assistance to Third World clients will in many cases be scaled back as agreements are renegotiated. Even allies of special importance (Cuba, Vietnam, Angola, Ethiopia, South Yemen, Nicaragua, and Afghanistan) are likely to feel the pinch, although they will continue to receive substantial aid.

- Given Moscow's limited economic capacities, the Soviets will continue to push arms sales for barter or hard currency. Military assistance will remain the primary feature of Soviet relations with many Third World countries and may be offered at favorable terms in order to help expand Soviet influence in countries of special importance to Moscow.

- It is highly unlikely that Moscow will become directly involved in military support to a leftist seizure of power in the Third World as it did in the 1970s.

- Moscow will give greater priority to relations with the newly industrializing countries and traditionally pro-Western states.

- Soviet military forces (primarily naval and naval air) will remain deployed to several Third World locations, particularly the eastern Mediterranean Sea. We believe there is a good chance, however, that Moscow may draw down its forces in some areas. We see some chance that Soviet naval forces will withdraw from Cam Ranh Bay during the time frame of this Estimate. Although the Soviets may in some cases seek to expand existing military access arrangements, we believe they are unlikely to seek any new foreign basing arrangements.

Moscow will be more supportive than in the past of negotiated settlements in regional conflicts, although its behavior will depend on the potential impact on relations with the West or other key regional powers, and also on the economic cost to Moscow of supporting such a conflict:

- In the Middle East, the policy of "neither peace nor war" no longer suits Soviet interests. The potential threat that a conflict poses to Soviet security and to relations with the Western powers ensures that Moscow will support a peace process in which it has a role, while leaning on its Arab clients and the PLO to be more cooperative in the process.

- In Central America, Moscow will counsel Nicaragua's President Ortega to take advantage of regional peace initiatives, limit support for regional leftist insurgencies, move toward more pragmatic economic policies, and seek economic aid from a variety of

13. *(Continued)*

Figure 3
Soviet Economic Aid Disbursements to Selected LDCs

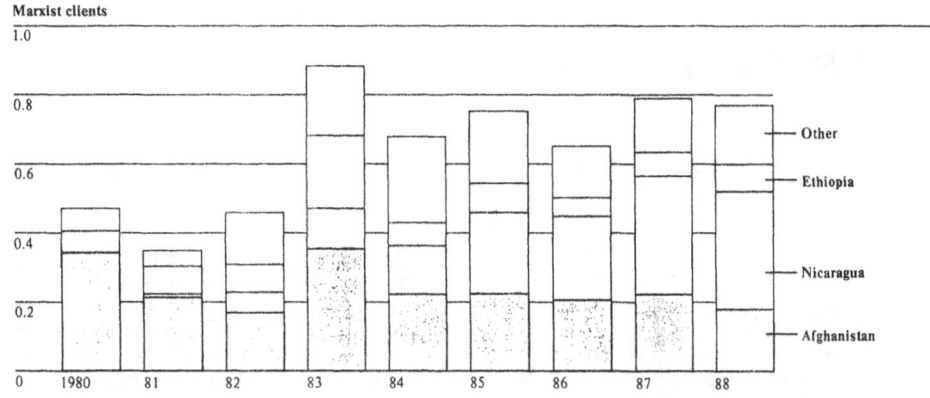

Note: The numbers for Communist countries have been revised as a result of recent study.

13. *(Continued)*

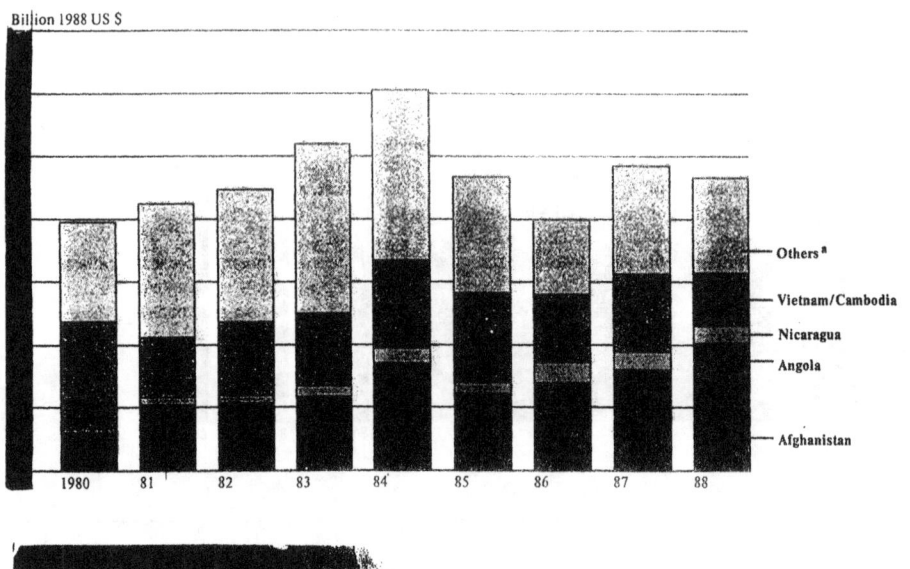

Figure 4
Soviet Arms Deliveries to Marxist and Communist Clients, 1980-88

donors. While encouraging internal reforms, the Soviets will work to keep Nicaragua a Marxist-Leninist state.

- Moscow sees the Horn of Africa as another potential arena for joint US-Soviet efforts to encourage a political settlement. (C-NF)

Prospects for Gains and Losses

These changes in Soviet approach have already produced some important successes for Moscow. To a substantial degree, Gorbachev has already undercut the fundamental mistrust that has sustained resistance in the West and most of the Third World to expansion of Soviet political, economic, and military influence. If current trends continue—and we believe they will—he is likely to make substantial progress toward the objectives that drive this change in approach:

- Building on the gains he has already made, Gorbachev will succeed in creating an extended respite from East-West tensions and a more stable international environment conducive to undertaking disruptive internal reforms.

13. *(Continued)*

- Existing pressures within the Western Alliance to slow the pace of defense modernization, reduce standing military forces, and limit defense spending will be further strengthened—with or without arms control agreements—thus facilitating Moscow's effort to reduce the defense burden, make additional troop cuts, and concentrate on rebuilding the Soviet economy.

- Western interest in broadening trade, technology sales, and financial and other economic ties to the USSR will increase as a result of a more lenient political attitude toward involvement in *perestroyka*. (Serious economic constraints, such as the difficulty of repatriating profits and Moscow's lack of hard currency, will remain.)

But Moscow is playing from a weak hand as it attempts to translate an improving image abroad into tangible, lasting benefits. Its use of military power as a lever of influence is likely to decline further, while it will face persisting economic and political weaknesses that *perestroyka* will do little to alleviate in the time frame of this Estimate. In particular, even if Gorbachev's reforms begin to take hold, the USSR is not likely to be a major global economic player until well into the next century, if then:

- *The Western Alliance.* New incentives will be created for individual Alliance members to pursue parochial agendas with Moscow. Changing attitudes toward the USSR in Western Europe will complicate Alliance management. Alliance unity on some key security issues will be seriously tested, but West European support for a US military presence on the Continent will not, in our view, be significantly eroded.

- *The Third World.* Many Third World countries will welcome the USSR's new international respectability as an opportunity to improve ties to Moscow—aiming to advance their own regional agendas and to gain some leverage on the United States. Moscow is likely to be able to capitalize by playing a larger role on regional issues—such as a Middle East peace settlement—where it has long been odd man out. Local opponents of US military facilities in the Third World will be emboldened to press their case as perceptions of a Soviet threat decline. Soviet activity and presence will increase, affording Moscow new opportunities for influence and intelligence operations. But the fundamental geopolitical interests of developing countries will incline them to continue good relations with the West, while economic weakness will significantly limit Moscow's relevance to the main issues confronting them.

Moscow may well suffer losses that will offset some of its potential gains—losses that could ultimately serve to discredit the course Gorbachev has set and give support to those who are arguing for a more cautious course:

- In a more relaxed climate, there is a significant chance that some East European countries—or populations—will try to move beyond even the expanded leeway for political and social change that Gorbachev seems to be allowing. Moscow's alliance structure and cohesion may be challenged even sooner than ours.

- Moscow's unorthodox foreign policy departures and its reductions of material support will lead some Soviet Third World clients to explore improved ties to the West.

Gorbachev and his allies in the leadership can nevertheless more easily point to the successes of their reform agenda in the international arena than they can at home, where political reforms have produced turmoil and economic reforms have yet to produce significant results. Successes on the foreign front will continue to strengthen their hand during the time frame of this Estimate, but will by no means ensure their survival or the success of the reforms.

The Future of Soviet Strategy: With and Without Gorbachev

Our reporting suggests that Gorbachev's radical departures from past policy have been and probably will continue to be controversial with elements of the elite. The radicalization of his agenda over the past year or so has evidently deepened the controversy:

- Public statements of Politburo members Ligachev and Chebrikov suggest that they are less enthusiastic supporters of "new thinking" than other members of the Politburo.

13. *(Continued)*

- Party conservatives and members of the military and security elites have criticized specific decisions such as the unilateral nuclear testing moratorium, the acceptance of asymmetrical reductions in the INF Treaty, and unilateral force reductions.

Scenarios Under Gorbachev

Nevertheless, Gorbachev has continued to outmaneuver his critics and to improve his ability to carry out his foreign policy and defense agenda. We believe a continuation and consolidation of current trends is the most likely scenario in the next few years:[6]

- It is widely recognized in Moscow that the Gorbachev foreign policy has contributed to a dramatic improvement in the USSR's international image and to its security.

- Gorbachev will continue to move cautiously to prepare the groundwork for potentially controversial initiatives.

- He will continue to gradually remove defenders of the old order. With his downgrading of leading conservative critic Ligachev last fall, he put naysayers on notice that they will pay a price for resisting his program.

- Gorbachev is shaking up the entire foreign policy and national security apparatus so that it will better serve his agenda. The foreign ministry and party foreign policy apparatus have already undergone substantial reorganization and the military, intelligence, and security services reportedly will soon do so as well.

Potentially Disruptive Developments

Gorbachev's reform agenda has so far produced considerable economic disruption and political turmoil, with few positive results to show for it. The situation is likely to get worse before it gets better. Short of the overthrow of Gorbachev, we believe the new leadership's strategy toward the West is relatively invulnerable to such bad news on the home front.

Up to a point, the prospect of continuing domestic turmoil is likely to reinforce sentiment in favor of a respite from East-West tensions. Continued economic decline could push Moscow to move more quickly to reduce trade barriers and elicit assistance from the West, especially on the consumer front. Political instability, on the other hand—particularly if it was nationality based—could lead Moscow on a selective basis to reimpose constraints on contacts between Soviet citizens and the West, limit travel opportunities, resume some jamming of Western radios, and tighten the constraints on *glasnost*.

Serious instability in Eastern Europe would probably pose the greatest risk to Gorbachev's approach to the West. Moscow is tolerating and even encouraging significant steps in the Bloc toward greater independence in domestic and foreign policy. Moscow's tolerance has fueled new and rapidly growing pressures for change in the region, especially in Poland and Hungary. Precipitous steps toward greater independence by an East European regime—raising the prospect of a loss of party dominance or a challenge to the integrity of the Pact—would raise alarms in Moscow and strengthen sentiment in favor of a crackdown in the region and the reimposition of tighter controls on East-West contacts.

A reescalation of US-Soviet tensions—perhaps provoked by a crackdown at home or in Eastern Europe—could also throw Gorbachev's strategy off track. There is already some sentiment in the leadership that Gorbachev has moved too quickly in his drive to improve relations with the Western powers and given away too much. A shift in Washington toward a harshly anti-Soviet policy could reinforce these concerns and lead Gorbachev to tack in a conservative direction.

This development would probably not lead the leadership to roll back initiatives already taken, but it would almost certainly strengthen those arguing that

---

[6] Our judgments about Gorbachev's staying power are based on his strong political skills, his willingness to tack with the political winds if necessary, and the success he has already achieved in outflanking conservative opponents in the party. These issues will be discussed in greater depth in the forthcoming NIE 11-18-89, *Prospects for Gorbachev and His Reform Agenda Over the Next Four Years*.

13. *(Continued)*

Moscow should "pause" in its efforts to forge better ties to the United States and place more priority on cultivating the West Europeans. It could also limit Gorbachev's freedom on maneuver in negotiations and his ability to transfer additional resources from defense to the civilian economy.

Scenarios Without Gorbachev

How Soviet policy would change without Gorbachev would depend on the timing and the circumstances surrounding his departure. We do not believe a return to the confrontational policies of the past is likely. But there could be some significant retrenchment from Gorbachev's more forthcoming approach to the West and a resulting increase in East-West tensions:

- If Gorbachev were to die in office, we believe his policies would survive him at least in the short run. Gorbachev would most likely be replaced by a moderate reformer or by one of several allies on the Politburo who seem as radical or more so than he is. Either would attempt to maintain the current course, although the removal of Gorbachev's forceful personality and political skills would be bound to slow the pace of change. Because Gorbachev probably will continue to remove opponents of his policies from the Politburo, over time the probability that Gorbachev's course would persist is likely to increase.

- If Gorbachev were to be ousted from office in the next few years, he most likely would be replaced by a more orthodox figure favoring a distinctly more cautious course on domestic and foreign policy. Such a leadership would probably voice support for *perestroyka* in general, while in practice moving to gut some of Gorbachev's most controversial initiatives to liberalize the political system and introduce market elements into the economy. It would be difficult for any regime to improve Soviet economic performance without constraining defense spending, but a more orthodox leadership would almost certainly be more supportive of military and defense industry interests. It would probably eschew meaningful unilateral arms control concessions or force cuts, be more supportive of leftist allies abroad, and take a more conservative approach to the reorganization of the military and security services. Such a regime would not necessarily pursue more confrontational policies, but its harder line on a range of foreign and domestic issues would probably lead to an increase in East-West tensions.

- We see little chance that any alternative regime would find it in the Soviet interest to revert to an openly confrontational strategy toward the West that would entail a major new military buildup or aggressive policies in the Third World. Political instability serious enough to threaten central control—while unlikely in our view—would increase the chances that a xenophobic leadership advocating such a course could come to power.

- We see even less chance of a leadership coming to power that attempts to pursue a more radical effort than Gorbachev to engage the West and integrate the USSR into the international community.

Implications for Western Policy

Under almost any scenario, the USSR will remain the West's principal military and political adversary. *Perestroyka*, however, is changing the nature of the Soviet challenge. Soviet policies that mute Cold War rhetoric and reduce the West's perception of hostility and danger threaten to undermine the philosophical and institutional framework the West has developed over the last 40 years for containing and combating Soviet and Communist expansionism. It will become increasingly difficult for the West to approach East-West relations from the same perspective, rhetoric, and policies as in the past. Western policies will have to sell in a more challenging market where the perception of threat is significantly reduced while competition remains strong.

At the same time, the processes Gorbachev has set in motion create new opportunities to realize objectives Western policy has long sought. These processes will continue to:

- Erode the xenophobia and two-camp mentality that have traditionally driven Soviet hegemonic ambitions.

13. *(Continued)*

Secret

> *The Long-Term Outlook*
>
> *There is general agreement in the Intelligence Community over the outlook for the next five to seven years, but differing views over the longer term prospects for fundamental and enduring change toward less competitive Soviet behavior:*
>
> - *Some analysts stress Gorbachev's political vulnerability, the opposition to real change in the party, military, and security elites, and the unpredictable consequences of the turmoil he has fostered in the system. They point to a history of failed attempts to reform the Soviet system and are reluctant to make long-range predictions about the future. In any event, they see Gorbachev's changes as largely tactical, driven by the need for a respite from the competition. They suspect that less confrontational policies may last only as long as necessary to achieve the expected gains in economic performance—albeit into the next century—and see a serious risk of a return to traditionally assertive behavior when that time arrives.*
>
> - *Other analysts stress Gorbachev's political strength and cunning and the strong forces—societal pressures and global trends—behind the reform process. They view the current effort at reform as far deeper and more comprehensive than past attempts and see current changes as driven by a fundamental rethinking of national interests and ideology as well as by more tactical considerations. They see temporary retrenchments as possible and even likely, but believe Gorbachev's changes will more likely than not have sufficient momentum to endure, producing lasting shifts in Moscow toward a more open society, more cooperative behavior in the Third World, and a significantly reduced emphasis on military competition.* (C NF)

- Pave the way for the significant reduction of forward-based Soviet military power in Europe.

- Weaken Soviet hegemony and expand individual liberties in Eastern Europe.

- Undercut support for radical leftists in the Third World.

- Further weaken the claims of the military on the Soviet budget.

- Facilitate movement toward institutional guarantees for individual liberties in the USSR. (C NF)

There are limits on the West's ability to influence this process:

- Gorbachev and his colleagues have made clear that they plan to proceed in current directions whether or not the West reciprocates.

- Western assistance can affect Soviet economic performance only at the margins.

- In the long run, Gorbachev's fortunes and the fate of his policies will rest more on domestic factors—the ability to control domestic disorder and to improve economic performance—than on foreign policy successes. (C NF)

Nevertheless, Western influence over Soviet foreign, defense, and domestic policies is probably greater than ever before:

- While Gorbachev has the initiative and the ability to make foreign policy innovations more quickly than the Western democracies, the USSR's domestic troubles give him the weaker hand and the greater need for a less confrontational relationship.

- Gorbachev recognizes that successes abroad help bolster his position at home. His ability to claim success will be dependent on how the West responds to his initiatives. (C NF)

Gorbachev will not endanger Soviet security or give in to what he perceives as blackmail, but he has already shown that he is prepared to force through dramatic changes in past Soviet policies—even at some risk to his political position—in order to address longstanding Western concerns. (C NF)

13. *(Continued)*

~~Secret~~

> *Origins of "New Thinking"*
>
> "New thinking" has come to stand for a number of theoretical tenets—from deemphasis on military struggle and class warfare to "reasonable sufficiency" in defense to a reassessment of the costs and benefits of Third World involvement—that Gorbachev has set forth as guiding principles of his foreign policy. (C NF)
>
> While Gorbachev has brought these new concepts to the fore, many of them have a long history. Some got their start under Khrushchev, in the thaw that followed Stalin's death:
>
> - Although he never used the term, Khrushchev made a number of basic theoretical alterations—discarding Stalin's dogma on the inevitability of war and resurrecting peaceful coexistence.
>
> - Many current "new thinkers," including Gorbachev, began their political and academic careers during the Khrushchev years. (C NF)
>
> The Brezhnev years were marked by a more conservative political tone. But the regime tolerated a broadening discussion in academic circles of many of the components of new thinking—such as the risks of regional conflicts, the changing nature of capitalist societies, and the meager prospects for Communist gains in the Third World. (C NF)
>
> The formation and growing prominence in the postwar years of a number of foreign policy think tanks under the auspices of the Academy of Sciences played a key role in the dissemination of new thinking. Most of the well-known proponents of new thinking have their origins in or still work in a handful of these institutes. (C NF)
>
> Most of the ideas that Gorbachev has touted under the rubric of new thinking in fact have their origins in the West. Well before new thinking, Western concepts such as "interdependence," balance of interests, and mutual security were appearing in Soviet academic journals and unofficial remarks. (C NF)
>
> Gorbachev has sought to institutionalize new thinking by promoting its proponents at every opportunity to positions of prominence in the party apparatus and the media. New thinkers are noticeably prominent in the major academic institutes and the foreign ministry. Were the political climate in Moscow to shift, however, proponents of more orthodox approaches to international affairs could again assume more influential positions. (C NF)

Indicators of Enduring Change

As evidence of Moscow's progress over the next two to three years toward fulfilling the promise of more responsible behavior, we will be watching for:

- Soviet acceptance of real liberalization in Eastern Europe.

- Full implementation of announced force reductions.

- A substantial conversion in the defense industry to production for the civilian economy. (C NF)

Over the longer term, we believe the most reliable indications of progress toward—or retrogression from—enduring change in the USSR will not be in any specific list of policy changes but in evidence of a more open society and relationship with the outside world:

- Institutional changes that implement a more pluralistic decisionmaking process on national security issues, such as establishing an effective mechanism for oversight of foreign policy and defense issues by the USSR Supreme Soviet (legislature).

13. *(Continued)*

- The institutionalization of *glasnost* in the national security realm, providing for release of significant data about the Soviet defense budget and sanctioning a vigorous debate about foreign and defense policy options.

- Playing a responsible, nonconfrontational role on transnational issues (such as terrorism, narcotics, and the environment) and in international bodies such as the United Nations.

- Significant steps toward greater interdependence with the global economy, making the ruble a convertible currency (not likely in the period of this Estimate) and exposing the Soviet economy to foreign competition.

- Progress toward the rule of law, including sharp curtailment of the security organs' extralegal activities.

- A significant relaxation of the barriers to free travel and emigration.

14. SNIE 37-89, November, 1989, *Afghanistan: The War in Perspective* (Key Judgments only)

 **Director of Central Intelligence**

SNIE 37-89

Afghanistan: The War in Perspective

Information available as of November 1989 was used in the preparation of this Special National Intelligence Estimate.

The following intelligence organizations participated in the preparation of this Estimate:
The Central Intelligence Agency
The Defense Intelligence Agency
The National Security Agency
The Bureau of Intelligence and Research, Department of State

also participating:
The Deputy Chief of Staff for Intelligence, Department of the Army
The Director of Naval Intelligence, Department of the Navy
The Assistant Chief of Staff, Intelligence, Department of the Air Force

This Estimate was approved for publication by the National Foreign Intelligence Board.

November 1989

14. (*Continued*)

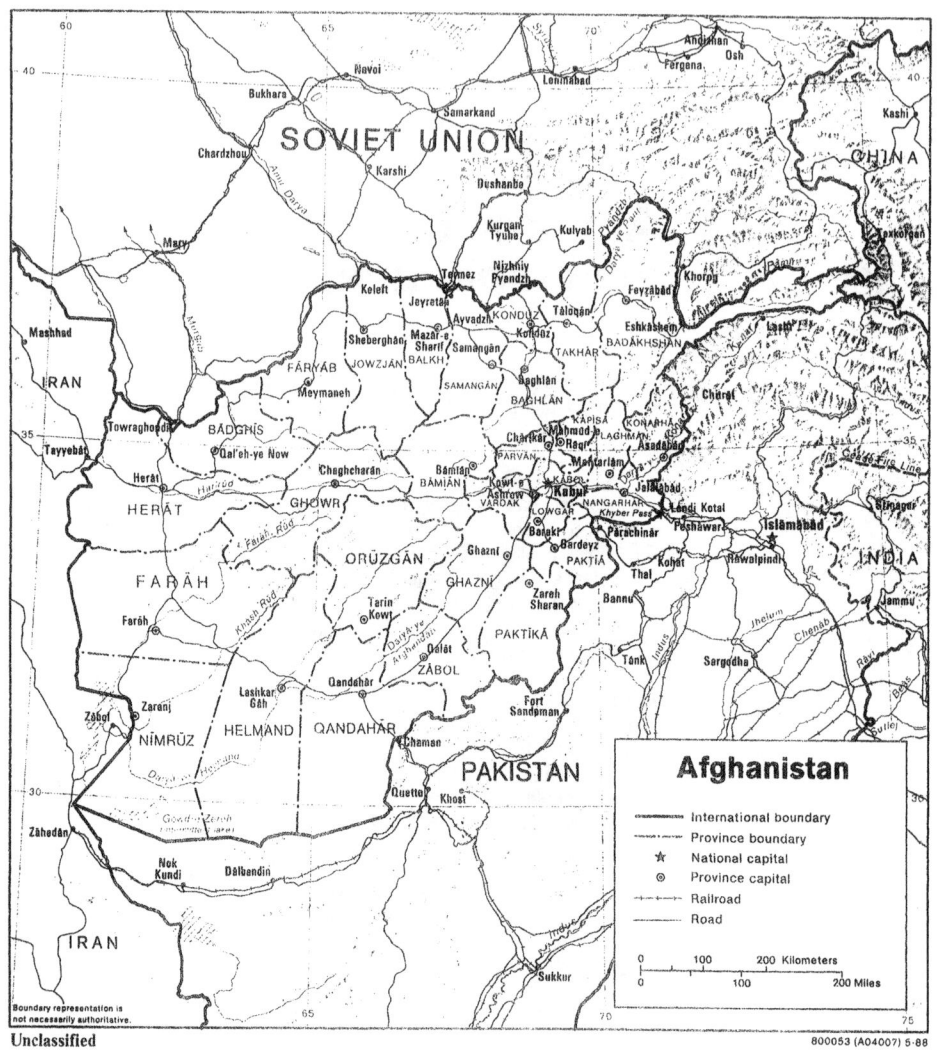

14. *(Continued)*

Key Judgments

The Kabul regime is weak, unpopular, and factionalized, but it will probably remain in power over the next 12 months. The war will remain at a near impasse. The regime will continue to resist Mujahedin pressure so long as the Soviet Union remains willing and able to continue its massive military supply program and the regime's internal problems remain manageable:

- The Mujahedin hold the military initiative *to the extent that* they move unhindered by the regime in most of the countryside and they choose when and where to fight. The resistance, however, will be unable to prevent the supply of Soviet materiel to regime forces. The resistance will remain a guerrilla force and will find it difficult to seize major regime garrisons.

- This conflict is best understood as an insurgency. Political/military elements, such as regime fragility, Mujahedin disunity, and local tribal factors will be at least as important to the final outcome as strictly military considerations.

- Despite extensive popular support, the highly factionalized resistance is unlikely to form a political entity capable of uniting the Mujahedin.

- The Afghan Interim Government and most major commanders will refuse to negotiate directly with Kabul, barring the departure of Najibullah and top regime officials, but we cannot rule out the possibility of indirect talks.

Pakistan will continue to support the resistance, whether Benazir Bhutto or her political opposition is in power. (S NF)

The Soviets will continue to search for a political settlement while providing massive support to Kabul over the next year. Soviet moves could include a dramatic new initiative, especially if Gorbachev saw it as a way to remove the Afghan issue from the US-Soviet agenda before the summit next year.

One way to break the impasse would be to alter the pattern of foreign support:
- A unilateral US cutoff of support to the resistance would alter the military balance in favor of the regime and give it the upper hand in dictating the terms of political arrangements.

14. *(Continued)*

- A unilateral Soviet cutoff of support to the regime would be devastating to Kabul's prospects.
- Mutual cuts by the United States and Soviet Union (negative symmetry) would be unpopular with the resistance but ultimately more damaging to the regime.
- Even with aid cuts, conflict would probably continue indefinitely, though at a lower level of intensity.

To reduce its vulnerability to determined efforts by the resistance to bring it down, the regime is likely to continue to seek separate deals with local resistance commanders.

15. NI IIM 91-10006, November 1991, *Soviet Tactical Nuclear Forces and Gorbachev's Nuclear Pledges: Impact, Motivations, and Next Steps* (Key Judgments only)

Director of
Central
Intelligence

~~Secret~~
~~NOFORN-NOCONTRACT~~
~~ORCON~~

Soviet Tactical Nuclear Forces and Gorbachev's Nuclear Pledges: Impact, Motivations, and Next Steps (C-NF)

Interagency Intelligence Memorandum

~~Secret~~

NI IIM 91-10006
November 1991

Copy 702

15. *(Continued)*

 Director of Central Intelligence

~~Secret~~
~~NOFORN-NOCONTRACT~~
~~ORCON~~

NI IIM 91-10006

Soviet Tactical Nuclear Forces and Gorbachev's Nuclear Pledges: Impact, Motivations, and Next Steps ~~(C-NF)~~

Information available as of November 1991 was used in the preparation of this Memorandum.

The following intelligence organizations participated in the preparation of this Memorandum:
The Central Intelligence Agency
The Defense Intelligence Agency
The National Security Agency
The Bureau of Intelligence and Research, Department of State

also participating:
The Director of Naval Intelligence, Department of the Navy
The Assistant Chief of Staff, Intelligence, Department of the Air Force

This Memorandum was approved for publication by the Chairman, National Intelligence Council.

~~Secret~~
November 1991

15. *(Continued)*

~~Secret~~
~~NOFORN NOCONTRACT~~
~~ORCON~~

Soviet Tactical Nuclear Forces and Gorbachev's Nuclear Pledges: Impact, Motivations, and Next Steps ~~(S-NF)~~

- If Gorbachev's *unilateral* initiatives to reduce tactical nuclear warheads are carried out, *almost 75 percent* of Moscow's inventory of these warheads will be *destroyed or placed in central storage.* ~~(S-NF)~~

- If Gorbachev's *reciprocal* proposals are implemented, all of the Soviet inventory of tactical nuclear warheads will be *destroyed or placed in central storage.* ~~(S-NF)~~

- The elimination process will take at least several years. ~~(S-NF)~~

- Soviet arms control positions probably are not fully worked out, but in the future Soviet negotiators are likely to become more flexible and abandon most old agenda items with the exception of dual-capable aircraft and the nuclear weapons of other countries. ~~(S-NF)~~

~~Secret~~
NI IIM 91-10006
November 1991

15. *(Continued)*

Key Judgments

The Potential Impact of Gorbachev's Proposals
The withdrawal of many Soviet units from Eastern Europe and reductions in the size and number of units within the Atlantic-to-the-Urals zone that have occurred over the past two years already have caused a sharp decline in the number of tactical nuclear systems in Soviet forces opposite NATO.

President Gorbachev's 5 October proposals, if implemented, further advance that process. We estimate that unilateral measures will lead to the destruction ▮▮▮▮▮▮▮▮▮▮▮▮▮▮▮▮▮▮ more than half the tactical nuclear warheads in Moscow's inventory. ▮▮▮▮▮▮▮ tactical naval nuclear warheads will be moved to central storage. (S NF)

A unilateral reduction on this scale will:
- Eliminate the nuclear capability of Soviet Ground Forces.
- Increase the amount of time the Soviet Navy will require to arm its ships, submarines, and aircraft with nuclear munitions.
- Take at least several years to implement.

Reciprocal measures proposed by Gorbachev would, if implemented:
- Eliminate the tactical nuclear capability of the Soviet Navy.
- Limit the air forces' quick-response tactical nuclear capability by placing warheads in central storage.

Motivations Behind the Proposals
The speed and content of Gorbachev's response to President Bush's initiative of 27 September reflect the high priority Soviet officials place on nuclear security:
- Elimination of all nuclear artillery projectiles and short-range ballistic missile (SRBM) warheads will remove most of the tactical nuclear warheads located in non-Russian republics.
- Gorbachev is using the US proposal to reassert himself as a reliable and credible negotiating partner, but his capability to fulfill completely his own proposals is questionable.

The Future of Soviet Tactical Nuclear Weapons and Negotiating Positions
Dismantling and destroying nuclear warheads is a complex and time-consuming process, and any new union, therefore, is likely to retain a tactical nuclear capability for the foreseeable future.

15. *(Continued)*

Because of continuing improvements in conventional weapon systems, the senior Soviet leadership has probably concluded that tactical nuclear warheads can be eliminated or stored without significantly compromising the war-fighting capabilities they will require.

The Soviets probably have not had enough time to think out fully their negotiating positions. We believe the Soviets are likely to:
- Be less insistent on old agenda items and display considerable flexibility, while trying to preserve the option to revisit issues, especially those affected by evolving relations between the center and the republics.
- Maintain a low-key approach to further negotiations to avoid kindling the interest of republic leaders in becoming full players in formal talks.

Carryovers from the old Soviet agenda, however, will include concern about US dual-capable aircraft and inclusion of other countries in discussions of tactical nuclear systems. This posture may reflect a greater concern about proliferation to the south and on the continent than about the United Kingdom and France.

At a minimum, the Soviets will seek a process of consultations during all phases of the implementation of US and Soviet reductions. They probably will also seek technical—and perhaps financial—aid in dismantling and destroying warheads.

Disarray in Moscow and evolving political relations will complicate the negotiating process for some time. Elements in the military may still be recalcitrant, and the republics—especially Russia, Kazakhstan, and Ukraine—want a greater say in the Kremlin's nuclear decisionmaking.

The Military Balance I
Conventional Forces in Europe

16. NIE 11-14-89, February 1989, *Trends and Developments in Warsaw Pact Theater Forces and Doctrine Through the 1990s*

Director of Central Intelligence

~~Secret~~

Trends and Developments in Warsaw Pact Theater Forces and Doctrine Through the 1990s

National Intelligence Estimate

Key Judgments and Executive Summary

These Key Judgments and Executive Summary represent the views of the Director of Central Intelligence with the advice and assistance of the US Intelligence Community.

~~Secret~~

NIE 11-14-89
February 1989
Copy 364

16. *(Continued)*

 **Director of Central Intelligence**

~~Secret~~
~~NOFORN-NOCONTRACT~~

NIE 11-14-89

Trends and Developments in Warsaw Pact Theater Forces and Doctrine Through the 1990s (U)

Information available as of 1 March 1989 was used in the preparation of this National Intelligence Estimate.

The following intelligence organizations participated in the preparation of this Estimate:
The Central Intelligence Agency
The Defense Intelligence Agency
The National Security Agency
The Bureau of Intelligence and Research, Department of State

also participating:
The Deputy Chief of Staff for Intelligence, Department of the Army
The Director of Naval Intelligence, Department of the Navy
The Assistant Chief of Staff, Intelligence, Department of the Air Force

This Estimate was approved for publication by the National Foreign Intelligence Board.

~~Secret~~
February 1989

16. *(Continued)*

Key Judgments

We judge that the Soviet leadership's security policies will produce, during the period of this Estimate, the most significant changes in Soviet general purpose forces since Khrushchev's drastic force reductions. We further assess these policies are designed primarily to help the Soviet leadership revitalize the Soviet economy by shifting resources from defense to civilian sectors. We also believe decisions already undertaken signal a sharp divergence from existing force development trends, and they have necessitated a dramatic alteration in our forecast of future Soviet general purpose forces.[1]

When Gorbachev came to power in 1985, he inherited a technologically backward economy that had experienced a decade of slowing growth characterized by industrial bottlenecks, labor and energy shortages, low and declining labor productivity, and decreasing efficiency of capital investment. Almost immediately after becoming General Secretary, he began to establish the political and ideological foundation for imposing his own priorities for resource allocations, clearly signaling a more intense competition between civilian and military needs. In doing so, he:

- Reaffirmed the traditional party authority for formulating military doctrine, which the Brezhnev regime had allowed to become dominated by the professional military hierarchy.
- Promoted a debate carried out in doctrinal terms over "reasonable sufficiency" and "defensive sufficiency," but which reflects a more fundamental examination of "How much is enough?" for defense.
- Attempted to dampen demand for defense spending by using arms control forums and foreign policy initiatives to reduce external threats.
- Broadened the Soviet concept of national security as part of the "new thinking" policy to give greater weight to its economic and political components.
- Embraced vigorously the position adopted by previous Soviet leaders that the impossibility of victory in nuclear war is basic to the political dimension of Soviet military doctrine, and that the pursuit of capabilities associated with achieving victory is too elusive and costly.

Gorbachev's initial "ground-laying" objectives were largely achieved during his first few years in office. The regime did not order cutbacks in military programs immediately, however, preferring instead to reduce the

---

[1] See Director, Defense Intelligence Agency, alternative key judgment on page ix. (S NF NC)

16. *(Continued)*

~~Secret~~

burden by attempting to increase the efficiency of the defense sector. Despite these efforts to alleviate what Soviet officials describe as a "crisis" in the economy, after four years Gorbachev has failed to bring about a rebound in economic growth. Determined to succeed in his revitalization campaign and recognizing that the defense industrial sector offers an important source of additional help for his modernization program, Gorbachev, in 1988, decided to take stronger action to invest more in consumer-oriented projects. He evidently decided to act at that point because, in addition to the obvious lack of progress on economic programs and the rise in consumer dissatisfaction, the regime was faced with some key deadlines in the preparation of the 1991-95 Five-Year Plan. The results have become most vividly evident with announced policy initiatives designed primarily to help the Soviet leadership reinvigorate the economy by shifting resources from defense to the civil sector:

- Unilateral reductions and restructuring of Soviet general purpose forces that will cut 500,000 personnel from peacetime forces by January 1991, including 240,000 personnel from Soviet forces west of the Urals and 50,000 personnel from those in Central Europe. Forces remaining opposite NATO will be converted into a "clearly defensive" structure.

- Cuts in overall defense spending of 14.2 percent and defense production levels of 19.5 percent over the next two years that clearly reflect plans for a reduced force structure and reductions in rates of equipment modernization.

- Increases in the defense industry's direct contribution to production of consumer and civilian investment goods that will cut significantly into defense output. ~~(S NF NC)~~

Despite these dramatic actions and their apparent far-reaching implications, there remains considerable uncertainty about the durability and consequences of Gorbachev's initiatives on military matters. The amount of progress that is achieved on economic revival will largely determine Gorbachev's ability to sustain his reforms, his willingness to undertake additional initiatives, his standing with the party leadership, the support he receives in pursuing related programs, and his ability to control the impact of external factors that could impinge on his objectives. ~~(S NF NC)~~

Nevertheless, we believe it is highly likely that further decisions to reduce planned defense spending and to shift investment from defense to the civil sector will become apparent during the coming 13th Five-Year Plan (1991-95). We reaffirm the recent assessment in NIE 11-23-88 ~~(Secret NF NC)~~, December 1988, *Gorbachev's Economic Programs: The Challenges Ahead*,

16. *(Continued)*

~~Secret~~

that Gorbachev will divert additional resources from the defense sector to the civil sector. Over the longer term, Gorbachev probably will continue to impose constraints on the defense budget, and we judge that Soviet defense spending will continue to decline as a portion of GNP through the turn of the century. (S NF NC)

We believe that the doctrinal concepts of "reasonable sufficiency" and "defensive sufficiency" have been articulated primarily to strengthen Gorbachev's control over defense resource decisions to support economic revival. We also believe that, by the turn of the century, these concepts probably will have become lasting features of Soviet national security policy, helping ensure continued party control over defense policy and defense spending. (S NF NC)

Decisions by the USSR and its Warsaw Pact allies to reduce their general purpose forces and cut defense spending over the next two years would reverse the long-term trend of continuing growth in size and offensive capabilities of these forces. As a consequence of the planned cuts, the offensive capabilities of Warsaw Pact theater forces will decline through the first half of the 1990s. (S NF NC)

We judge that the USSR will maintain large general purpose forces in the Atlantic-to-the-Urals zone to reinforce its status as a superpower, to deter aggression, to carry out wartime missions, and to underwrite its political objectives in the region. Within emerging economic constraints, we also believe the Soviets will modernize their still formidable general purpose forces. Furthermore, the Soviets will want to minimize the erosion of their relative military position due to both Warsaw Pact force reductions and continuing improvements in NATO military capabilities. Absent a far-reaching conventional arms control agreement, the Soviets will maintain the capability to conduct large-scale offensive operations deep into NATO territory but only after general mobilization. For the period of this Estimate, Warsaw Pact forces, led by the USSR, will remain the largest aggregation of military power in the world, and the Soviets will remain committed to the offensive as the preferred form of operations in wartime. (S NF NC)

Even with reductions in defense spending and procurement, the Soviets will continue to maintain the world's highest level of weapons production through the turn of the century. Although Soviet weapons projected through the 1990s will involve mostly evolutionary improvements over present types, a steady stream of better military technology will be available to Soviet force developers throughout this period. Indeed, the military expects *perestroyka* to yield significantly improved military technologies. (S NF NC)

16. *(Continued)*

~~Secret~~

In addition to reductions in procurement funds, the significantly increased unit costs of high-technology weapon systems will further reduce traditionally high Soviet procurement rates. The increased effectiveness of these weapons, however, will reduce the number of such systems required to maintain the combat capabilities of Soviet general purpose forces. These factors will almost certainly lead to a less than 1-for-1 replacement rate for more advanced Soviet weapon systems over the course of this Estimate. As a consequence, we expect to see a continuation in the recent trends of declining production rates and deployment patterns for high-technology equipment.

Since the late 1970s, the Soviets have improved their capabilities to conduct longer and more intensive conventional operations against NATO, including increased training for defensive operations against attacking NATO forces. The Soviets assess NATO to be a tougher military opponent on the conventional battlefield today than in past decades. Furthermore, they believe improvements in NATO doctrine and projected force modernization will make NATO an even more formidable conventional opponent over the course of this Estimate.

Soviet pessimism regarding the utility of nuclear war and NATO's increased conventional capabilities have caused the Soviets to prepare for the possibility that a NATO-Pact war might remain conventional.[2] But they believe they must also prepare for nuclear war both to deter it and to wage it if it happens. Indeed, we judge that the Soviets still believe a NATO-Pact war is likely to escalate to the nuclear level due to NATO's doctrine of flexible response. Therefore, we expect the Soviets to maintain sizable nuclear forces subject to limitations imposed by current and future arms control agreements. Furthermore, we believe that, should an agreement with NATO governing quantities and modernization of short-range nuclear forces not materialize, the Soviets will continue to expand and modernize their tactical nuclear missile force by the mid-1990s.

Following a trend we identified in ▓▓▓▓ we believe the overall peacetime readiness posture of Warsaw Pact general purpose forces opposite NATO during the period of this Estimate will be designed to accommodate the following:
• Primary emphasis will be placed on the ability to mobilize and deploy large reinforcements before hostilities, not on the ability of forward forces to initiate a quick, unreinforced attack.

~~Secret~~

16. *(Continued)*

- In line with the Warsaw Pact's recent decisions to reduce and restructure its theater forces, these forces will be maintained at sufficient readiness to defend against a sudden attack and act as a defensive shield to allow for the full mobilization and deployment of Pact forces. (S NF NC)

We consider Pact initiation of hostilities without mobilization to be extremely unlikely. We cannot, however, rule out the possibility that the Pact might initiate hostilities from a condition of partial mobilization if it perceives an opportunity to achieve decisive results against NATO, or a need to forestall NATO from achieving decisive results against the Pact. (S NF NC)

Our judgments regarding Warsaw Pact sustainability in a future war with NATO differ substantially from those made several years ago. In 1985 we stated unconditionally that the Warsaw Pact logistic structure in Central Europe could support 60 to 90 days of theater offensive operations against NATO. We now judge that overall Pact sustainability is a function of the resilience of NATO's forward defenses. If NATO's forward defenses were to collapse within three days of intensive operations, ammunition stocks in the Western Theater of Military Operations (TMO) would be sufficient to support the Pact's Theater Strategic Operation for up to 90 days. If, on the other hand, Pact forces were to require at least two weeks of high-intensity operations to achieve a decisive breakthrough, the Pact would not have enough ammunition in the Western TMO to sustain a theater strategic operation beyond a total of about 30 to 45 days. If confronted with the prospect of some shortfall in ammunition supply, the Pact would move additional ammunition stocks from elsewhere to the Western TMO, or adjust war plans to avoid or at least minimize any adverse impact on combat operations. (S NF NC)

Soviet general purpose forces are fielding new weapons of virtually every type, and we believe this trend will continue through the end of the century. Motivated by the need to counter NATO's deep-attack, high-technology conventional weapons and extended-battlefield concepts, for example, the Soviets have been able to match or exceed NATO's capabilities in nearly every major ground forces' weapons category. Rates of equipment modernization probably will decrease through the end of the century as the Soviets reduce defense production to free resources for the civil sector. However, we expect that the Soviets will resist cutting substantially research, development, testing, and evaluation in an effort to close the military technology gap with the West. As in the past, Soviet forces in the Western TMO will likely be the first to receive new equipment. (S NF NC)

16. *(Continued)*

The Ground Forces are the largest element of the Soviet armed forces, and their development determines the overall direction of Soviet theater forces development. We see no evidence that this will change. We now judge, based on the plans for reductions in force levels, defense spending and military procurement, that a 25-year period of Soviet Ground Forces growth has ended, and the decline in their overall size could go beyond that already announced. We further judge that a resumption of growth in the Ground Forces is highly unlikely before the turn of the century.

In order to meet the targets for reductions set by Gorbachev for January 1991, Soviet Ground Forces will be considerably restructured over the next two years, but we cannot confidently predict their final form. Before Gorbachev's cuts, the Soviets had begun to move toward combined-arms formations. Although the final balance of tanks and mechanized infantry is still in flux, we believe that combined-arms doctrine will guide Soviet force restructuring through the 1990s.

Despite cuts in defense spending and procurement, we judge the Soviets will continue to modernize their Air Forces, albeit more slowly than in the past. Beginning in the mid-1990s and continuing through the turn of the century, the Soviets are expected to introduce light, medium, and Stealth bombers, Stealth and non-Stealth fighter-bombers, and at least one new fighter. The announced reduction of 800 combat aircraft from the Air Forces, however, signals a significant change in the pattern of force expansion of the past two decades. We now judge that the Soviet Air Forces will remain at their post-reduction levels until after the end of the century.

Soviet naval general purpose forces continue to have the major missions of protecting the Soviet missile-launching submarine force and defending the USSR against NATO strategic and theater forces. Although the Navy can be expected to bear a share of spending reductions, major emphasis will be placed on improving antisubmarine and antisurface combatant operations, gradually modernizing Soviet naval aviation, and increasing the availability of sea-based airpower as larger aircraft carriers enter service during the 1990s. Support for land TMOs remains a primary wartime task of naval theater forces, and we project a slow continuation of several organizational and weapon trends that should provide land theater commanders with more capable naval forces for combined-arms operations.

Non-Soviet Warsaw Pact defense industries have been expanding and producing a larger share of the NSWP military inventory. But announced defense spending cuts and the weakened state of NSWP economies will cause military production in the NSWP countries to decline during the period of this Estimate. We also judge that NSWP forces will fall further

16. *(Continued)*

behind Soviet forces in technology and organization during this same period. The relative contribution of the NSWP armies to overall Warsaw Pact military capability is also likely to decline somewhat over the next few years. (S NF NC)

A major objective of the Soviet leadership's current foreign policy is to reduce political support in the NATO countries for increased defense spending to support NATO's force modernization program. Gorbachev will continue to negotiate for conventional arms control agreements to slow Western military modernization and facilitate his own defense program. In addition, Warsaw Pact foreign policy over the period of this Estimate will seek to weaken the position of the United States and Canada within the North Atlantic Alliance. (S NF NC)

Alternative Key Judgment. The Director, Defense Intelligence Agency, while recognizing the significance of the ongoing changes in the Soviet Union, believes the likelihood of large unilateral reductions in military expenditures beyond those already proclaimed by Soviet leaders is not as high as implied by the majority view in the Estimate, particularly for the longer term. Notwithstanding the potential importance of new developments in Soviet military policies discussed in this Estimate, the Director, DIA, believes present evidence and future uncertainties make the elements of continuity in Soviet military policy as important as the changes for US national security and defense planning. (S NF NC)

16. *(Continued)*

Executive Summary

A Time of Change in Soviet General Purpose Forces and Policy

We judge that the Soviet leadership's current security policies will produce during the period of this Estimate the most significant changes in Soviet general purpose forces since Khrushchev's drastic force reductions. We further assess that these policies are designed primarily to help the Soviet leadership revitalize the Soviet economy by shifting resources from defense to civil sectors. We also believe decisions already undertaken signal a sharp divergence from existing force development trends, and they have necessitated a dramatic alteration in our forecast of future Soviet general purpose forces.[3]

When Gorbachev came to power in 1985, he inherited a technologically backward economy that had experienced a decade of slowing growth characterized by industrial bottlenecks, labor and energy shortages, low and declining labor productivity, and decreasing efficiency of capital investment. Almost immediately after becoming General Secretary, he began to establish the political and ideological foundation for imposing his own priorities for resource allocations, clearly signaling a more intense competition between civilian and military needs. In doing so, he:

- Reaffirmed the traditional party authority for formulating military doctrine, which the Brezhnev regime had allowed to become dominated by the professional military hierarchy.

- Promoted a debate carried out in doctrinal terms over "reasonable sufficiency" and "defensive sufficiency," but that reflects a more fundamental examination of "How much is enough?" for defense.

- Attempted to dampen demand for defense spending by using arms control forums and foreign policy initiatives to reduce external threats.

- Broadened the Soviet concept of national security as part of the "new thinking" policy to give greater weight to its economic and political components.

- Embraced vigorously the position adopted by previous Soviet leaders that the impossibility of victory in nuclear war is basic to the political dimension of Soviet military doctrine, and that the pursuit of capabilities associated with achieving victory is too elusive and costly.

Gorbachev's initial "ground-laying" objectives were largely achieved during his first few years in office. The regime did not order cutbacks in military programs immediately, however, preferring instead to reduce the burden by increasing the efficiency of the defense sector. Despite these efforts to alleviate what Soviet officials describe as a "crisis" in the economy, after four years Gorbachev has failed to bring about a rebound in economic growth. Determined to succeed in his revitalization campaign and recognizing that the defense industrial sector offers an important source of additional help for his modernization program, Gorbachev, in 1988, decided to take stronger action to invest more in consumer-oriented projects. He evidently decided to act at that point because, in addition to the obvious lack of progress on economic programs and the rise in consumer dissatisfaction, the regime was faced with some key deadlines in the preparation of the 13th Five-Year Plan (1991-95). The results have become most vividly evident with announced policy initiatives designed primarily to help the Soviet leadership reinvigorate the economy by shifting resources from defense to the civilian sector:

- Unilateral reduction and restructuring of Soviet general purpose forces that will cut 500,000 personnel from peacetime forces by January 1991, including 240,000 personnel from Soviet forces west of the

---
[3] See Director, Defense Intelligence Agency, alternative judgment on page 13.

16. *(Continued)*

Urals and 50,000 personnel from those in Central Europe. Forces remaining opposite NATO will be converted into a "clearly defensive" structure.

- Cuts in overall defense spending of 14.2 percent and defense production levels of 19.5 percent over the next two years that clearly reflect plans for a reduced force structure and reductions in rates of equipment modernization.

- Increases in defense industry's direct contribution to production of consumer and civilian investment goods that will cut significantly into defense output.

Despite these dramatic actions and their apparent far-reaching implications, there remains considerable uncertainty about the durability and consequences of Gorbachev's initiatives on military matters. The amount of progress that is achieved on economic revival will largely determine Gorbachev's ability to sustain his reforms, his willingness to undertake additional initiatives, his standing with the party leadership, the support he receives in pursuing related programs, and his ability to control the impact of external factors that could impinge on his objectives.

Nevertheless, we believe it is highly likely that further decisions to reduce planned defense spending and to shift investment from defense to the civil sector will become apparent during the upcoming 13th Five-Year Plan. We reaffirm the recent assessment in NIE 11-23-88, December 1988, *Gorbachev's Economic Programs: The Challenges Ahead*, that Gorbachev will divert additional resources from the defense sector to the civil sector. Over the longer term, Gorbachev probably will continue to impose constraints on the defense budget, and we judge that Soviet defense spending will continue to decline as a portion of GNP through the turn of the century.

Gorbachev and the Formulation of Defense Policy

Gorbachev's decision to include the military as one target of his *perestroyka* ("restructuring") campaign has brought into sharp relief his attempts to tighten party control over the Soviet armed forces. Soon after taking office as General Secretary in early 1985, Gorbachev and his allies moved quickly to reaffirm party control over military issues, in particular its authority for formulating military doctrine. Although most attention has focused on the defense spending implications of Gorbachev's programs, it has become clear that he is also using *perestroyka* as a tool to tighten the party's grip on the military's political accountability. The mid-1988 19th Party Conference and subsequent remarks by Foreign Minister Shevardnadze calling for oversight of the Soviet military by nationwide elected bodies provide strong indications of the leadership's determination to broaden and intensify review of national security matters, especially defense spending.

Reasonable and Defensive Sufficiency. The concept of "reasonable sufficiency" is emerging as a major announced theme of Soviet security policy, and it is being linked closely to Gorbachev's new formulations of military requirements. Sufficiency has been generally defined by Gorbachev and other party officials as a level of military power adequate "to repel aggression, but insufficient to conduct offensive operations." The concept remains under discussion in the Soviet Union, and the debate has largely focused on three central issues:

- A contest over resources as Gorbachev seeks a doctrinal basis for strengthening his control over defense resource decisions.

- The need to influence Western audiences in a direction favorable to Soviet defense and economic policy objectives.

- The belief by at least some leaders that Soviet national security can be better ensured if both sides reduce their military forces.

We judge that in presenting this concept the Gorbachev leadership is attempting to establish a new basis for determining "How much is enough?" for defense. It has been linked to two other announced policy outlooks: that overall defense posture should be judged by "qualitative" as well as quantitative measures; and, that further increases over existing force

16. *(Continued)*

levels do not necessarily result in greater security. By advocating these concepts, Gorbachev seeks to promote policies that will benefit his economy by reducing the burden of military spending, mitigate the effects of reduced spending by attempting to manage the future military threat through aggressive arms control policies, and reap political benefits that would contribute to his goals by reducing the Western perception of the Soviet threat. We believe that the concept's long-term implications are inextricably linked to the fate of Gorbachev's reform programs. We further judge that, as long as leadership backing within the party for his emphasis on industrial modernization holds up, and, barring an unforeseen deterioration in US-USSR relations, Gorbachev's concept of sufficiency will provide the basis for Soviet security policy.

Over the last few years, the principle of reasonable sufficiency has also been linked to the term "defensive sufficiency" (also translated as "defensive defense"). In this context it has been proposed by Gorbachev and other high-ranking Soviet officials as a basis for determining the organization, size, disposition, and strategy of Pact and NATO forces in Europe. Not surprisingly, even many Soviet military sources have been particularly skeptical about defensive doctrine, and several high-ranking officers have asserted that, while defense can prevent the enemy from defeating the USSR, it does not defeat the enemy.

Although usually placed by Soviet spokesmen in the context of its mutual applicability to both alliances, Gorbachev linked his late 1988 unilateral troop reduction and reorganization announcement to Soviet forces adopting a "clearly defensive" structure. The leadership's championing of reasonable and defensive sufficiency derives much of its impetus from economic requirements, and we believe its success ultimately will be determined by the policy agenda and political power of the party leadership rather than by resolution of a doctrinal discourse between military and civilian writers. We further assess, nevertheless, that, by the turn of the century, these concepts probably will have become a lasting feature of Soviet national security policy, helping ensure continued party control over defense policy and defense spending.

Alternative Judgment: The Director, Defense Intelligence Agency, believes that Soviet objectives in promulgating the concept of reasonable sufficiency are designed not only to avoid the costs of an unabated continuation of the arms race, but are primarily to establish the basis for arms reduction proposals, to raise Western expectations regarding the prospects for substantial force reductions, and to undermine support for NATO modernization. Its long-term importance will depend primarily on how the West responds to Soviet initiatives and the progress made in the arms control arena. Should Gorbachev fail to achieve his minimum goals by the mid-1990s, the Soviets most likely would, despite the extremely high costs, revert to their traditional resource-intensive approach to develop the next generation of weapons and modernize their forces.

Arms Control

In parallel with the doctrinal changes involving sufficiency Gorbachev has advocated "new thinking" on foreign policy. This "new thinking" emphasizes the political and economic dimensions of national security and the limits of military power. An important element of this "new thinking" has been an aggressive public pursuit of conventional arms control since early 1986. The Warsaw Pact's efforts at conventional arms control have featured a number of proposals by Gorbachev, by the Warsaw Pact's Political Consultative Committee, and, in addition, hundreds of statements and press articles by lower-ranking officials, all stressing the Soviet Union's desire for a conventional arms reduction agreement.

We judge that the Soviets and their allies have a number of interrelated military, political, and economic reasons to engage the West in conventional arms control:

- To improve the correlation of forces and reduce what they perceive as NATO's capability to launch a surprise attack.

- To impede NATO's force modernization plans and prevent or impede NATO's deployment of advanced-technology weapons, thus reducing the urgency on the part of the Soviet Union to match or better NATO's high-technology modernization programs.

- To make it politically easier to allocate economic resources within the Soviet Union from the defense sector to the civilian sector to carry out *perestroyka*.

- To appeal to public opinion at home and abroad in a generalized way, while adding to Moscow's overall arms control posture and enhancing the USSR's image as a trustworthy and rational player in the international arena. (S NF NC)

In early December 1988, Gorbachev announced major unilateral cuts in Soviet military manpower and equipment to occur during the next two years. A month later he announced major reductions in defense spending and defense production (see the table). While we believe that a mixture of economic, political, and military considerations went into these decisions, in our judgment, economic considerations—providing resources and manpower to the civilian economy—were the primary factor. Had the cuts been designed solely for political or propagandistic effect, we believe the withdrawal of the six tank divisions from Central Europe would have been sufficient. Politically, the reductions are designed to put pressure on NATO to move toward conventional arms control negotiations that would involve multilateral force reductions. The unilateral cuts are also intended to influence NATO electorates to withdraw support for new weapons procurement programs and expanding military budgets. Indeed, over the long term, the potential for slowing NATO's modernization is probably a more important factor in Moscow's calculations than the direct savings expected from the unilateral force cuts. Slowing or reversing NATO's modernization reduces the pressure to develop matching programs and permits the Soviet leadership to concentrate on its economic problems. (S NF NC)

Depending on the West's response, Gorbachev might advance other initiatives, especially in the context of the conventional arms reduction talks, designed to keep political pressure on the West while holding down the defense burden at home. We believe further major unilateral force reductions would generate strong opposition which would coalesce within the defense establishment and among its allies in the political leadership. This opposition could be largely neutralized, however, if Gorbachev could demonstrate that NATO's military forces were also being reduced unilaterally. (S NF NC)

Soviet Doctrine on Theater War Against NATO
Nature of Future War. We believe that Soviet views on the nature and results of a theater war between NATO and the Warsaw Pact have changed in recent years. Soviet planning through the mid-1970s was based on a belief that NATO's conventional capabilities were relatively weak and the alliance was almost certain to initiate nuclear warfare early in a conflict in an effort to avoid conventional defeat. (S NF NC)

The Soviets now perceive that NATO's conventional forces have become substantially more difficult to defeat. Consequently, NATO has become more capable of delaying and perhaps averting the collapse of its conventional defenses, and the necessity for NATO to resort to early use of nuclear weapons has decreased. The Soviets may also believe that the USSR's ability to at least match NATO's nuclear strength at the tactical, theater, and strategic levels has reduced NATO's incentive to initiate nuclear use early. Nevertheless, we judge that, even under contemporary conditions, the Soviets generally assess a NATO-Pact war as likely to escalate to the nuclear level, and they continue to believe that escalation to general nuclear war is likely to be the outcome of the use of any nuclear weapons in the theater. (S NF NC)

The Soviets may also have come to believe, however, that a NATO-Pact war might terminate before the use of nuclear weapons.

16. *(Continued)*

Announced Warsaw Pact Unilateral Reductions To Take Place During 1989-90

	Military Manpower	Force Structure	Tanks	APC/IFV	Artillery Systems	Short-Range Missile Launchers	Combat Aircraft	Defense Budget (*percent*)
USSR								
Announced Total	500,000	...[a]	...[a]		...[a]	24	...[a]	14.2 (1989-90)
Eastern USSR	200,000	...[a]	...[a]		...[a]		...[a]	
Southern USSR	60,000	...[a]	...[a]		...[a]		...[a]	
Atlantic-to-the-Urals	240,000	...[a]	10,000		8,500		800	
Central Europe [b]	50,000	6 divisions	5,300		650 [c]	24	260	
Non-Soviet Warsaw Pact								
Computed Total [d]	81,300	7 divisions, 6 regiments	2,751	895	1,530	6	210	
East Germany	10,000	6 regiments	600				50	10 (1989-90)
Poland [e]	40,000	4 divisions [f]	850	700	900	6 [g]	80	4 (1989)
Czechoslovakia [h]	12,000	3 divisions	850	165			51	15 (1989-90)
Hungary	9,300		251	30	430		9	17 (1989)
Bulgaria	10,000		200		200		20	12 (1989)
Romania [i]								
Warsaw Pact Computed Totals [d]								
Atlantic-to-the-Urals	321,300	13 divisions, 6 regiments	12,751	895	10,030	30	1,010	
Eastern Europe	131,300	13 divisions, 6 regiments	8,051	895	2,180	30	470	
Central Europe [b]	121,300	13 divisions, 6 regiments	7,851	895	1,980	30	450	

[a] Soviet statements express or imply reductions in these categories, but no specific quantities have been announced.
[b] Central Europe includes Czechoslovakia, East Germany, Hungary, and Poland.
[c] This figure is assessed from units announced to be withdrawn.
[d] Announced Warsaw Pact totals are currently lagging the computed totals of the reductions announced by individual countries.
[e] In addition, Poland has announced that in the past two years (1987-88) 15,000 men, two divisions, unspecified other units, 419 tanks, 225 APCs, 194 aircraft, and other types of equipment were removed from its forces.
[f] Two of the divisions are to be eliminated, and two are to be reduced in strength.
[g] This figure is based on the announced elimination of an "operational-tactical" (Scud) missile brigade (probably in the Warsaw Military District).
[h] Czechoslovakia has announced a reduction of 12,000 men in combat units but is transferring these men and 8,000 men from support units to the military construction troops.
[i] A slight increase in defense spending (1.7 percent) was announced for 1989. No force cuts were announced.

This table is Secret Noforn Nocontract.

 Although our evidence indicates that the Soviets would neither begin a NATO-Pact conventional war for limited goals nor conduct initial operations with limited goals in mind, they may be willing to accept partial achievement of their objectives rather than increase the risk of nuclear escalation.

Nuclear Doctrine. There is no indication that the Soviets have ever been sanguine about the consequences they would expect to suffer in a nuclear war. Moreover, evidence from the 1980s indicates the Soviets doubt they could prevail in any traditionally meaningful military-political sense because of the expected high levels of damage both sides would sustain from nuclear attacks. Since the early 1980s, Soviet leaders have explicitly renounced the possibility of achieving victory in a general nuclear conflict. We judge that the "no victory in nuclear war" position—publicly endorsed by Gorbachev and incorporated in the 1986 27th Party Congress Program—is basic to the political dimension of Soviet military doctrine.[5]

The Soviet leaders' public portrayal of their nuclear policy clearly serves their political interests and it does not mean a deemphasis of Soviet nuclear weapons development. The Soviets continue to recognize that circumstances might compel them to fight a nuclear war—regardless of whether they think a traditional victory can be achieved—and they intend to achieve the best possible outcome if it ever happens. At the same time, the Soviet leadership believes the best possible nuclear-war-fighting capability will produce the best possible nuclear deterrent as well. For these reasons, subject to an arms control agreement, we expect the Soviets to maintain a sizable nuclear delivery force and to continue to improve those weapon systems that constitute this force.

We have not detected any changes in the military-technical dimension of Soviet military doctrine that clearly demonstrate that the Soviets have changed their nuclear-war-fighting doctrine under Gorbachev. The coming 13th Five-Year Plan presents a key opportunity for him to affect decisions involving the future of the Soviet armed forces. Consequently, if the Soviets determine that the pursuit of capabilities associated with traditional Soviet means of victory is too elusive and costly, we would expect, by the mid-to-late 1990s, to acquire evidence of basic changes in the structure and development of the USSR's nuclear forces.

Conventional Doctrine. The Soviets have devoted considerable emphasis during the 1980s to the changing nature of conventional warfare. Their interest has largely centered on three themes:

- Should a war between NATO and the Warsaw Pact occur, it might be a protracted, worldwide conflict fought with conventional weapons and continuing for weeks or months, perhaps even longer.

- Conventional weapons are becoming so accurate and lethal that the destructiveness of some now approaches that of low-yield nuclear weapons. They can be employed, therefore, to destroy many targets that previously required nuclear strikes. Their use, however, does not necessarily incur the risks of escalation to general nuclear war inherent in the use of even a single nuclear weapon.

- Military advantages afforded the USSR by its numerical advantages in conventional forces against NATO may be mitigated by Western progress in

---

[5] The Soviets define military doctrine as a system of basic views on the prevention of war, military organizational development, preparation of the country and the armed forces for repelling aggression, and methods of conducting warfare. It is based on the principles of Soviet military science and has two elements: sociopolitical and military-technical. The first establishes the geostrategic and ideological context in which warfare occurs, and its content is the responsibility of the Soviet political leadership; the second guides the planning and conduct of combat operations, and its formulation is primarily the responsibility of the Soviet General Staff. As Soviet military leaders have publicly acknowledged, the military-technical component is strictly subordinate to the sociopolitical dimension. Doctrine is approved by the highest Soviet civilian and military command authorities and therefore has the status of state policy.

advanced-technology conventional weapons, especially precision-guided, long-range weapons.

The acquisition of new conventional battlefield technologies by the West would create two problems for Pact operational planners during a war. First, the development and widespread fielding of such weapons by NATO could increase significantly the losses sustained by the Pact in conventional combat, thus raising the possibility of even otherwise successful operations becoming prohibitively expensive. Instead of the previous expectation of rapid breakthroughs and high-speed exploitation operations, the Soviets are now concerned that offensive operations would assume the agonizing character of "gnawing through" numerous defensive lines. Second, long-range high-technology weapons could be used to isolate the European battlefield from Pact reinforcements. Without substantial, early reinforcement by mobilized forces from the USSR, the Soviets believe that they might not attain a sufficient correlation of military forces to ensure a rapid rate of advance.

In our view, these concerns have led to a vigorous advocacy by Soviet military leaders over the last several years for modernizing conventional forces through greater exploitation of new technologies. The military's concerns for the high-technology conventional battlefield of the future have given them a strong incentive to support Gorbachev's industrial modernization strategy, which is intended to keep the Soviet Union from lagging even further behind in the development of new weapon technologies. We believe, therefore, that through the mid-1990s the military will accept the promises of future benefits and will refrain from pushing for vigorous development and full-scale fielding of weapons incorporating costly technologies.

Soviet Doctrine on War Initiation

Outbreak of War. We judge the Soviets believe that a period of crisis—possibly of very short duration but probably lasting weeks and even months—will precede a war. The Soviets generally dismiss the notions of an accidental outbreak of a major war or a massive attack launched outside the context of a major crisis. However, as a result of NATO's improved capabilities, the Soviets have expressed a growing concern that their opportunity to detect enemy preparations for an attack may have grown shorter. Soviet emphasis on defensive operations in their training, while undertaken for a variety of reasons, is consistent with the assessment that the Pact may have less warning and mobilization time than it previously believed. Nevertheless, we believe that the Soviet military still has confidence in its ability to detect enemy preparations for war at a preliminary stage—early enough to take effective action to deprive the West of gaining significant advantage from surprise.

Force Mobilization. The ability to mobilize large forces rapidly instead of maintaining immediate combat readiness of the entire force is the goal of Pact planners, based on their perception that a war in Europe will be preceded by a period of crisis. The Soviets expect that the forces of both sides will be fully or almost fully mobilized and prepared for combat before the onset of hostilities. We judge that Warsaw Pact theater forces positioned in Central Europe are maintained at sufficient readiness in peacetime to defend against a sudden attack and to act as a defensive shield to allow for the further mobilization and deployment of Pact forces.

The Pact would take steps during a period of tension to allow for a faster mobilization and transition to higher stages of combat readiness as the situation became more threatening. We estimate that the Soviets currently need at least two to three weeks to fully prepare their current forces in Central Europe for sustained offensive operations at authorized wartime strength.

We judge that, at the same time, situations could occur during the prehostilities phase that would convince the Soviets to launch a preemptive attack before reaching full mobilization. Such circumstances might include the belief that their mobilization progress had permitted them a decisive, albeit temporary, advantage in relative force preparedness. Alternatively, concern that NATO's buildup was shifting the correlation of forces against the Pact could persuade the Soviets to attack. After the announced force reductions are completed by 1991, however, Soviet capabilities to attack from a condition of partial mobilization

16. (*Continued*)

will be significantly reduced. Therefore, by the early 1990s, the likelihood that the Warsaw Pact would exercise such an option will decline accordingly.

In addition to diminishing Soviet capabilities for conducting a short-warning attack, Gorbachev's proposed force reductions in the Atlantic-to-the-Urals zone—particularly the 50-percent tank cut in Central Europe—will have a significant effect on the preparation time required for the Warsaw Pact to conduct offensive operations against NATO. Substantial reinforcement of Soviet forces in Central Europe by units from the western USSR and the mobilization of the logistic support structure are already required to launch a sustained theater offensive operation. Tank reductions in the forward area on the announced scale will create the need for even greater reinforcement. The scale of the reinforcement required to conduct a deep theater offensive operation will vary with the structure selected for the forces remaining in Central Europe. Although forces for a theater offensive operation will still be available, the bulk of two fronts will have to be moved forward from the Soviet Union before the onset of offensive operations. This movement will increase the preparation time beyond the two to three weeks we currently assess the Soviets require to prepare their forces for a sustained theater offensive.

Resource Allocations to the Military

Although he came to power intent on restructuring the Soviet economy, Gorbachev did not initially order cutbacks in military programs. In fact, our estimates of Soviet defense spending since 1985 indicate that it has continued to grow in real terms by about 3 percent per year. Thus far, we have not seen any scaling back or stretching out of major weapons development or production programs that can be directly linked to Gorbachev's economic initiatives. Gorbachev's announcement, however, that overall defense spending will be reduced by 14.2 percent and outlays for arms and equipment by 19.5 percent over the next two years indicates a significant change in the course of future defense spending. In addition, the defense industry has been directed to accelerate its contribution to the production of consumer and civilian investment goods. The cuts are clearly meant to help alleviate the economic burden of defense, and they could provide a meaningful boost to the civilian economy over the longer term.

In transferring resources from defense to civilian programs, Gorbachev probably will not limit the impact to any particular service or mission. A host of military, economic, domestic political, and foreign policy considerations will influence the implementation of spending cuts, and we believe that no element of the force will remain totally unscathed. We believe that we will get fairly clear signs early on of broad-based cuts in Soviet weapons procurement or changes in military activity, but measuring precise changes or the exact level of defense spending will be more difficult.

Weapons Modernization

Even with a reduction in defense spending, the Soviets will continue to maintain the world's highest level of weapon production through the turn of the century. A steady stream of improved Soviet military technology developments will be available to Soviet planners and design engineers throughout this period. Indeed, the military's future development of high-technology weapons is dependent on the same technologies which *perestroyka* is intended to improve. Nevertheless, we judge the major portion of Soviet systems projected through the year 2000 will involve evolutionary improvements in systems now in service, rather than dramatic technological breakthroughs.

Manpower Issues

Since 1980, the number of draft-age males has declined, reflecting the demographic "echo" of the lower birthrate during World War II. The draft-age conscription pool reached its nadir in 1987, however, and, for the first time since the war, the USSR can count on a basically stable youth population. The shrunken conscript pool, nevertheless, has caused the Soviet military serious problems. It has had to lower its mental and physical standards significantly in order to provide the same number of draftees. In addition, the problems of managing a multiethnic military have become increasingly prominent. Soviet military writings have cited minorities' lower educational achievement, Russian language deficiencies, and higher levels of ethnic tension within units. The announced reduction of 500,000 personnel in the Soviet military—nearly 10 percent of the 5.5 million estimate of Soviet military manpower—should alleviate somewhat the military's difficulties in finding suitable conscripts to fulfill manpower requirements.

16. (Continued)

Sustainability

████████████ we stated unconditionally that the Warsaw Pact's logistic structure in Central Europe could support 60 to 90 days of combat operations against NATO. We now judge, however, that overall Pact sustainability will depend to a significant extent on how long NATO's defenses hold and whether NATO can seal off any breakthroughs:

- If Pact forces break through NATO defenses in three days and reach their immediate frontal objectives by D+14 or 15, we judge that sufficient ammunition stocks exist within the Western TMO to support fully such a campaign for 60 to 90 days.

- If Pact forces require about a week of high-intensity operations to achieve a major breakthrough, the Pact's total stocks in the Western TMO could support combat operations for approximately 60 to 75 days.

- If Pact forces require about two weeks of high-intensity operations to achieve a breakthrough or if NATO manages to seal any earlier major Pact breakthrough, the Pact would not have enough ammunition in the Western TMO to sustain combat operations beyond 30 to 45 days. (S NF NC)

If confronted with the prospect of a shortfall in ammunition supply, Pact leaders would adjust wartime plans to avoid, or at least minimize, any adverse impact on combat operations. In addition, the Soviets would move stocks from elsewhere, such as the Strategic Reserve, to the Western TMO. (S NF NC)

Future Soviet General Purpose Forces

Although the Soviets have announced that they will cut their general purpose forces, defense spending, and defense production over the next two years, we believe that the Soviets are determined to maintain large general purpose forces through the period of this Estimate. In addition to supporting their claim to be a superpower, the Soviets believe such forces are necessary to deter aggression, to carry out wartime missions, and to underwrite their political objectives in the region. We judge that these factors will continue to guide Soviet force development in the future. Absent a far-reaching conventional arms control agreement, the Soviets will maintain the capability to conduct large-scale offensive operations deep into NATO territory, but only after general mobilization. Furthermore, for the period of this Estimate, Pact forces, led by the USSR, will remain the largest aggregation of military power in the world, and the Soviets will remain committed to the offensive as the preferred form of operations in wartime. (S NF NC)

Ground Forces. The Soviet Ground Forces are the largest element of Soviet general purpose forces, and their development largely determines the overall direction of theater forces development. We see no evidence that either of these conditions will change. Cuts in the size of the ground forces announced by the Soviets, however, signal a significant change in the overall developmental path of the force. Before the announcement, the Soviet ground forces were expected to grow gradually in their overall size. The cuts—the most sizable since the early 1960s—diverge considerably from existing trends, and they alter significantly our forecast of future Soviet forces. Ambiguity persists concerning the actual implementation of announced force cuts and the restructuring of forces remaining after the withdrawal into what the Soviets term a "clearly defensive" orientation. We now judge, nevertheless, that a 25-year period of Soviet ground force growth has ended, and that the force will experience a decline in its overall size that could very well go beyond the magnitude of that already announced by the Soviets. We further judge a resumption of force growth, barring an unforeseen deterioration in the international environment, to be highly unlikely before the turn of the century. (S NF NC)

Our assessment of current trends in Soviet force development leads us to conclude that restructured combined-arms formations based on mechanized infantry and tanks supported by artillery have replaced predominantly tank formations as the main component of land combat power. We believe this trend toward combined-arms formations will continue, but we cannot predict with any certainty the final organization of these units. (S NF NC)

The Soviet ground forces are fielding new equipment in virtually every weapon category. This pattern of weapon modernization will continue for the foreseeable future but at a slower pace than in the past:

- The Soviets probably have begun fielding a tank referred to by the Intelligence Community as the

16. *(Continued)*

Future Soviet Tank-I (FST-I), with the capability to fire antitank guided missiles through its main gun. A new design, the FST-II, is expected to reach serial production by the mid-1990s. It will likely incorporate incremental improvements over previous designs and may, in addition, have a larger caliber gun.[6]

- In addition to improving the firepower and protection of their current infantry fighting vehicles, the Soviets should field a new IFV within the next year. A new armored personnel carrier also is under development. These new systems are designed to have improved protection and firepower and reflect the increasing role for these systems in Soviet combined-arms operations against NATO.

- The Soviets will field several new models of tube artillery by the end of the century. Primary improvements will include fully automatic ammunition loaders, new fire-control systems, increased armor protection, improved metallurgy for the cannon and chassis, and a longer tube for greater range in some models. In addition, the Soviets are developing improved artillery munitions.

- The Soviets will continue their ambitious short-range ballistic missile (SRBM) research and development program, and we project that they will continue to expand and modernize their tactical nuclear forces by improving the accuracy of their missiles and fielding an extended-range SS-21 and a solid-fueled follow-on to the Scud. A series of improved conventional munition warheads also are being developed to improve the effectiveness of SRBMs in conventional operations.

- The Soviets are projected to field several new air defense weapons to maximize their future air defense capabilities against helicopters and high-performance aircraft. Improvements will include improved seekers for better low-altitude engagement capability, multiple engagement radar, and more lethal warheads.

[6] *The Deputy Chief of Staff for Intelligence, US Army, believes that FST-II may have an unconventional design, possibly with a reduced turret.*

Air Forces. Even before Gorbachev's announcement of force cuts, we had expected the size of the Soviets' air forces to remain relatively constant as they attempted to catch up with the West qualitatively. We now judge that the air forces will be maintained at their postreduction levels until after the turn of the century. We also judge that the Soviets will continue to modernize their air forces, albeit more slowly, during the period of this Estimate in an attempt to narrow major technological gaps with the West. There is considerable uncertainty, nevertheless, over how the Soviets will implement the announced reduction in aircraft and how the air forces will implement spending and procurement cuts. Senior Soviet military leaders have placed great importance on retaining approximate air parity in the Central European air balance, and they have emphasized the importance of new weapon systems in developmental programming:

- Modernization of the Soviet fighter force probably will be based almost entirely on variants of the Fulcrum, Foxhound, and Flanker. We judge that the first follow-on fighter to appear would probably be a Fulcrum replacement.

- The Soviets will most likely continue to modernize their medium bomber force with improved variants of the Backfire, and we estimate that a new medium bomber will succeed the Backfire about the turn of the century. We further project that a new light bomber, ███████████ will begin to replace strategic aviation Fencer aircraft in the mid-1990s.

- The Fencer probably will continue to replace less capable fighter-bombers in front aviation ground attack units into the early to mid-1990s. We estimate that the Soviets will develop a new fighter-bomber around the turn of the century. This aircraft would probably have a substantial payload-radius capability, incorporate low-observable technology to improve its survivability, and be equipped with advanced navigation and weapons delivery avionics.

16. *(Continued)*

- The Mystic high-altitude reconnaissance aircraft is expected to enter service in the early 1990s. The Soviets are also augmenting their aerial reconnaissance capability by fielding a family of drones, including the soon-to-be-fielded DR-X-4.

- The Hind continues to be the workhorse of the Soviet attack helicopter force, and variants with improved capabilities continue to replace older models. Two new armed helicopters, the Hokum and Havoc may begin deployment in the early 1990s. Developmental programs are under way for a medium-tiltrotor and a heavy-tiltrotor helicopter, but they are unlikely to be fielded in significant numbers during the period of this Estimate.

- A new V/STOL aircraft is under development, and it may enter service with the Soviet air forces. The Soviets are also developing Stealth aircraft including a bomber and a fighter-bomber.

The Soviet strategic bomber force is currently undergoing its second reorganization of this decade. While we do not yet have enough evidence to firmly determine the intent or operational significance of the latest reorganization, it appears designed to give the Soviets greater flexibility in allocating heavy bombers between theater and intercontinental missions.

Soviet Homeland Air Defense Forces
The Soviets are continuing to modernize their Strategic Air Defense Force including the air surveillance network, the interceptor force, and the surface-to-air missile (SAM) force. This effort, with its emphasis on systems with good capabilities against low-altitude targets, appears to be focused on two main objectives: the development of a long-range capability to shoot down cruise missile carriers before they can release their weapons, and the development of a terminal defense to intercept penetrators that make it through the outer barrier. In addition to improving the capabilities of their current interceptor force, we expect the Soviets to deploy follow-ons to the Fulcrum, Flanker, and Foxhound over the next 10 to 15 years. Performance improvements on the follow-ons will include a radar capable of tracking multiple targets with small radar cross sections in lookdown operations, better maneuverability, and—in the Foxhound follow-on—a capability to intercept cruise-missile-carrying aircraft before they can launch their missiles. The SA-10 system, including future modifications, will dominate strategic SAM force modernization through the next 10 years. An SA-5 follow-on is projected to begin deployment in the 1990s, but we are unsure whether it will be a modification or a new design. In addition, the Soviets will develop one or more lasers with an air defense application, including those capable of causing structural damage and damage to electro-optical sensors.

The Soviets have reorganized their Strategic Air Defense Forces in the peripheral areas of the USSR by giving them back to the national air defense system. This probably was brought about by national air defense authorities to ensure that they controlled the forces required for territorial defense, and perhaps also to improve the responsiveness of Soviet air defenses to peacetime airspace violations.

Naval Forces. Although we do not know how the personnel and budget cuts announced by Gorbachev will be apportioned among the five services, these reductions could have a significant effect on the Soviet Navy's size and mix of forces. The Navy may be trying initially to meet some of its personnel and overall budget reductions by further reducing its operational tempo and retiring older combatants, and the Soviets have already accelerated the rate at which they are scrapping older surface combatants and submarines. Retirements, however, will have no impact on the Navy's need to cut procurement expenditures, and some major programs may have to be reduced, stretched out over time, or eliminated altogether. Surface combatants are likely to take the largest share of "hardware" cuts because of the traditional Soviet bias in favor of submarines and the fact that surface combatants are the most manpower intensive naval systems. Despite such reductions, we expect to see the Soviets continue to make qualitative improvements in their Navy that focus on its most important mission areas.

We see no significant operational change in Soviet naval support for land TMOs. We anticipate the slow continuation of several naval organizational and weapon trends that should provide land theater commanders with more capable forces for combined-arms operations as a major wartime task of the Soviet Navy. Chief among these are:

- Integration of the newly developed SS-N-21 long-range land-attack nuclear submarine-launched cruise missile in theater nuclear strike plans. The high-altitude SS-NX-24 is now in development and it will also have a theater mission when it is initially deployed in the early 1990s.

- Continuing efforts to develop more effective seaborne air defenses against enemy aircraft armed with air-launched cruise missiles or improved air-to-surface missiles.

- Continued gradual replacement of older naval Tu-16 Badgers with Tu-22M Backfire-C bombers, giving Soviet naval aviation greater potential for in-theater maritime strikes.

Non-Soviet Warsaw Pact Forces

Following the Soviets' lead, and undoubtedly with Moscow's approval, all non-Soviet Warsaw Pact (NSWP) countries, except Romania, announced force and defense spending reductions in January 1989. As in the Soviet case, there is a mixture of economic, political, and military considerations to these decisions. Nevertheless, we judge that weaknesses in the NSWP economies constituted the primary motivation for their decision to cut forces and defense spending. The reductions, however, do not represent as sharp a departure in force and spending trends as represented by the Soviet cuts. NSWP military procurement began slowing in the mid-1970s, and it has dropped significantly since the early 1980s. NSWP force size has been largely static since the 1970s. For these reasons, we had projected no force growth and slow rates of modernization even before the cuts were announced.

NSWP force cuts range between 5 and 20 percent of currently assessed force levels, and we judge that virtually all equipment cuts will be taken in older equipment that dominates the NSWP inventory (see the table on page 5). While considerable uncertainty exists regarding the individual impact of defense spending and procurement cuts on the armed forces' acquisition of newer equipment, we project that rates of modernization will slow beyond their already gradual pace. This may be offset somewhat by the reduced size of the NSWP forces and the elimination of the oldest equipment in their inventories.

NSWP countries maintain important defense industries, and their role in weapons production has increased substantially. They now account for about one-fifth of total Pact land arms production (a much smaller share of aircraft and ships), although the equipment they produce tends to be relatively less sophisticated and easier to manufacture than systems simultaneously in production in Soviet plants. We believe that, over the next decade, the Soviets expect NSWP industry to relieve Soviet industry of more of the burden of equipping NSWP forces while providing increased support for the modernization of Soviet industry.

We foresee modest improvements in NSWP forces during the projections period that, while insufficient to close the modernization gap between their forces and Soviet force standards in Eastern Europe, will enable them to fulfill important roles in Warsaw Pact plans for war against NATO. We project NSWP forces will gradually modernize their equipment and reorganize along Soviet lines through the end of this century:

- Ground force equipment modernization will consist primarily of T-72 series tanks, self-propelled artillery, surface-to-air missiles, and newer infantry fighting vehicles. Major restructuring may occur in the ground forces which could follow the lines adopted by the Hungarian ground forces.

- NSWP air force modernization will be a gradual process. The ground attack replacement is the Fitter-K, while the air defense forces will be improved through the fielding of the Fulcrum.

16. *(Continued)*

- The NSWP countries with naval forces do not appear willing or able to significantly increase their naval expenditures. Over the long term, older and less capable weapon systems in the inventories of the NSWP navies gradually will be replaced by more capable systems, though on a less than 1-for-1 basis due to budget constraints.

The Soviets almost certainly are resigned to accept NSWP force inadequacies, and we judge that they will continue to tolerate such deficiencies while insisting that the most glaring faults be rectified. The Soviets almost certainly are aware of the operational price they will pay if their NSWP allies are not able to perform their assigned missions alongside Soviet forces. The impact of these force deficiencies on operational planning will become more apparent to the Soviets after their force reductions in Central Europe and the western USSR are completed. In general, we forecast that the uneasy, and at times strained, relationship that exists between the Soviets and their allies regarding force modernization and reorganization will remain for the foreseeable future.

Soviet Policy Toward NATO

The major objective of Soviet policy toward NATO is to reduce European governmental and popular support for increased defense spending that would support NATO's force modernization program. If this policy is successful, it would reduce internal Soviet perceptions of the NATO threat, thereby enabling Gorbachev to make major shifts of resources from the defense to the civil sector without being accused of reducing Warsaw Pact security.

Soviet and Warsaw Pact policy toward NATO for the foreseeable future will likely follow two interrelated tracks. First, the Pact will engage the West in arms control negotiations at all levels. Second, it will pursue an aggressive course of public diplomacy, active measures, and unilateral initiatives aimed at influencing NATO governments and electorates to reduce defense spending and slow NATO modernization. Warsaw Pact public diplomacy will also exploit popular opposition in Western Europe to current NATO out-of-country basing policies and publicly burdensome NATO military training programs.

Warsaw Pact foreign policy over the period of this Estimate can also be expected to support another Soviet objective vis-a-vis NATO: the weakening of the position of the United States and Canada within the North Atlantic Alliance. In addition to reducing the apparent threat from the Soviet Union in the eyes of West Europeans—thus reducing the need for NATO's continued dependence on the United States—the Soviets will encourage other NATO members to deal directly with the Soviet Union. Warsaw Pact foreign policy will also complicate NATO's efforts to reach agreement on positions for the Conventional Stability Talks (CST). An apparently accommodating Soviet security policy will undermine tough Western bargaining positions in the CST and increase pressure on the NATO allies to meet Soviet negotiating concerns, such as NATO ground attack aircraft and forward based systems.

A critical issue confronting NATO over the next decade is to identify, interpret, and react correctly to developments in Warsaw Pact general purpose forces. As decisions on the size and composition of Pact future general purpose forces become apparent, NATO will have to sort out the real from the declared changes in Warsaw Pact capabilities and intentions. Furthermore, NATO will have to accomplish this in an environment of increasing public skepticism about the Warsaw Pact "threat" and sagging support for NATO defense spending.

Even under the most favorable conditions of East-West relations over the course of this Estimate, NATO can expect to face a formidable Pact military force. We judge that military forces will remain, from the USSR's perspective, the primary basis of its superpower status. Thus, despite significant shifts of resources from the defense sector, the Soviet Union will continue to plan for and invest heavily in its general purpose forces while seeking to build a more capable economy to underpin Soviet military capabilities in the future.

Alternative Judgment. The Director, Defense Intelligence Agency, while recognizing the significance of the ongoing changes in the Soviet Union, believes the

16. *(Continued)*

likelihood of large unilateral reductions in military expenditures beyond those already proclaimed by Soviet leaders is not as high as implied by the majority view in the Estimate, particularly for the longer term. Notwithstanding the potential importance of new developments in Soviet military policies discussed in this Estimate, the Director, DIA, believes that present evidence and future uncertainties make the elements of continuity in Soviet military policy as important as the changes for US national security and defense planning.

17. M/H NIE 4-1-84, September 1989, *Warning of War in Europe: Changing Warsaw Pact Planning and Forces* **(Key Judgments only)**

Director of
Central
Intelligence

~~Secret~~

Warning of War in Europe: Changing Warsaw Pact Planning and Forces

National Intelligence Estimate
Memorandum to Holders

This Memorandum to Holders represents the views of the Director of Central Intelligence with the advice and assistance of the US Intelligence Community.

~~Secret~~

NIE 4-1-84
September 1989

Copy 627

17. *(Continued)*

 **Director of Central Intelligence**

~~Secret~~

NIE 4-1-84

Warning of War in Europe: Changing Warsaw Pact Planning and Forces

Information available as of 28 September 1989 was used in the preparation of this Memorandum to Holders.

The following intelligence organizations participated in the preparation of this Memorandum:
The Central Intelligence Agency
The Defense Intelligence Agency
The National Security Agency
Bureau of Intelligence and Research, Department of State

also participating:
The Deputy Chief of Staff for Intelligence,
Department of the Army
The Director of Naval Intelligence,
Department of the Navy
The Assistant Chief of Staff, Intelligence,
Department of the Air Force
The Director of Intelligence, Headquarters,
Marine Corps

This Memorandum was approved for publication by the National Foreign Intelligence Board.

~~Secret~~
September 1989

17. *(Continued)*

~~Secret~~
~~NOFORN-NOCONTRACT~~

Warning of War in Europe: Changing Warsaw Pact Planning and Forces (u)

- *The warning times we associate with possible Warsaw Pact preparations for war with NATO in Central Europe have increased significantly from those set forth in 1984.* ~~(S NF)~~

- *Pact military planners would prefer and are most likely to attempt to conduct a well-prepared attack involving five to six fronts with four fronts in the first strategic echelon. We should be able to provide about four to five weeks of warning of such an attack.* ~~(S NF)~~

- *We recognize that circumstances could cause the Pact to commit its forces to an attack after the completion of mobilization and movement, but before completing the postmobilization training necessary for minimum offensive proficiency. The warning times would be shorter, but the Soviets would judge such an attack as highly risky.* ~~(S NF)~~

- *Announced Soviet and non-Soviet Warsaw Pact unilateral reductions, if completed, and given no reduction in NATO capabilities, should significantly extend preparation time because of the greater need in the first echelon for currently low-strength divisions from the western USSR.* ~~(S NF)~~

17. *(Continued)*

Figure 1
Projected Warsaw Pact Echelons
in the Western Theater of Military Operations (TMO)—Four-Front Attack

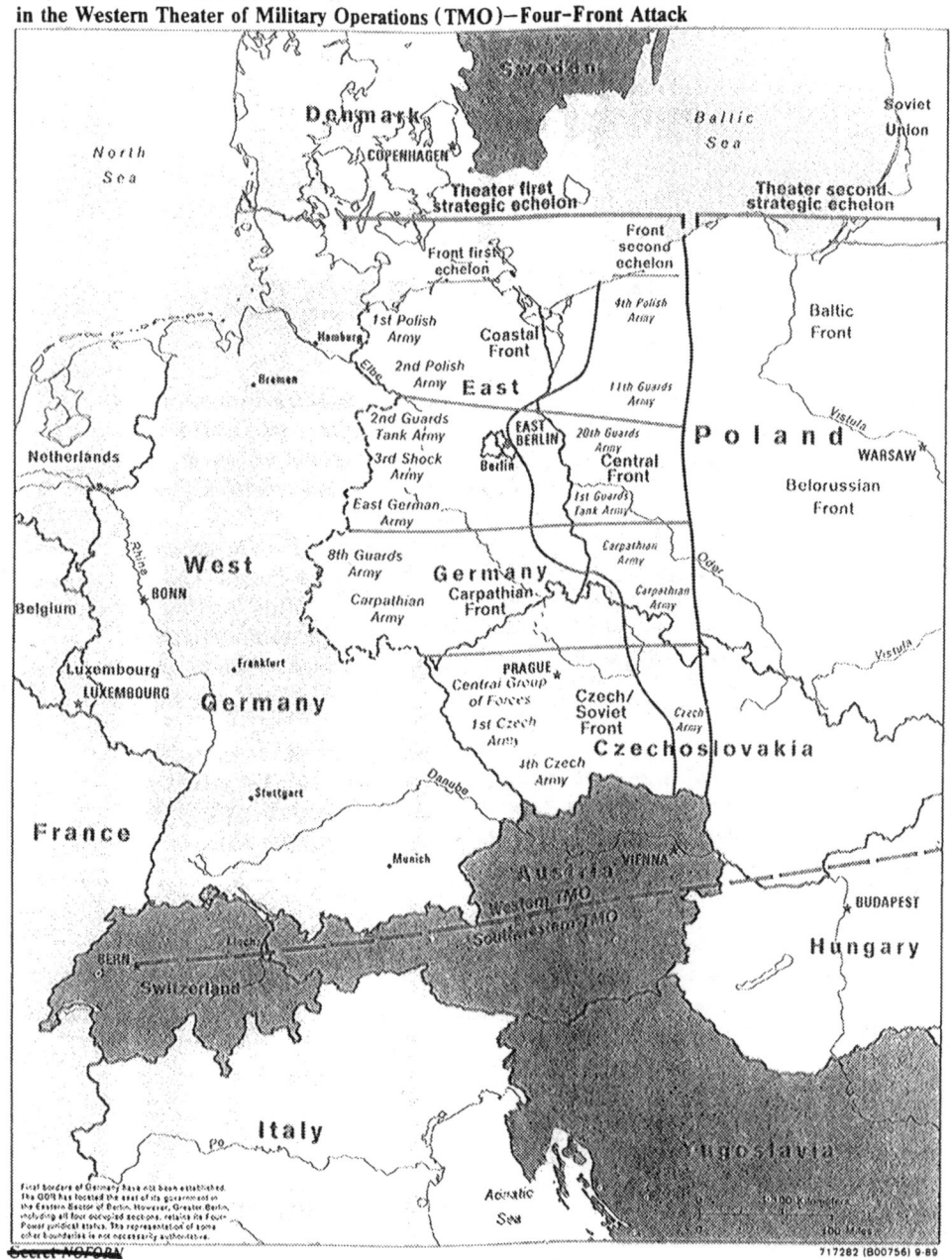

17. (*Continued*)

Key Judgments

The warning times we associate with possible Warsaw Pact preparations for war with NATO in Central Europe have increased significantly from those set forth in NIE 4-1-84. These changes are a direct consequence of Soviet assessments of improved NATO military capability, our improved understanding of the Soviet process of transitioning to war, and changes in Soviet peacetime readiness. Accordingly, before unilateral force reductions, we assess that:

- Pact military planners would prefer and are most likely to attempt to conduct a well-prepared attack involving five to six fronts with four fronts in the first strategic echelon. We should be able to provide about four to five weeks of warning of such an attack. The increased time needed to prepare this attack option results from increased reliance in the first echelon on "not ready" divisions from the western USSR.

- An attack with three fronts in the first echelon remains a possibility in some circumstances. We should be able to provide about two to three weeks of warning of such an attack. Our assessment of the increased time needed to prepare these fronts for sustained offensive operations results from new judgments about the time required to prepare Soviet forces based in Eastern Europe.

- We recognize that circumstances could cause the Pact to commit its forces to an attack after the completion of mobilization and movement but before completing postmobilization training necessary for minimum proficiency for offensive operations. If so, we could provide at least two weeks of warning of a four-front attack or at least one week warning of a less likely three-front attack. We believe, however, the Soviets would judge attacks before completion of postmobilization training as highly risky because of the reliance on reserves lacking such training.

17. *(Continued)*

**Figure 2
Announced Warsaw Pact Unilateral Force Reductions
in the Western Theater of Military Operations**

17. *(Continued)*

~~Secret~~
~~NOFORN-NOCONTRACT~~

Announced Soviet and non-Soviet Warsaw Pact unilateral force reductions, if completed, should significantly extend preparation time because of the greater need in the first echelon for currently low-strength divisions from the western USSR. Warning of our assessed most likely attack option—four fronts in the first echelon—would increase by about two weeks. If the Soviets elected to attack after only mobilization and movement, warning times would increase by almost a week.

These preparation and warning times after unilateral reductions assume that NATO capabilities remain at current levels. Unilateral NATO reductions could diminish Pact perception of their requirements for success and, therefore, reduce warning time.

The ongoing Conventional Forces in Europe (CFE) Talks are likely to result in an agreement establishing numerical parity between NATO and Warsaw Pact forces below current NATO levels within the Atlantic-to-the-Urals zone. From peacetime parity, the Soviets would have to reestablish major forces in order to generate the capability to attack successfully and sustain the offensive to the depth of the theater. This requirement would increase preparation time considerably over what we have assessed in this Memorandum. Alternatively, the Soviets could increase the readiness and combat power of residual forces through higher manning levels and acquisition of modern equipment. This would require reinvesting the savings achieved by reducing their forces under CFE into defense and restructuring their forces and redistributing their equipment. These smaller forces would be capable of launching attacks for limited objectives with warning times more like we are accustomed to today. We do not believe such attacks for limited objectives would be attractive to Pact planners because the risks, to include escalation to nuclear war, would far outweigh any potential short-term gains.

We are confident that for the period of this Estimate we will be able to detect and report significant disruptions or a reversal of present political, social, and economic trends in the Warsaw Pact countries. Although these indicators will remain ambiguous with regard to actual national war preparations, they will continue to signal that the potential for a crisis had increased.

~~This information is Secret Noforn.~~

National Intelligence Council

~~Secret~~

Memorandum

The Post-CFE Environment in Europe

~~Secret~~

NIC M 89-10002
September 1989
Copy 635

18. *(Continued)*

National Intelligence Council

~~Secret~~
~~NOFORN-NOCONTRACT~~

NIC M 89-10002

The Post-CFE Environment in Europe (U)

Information available as of 1 September 1989 was used in the preparation of this Memorandum, which was prepared by the National Intelligence Officers for General Purpose Forces, USSR, and Europe. (U)

~~Secret~~
September 1989

18. *(Continued)*

Secret
NOFORN-NOCONTRACT

Key Judgments

- The era following the Conventional Forces in Europe (CFE) Talks will be a transitional period in Europe, marked by the reevaluation and redefinition of longstanding economic, political, and military relationships between and within the existing alliances. (S NF)

- The overall threat to NATO will diminish in a post-CFE environment, and barring a precipitous decline in NATO, the currently unfavorable balance of forces will be largely eliminated. Remaining Warsaw Pact forces will need even longer and more massive mobilization to be able to carry out deep strategic operations in Central Europe. (S NF)

- West European publics and leaders already perceive a reduced military threat from the Warsaw Pact and will expect continued attempts by the Soviet Union and its East European allies to focus on political and economic relationships with the West, reduce the size of their military forces, and shift resources from defense to civil production. (S NF)

- Continued US leadership of NATO will be challenged by the emergence of a stronger Eurocentric approach emphasizing the importance of political and economic over military matters as West European concerns about the Warsaw Pact threat diminish, and domestic pressures for reallocating defense budgets to civilian needs, such as the environment, and emphasis on East-West cooperation rather than confrontation increase. (S NF)

- There will be an increased prospect of instability in some East European countries if their economies fail to improve significantly—a likely prospect if they are unable to profitably exploit their greater access to the West. (S NF)

18. *(Continued)*

Secret
NOFORN NOCONTRACT

Discussion[1]

Intelligence Community analysts believe that the next decade—following the Conventional Forces in Europe (CFE) talks—will likely see long-established military, political, and economic relationships between and among European nations and their superpower partners reevaluated and redefined. CFE is an important element in a larger process of enhanced West European economic integration, the assertion of independent European political interests, and the political and economic reforms and reallocations under way in Eastern Europe and the Soviet Union. Excepting upheaval in Eastern Europe, Community analysts foresee more direct policy concerns for the United States emerging from the changes in Western Europe than from those in either Eastern Europe or the Soviet Union. (S-NF)

Post-CFE Warsaw Pact military forces will be incapable, without significant, costly, and time-consuming mobilization, of carrying out the deep strategic operations in Central Europe that have been characteristic of Soviet military planning for several decades. Both the East and the West will be forced to revise their views of war in Europe; current Soviet military reductions and restructuring probably reflect the early stages of such a reevaluation process. Although Soviet strategy and doctrine are clearly changing in reaction to new political instructions and economic imperatives, their final shape is not yet discernible. Nevertheless, Soviet military objectives against NATO would be likely to be much more limited, *replacing* those of the traditional Theater Strategic Operation, which projects Soviet military operations throughout Western Europe. (S-NF)

[1] This Memorandum synthesizes the results of three meetings convened in mid-August 1989 by the National Intelligence Council to discuss Intelligence Community analysts' views of the military, political, and economic implications of a post-CFE Europe. Recognizing the great uncertainties posed by the current political environment in Eastern Europe and the USSR, the discussion focused on projected conditions in the latter half of the 1990s, with the assumption of a CFE agreement based on current proposals. Although coordinated, this memorandum is speculative and not limited to evidence on hand. (S-NF)

Post-CFE Soviet forces—although smaller—may be on average better equipped, depending on the Soviet's willingness to reinvest potential savings into the military. Some analysts believe that through this modernization and restructuring the Soviet's readiness posture is likely to improve. Despite potential improvements, however, the overall military threat to NATO will diminish, and, unless there is a precipitous decline in NATO forces, the currently unfavorable balance of forces would be largely eliminated. Under the Warsaw Pact's proposal, a CFE agreement would force the Pact to give up nearly half of its reinforcement capability in the Atlantic-to-the-Urals zone; NATO's reinforcement capability, however, would be significantly less affected. Further, the Soviet Union will not likely be able to regenerate rapidly the force structure required for deep offensive operations. Strategic surprise in Europe, therefore, will be even less likely, although tactical surprise would remain possible, for example, to obtain limited objectives. (S-NF)

Overall, there will be a continued shift in Soviet emphasis away from military power and toward political and economic interaction with the West. Through CFE, Gorbachev apparently intends to validate the basic assumption of his "new" foreign policy line: that national security will no longer be founded primarily on military strength but on a broader based combination of diplomacy, negotiation, economic power, and military strength. (S-NF)

On the NATO side, political and budgetary constraints together with perceptions of a reduced Soviet threat will result in a decreasing commitment by European nations to the maintenance of large standing forces, leading to continued force reductions, beyond those agreed to at the CFE Talks. Depending on where such additional cuts were taken, and how far they went in relation to Pact forces, such reductions

Secret

18. *(Continued)*

would probably force major changes in NATO's defense strategy. Simultaneously, a CFE agreement would contribute to the political momentum toward denuclearization in Europe and lead to changes in Alliance nuclear use policies. In general, the post-CFE situation will be dynamic as both military alliances develop new objectives and strategies and design and field forces to implement them.

In a post-CFE Europe, the Soviet Union's dominant role in most of Eastern Europe will decline significantly and depend primarily on formal adherence to the Warsaw Pact and economic ties. East European countries will also become increasingly independent. This could weaken the military rationale for the Warsaw Pact and precipitate increased East European pressure to reorient the Pact toward more of a political alliance.

Moscow's East European allies, lacking strong Bloc identity, will probably prefer to establish individual bilateral relations with West European nations. With Soviet military presence and political influence in Eastern Europe reduced, the reliability of the political underpinnings of the current military and economic relationships such as the Warsaw Pact and CEMA will be called into question. Traditional national animosities and historical grievances among the East European countries—already reemerging as the imposed Bloc identity recedes—will worsen in the post-CFE era. If military drawdowns through CFE proceed too quickly—contributing to mounting internal and external pressures for reform—this could lead to social and political unrest in one or more of the East European regimes and result in a regime crackdown that could stall East-West relations.

In contrast, events within the European Community (EC)—notably 1992 market integration and significant progress toward European political cooperation—are bolstering and broadening the West European sense of common purpose and community. As West European countries move away from their dependence on a US-led Atlantic Alliance and toward a more intra-European perspective, they will become increasingly parochial in their security concerns and less prone to take a US view. They may attempt to craft a "Common European House" built to EC rather than Soviet or US specifications. EC member states' vested interests in an economically strong, politically cohesive EC would prevent the admission of any current CEMA state during the next decade. The Council of Europe is the more likely venue for trans-European policy dialogue and cooperation.

CFE will strengthen widely held perceptions among West Europeans of a diminished threat. In the aftermath of a CFE agreement, there will be an increased number of politically powerful voices in the West calling into question the need for military alliances. But as long as there remains a substantial—even though reduced—US military presence in Europe, however, the broad foundations of NATO will essentially remain intact. Even in countries where antinuclear sentiments and pro-arms-control views are strongest, the majority of the public today still favors membership in NATO.

On the economic side, CFE will contribute to a more positive environment for East-West trade, although the continued presence of cumbersome bureaucracies and trade barriers will hinder prospects for significantly increased trade. The East Europeans are anxious to expand economic relationships, singly and in groups, with the European Community. They are unlikely, however, either to increase trade rapidly or to take advantage of technology transfer to offset adverse economic conditions. Some analysts feel that the West European nations are already beginning to

18. *(Continued)*

determine what they could do to improve the East European economies and would continue to do so. Most believe, however, that the EC nations, though conscious of East European need for economic assistance and outside investment, now appear unwilling and unable to provide investment or economic assistance in large enough quantities to achieve long-term fundamental changes in the economic relationship. Despite some interest on the part of the West Europeans, most believe that they are unlikely to make the massive investment needed to assist East European economies. Individual East European nations will also have to contend with the unified decision apparatus represented by the EC with no counterpart economic coalition to represent their interests. Indeed, CEMA will become increasingly ineffective in the projected environment, as individual East European nations seek to expand their own relations based on economic needs and potential. (S NF)

The likely effects of CFE on the Soviet Union's economy are less clear. CFE could have enormous implications over time for the Soviet economy, particularly in terms of reduced resources devoted to defense production. Because the Soviet Union spends more than three times more on conventional forces than it does on strategic offensive nuclear forces, a CFE accord offers the potential for much greater resource savings and industrial reorientation than the INF and START agreements combined. Savings can be realized in procurement, force structure, operations and maintenance expenditures, and manpower utilization. Overall, a CFE agreement could allow the Soviets to save up to 15-18 billion rubles per year, or about 15 percent of total investment and operating expenditures. To put such savings into perspective, the amount is almost equal to Soviet investment in the critical machine-building sector and over half the amount invested in housing. (S NF)

At the same time, problems in the Soviet economy and the requirements of future forces will probably prevent the Soviets from realizing the full economic benefits of CFE. There is considerable doubt about the ability of the Soviets to effectively redistribute resources from defense to civilian uses. Factors inhibiting conversion include reluctance to reorient military research and development programs; difficulties in transferring skilled workers from military industries and absorbing released military manpower into the already inefficient and underemployed Soviet industrial labor pool; and the technical problems involved in converting specialized industrial processes. Moreover, an unknown percentage of these savings, in the early years, would have to be spent on modernization and restructuring stemming from shifts in Soviet strategy and weapons requirements. For example, some Soviet officials have stated that, in keeping with the new defensive doctrine, greater emphasis will be placed on "defensive" weapons. Other modernization and potential increases in the costs of maintaining residual forces at higher levels of readiness—should the Soviets do so—could also cut into the projected savings. (S NF)

19. NIC M 89-10003, October 1989, *Status of Soviet Unilateral Withdrawals*

National Intelligence Council

~~Secret~~

Memorandum

Status of Soviet Unilateral Withdrawals

~~Secret~~

NIC M 89-10003
October 1989

Copy 632

19. *(Continued)*

NIC M 89-10003

Status of Soviet Unilateral Withdrawals (U)

Information available as of 1 September 1989 was used in the preparation of this Memorandum, which was prepared by the National Intelligence Officer for General Purpose Forces. The Memorandum was coordinated with representatives of the Defense Intelligence Agency and the Central Intelligence Agency; coordination was chaired by the National Intelligence Officer for General Purpose Forces.
(U)

19. *(Continued)*

Status of Soviet Unilateral Withdrawals

- *Soviet reductions in Eastern Europe are proceeding in a manner consistent with Gorbachev's commitment; they will result in a significant reduction in the combat capability of Soviet forces in Eastern Europe.*

- *Current Soviet activities comprise four simultaneous processes: withdrawal, reduction, restructuring, and modernization.*

- *In Eastern Europe the Soviets, at roughly halfway through the period, have withdrawn about 50 percent of the equipment and units promised. Percentages are much lower for reductions in the overall Atlantic-to-the-Urals zone and for east of the Urals.*

- *Soviet restructuring and modernization activities will produce a smaller, more versatile, standing force optimized for defense, but still capable of smaller scale offensive operations.*

19. *(Continued)*

Discussion

This paper presents the latest assessment of the ongoing unilateral Soviet withdrawal of forces from Eastern Europe and reductions in the so-called Atlantic-to-the-Urals (ATTU) zone. It provides the latest figures of forces withdrawn and reduced, the current understanding of the restructuring of the forces remaining, and the best estimates of the factors affecting the combat capabilities and potential missions of those residual forces.

We have reached two bottom-line judgments. First, we believe that the Soviet withdrawal is real and that it will result in a reduction in the combat capability of the remaining Soviet forces in Eastern Europe; second, all of the changes we are seeing, and those we anticipate, are consistent with our understanding of General Secretary Gorbachev's policy objectives—reducing Western perceptions of the Warsaw Pact threat, inducing a relaxation in NATO's defense efforts, achieving an agreement on Conventional Forces in Europe (CFE), and lowering the defense economic burden on the USSR.

Although "withdrawal" or "reduction" are the terms generally associated with the current Soviet activity, there are actually four processes occurring simultaneously: first, a *withdrawal* of Soviet units and equipment from the traditional "forward areas" in Eastern Europe; second, a *reduction* in the overall Soviet force posture, with a particular emphasis on those areas facing NATO; third, a *restructuring* of the remaining forces intended to bring their capabilities into line with anticipated missions, objectives, and conditions; and, fourth, a continuation of programatic *modernization* intended to raise the combat effectiveness of Soviet forces. All of this activity is totally unilateral. The Soviets are under no formal obligation to carry through and are free to adjust the process as they proceed. Nevertheless, Gorbachev has a strong interest in demonstrating that he is fulfilling his promises.

In assessing what is going on, the best place to start is with the dramatic 7 December 1988 speech at the UN by Gorbachev. He made the following key statements of Soviet intentions, that over the next two years the Soviets would:

- *Reduce* the overall size of their armed forces by 500,000 personnel.

- *Reduce* the size of their forces in East Germany, Czechoslovakia, and Hungary by 50,000 persons and 5,000 tanks. This was later increased to 5,300 tanks with the inclusion of reductions in Soviet forces in Poland.

- *Reduce* 10,000 tanks, 8,500 artillery systems, and 800 combat aircraft from Eastern Europe and the Western USSR (the ATTU zone).

- *Withdraw* and *disband* six tank divisions from East Germany, Czechoslovakia, and Hungary.

- *Withdraw* assault landing formations and units and assault river crossing forces.

- *Restructure* the remaining forces to present an "unambiguously defensive" posture.

He made additional promises concerning Asia.

Gorbachev's speech was met with many questions and much skepticism in the West. Between late December and late February, official Soviet spokesmen asserted that the six Soviet divisions to be withdrawn from Eastern Europe would be withdrawn in their entirety, that all of their combat equipment would be destroyed, and that the other tanks removed from Eastern Europe would be destroyed or converted.

19. (*Continued*)

As the withdrawals and restructuring have progressed, it has become increasingly clear that, although the Soviets are generally moving toward meeting Gorbachev's initial commitments, they are not being implemented in the manner described by some subsequent spokesmen. The tank regiments, other units, and all of the tanks of the three divisions scheduled for removal in 1989 have been withdrawn, along with many tanks from other divisions. Other units—and almost all of the artillery and armored troop carriers—however—are being used in the restructuring of the remaining divisions, each of which is losing two battalions of tanks as one tank regiment is converted to a motorized rifle regiment. Moreover, the tanks being removed from Eastern Europe are not being destroyed.

The Soviets are beginning to acknowledge deviations from some of their statements, but they have still not been entirely forthright about some of the consequences, notably:
- That the artillery in the remaining divisions is being increased by the addition of one artillery battalion in tank divisions and that artillery battalions in divisions are being expanded from 18 to 24 guns.
- That the restructuring of the remaining divisions may eventually require the introduction of some 2,000 additional armored troop carriers.

Most of what the Soviets are doing makes military sense. Indeed, it is generally what we would have expected until the Soviets began making additional statements. Despite these deviations, the overall result will still be a very significant reduction in the offensive combat power of Soviet forces in Eastern Europe.

How close have the Soviets come to meeting Gorbachev's 7 December promises as we approach the midway point? Tables 1-3 illustrate our answer. Table 1 provides the scorecard for forces withdrawn from Eastern Europe. Column one gives the reportable items; column two, the total number of those items in that area as of 1 January 1989; column three, the specific reductions announced for each of the items; column four, the reductions the Soviets have announced as of 1 August 1989; column five, our assessment of reductions as of 1 September 1989; and, finally, column six provides the percentage that our assessment represents of the total announced reduction. At halfway through the period, the percentages are in the neighborhood of 50 percent complete. We believe that up to 2,800 tanks; 180 combat aircraft; four air assault units; and two assault crossing units have been withdrawn; and three tank divisions have been removed from the force structure. No percentage is offered for artillery because no specific withdrawal of artillery from the forward area was promised in Gorbachev's speech.

Turning to table 2, we see a similar picture, although the percentages are somewhat reduced. For example, we have not detected that the Soviets have reduced the total number of tanks in the ATTU zone to the same degree that they have withdrawn the promised number of tanks from Eastern Europe. Finally, table 3 provides a picture of the status of the reductions from east of the Urals. Overall, the Soviets, within the limits of our ability to observe and assess, seem to be proceeding with the unilateral withdrawals as outlined by Gorbachev.

Questions have arisen concerning the spirit and letter of their promise. Are they doing what they promised? Is the force size really changing? Even if it is, are the residual Soviet forces more capable? In short, is there less here than meets the eye?

Let us look at the tank issue first. Following Gorbachev's 7 December speech, statements by Soviet officials indicated that most or all of the of the 5,300 tanks to be withdrawn from Eastern Europe would be destroyed and that most of the 4,700 others to be reduced in the western USSR would be converted to civilian use. Some subsequent statements have indicated that tanks would also be placed in storage or used to upgrade units. The inconsistency and ambiguity of these statements make it difficult to determine how many tanks the Soviets now intend to dismantle or destroy, but virtually all of them will be older models from within the USSR and not the relatively more modern tanks being withdrawn from Eastern Europe. Moreover, some evidence indicates that Moscow is planning to store a significant number of the tanks removed from units in the ATTU zone east of

19. *(Continued)*

Secret

Table 1
Soviet Forces Withdrawn From Eastern Europe to the USSR [a]

	Total in Units (As of 1 January 1989)[b]	Announced Withdrawals (to be implemented by 1 January 1991)	Withdrawals Claimed (completed as of 1 August 1989)	Assessed Withdrawals (as of 1 September 1989)	Percent of Announced Withdrawals Completed
Ground forces divisions	30	6	3	3 [c]	50
Tanks	10,600	5,300	2,700 to 3,100 [d] (1,988 from East Germany)	2,700 to 2,800 [e] (2,000 from East Germany)	51 to 53
Artillery	7,000 [f]	Unspecified	690 to 700 [g] (169 from East Germany)	36 [h]	
Combat aircraft	1,600 [i]	260 to 321 [j]	120 to 162 [k]	180	56 to 69
Air assault units	8	8	4	4 [l]	50
Assault crossing units	7	7	2	2 [m]	29
Manpower	600,000	50,000	31,800 [n] (11,400 from East Germany)		

[a] This table includes forces the Soviets are removing from Eastern Europe. It does not include the disposition of these forces in the Soviet Union.
[b] Aircraft totals are as of 1 January 1988.
[c] Major elements of the 25th Tank Division (TD) and 32nd Guards Tank Division (GTD)—including all tanks and the air defense regiment, reconnaissance battalion, and multiple rocket launcher battalion from each division—have departed from East Germany. Both divisions transferred their motorized rifle regiment to another division, but a tank regiment from these divisions was removed in their place. Most of the artillery and virtually all motorized rifle elements from the 25th TD and 32nd GTD probably have been retained in East Germany to facilitate the restructuring of remaining Ground Forces units.
   Major elements—and perhaps all—of the 13th Guards Tank Division have departed from their garrisons in Hungary. Only tanks from the division, however, have been identified at bases in the USSR.
[d] Some Soviet spokesmen have indicated that from 2,700 to 3,100 tanks are being or have been withdrawn from "abroad." In each instance, their statements may include tanks removed from Eastern Europe and Mongolia. Most recently, another Soviet spokesman stated that some 2,700 tanks had departed from Eastern Europe.
[e] Tanks from as many as five maneuver regiments and a tank training regiment may have departed from Hungary.
[f] This total is for all Soviet artillery 100 mm and above, including mortars, multiple rocket launchers, and antitank guns.
[g] Soviet spokesmen have stated that from 690 to 700 "guns" or artillery pieces have been withdrawn from "abroad." Their statements either specifically or probably include artillery removed from Eastern Europe and Mongolia.
[h] Because of force restructuring requirements, most—perhaps all—self-propelled artillery pieces probably remain in Eastern Europe; some 36 BM-21 multiple rocket launchers were observed on railcars and apparently departed from East Germany.
[i] This total excludes helicopters and AWACS.
[j] Soviet spokesmen have stated that from 260 to 321 combat aircraft will be removed from Eastern Europe.
[k] Soviet spokesmen have stated that from 120 to 162 combat aircraft have been withdrawn from "abroad." Their statements either specifically or probably include aircraft removed from Eastern Europe and Mongolia.
[l] In addition to the four air assault battalions apparently removed from Eastern Europe, the air assault brigade at Cottbus in East Germany is in the process of withdrawing and probably has been eliminated from the structure of the Western Group of Forces.
[m] Some assets from withdrawn assault crossing battalions apparently have been reassigned to units remaining in East Germany.
[n] Soviet spokesmen have stated that 31,800 servicemen have been withdrawn from "abroad." Their statements probably include personnel removed from Eastern Europe and Mongolia. One spokesman said that 11,400 men had departed from East Germany.

the Urals. There is also evidence that the Soviets will upgrade divisions in the USSR, including those in the ATTU zone, with more modern tanks withdrawn from Eastern Europe.

In general, we believe that tanks withdrawn from Eastern Europe are replacing older tanks that had been in cadre units or storage in the USSR. To the best of our knowledge, the Soviets are taking the opportunity created by this withdrawal to retain their most modern equipment in their residual forces. Thus, in East Germany, the residual force will be entirely equipped with T-80s. The withdrawn T-64s replace T-10s, T-55s, T-54s, and the oldest T-64s that had

19. *(Continued)*

Table 2
Soviet Force Reductions in the Atlantic-to-the-Urals Zone [a]

	Total in the Force (as of 1 January 1989)[b]	Announced Reductions (to be implemented by 1 January 1991)	Assessed Reductions (as of) September 1989	Percent of Announced Reductions Completed
Ground Forces divisions	144	Up to 50[c] percent	20[d]	28
Tanks	44,000	10,000	1,600[e]	16
Artillery	52,500[f]	8,500	1,400[a]	16
Combat aircraft	11,500[g]	800	530[h]	66
Manpower	2,424,000[i]	240,000		

[a] This table includes equipment apparently removed from the force but most of which remains unaccounted for.
[b] Aircraft totals are as of 1 January 1988.
[c] Soviet spokesmen have stated that as many as half of Soviet Ground Forces divisions will be eliminated.
[d] This total includes those divisions that have physically disbanded or deactivated to mobilization bases (2nd TO&E divisions). An additional six divisions apparently are in the process of disbanding or deactivating.
[e] Some 2,700 to 2,800 tanks have been withdrawn from Eastern Europe (see Table 1, footnote f). Most of these are T-64s, which have been accounted for in units or bases in the USSR. Some 1,600 additional tanks—mostly T-10s and T-54/55s—were removed from army corps or divisions deactivating or disbanding in the western Soviet Union. Most of these tanks remain unaccounted for.
[f] This total includes antitank guns in units and artillery pieces stored in depots.
[g] This total excludes helicopters, sea-based naval air, heavy bombers, tankers, and AWACS.
[h] These aircraft have been removed from active units. A senior Soviet officer has indicated that some of these aircraft will be scrapped, some used for training or as flying targets, and some mothballed. To date, no scrapping has been confirmed.
[i] This total includes 1,309,000 in the Ground Forces; 358,000 in the Air Defense Forces; 263,000 in the Air Forces; 280,000 in the Navy; and 214,000 in the Strategic Rocket Forces. It does not include construction and railroad troops or civil defense and internal security forces.

been held for many years in cadre units or in long-term depot storage in the interior of the Soviet Union and east of the Urals.

What does this mean for Soviet capabilities? There has been no net increase in the number of T-72 and T-80 tanks in the forward area, and only modest increases are anticipated in the next few years. Therefore, the overall number of "most modern tanks" is not affected by the restructuring. In fact, the net number of tanks is being reduced by a significant number of older, yet fully capable T-64 tanks. Whereas the Soviets had 30 divisions with 120 maneuver regiments before the withdrawal began, after the withdrawals are concluded they will have 24 divisions with 96 maneuver regiments.

The manner in which the Soviets are carrying out their restructuring has, however, provoked serious questions that have not yet been answered. Clearly, although they have adhered to their promise to withdraw tanks and have removed three divisions from their force structure in Eastern Europe, equipment other than tanks from those units is being used to modernize and expand the equipment holdings of the remaining divisions.

The inconsistency of certain features of the reduction and restructuring programs with some Soviet descriptions of these activities probably reflects adjustments made by the General Staff as the programs have

19. *(Continued)*

Secret

Table 3
Soviet Force Reductions East of the Urals a

	Total Deployed (As of 1 January 1989 b)	Announced Reductions (To be implemented by 1 January 1991)	Assessed Reductions (As of 1 September 1989)	Percent of Announced Reductions Completed
Ground Forces army corps	5		2 c	
Ground Forces divisions	75	15 divisions in "eastern" USSR d	5	13 to 33 e for divisions in "eastern" USSR
Tanks	22,600		650	
Artillery	31,000 f		1,050	
Combat aircraft	3,930 g	15 h regiments in "eastern" USSR	115 aircraft i	
Manpower	967,000 j	260,000 k		

a This table includes equipment apparently removed from the force but most of which remains unaccounted for.
b Aircraft totals are as of 1 January 1988.
c This total includes army corps headquarters that have been disbanded along with their nondivisional units. The divisions subordinate to the army corps have not all been disbanded. They are included in the figures for divisions. An additional army corps may be deactivating.
d The Soviets have announced that 15 divisions will be eliminated in the "eastern" USSR. They have not specified, however, which areas and forces are included in the "eastern" USSR. Because Soviet spokesmen also have stated that as many as half of all Soviet Ground Forces divisions will be eliminated, this would total 38 of the 75 divisions east of the Urals if the reduction is apportioned evenly.
e The lower percentage excludes force reductions resulting from the Afghan withdrawal from the "eastern" USSR total; the higher figure includes these reductions.
f This total includes an estimated 3,000 antitank guns and an undetermined number of artillery pieces with a caliber less than 100 mm stored in depots.
g This total excludes helicopters, sea-based naval air, heavy bombers, tankers, and AWACS.
h This total includes the four regiments to be withdrawn from Mongolia. The Soviets have not specified which other regiments and how many additional aircraft are included.
i These aircraft have been removed from active units and remain unaccounted for. Because the Soviets have not specified the number of aircraft to be reduced, we cannot determine what percentage 115 is of the total they plan to eliminate.
j This total includes 491,000 in the Ground Forces; 157,000 in the Air Defense Forces; 94,000 in the Air Forces; 120,000 in the Navy; and 105,000 in the Strategic Rocket Forces. It does not include construction and railroad troops or civil defense and internal security forces.
k This total includes 200,000 in the "eastern" USSR and 60,000 for the "southern" USSR, the latter probably being servicemen withdrawn from Afghanistan.

evolved. With the withdrawal program originally having been imposed from above, the General Staff probably has been given considerable flexibility in organizing remaining Soviet forces within the constraints imposed by "defensive" restructuring.

The character of the restructured residual force, therefore, is a major question. To discuss that force, however, requires some explanation of the overall Soviet motivation for the process. We believe that the ongoing unilateral reductions and restructuring are intended largely to foster a perception of reduced threat in the West and to maintain the momentum toward a CFE agreement that would allow Gorbachev to reduce his forces further, reap potential economic benefits, and simultaneously reduce NATO force capability. We believe the Soviets remain committed to this end game and will not jeopardize it in an effort to obtain short-term military advantages that almost certainly would be quickly discovered by the West.

Gorbachev's economic agenda is an overriding consideration as we assess the scope of the Soviet's reductions and withdrawals. But what of the restructuring and modernization? As long ago as the middle-to-late 1970s, the Soviets recognized that the type of war that would probably be fought in Central Europe had

Secret

19. *(Continued)*

Key Statements on Soviet Tank Reductions

22 December 1988
Major General Lebedev of the Soviet General Staff states that entire units with their materiel will be withdrawn from Eastern Europe. The units will be disbanded, and much of their equipment—including the latest model tanks—will be scrapped. Tank engines and auxiliary equipment will be turned over to the civilian economy. (Lebedev's statement was referring specifically to the tanks in the six divisions to be withdrawn; however, the context of his remarks indicate he may have been referring to all tank units removed from Eastern Europe.)

16 January 1989
Marshal Akhromeyev states that six tank divisions will be withdrawn from East Germany, Czechoslovakia, and Hungary. In addition, 3,300 tanks will be removed from Soviet motorized rifle divisions and other units in Eastern Europe. All 5,000 tanks to be withdrawn will be destroyed, and most of the tanks to be reduced west of the Urals will be dismantled.

17 January 1989
Marshal Kulikov asserts that "withdrawn forces" will not be stationed in the western military districts, although some would be stationed east of the Urals.

18 January 1989
General Secretary Gorbachev announces that half of the 10,000 tanks will be destroyed and half will be converted to civil use.

24 January 1989
Deputy Foreign Minister Karpov says that, of the 10,000 tanks to be reduced, half would be scrapped and the other half converted to civil or training use. The reduction involved 5,300 of the "most modern" tanks and, of these, 3,300 would be from divisions remaining in Eastern Europe. The 2,000 tanks in the six tank divisions withdrawn from Eastern Europe would be "dismantled."

17 April 1989
Army General Snetkov, commander of Soviet forces in East Germany, states that the tanks removed from the GDR will be sent beyond the Urals; some will be "mothballed" and some modified for use in the national economy.

5 May 1989
Lieutenant General Fursin, Chief of Staff of Soviet forces in East Germany, announces that 1,000 tanks are already beyond the Urals, where they will be turned into bulldozers.

12 May 1989
Colonel General Chervov of the Soviet General Staff states that, of the 10,000 tanks to be eliminated, 5,000 will be destroyed and 5,000 will be used as towing vehicles or targets for firing practice.

19 May 1989
Soviet General Staff Chief Moiseyev says that Moscow reserves the option to retain rather than destroy equipment withdrawn from Eastern Europe.

23 May 1989
General Markelov, Chief of the General Staff Press Center, announces that older, wornout tanks will be smelted, and that newer tanks will be remodeled to serve as tractors for civilian purposes. He also states that a steel works at Chelyabinsk in the Urals is already smelting tanks.

19. *(Continued)*

Key Statements on Soviet Tank Reductions (continued)

23 May 1989
Major General Shchepin, Chief of Staff of the Soviet Central Group of Forces, states that some of the T-72 tanks removed from Czechoslovakia will be scrapped or converted for civilian use at the Black Sea port of Novorossiysk in the North Caucasus Military District.

3 June 1989
General Staff spokesman Lieutenant General Petrov states that more than 2,750 tanks and artillery pieces have been dispatched to storage bases or for destruction.

30 June 1989
Colonel General Omelichev, First Deputy Chief of the General Staff, states that more than 3,000 tanks have been withdrawn from Eastern Europe and Mongolia. He adds that units being withdrawn will be disbanded and some of their equipment will be destroyed, some transferred to storage bases, and some used in the national economy.

3 July 1989
Defense Minister Yazov states that some tanks withdrawn from Eastern Europe are being used to upgrade units in the USSR, some are being mothballed, and "old" tanks made in the 1950s and 1960s are being destroyed.

3 July 1989
Colonel General Krivosheyev of the General Staff states that the smelting of tanks has begun and that their engines and other components are being used in the economy; other tanks are being converted for civilian use. In 1989, 5,000 will be scrapped and 2,000 will be converted. Those being scrapped are heavy tanks like the T-10, which are unsuitable for civilian use.

---

changed. Where once the use of nuclear weapons was expected, causing the Soviets to plan for rapid breakthrough and exploitation, the Soviets began to foresee a largely or wholly conventional war, where both sides' nuclear arsenals might be checked by parity. At the same time, they saw changes in NATO conventional forces that made those forces more and more capable of withstanding a conventional Soviet breakthrough operation. With the advent of densely deployed, relatively cheap, and highly effective antitank weapons systems, the Soviets began to talk about "gnawing" rather than "slicing" through NATO defenses. As Soviet General Staff attention turned toward the demands of a high-tech conventional battlefield, the Soviets recognized an increasing need to train for defensive operations. They also saw that their heavy tank forces were becoming more vulnerable, but only after the December initiative did they alter the planned expansion of their tank forces. In general terms, the current Soviet military response to NATO conventional capabilities is more infantry and artillery up front, backed by tank forces.

It is the reduction in the force and the change in the missions it is structured to perform that reflect Gorbachev's impact. Gorbachev has reasserted the Party's leading role in determining the sociopolitical content of Soviet military doctrine. The Communist Party and its leaders decide matters of national security, determine the potential opponents, the strategic likelihood of war, and the resources to be allocated to defense. Gorbachev's views of Soviet economic problems, and his assessment that near-to-midterm conflict with the West was unlikely, led him to conclude that reductions were a feasible method of contributing to his economic and political objectives.

19. *(Continued)*

The Soviet leadership's reductions and restructuring programs will produce over the next few years the most significant changes in Soviet general purpose forces opposite NATO since Khrushchev's drastic force reductions of the late 1950s and early 1960s:

- As a consequence of decisions by the USSR and its Warsaw Pact allies to cut their general purpose forces over the next two years, the offensive capabilities of Pact theater forces will decline through the first half of the 1990s.

- The announced withdrawals of Soviet forces from Central Europe, when completed, will significantly reduce Soviet prospects for attacking from a less than fully prepared force posture and lengthen considerably the amount of time required for the Pact to prepare and position forces for sustained offensive operations against NATO.

- Residual forces would be sufficient to mount a hastily constituted but still effective defense against NATO forces until reinforcements could be mobilized and moved forward.

As the Soviets move to an infantry-heavy force structure through restructuring, there may be a dramatic increase in the number of BMP infantry fighting vehicles. Although effective in combat operations, BMPs are not tanks, and we judge:
- Regardless of how the Soviets choose to restructure their forces, the loss of half the tanks previously stationed in Eastern Europe will significantly degrade Pact offensive capabilities.
- Even a large addition of well-equipped infantry would not totally offset this loss of armored striking power.

The Soviets, nevertheless, have no intention of disarming themselves, nor do they intend to maintain obsolete forces. Quite the contrary, Gorbachev's economic reforms, if successful, would prevent such outcomes. It is consistent with stated objectives, therefore, simultaneously to withdraw tanks, reduce the size of forces overall, and restructure and modernize residual forces using existing equipment to maximize their potential effectiveness against NATO.

Although we have a pretty good perspective on the general impact of these changes, there are still some important uncertainties. We do not know the actual shape that Soviet forces will take. Will Soviet objectives for their restructured forces change? They seem unlikely to have a capability to conduct breakthrough operations without mobilization—will that change? Will the residual forces be maintained at a higher level of readiness? On all these questions, opinions will abound, but until evidence or trends appear, conclusions are premature.

We conclude that the Soviet withdrawals and reduction observed to date are generally consistent with Gorbachev's initial statement. We also conclude that Soviet restructuring and modernization activity—consistent with emerging Soviet military doctrinal views of war in Europe and the nature and capability of NATO—will result in a smaller standing force optimized for defense, but still capable of smaller scale offensive operations. Such a force would require a massive and lengthy mobilization in order to perform deep strategic offensive operations against NATO.

20. NIC M 89-10005, November 1989, *Soviet Theater Forces in 1991: The Impact of the Unilateral Withdrawals on Structure and Capabilities* (Key Judgments only)

National Intelligence Council

~~Secret~~

Memorandum

Soviet Theater Forces in 1991: The Impact of the Unilateral Withdrawals on Structure and Capabilities

~~Secret~~

NIC M 89-10005
November 1989

Copy 598

20. (*Continued*)

National Intelligence Council

Secret
NOFORN NOCONTRACT

NIC M 89-10005

Soviet Theater Forces in 1991: The Impact of the Unilateral Withdrawals on Structure and Capabilities (U)

Information available as of 22 November 1989 was used in the preparation of this Memorandum, which was prepared by the National Intelligence Officer for General Purpose Forces. The Memorandum was coordinated throughout the Intelligence Community by the National Intelligence Officer for General Purpose Forces. (U)

Secret
November 1989

20. (*Continued*)

~~Secret~~
~~NOFORN-NOCONTRACT~~

Key Judgments

Implementation of the two-year program of unilateral troop reductions announced by Soviet President Mikhail Gorbachev in December 1988 appears to be roughly on schedule. To date, the Soviets have withdrawn almost 2,000 tanks from the German Democratic Republic; however, reorganization and modernization in the Western Group of Forces (WGF) will partially offset the resulting reduction in force capabilities.

At the end of 1990, the WGF will consist of five armies and 15 divisions (seven tank and eight motorized rifle). It appears that the divisions will consist of four maneuver regiments: tank divisions will have two tank and two motorized rifle regiments, while motorized rifle divisions will have four motorized rifle regiments. Regiments apparently will not have combined arms battalions. It is not yet clear whether motorized rifle regiments in tank divisions will have two or three motorized rifle battalions (along with one tank battalion).

Complete reorganization of units in the WGF will require the Soviets to introduce approximately 1,800 armored troop carriers (ATCs), 400 artillery pieces (122 mm and 152 mm) and 200 antitank guns. Only about 450 ATCs, about 100 artillery pieces, and about 100 antitank guns have been introduced. Therefore, although the reorganization could be completed by the end of 1990, the current pace of equipment introduction would need to be increased significantly.

The restructuring of WGF tank and motorized rifle divisions will result in greater changes in their capabilities than are apparent from the changes in their aggregate combat potential scores. The divisions—and the WGF—will have substantially less armored striking power. Moreover, the new division organization makes it more difficult to concentrate tank forces.

Manpower reductions, coupled with the requirements of the reorganization, will not allow division-level readiness to be increased in the foreseeable future. Divisions will probably continue to be manned at about 85-percent strength.

Secret
NIC M 89-10005

20. *(Continued)*

The unilateral air reductions and restructuring will, when completed, result in a Soviet aircraft mix weighted toward air-to-air fighters over ground attack aircraft in East Germany. The aircraft force mix in the Western Theater of Military Operations as a whole, however, will be weighted more heavily than before toward ground attack aircraft. The number of deep attack aircraft remains unchanged. Although this new force structure will be more capable of defending against a surprise NATO air offensive, it will not further impair the Soviets' ability to conduct offensive air operations.

The unilateral reductions are consistent with the announced Soviet shift toward a more defensive doctrine. Pursuant to the new doctrine's "War Prevention" tenet, the reductions will virtually eliminate the Soviets' already limited short warning attack capability. By lengthening Soviet timelines to transition to war, the reductions increase the prospects for successful crisis management.

We believe the General Staff would have mid-to-high-level confidence in its ability to prosecute deep offensive operations against NATO forces in the Central Region, given sufficient time for force generation. However, the need to draw substantially on forces in the western USSR would severely constrain Soviet options in a multitheater war.

21. NIC M 90-10002, April 1990, *The Direction of Change in the Warsaw Pact*

National Intelligence Council

~~Secret~~
~~NOFORN NOCONTRACT~~

Memorandum

The Direction of Change in the Warsaw Pact (C NF)

~~Secret~~

NIC M 90-10002
April 1990
Copy 680

21. (*Continued*)

National Intelligence Council

~~Secret~~
~~NOFORN NOCONTRACT~~

NIC M 90-10002

The Direction of Change in the Warsaw Pact ~~(C-NF)~~

Information available as of 1 March 1990 was used in the preparation of this Memorandum. The Memorandum was drafted and coordinated within the Intelligence Community by the National Intelligence Officer for General Purpose Forces to whom comments may be directed at secure 37311.

~~Secret~~
April 1990

21. *(Continued)*

Key Judgments

Recent political events in Eastern Europe will further erode Soviet confidence in their allies. Moscow can *not* rely upon non-Soviet Warsaw Pact forces; it must question its ability to bring Soviet reinforcements through East European countries whose hostility is no longer disguised or held in check. On the basis of completed unilateral Warsaw Pact cuts without NATO reciprocation and considering current political turmoil, we now believe that the capability to conduct an unreinforced conventional Pact attack on NATO would be virtually eliminated.

Should current CFE proposals for both sides be implemented, we believe that Soviet defense planners would judge Pact forces *incapable* of conducting a theater strategic offensive *even after full mobilization of reserves and deployment of standing forces within the Atlantic-to-the-Urals (ATTU) Zone.* Conduct of an attack upon NATO in such conditions would require generation of additional forces and equipment.

The unilateral reductions begun a year ago by the Soviet Union will probably be completed on schedule. The recent Soviet agreements to remove all forces stationed in Czechoslovakia and Hungary by mid-1991 will nearly double the originally announced unilateral withdrawal in ground forces (at least 11 rather than six divisions).

The large unilateral reductions in Soviet forces due to be completed by the end of 1990 are forcing widespread restructuring of military units, substantially reducing the armor in Soviet ground force divisions, eliminating some specialized assault units, and reducing ground attack capabilities of tactical air units.

The originally announced Central European reductions (nearly 10 percent in manpower, 20 percent in aircraft, and 50 percent in tanks) will reduce the offensive capabilities of Pact Forces and, along with sweeping Soviet CFE proposals, are convincing indicators of Soviet intent to cut their military burden and are consistent with a movement toward a defensive doctrine.

21. *(Continued)*

~~Secret~~
~~NOFORN NOCONTRACT~~

In the aggregate, the above changes lessen the state "combat potential" of forward Soviet units. We believe that Soviet planners recognize that these reductions (assuming no change in NATO forces) would require substantially greater forces to be brought forward from the USSR for the conduct of sustained theater offensive operations. On the basis of these military changes alone, in September 1989 we judged that NATO would have 40 to 50 days of warning of a four-front Pact attack. Current political changes would probably increase this warning time.

~~This information is Secret Noforn Nocontract WNINTEL.~~

21. *(Continued)*

~~Secret~~
~~NOFORN NOCONTRACT~~

Contents

	Page
Key Judgments	iii
Discussion	1
Background	1
Traditional Soviet Views of Operations Against NATO	1
The Soviets Modernize	1
The NSWP Lags	1
Reassessing the Doctrine	2
The Warsaw Pact in Transition	2
Soviet Cutbacks	2
The Halfway Point	4
Restructuring	6
Effects of the Changes	8
Combat Potential	8
How the Changes Affect Soviet Perceptions of the Balance	9
Annex: Warning Implications of Warsaw Pact Unilateral Force Reductions	15

21. *(Continued)*

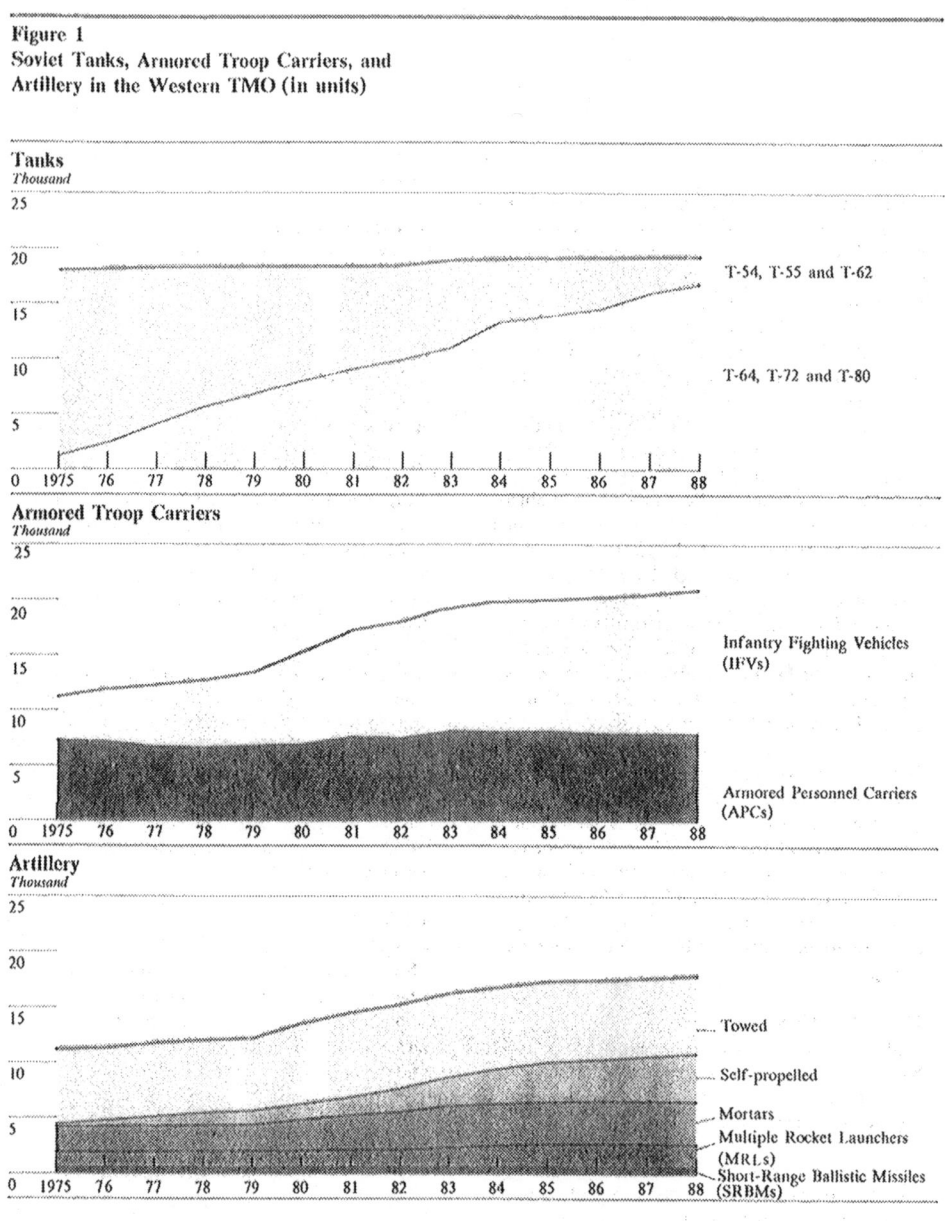

Figure 1
Soviet Tanks, Armored Troop Carriers, and Artillery in the Western TMO (in units)

21. *(Continued)*

~~Secret~~
~~NOFORN NOCONTRACT~~

Discussion

Background

Traditional Soviet Views of Operations Against NATO
The Soviet General Staff based its war plans on the assumption that, if it had to fight a war with the West, the Soviet Union would be able to achieve classic military victory through the destruction of NATO forces and the occupation of NATO territory, principally Western Europe. Occupation of Germany and the political imperative for control of Eastern Europe led to the stationing of substantial Soviet forces in the forward area. By the middle-to-late 1970s, however, Soviet perceptions of their ability to prevail were changing. Where once Soviet forces, using nuclear weapons, could obtain planned objectives with relatively little assistance from their smaller, less well-equipped allies, the prospect of war with at least an initial conventional phase changed the situation to one that required the participation of East European forces and relied upon the long lines of communication that fed supplies from the USSR through Eastern Europe to attacking Soviet forces. Influenced to a large degree by their perception of greatly improved NATO conventional defenses, the Soviet General Staff considered even the large Soviet force in the forward area no longer adequate to the task, and foresaw the need to draw additional forces from the Soviet Union for its planned Theater Strategic Operation. Thus, by the mid-1980s, Soviet staff planners forecast a prolonged conventional war with NATO in which non-Soviet Warsaw Pact forces were included in the initial attack and which relied upon major reinforcements from the Soviet Union for success.

The Soviets Modernize
When Mikhail Gorbachev took over as party General Secretary in early 1985, the Soviet military already was implementing a long-term program of force restructuring, expansion, and modernization:

- *Restructuring* of 36 active divisions from the late 1970s through the end of 1984 had made them larger, more mobile, and more flexible, with enhanced combined-arms capability and increased firepower.

- *Ground force mobilization bases*—units created by the Soviets in the 1960s to stockpile older equipment for inactive divisions—were gradually being activated with small cadre elements that could facilitate rapid expansion to wartime strength and readiness. More than 20 such bases were activated between 1975 and 1984, while the overall number of active tank, motorized rifle, and airborne divisions increased from 176 to 200.

- *Ground equipment modernization*, begun as early as the mid-1960s, had become persistent and even paced. For example, the quantity and quality of tanks, armored troop carriers and artillery in the Western Theater of Military Operations (TMO) opposite NATO's central region had been increasing dramatically (see figure 1).

- *Attack helicopters* also increased significantly—by more than 60 percent from 1981 to 1985 in the Atlantic-to-the-Urals Zone (see figure 2).

- *Air forces modernization* introduced the Su-24 Fencer light bomber and Tu-22M Backfire medium bomber in the 1970s and fourth-generation MiG-29 Fulcrum and Su-27 Flanker fighter-interceptors in the 1980s (see figure 3).

The NSWP Lags
The non-Soviet Warsaw Pact (NSWP) forces lagged the Soviets in force modernization, yet the Soviets depended on them to play a significant, perhaps vital, role in a war with NATO. If NSWP forces were no longer available, Soviet staffs would need to rethink operations against NATO. Soviet confidence in the reliability of non-Soviet Pact forces was the result of strategic interests generally shared with East European Communist leaderships, as well as a carefully planned Soviet-dominated command and control structure to

21. *(Continued)*

Figure 2
Soviet Attack Helicopters in the ATTU Zone [a]

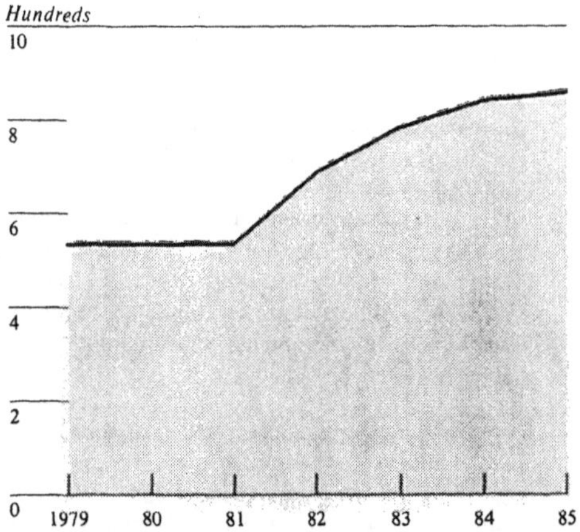

[Chart showing helicopter numbers in hundreds from 1979 to 1985, rising from about 5 hundred to about 8 hundred]

[a] Includes Hip E, Hind D, E, and F helicopters.

which the East Europeans acceded. Although that architecture gave the Soviet General Staff executive authority for wartime decisionmaking and command generation of Warsaw Pact forces, it relied upon national general staffs to pass orders. Therefore, the Pact command and control structure was, and remains, dependent upon the cooperation of the highest political and military leaders in each Pact country. Since it was clear that their interests in most crisis situations through the mid-1980s would be congruent with the Soviets' interests, we formerly assessed—and believed that Soviet planners also assessed—that the East European forces were at least initially reliable and would respond to commands to fight.

Reassessing the Doctrine
By 1985 Soviet theater forces were structured for fast-paced, offensive operations lasting for an extended period of time (weeks—perhaps months) in a nonnuclear environment. Soviet and Pact exercise patterns tended to confirm that they planned on such a scenario. In building to this capability, however, the Soviets had traded decreased readiness for increased combat power after full preparation. Soviet forces in Central Europe were manned some 170,000 below full wartime strength and were assessed to require two to three weeks to prepare for offensive operations.

Soon after coming to power, Gorbachev held talks with his military leadership. He agreed with the need to modernize Soviet conventional forces but understood that conventional modernization would be enormously expensive. He probably concluded that the USSR could not afford a buildup of both nuclear and conventional forces. In 1986 and 1987, there was mounting evidence that the Soviets were reassessing their military doctrine. High-level Soviet military leaders told their Western counterparts that Soviet/Warsaw Pact doctrine had changed, and that evidence of such change should be clear to observers of Pact exercises and training patterns. There were also indications that the "defensive doctrine" being stressed by the Soviets was not understood or accepted uniformly throughout the Soviet military leadership.

The Warsaw Pact in Transition

Soviet Cutbacks
In December 1988, Gorbachev announced at the United Nations that significant unilateral reductions of Soviet forces would take place in 1989 and 1990. His statement was followed by various explanations of Soviet reduction plans and additional announcements concerning cuts in defense spending and production (see inset). Soon after Gorbachev's announcement, each of the USSR's Warsaw Pact Allies except Romania announced force and defense spending cuts. These cuts—to be completed by the end of 1990—roughly parallel the Soviet cuts in types and proportional amounts of equipment, manpower, and expenditures (see table 1). These announcements of cuts, which almost certainly had Moscow's prior approval, contradicted earlier indications that the Soviets would require their allies to make up any unilateral Soviet force reductions.

21. (Continued)

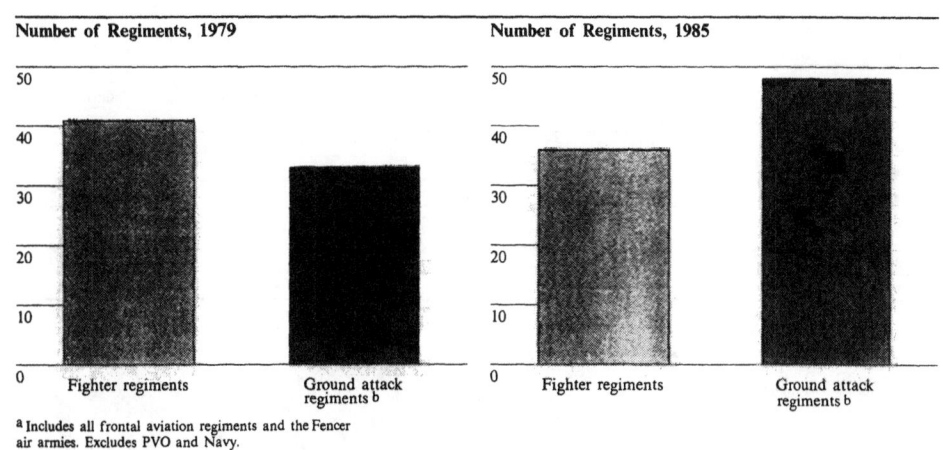

Figure 3
Force Composition in the ATTU Zone, 1979 and 1985 [a]
Soviet Tactical Air Force

Number of Regiments, 1979 — Fighter regiments, Ground attack regiments [b]
Number of Regiments, 1985 — Fighter regiments, Ground attack regiments [b]

[a] Includes all frontal aviation regiments and the Fencer air armies. Excludes PVO and Navy.
[b] Ground attack regiments (light bombers and fighter-bombers).

Soviet Unilateral Force Reductions Announced by President Gorbachev on 7 December 1988 (To Be Implemented by 1 January 1991)

Reduced from the Soviet Armed Forces	500,000 personnel
Withdrawn from Eastern Europe	Six tank divisions 50,000 personnel 5,000 tanks Assault landing units Assault crossing units
Reduced in the Atlantic-to-the-Urals Zone	10,000 tanks 8,500 artillery systems 800 combat aircraft

In Central Europe alone, Gorbachev's announced Soviet reductions would entail:

- A total of 50,000 men and 5,000[1] tanks to be withdrawn from Soviet forces in Eastern Europe. As part of this reduction, six Soviet divisions—four from East Germany, and one each from Czechoslovakia and Hungary—were to be withdrawn. The removal of 50,000 Soviet military personnel would reduce Soviet strength in the forward area by nearly 10 percent. The withdrawal of 5,300 tanks would cut total Soviet tank strength in Central Europe in half (see figure 4).

- From the air forces, 320 combat aircraft to be removed from Central Europe; this is a 20-percent reduction in Soviet combat aircraft stationed in Central Europe.

[1] Later increased to 5,300 with the inclusion of Soviet forces in Poland. (U)

21. *(Continued)*

~~Secret~~

Table 1
Announced Non-Soviet Warsaw Pact Unilateral Reductions

	Military Manpower	Force Structure	Tanks	Combat Aircraft	Defense Budget (*percent*)
Total	81,300		2,751	210	
East Germany	10,000	6 regiments	600	50	10 (1989-90)
Poland	40,000	4 divisions [a]	850	80	4 (1989)
Czechoslovakia	12,000 [b]	3 divisions	850	51	15 (1989-90)
Hungary [c]	9,300	1 tank brigade	251	9	17 (1989)
					30 (1990)
Bulgaria	10,000		200	20	12 (1989)
Romania					1.7 (1989)

[a] Two to be eliminated; two to be reduced in strength.
[b] Being transferred to construction troops.
[c] Excludes November-December 1989 announcements.

This table is Secret Noforn WNINTEL.

- A total of 10,000 tanks, 8,500 artillery systems, and 800 combat aircraft to be eliminated from the Atlantic-to-the-Urals (ATTU) Zone. A 10,000-tank reduction in the ATTU zone would cut the number of Soviet tanks in operational units by about one-fourth. Cutting 800 aircraft represents a reduction of more than 8 percent of the Soviet combat aircraft in units opposite NATO.

- A "major portion" of troops in Mongolia to be withdrawn, later clarified as a cut in ground forces of 75 percent, with the air forces there to be eliminated.

Although unilateral Navy reductions were not part of Gorbachev's speech, the Soviets have embarked on a program of naval measures. In 1989, 46 ships and submarines departed Soviet naval facilities to be scrapped in foreign yards. All but one were at least 30 years old; only one was operational. We have identified an additional 120 units that are candidates for scrapping in 1990. The Soviets have also reduced out-of-area deployments by both ships and Soviet naval aircraft. At the same time, the Soviets continue with force modernization and construction of aircraft, submarines, and surface combatants, including three conventional takeoff and landing (CTOL) aircraft carriers, although there is debate within the USSR over the need for carriers.

The Halfway Point

One year into the two-year unilateral withdrawal/reduction period announced by Gorbachev, the first phase of the program is complete (see inset). Moscow has withdrawn at least 50 percent of the tanks and approximately 60 percent of the combat aircraft from Eastern Europe that Gorbachev said would be removed, and it has withdrawn about half of the tanks and a quarter of the combat aircraft to be removed from Mongolia. In Eastern Europe, of the six Soviet tank divisions to be withdrawn by the end of 1990, Moscow has withdrawn the major elements of three (two from East Germany, one from Hungary). The number of Soviet tactical aviation units (for which no reductions were announced) remains about the same, but the units are losing assigned aircraft.

21. *(Continued)*

Figure 4
Soviet Ground Forces in Central Europe, March 1990

	Current	To be withdrawn	Percentage to be withdrawn	To remain
Maneuver divisions	30	6	20	24
Tanks	10,600	5,300	50	5,300
Combat aircraft	1,600	320	20	1,280
Personnel	600,000	50,000	8.3	550,000

Announced Soviet Unilateral Withdrawals From Central Europe

21. *(Continued)*

Assessed Unilateral Soviet Force Reductions, 1 January 1990	
Withdrawn from Eastern Europe	Three tank divisions (major elements) 2,600–2,775 tanks Four air assault units Two assault crossing units
Reduced in the Atlantic-to-the-Urals Zone	3,260 tanks 2,120 artillery systems 580 combat aircraft
Reduced from the Soviet Armed Forces	Total: 26 divisions ATTU Zone: 16 divisions disbanded and three deactivated Non-ATTU Zone: four divisions disbanded and three deactivated

Restructuring

To accommodate such radical equipment changes and claimed changes in doctrine, many units are being restructured:

- *Ground force restructuring.* About two-thirds of the 27 Soviet divisions that remained in Eastern Europe at the end of 1989 are probably being restructured (figure 5), as are up to four divisions in the USSR:

  —*Tank divisions*, which had three tank regiments and one motorized rifle regiment, will now have two tank regiments and two motorized rifle regiments. Most divisions will lose 69 tanks, or 22 percent of their original holdings.

  —*Motorized rifle divisions*, which had one tank regiment and three motorized rifle regiments, will now have four motorized rifle regiments. They are also losing tanks from other divisional elements. These changes reduce the number of tanks by 105 per division in most motorized rifle divisions in Eastern Europe and by 65 per division in the USSR—40 and 30 percent respectively of their original holdings.

  —Some of the personnel and most of the armored troop carriers and artillery from the units being withdrawn are being used to meet the needs of the restructured divisions remaining in Eastern Europe. Additional armored troop carriers—some 450 observed thus far—have arrived from the USSR. Some 2,000 additional armored troop carriers would be required to restructure the 24 Soviet divisions in the originally planned residual force in Eastern Europe. Artillery battalions continue to increase from 18 to 24 guns, and a third artillery battalion appears to be being added to the artillery regiments of tank divisions.

  —In addition, some river-crossing and air assault units are to be withdrawn to the USSR.

- *Tactical air force restructuring* (figure 6).

  —Few units are being disbanded; instead, the average strength of tactical air regiments is being reduced by about 10 aircraft each. Overall, there will be about 17 percent fewer aircraft opposite NATO (bars 1 and 2).

  —The most modern of the displaced aircraft are going to regiments with older aircraft (MiG-21/MiG-23/Su-17), which are leaving active service.

  —The predominance of ground attack regiments over fighter regiments in East Germany has changed to a more balanced force.

  —Half the light bombers (Fencers) in the forward area have been relocated to the Western USSR. These aircraft could be rapidly reintroduced into Eastern Europe.

21. *(Continued)*

Figure 5
Soviet Division Restructuring

Tank Division [a]

Total equipment: 250 tanks (22- or 31-percent decrease)
   340 to 432 IFVs/APCs

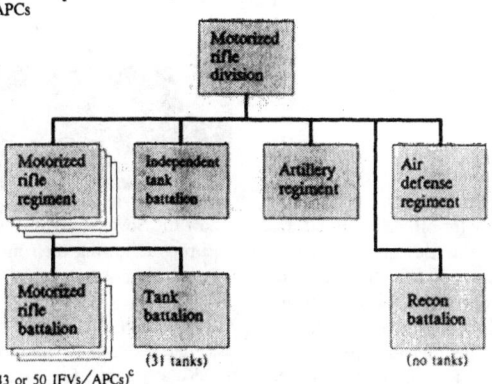

[a] Soviet tank divisions in Eastern Europe have had 319 or 363 tanks and 251 IFVs/APCs, not including command and reconnaissance variants.

Motorized Rifle Division [b]

Total equipment: 155 tanks (40- or 44-percent decrease)
   655 IFVs/APCs

(43 or 50 IFVs/APCs)[c]

[b] Soviet motorized rifle divisions in Eastern Europe have had 260 and 277 tanks and 455 IFVs/APCs, not including command and reconnaissance variants.

[c] Varies depending on whether the regiment is BMP or BTR equipped. Soviet motorized rifle divisions in Eastern Europe that have been restructured have two BMP-equipped regiments and two BTR-equipped regiments.

Figure 6
Reduction and Restructuring, 1988 and 1990
Soviet Air Forces in the ATTU Zone

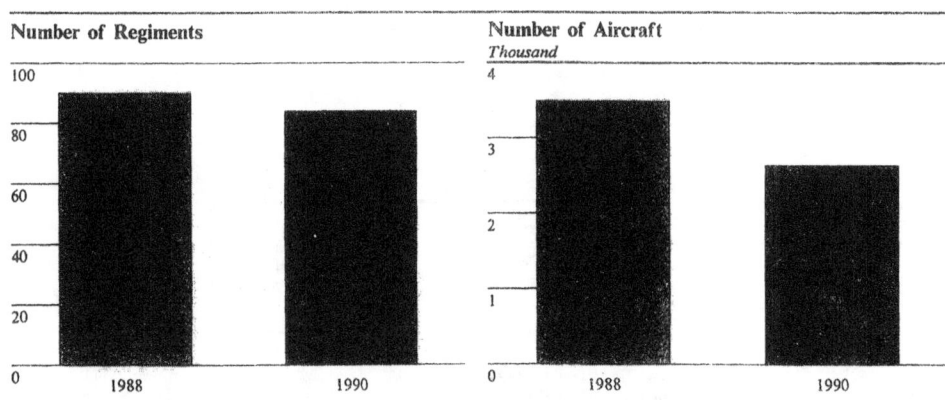

- The certainty of complete withdrawal from Czechoslovakia and Hungary and the high likelihood of other reductions beyond those originally announced raise the prospect of further changes in Soviet plans for restructuring.

Effects of the Changes

Reductions and restructuring will significantly degrade the ability of Soviet forces to concentrate combat power, particularly for offensive operations. Armored striking power, in particular, is reduced and fragmented. The new motorized rifle divisions are well suited for defensive operations but are not organized specifically to conduct large-scale attacks or counterattacks. The new tank divisions are "balanced"—thus, better suited for holding ground than the previous standard tank divisions—but they retain substantial offensive punch.

Combat Potential

To gauge the probability of mission success, Soviet staff officers often compare the relative strength of opposing forces in terms of their calculated "combat potential." How the Soviets come up with combat 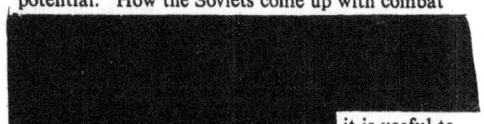 it is useful to essay a Soviet-style combat-potential analysis to see how the Soviets might view the correlation of forces in Europe following their unilateral reductions and restructuring.

Application of such analysis to the portion of the Soviet *Western Group of Forces* (WGF) in East Germany shows (see figure 7) that the 1991 force will

21. *(Continued)*

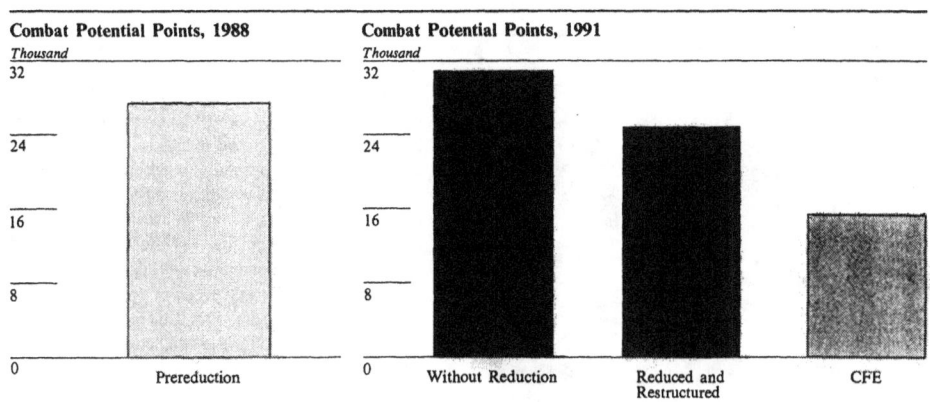

Figure 7
Western Group of Forces, 1988 and 1991

be large, modern, and will possess major combat potential. But it will possess *less* offensive combat potential than the Intelligence Community assessed it would have had in the absence of the unilateral reductions. In fact, a reduced and restructured WGF in 1991 has less combat potential than the 1988 WGF, even though some modernization will have taken place. The projected WGF structure for 1991 (without reductions) would have derived over half its offensive combat potential from tanks, but the force projected for 1991 *after* reductions will draw less than 40 percent of its offensive potential from its tanks.

The *air* assessment is different. The Soviets probably expect most of the effect of the unilateral reductions in air forces to be offset by modernization by the late 1990s. We believe, using Soviet-style combat-potential calculations, that the Soviets expect the unilateral force reductions to result in a modest shift in the Central European air balance to the *advantage* of NATO, but the current situation of near parity would not be upset (see figure 8). These changes in Warsaw Pact air forces probably would *not* substantially alter the Pact's overall prospects in an air war in Central Europe.

How the Changes Affect Soviet Perceptions of the Balance

Taken together, the reductions and restructuring reinforce our mid-1980s judgment that the Soviet General Staff did not have high confidence in its ability to conduct a deep attack on NATO without introducing significant reinforcements from the Soviet Union before D-Day. After reducing the shock power of forward area forces by 5,300 tanks, the General Staff would consider the Pact even less capable of conducting an attack without substantial reinforcement to

21. *(Continued)*

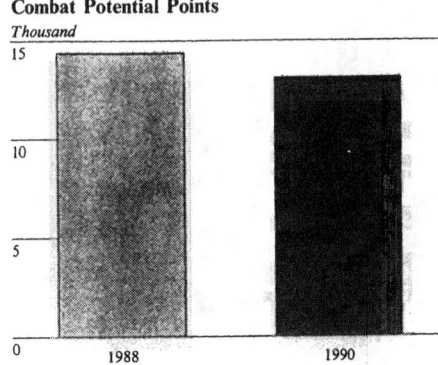

Figure 8
Soviet Air Forces in the ATTU Zone, 1988 and 1990

bring four fronts into the offensive (see figure 9). The need to bring forward tank-heavy forces from the Western USSR extends Soviet timelines to transition to war and virtually eliminates Soviet capability to execute a successful short warning attack (24 to 48 hours).

While the influx of armored troop carriers and artillery creates a more balanced force in the forward area, it would not make an unreinforced (three-front) attack option appear more attractive to the General Staff. The General Staff would perceive an even greater need to bring forces forward from the western USSR before D-Day to restore the offensive combat power lost with the removal of those tanks as well as the considerable reductions in East European forces. In turn, this would require the Soviets to shift a comparable number of divisions from the strategic reserve to the second strategic echelon—the follow-on fronts necessary to carry an offensive to strategic objectives beyond the Rhine into France.

Considering only the effects of the originally announced Soviet unilateral withdrawal, we believe that the residual Soviet forces would be unable to mount a "short warning" attack and that the Soviets would not be even moderately confident of success in pursuing deep theater objectives unless their attack was preceded by a lengthy mobilization period. But events in Eastern Europe have an even greater effect. By mid-1991, Soviet forces will be completely withdrawn from Czechoslovakia and Hungary. Moreover, the fundamental political changes occurring in the individual Warsaw Pact nations and their effect on the reliability of the non-Soviet Warsaw Pact military forces lead us to conclude that the Warsaw Pact does not at this time represent a significant offensive threat to NATO. The rate and scope of political change in Eastern Europe in recent months have outpaced our ability to assess completely the consequences for East European military capabilities. We judge that Soviet planners face the same uncertainties.

Recent and continuing political developments in Eastern Europe have undoubtedly eroded the confidence of Soviet war planners. Non-Soviet Warsaw Pact forces traditionally have made up nearly 50 percent of the Pact's first strategic echelon in Central Europe, and local transportation and security services would be crucial in moving Soviet forces into the forward area. NSWP forces were counted on to play critical roles in operations on both flanks in a NATO-Pact war. Now, the nonavailability of NSWP forces for Soviet offensive war plans and the increased potential of civil resistance to Soviet transit as the result of recent political changes will have far-reaching and adverse impacts on Soviet force commitments, dispositions, and objectives.

The military changes outlined in this memorandum have led to important lengthening of estimated preparation times for Soviet attack options (see table 2 and, for more detail, the annex). When the effects of the announced cuts under way in most of the NSWP states and the ongoing political developments in Eastern Europe are coupled with Soviet unilateral reductions and restructuring, we believe that Warsaw Pact

21. *(Continued)*

Figure 9
Projected Warsaw Pact Echelons
in the Western Theater of Military Operations (TMO)—Four-Front Attack

21. *(Continued)*

~~Secret~~

Table 2
Estimated Preparation Times for Soviet Attack Options

Days

	NIE 4-1-84	Before Warsaw Pact Unilateral Reductions ᵃ		After Warsaw Pact Unilateral Reductions ᵃ	
		Mobilization and Movement	Minimum Preparation for Offensive Combat	Mobilization and Movement	Minimum Preparation for Offensive Combat
Three fronts in first echelon	10 to 12	7 to 14	14 to 21	9 to 16	35 to 45
Five- to six-front attack with four fronts in first echelon	Not addressed	14 to 21	28 to 35	18 to 25	40 to 50

ᵃ Based on conditions in Eastern Europe in September 1989.

~~This table is Secret Noforn.~~

capability to conduct an unreinforced conventional attack against NATO is virtually eliminated (assuming that NATO remains at current force levels). ~~(S NF WN)~~

We assess that Soviet General Staff planners will probably conclude that—without reinforcements from the western USSR roughly equal to at least two fronts—their forces remaining in Eastern Europe after the unilateral cuts would *not* possess the advantage needed to initiate and sustain offensive operations to the depth of the theater against current NATO forces. On the basis of this assessment, we concluded in September 1989 that NATO would have a 40- to 50-day warning time to prepare for a conventional force attack. The current political changes in Eastern Europe, not considered in that assessment, would probably increase warning time. ~~(S NF WN)~~

The arms reduction proposals unveiled by both the Warsaw Pact and NATO for the Conventional Armed Forces in Europe (CFE) negotiations would result in further substantial cuts in Pact conventional forces in the Atlantic-to-the-Urals (ATTU) Zone (see table 3). Moscow would possess by far the largest national force structure in a post-CFE Europe but has already agreed to 30,000 more US than USSR stationed forces, in recognition of its large force advantage on the Continent. After such cuts, and assuming that equipment is destroyed and that NATO maintains parity, we believe that the Soviets would judge Warsaw Pact Post-CFE Forces incapable—*even after full mobilization of reserves and deployment of standing forces within the ATTU Zone*—of achieving the political-military objectives traditionally associated with Soviet strategy for a theater-strategic offensive. Their CFE proposal serves as one of the most convincing indicators to date of the defensive reorientation of their military doctrine and their intent to decrease the economic burden of the Soviet theater force structure through aggressive pursuit of conventional arms control. ~~(S NF)~~

21. *(Continued)*

Table 3
Post-CFE Warsaw Pact Force Structure
Atlantic-to-the-Urals Zone

	1988			1997		
	Soviet	NSWP	Total	Soviet	NSWP	Total
Tanks	35,002	14,809	49,811	12,000 14,000	8,000 6,000	20,000 20,000
Armored troop carriers	36,202	15,948	52,150	16,800 18,000	11,200 10,000	28,000 28,000
Artillery	32,523	10,312	42,835	10,000 17,000	6,500 7,000	16,500 24,000

Blue = Western proposal.
Red = Eastern proposal.

21. *(Continued)*

Annex
Warning Implications of Warsaw Pact Unilateral Force Reductions [2,3]

The announced reductions of Soviet forces in Eastern Europe and East European national forces, if fully implemented, will significantly lower Pact force levels in the forward area. Six Soviet tank divisions, plus critical combat support units such as bridging, and substantial amounts of additional equipment are scheduled to be withdrawn. Scheduled tank reductions amount to about half the Soviet tanks in Eastern Europe. Non-Soviet Warsaw Pact forces, which currently comprise a large proportion of the forces in Eastern Europe, are also to be reduced. Moreover, forces inside the Soviet Union are to be restructured and are to lose tanks and possibly artillery from their structure. Equipment modernization and restructuring of remaining Soviet forces in Eastern Europe may offset to some extent the loss of combat capability, but Non-Soviet Warsaw Pact forces are not taking similar steps.

These reductions—which are well under way—probably will render an unreinforced Pact attack practically impossible and will require the Pact to rely more heavily on currently nonready divisions to support either a two-, three-, or four-front attack. Pact planners will probably conclude that—without reinforcements from the western USSR roughly equal to two fronts—their forces remaining in Eastern Europe after the unilateral cuts would not possess the advantage over current NATO forces needed to initiate and sustain offensive operations to the depth of theater. The Soviets probably would believe that, to attain sufficient combat power in the theater, they would have to generate enough not-ready divisions to replace the withdrawn Soviet divisions, as well as the disbanded East European formations. Such greater reliance on the early commitment of currently not-ready divisions from the Soviet Union for sustained offensive operations would stretch out Pact preparations to 40 to 50 days. We cannot rule out the possibility that the Soviets might judge circumstances as compelling them to commit their forces without the minimum postmobilization training necessary for offensive operations in as little as 18 to 25 days (see table 4).

Our assessment of preparation and warning times after the Pact's unilateral reductions are complete assumes that NATO remains at current force levels. The extent of Pact preparations—reinforcement of forces in Eastern Europe and training—required to conduct a potentially successful offensive campaign is driven in large measure by Pact assessments of NATO military capability. As a result, unilateral NATO reductions outside the context of a conventional force reductions agreement could diminish the Pact's assessment of its force requirements for success and thus reduce the preparation time needed for the Pact and the warning time available to NATO.

---

[2] Extract from Memorandum to Holders of NIE 4-1-84 (Secret NF NC), September 1989, *Warning of War in Europe: Changing Warsaw Pact Planning and Forces*.
[3] Note that the preparation times assessed in this annex were based on the Eastern Europe of September 1989. Political turmoil since then would likely *increase* these preparation time estimates. (S NF)

21. *(Continued)*

~~Secret~~

Table 4
Estimated Preparation Times for Soviet Attack Options *Days*

	NIE 4-1-84	Before Warsaw Pact Unilateral Reductions		After Warsaw Pact Unilateral Reductions [b]	
		Mobilization and Movement	Minimum Preparation for Offensive Combat [a]	Mobilization and Movement	Minimum Preparation for Offensive Combat [a]
Three fronts in first echelon	10 to 12	7 to 14	14 to 21	9 to 16	35 to 45
Five- to six-front attack with four fronts in first echelon	Not addressed	14 to 21	28 to 35	18 to 25	40 to 50

~~Secret~~

The Military Balance II
Strategic Nuclear Weapons

22. NIE 11-3/8-88, December 1988, *Soviet Forces and Capabilities for Strategic Nuclear Conflict Through the Late 1990s* (Key Judgments and Executive Summary)

Director of
Central
Intelligence

~~Secret~~

Soviet Forces and Capabilities for Strategic Nuclear Conflict Through the Late 1990s

National Intelligence Estimate

Key Judgments and Executive Summary

These Key Judgments and Executive Summary represent the views of the Director of Central Intelligence with the advice and assistance of the US Intelligence Community.

~~Secret~~

NIE 11-3/8-88
1 December 1988
Copy 0538

22. *(Continued)*

 **Director of Central Intelligence**

~~Secret~~
~~NOFORN-NOCONTRACT~~

NIE 11-3/8-88

Soviet Forces and Capabilities for Strategic Nuclear Conflict Through the Late 1990s (U)

Information available as of 1 December 1988 was used in the preparation of this National Intelligence Estimate.

The following intelligence organizations participated in the preparation of this Estimate:
The Central Intelligence Agency
The Defense Intelligence Agency
The National Security Agency
The Bureau of Intelligence and Research, Department of State
The Office of the Deputy Assistant Secretary for Intelligence, Department of Energy

also participating:
The Deputy Chief of Staff for Intelligence, Department of the Army
The Director of Naval Intelligence, Department of the Navy
The Assistant Chief of Staff, Intelligence, Department of the Air Force
The Director of Intelligence, Headquarters, Marine Corps

This Estimate was approved for publication by the National Foreign Intelligence Board.

~~Secret~~
1 December 1988

22. *(Continued)*

~~Secret~~
~~NOFORN NOCONTRACT~~

NOTE

This Estimate is issued in several volumes:

- **Key Judgments** and **Executive Summary.**

- **Volume I** contains the Key Judgments, an overview of major Soviet strategic force developments in the 1980s, and a summary of Soviet programs and capabilities believed to be of greatest interest to policymakers and defense planners.

- **Volume II** contains:

  – Discussion of the Soviets' strategic policy and doctrine under Gorbachev, including their objectives in the event of a US-Soviet nuclear conflict and how the Soviet national command authority would operate.

  – Descriptions of Soviet programs for the development and deployment of strategic offensive and defensive forces and supporting systems.

  – Projections of future Soviet strategic forces.

  – Description of Soviet command, control, and communications capabilities and discussion of the peacetime posture of Soviet strategic forces.

  – Discussion of Soviet concepts and plans for the operations of strategic forces during the several phases of a global conflict.

  – Trends in the USSR's capabilities to carry out some missions of strategic forces in nuclear conflict.

- **Volume III** contains tables with detailed force projections and weapon characteristics.

~~This information is Secret Noforn.~~

22. (*Continued*)

Key Judgments

We have prepared this year's Estimate against the backdrop of considerable ferment in the national security arena in the Soviet Union that could over time result in a change in the Soviets' military outlook. Gorbachev has shown himself willing and able to challenge long-cherished precepts in this as in other policy areas. The evidence presented in this Estimate indicates, however, that, in terms of what the Soviets spend, what they procure, how their strategic forces are deployed, how they plan, and how they exercise, the basic elements of Soviet defense policy and practice thus far have not been changed by Gorbachev's reform campaign.

Given the turmoil that Gorbachev has set in motion over many of these issues, Soviet strategic goals and priorities over the long term have become more difficult for us to predict, and a major change toward a less threatening nuclear doctrine and strategic force structure could occur. However, we believe it is prudent to adopt a wait-and-see attitude toward the prospects for longer term change in the Soviets' fundamental approach to war. Many key doctrinal issues are far from settled among the Soviets themselves. Furthermore, if we are witnessing a transition in Soviet military thinking, substantial tangible evidence of any change in some areas may not be immediately forthcoming.

Ongoing development and deployment efforts indicate that all elements of Soviet intercontinental nuclear forces will be extensively modernized between now and the late 1990s. The Soviets will move from a force that has primarily consisted of fixed, silo-based ICBMs to one in which mobile platforms constitute well over half the deployed forces:

- *ICBMs*. In 1988 the Soviets began to deploy two new silo-based ICBMs that will be increasingly more vulnerable as US countersilo capabilities improve, but will enhance the Soviets' capabilities for prompt attack on hard and soft targets. The Soviets also began to deploy their first rail-mobile ICBM, and continued deploying road-mobile ICBMs, which will significantly improve Soviet force survivability.

- *SLBMs*. The Soviet ballistic missile submarine (SSBN) force of the future will contain fewer submarines but more long-range missiles and more warheads, and will generally be much more survivable. The Soviets have recently deployed their first submarine-launched ballistic missile (SLBM) with some capability to attack hardened targets, but SLBMs during the next 10 years will not be nearly as effective for this role as Soviet silo-based ICBMs.

22. *(Continued)*

- *Bombers and cruise missiles.* The heavy bomber force will have a greater role with more weapons and greater force diversity. In 1988 the Soviets began to deploy their new supersonic strategic bomber—the Blackjack—capable of carrying long-range, air-launched cruise missiles (ALCMs) and supersonic short-range missiles. ███████████████████████ In 1988 the Soviets launched their second Yankee Notch submarine as a dedicated launch platform for long-range, land-attack, sea-launched cruise missiles (SLCMs). In addition, ALCM and SLCM versions of a large, long-range, supersonic cruise missile are likely to become operational in 1989 and 1990, respectively. (S NF WN)

The Soviets continue to invest about as heavily in active and passive strategic defenses as they do in offensive forces, and their capabilities are improving in all areas:

- *Air defense.* Soviet capabilities against low-flying bombers and cruise missiles are increasing because of continuing deployments of all-altitude surface-to-air missiles and fighter and support aircraft.

- *Ballistic missile defense.* The new Moscow antiballistic missile (ABM) defenses should be operational in 1989 and will provide an improved intercept capability against small-scale attacks on key targets around Moscow. It is unlikely through at least the mid-1990s that the Soviets would make widespread ABM deployments that would exceed treaty limits, although they have developed a capability to do so. Also, improving technology is blurring the distinction between air defense and ABM systems.

- *Leadership protection.* A primary Soviet objective is to protect and support the leadership from the outset of crisis through a postattack period. The Soviets have had a 40-year program for leadership protection that includes facilities deep below Moscow and elsewhere that would be very difficult to destroy.

- *Laser weapons.* There is strong evidence of Soviet R&D efforts in high-energy laser weapons for air defense, antisatellite (ASAT), and ballistic missile defense (BMD) applications. The Soviets appear to be considering space-based lasers for BMD, but we do not expect them to be able to deploy an operational system until well after the year 2000.

- *Antisubmarine warfare (ASW).* The Soviets currently lack an effective means of locating US SSBNs in the open ocean. We judge that they will not deploy such a capability in the 1990s, and we see no Soviet solution to

22. *(Continued)*

the problem on the horizon. On the other hand, the Soviets will increase the threat to US attack submarines attempting to operate in areas close to the Soviet Union.

Without START constraints, if the Soviets were to modernize their forces in a manner that generally follows past efforts, in the next 10 years intercontinental nuclear weapons would probably grow from the current level of about 10,000 to between 12,000 and 15,000. In the absence of an arms control process, the Soviets would not necessarily expand their intercontinental attack forces beyond these figures, but they clearly have the capability for expansion in the late 1990s to 16,000 or even 18,000 if, for example, they decided to expand forces in response to a US deployment of strategic defenses. As a result of the assessed operational payloads of Soviet bombers and assumed rules for counting bomber weapons, a Soviet force of 6,000 accountable weapons under a START agreement would in fact probably contain 8,000 weapons. In a crisis or wartime situation, the Soviets might be able to deploy a few thousand additional weapons, by augmenting their force with nondeployed mobile missiles and by uploading some missiles to their maximum potential payloads, higher than the accountable number of warheads on these missiles. We note that efforts to deploy additional warheads in crisis or wartime would involve some operational and planning difficulties.

An alternative view holds that ▓▓ deploying additional warheads in crisis or wartime (assuming they were available) would be time consuming, disruptive to force readiness and operations, and potentially detectable.[1]

The Soviets apparently believe that, in the present US-Soviet strategic relationship, each side possesses strategic nuclear capabilities that could devastate the other after absorbing an attack and that it is highly unlikely either side could achieve a decisive nuclear superiority in the foreseeable future. Nevertheless, they continue to procure weapons and plan force operations intended to secure important combat advantages and goals in the event of nuclear war, including, to the extent possible, limiting damage to Soviet forces and society. Although we do not have specific evidence on how the Soviets assess their prospects in a global nuclear war, we judge that they would not have high confidence in the capability of their strategic offensive and defensive forces to accomplish all of their wartime missions—particularly limiting the extent of damage to the Soviet homeland.

---

[1] *The holder of this view is the Assistant Secretary of State for Intelligence and Research, Department of State.*

22. *(Continued)*

Thus far, we see no convincing evidence that the Soviets under Gorbachev are making basic changes in their approach to actually fighting nuclear war. Our evidence points to continuing Soviet programs to develop and refine options for both conventional and nuclear war, and the Soviets are preparing their forces for the possibility that both conventional and nuclear war could be longer and more complex than they previously assumed.

There is an ongoing debate among the leadership concerning how much is enough for defense, focused on the concept of "reasonable sufficiency." Although couched in doctrinal terms and aimed in part at Western audiences, the debate at this point appears to be primarily about resource allocations. (See page 15 for an alternative view.) To date, as demonstrated in the strategic force programs and resource commitments we have examined, we have not detected changes under Gorbachev that clearly illustrate that either new security concepts or new resource constraints are taking hold.

The large sunk costs in production for new strategic weapons and the fact that such production facilities cannot readily be converted to civilian uses mean that Gorbachev's industrial modernization goals almost certainly will not have major effects on strategic weapons deployments through the mid-1990s. Gorbachev might attempt to save resources by deferring some strategic programs, stretching out procurement rates, and placing more emphasis on replacing older systems on a less than 1-for-1 basis. Major savings could be achieved in the next several years only through cutbacks in general purpose forces and programs, which account for the vast majority of Soviet defense spending. Further, for both political as well as military reasons, Gorbachev almost certainly would not authorize unilateral cuts in the size of the strategic forces. Nevertheless, concerns over the economy's performance, as well as perceived foreign policy benefits, heighten Moscow's interest in strategic and conventional arms control agreements, and have contributed to the greater negotiating flexibility evident under Gorbachev's leadership. We judge, however, that Soviet force decisions, including potential arms control agreements, will continue to be more strongly influenced by the requirement to meet military and political objectives than by economic concerns.

The Soviets' recent positions on strategic arms control should not be taken as an indicator of whether or not they are implementing fundamental change in their approach to nuclear war. The asymmetric reductions and acceptance of intrusive on-site inspections entailed by the INF Treaty and the apparent Soviet willingness to accept deep strategic force reductions in START do reflect a marked change in political attitude on security issues under Gorbachev. Overall, however, we do not see Moscow's recent arms control positions resulting in strategic forces that the Soviets would perceive as less capable of waging a nuclear war.

22. *(Continued)*

Executive Summary

A Time of Change in Soviet Strategic Policy?
We have prepared this year's Estimate against the backdrop of considerable ferment in the national security arena in the Soviet Union that could over time significantly alter Soviet strategic programs and policies, and thus the overall strategic threat. We take the possibility of such change seriously because Gorbachev has shown himself willing and able to challenge long-cherished precepts in this as in other policy areas. We conclude that sufficiently compelling evidence is lacking to warrant a judgment in this Estimate that the Soviets already have begun to implement fundamental changes in their approach to warfare under Gorbachev. This year, in our assessments of the various elements of Soviet strategic programs and capabilities traditionally presented in this Estimate, we have paid particular attention to indications from the available evidence of whether major change is in the offing. In terms of what the Soviets spend, what they procure, how their strategic forces are deployed, how they plan, and how they exercise, the basic elements of Soviet defense policy and practice appear thus far not to have been changed by Gorbachev's reform campaign.

Given the turmoil that Gorbachev has set in motion over many of these issues, Soviet strategic goals and priorities over the longer term have become more difficult for us to predict, and a major change toward a less threatening nuclear doctrine and strategic force structure could occur. We believe, however, it is prudent to adopt a wait-and-see attitude toward the prospects for longer term change in the Soviets' fundamental approach to war. Many key doctrinal issues are far from settled among the Soviets themselves. Furthermore, if we are witnessing a transition in Soviet military thinking, substantial tangible evidence of any change in some areas may not be immediately forthcoming.

Strategic Offensive Forces
Evidence and analysis of ongoing development and deployment efforts over the past year have reaffirmed our judgment that all elements of Soviet intercontinental forces will be extensively modernized between now and the late 1990s, and will be more capable, diverse, and generally more survivable. The Soviets will move from a force that has primarily consisted of fixed, silo-based ICBMs to a force in which mobile systems (mobile ICBMs, SLBMs, and bombers) constitute well over half the deployed forces. A START agreement could have a significant impact on the size and composition of Soviet strategic offensive forces, although we expect most of these modernization efforts to continue in any case. Major changes in the force include:

- *ICBMs.* The Soviets began deployment in 1988 of two new silo-based ICBMs—the SS-18 Mod 5 heavy ICBM with an improved capability to destroy hardened targets and the SS-24 Mod 2, a medium, solid-propellant ICBM with 10 warheads that is replacing the six-warhead SS-19 liquid-propellant ICBM. The new silo-based systems will be increasingly more vulnerable as US countersilo capabilities improve, but will enhance the Soviets' capabilities for prompt attack on hard and soft targets. Over the past year the Soviets also deployed the SS-24 Mod 1 rail-mobile ICBM. These rail-mobile deployments, continued deployments of the road-mobile SS-25 (a single-warhead ICBM), and expected improvements and follow-ons to both missiles will significantly improve Soviet force survivability.

- *SLBMs.* The proportion of survivable Soviet weapons also will grow through the deployment of much better nuclear-powered ballistic missile submarines (SSBNs) and new submarine-launched ballistic missiles (SLBMs). The new submarines are quieter and are capable of operating from deep under the icepack. Equipped with new long-range SLBMs that have many warheads (four to 10), the Soviet SSBN force of the future will contain fewer submarines

22. *(Continued)*

22. *(Continued)*

22. (Continued)

but more warheads and will be much more survivable. We expect the Soviets to build additional Typhoon and Delta-IV submarines; we judge they will also introduce at least one and possibly two new SLBMs in the 1990s, and probably a new class of SSBN. The Soviets' recently deployed SS-N-23 Mod 2 on the Delta-IV gives them an emerging sea-based capability to destroy hardened targets. We expect, as the Soviets improve the accuracy and responsiveness of their SLBMs, that they will have greater confidence in their ability to attack US ICBM silos, but SLBMs during the next 10 years will not be nearly as effective for this role as Soviet silo-based ICBMs.

- *Bombers and cruise missiles.* Ongoing modernization will give the heavy bomber force a greater role in intercontinental attack, with more weapons and greater force diversity. Production of the Bear H, which carries AS-15 long-range, subsonic, air-launched cruise missiles (ALCMs), seems to be winding down. A force size of 80 is projected. The new supersonic Blackjack, which can carry ALCMs and short-range air-to-surface missiles, achieved initial operational capability in 1988; the Soviets will likely deploy some 80 to 120 by the late 1990s. The Soviets continue to deploy the Midas—their first modern tanker—in support of the heavy bomber force. We expect up to about 150 Midas to be built by the late 1990s to support both strategic offensive and defensive operations. In 1988 the Soviets launched their second Yankee Notch submarine as a dedicated platform for up to 40 SS-N-21 long-range, subsonic, land-attack, sea-launched cruise missiles (SLCMs). In addition, ALCM and SLCM versions of a large, long-range, supersonic cruise missile are likely to become operational in 1989 and 1990, respectively. we estimate that they may develop low-observable or Stealth cruise missiles for deployment in the mid-to-late 1990s.

Strategic Defensive Forces

The Soviets continue to invest about as heavily in active and passive strategic defenses as they do in offensive forces, and their capabilities are improving in all areas:

- *Air defense.* Soviet capabilities against low-flying bombers and cruise missiles are increasing because of continuing deployments of the SA-10 all-altitude surface-to-air missile and three different types of new lookdown/shootdown aircraft. These will be supported by the Mainstay airborne warning and control system (AWACS) aircraft, which became operational in 1987.

- *Ballistic missile defense.* The new Moscow antiballistic missile (ABM) defenses, eventually with 100 interceptors, should be operational in 1989 and will provide an improved intercept capability against small-scale attacks on key targets around Moscow. The Soviets have developed all the required components for an ABM system that could be used for widespread deployments that would exceed treaty limits. However, we judge that such a widespread deployment is unlikely through at least the mid-1990s. some new ABM components may be under development and might begin testing in the next year or two; if so, a new ABM system could be ready for deployment as early as the late 1990s for Moscow or possibly as part of a widespread system. Also, improving technology is blurring the distinction between air defense and ABM systems—for example, the capabilities of the SA-12 system.

- *Leadership protection.* A primary Soviet objective is to protect and support the leadership from the outset of crisis through a postattack period. The Soviets have had a 40-year program for providing

22. *(Continued)*

hardened and dispersed facilities for the survival of their leadership and for wartime management during a nuclear war. This program includes deep underground facilities, many of which are beneath Moscow or nearby, that would be very difficult to destroy ▮▮▮▮▮▮▮

- *Laser weapons.* There is strong evidence of Soviet R&D efforts in high-energy lasers for air defense, antisatellite (ASAT), and ballistic missile defense (BMD) applications. There are large uncertainties, however, about how far the Soviets have advanced, the status and goals of any weapon development programs, and the dates for potential prototype or operational capabilities. We expect the Soviets to be able to develop mobile tactical air defense lasers in the 1990s, followed by more powerful strategic systems, although there is a serious question as to whether the Soviets will field many dedicated laser weapons for air defense. Limited capability prototypes for ground-based and space-based ASAT could be available around the year 2000, possibly earlier. If ground-based BMD lasers prove feasible and practical, we expect Soviet technology would allow the Soviets to build a prototype for testing around 2000, maybe a few years earlier, although operational systems probably would not be available for some 10 years after initial prototype testing. The Soviets most likely are considering space-based lasers for BMD. We do not think they will be able to test a feasibility demonstrator before the year 2000, and we estimate that an operational system would not be deployable until much later, perhaps around 2010.

- *Other advanced technologies.* The Soviets are also engaged in extensive research on other technologies that can be applied to ASAT and BMD weapons. ▮▮▮▮▮▮▮ there is potential for a surprise development in one or more of these areas. However, the Soviets probably are at least 10 to 15 years away from testing any prototype particle beam weapon for ASAT or BMD. The Soviets might be able to test a ground-based radiofrequency ASAT weapon by the early 1990s. We believe it is possible a space-based, long-range, kinetic-energy BMD weapon could be deployed, but probably no earlier than about 2005.

- *Antisubmarine warfare (ASW).* The Soviets currently lack an effective means of locating in the open ocean either US SSBNs or modern attack submarines (SSNs) carrying land-attack cruise missiles. We see no Soviet solution to this problem on the horizon. We base this judgment on the difficulty we expect the Soviets to encounter in exploiting the basic phenomena of wake detection, and the technological hurdles they face in sensors, high-speed signal processing, and data relay.

- There is a possibility that the Soviets will introduce a space-based submarine detection system during the 1990s that, while it would have little or no ability to detect properly operated SSBNs, might have a very limited capability against US SSNs, under favorable conditions. Missions for such a system would be to detect SSNs operating in Soviet SSBN bastion areas or seeking to launch land-attack cruise missiles near the USSR. Technological and operational difficulties associated with building a complete ASW system would push system operational capabilities well into the first decade of the next century. Surface-towed passive surveillance sonar arrays and low-frequency active sonars will likely be deployed by the mid-1990s for local-area ASW surveillance. We assign a moderate probability to the deployment of an airborne radar by the late 1990s, intended to detect submarine-induced surface phenomena.

- Judgments on future Soviet ASW capabilities must be tempered by the difficulties inherent in forecasting Soviet ASW advances ▮▮▮▮▮▮▮▮▮▮▮▮▮▮▮▮

Projected Offensive Forces

This year, we have projected five alternative Soviet strategic forces to illustrate possible force postures under various assumptions about the strategic environment the Soviets will perceive over the next 10 years:

- Under a START agreement, as a result of the assessed operational payloads of Soviet bombers and

22. (Continued)

~~Secret~~

assumed rules for counting bomber weapons, a Soviet force of 6,000 accountable weapons would in fact probably contain about 8,000 weapons. In a crisis or wartime situation, the Soviets might be able to deploy a few thousand additional weapons, by augmenting their force with nondeployed mobile missiles and by uploading some missiles to their maximum potential payloads, higher than the accountable number of warheads on these missiles. We note that efforts to deploy additional warheads in crisis or wartime would involve some operational and planning difficulties.

- An alternative view holds that ████████ ████████████████████████████████████ deploying additional warheads in crisis or wartime (assuming they were available) would be time consuming, disruptive to force readiness and operations, and potentially detectable.[2]

- Two of the other projected forces are premised on a Soviet belief that relations with the United States are generally satisfactory and, although a START agreement has not been concluded, arms control prospects look good. Intercontinental weapons would probably grow over the next five years from the current number—about 10,000—to between 12,500 and 15,000 depending on modernization and growth rates and military spending levels. (Online weapons, those available after a short generation time, would be about 1,000 to 1,500 fewer, because of submarines in overhaul or empty ICBM silos being modified.) The increase in weapons results from deployment of new systems (SS-24, SS-N-20 follow-on, SS-N-23, Blackjack, Bear H) with more weapons than the systems they replace and not from any increase in launchers. We would expect no additional growth in warheads through the late 1990s.

- In the absence of an arms control process, the Soviets would not necessarily expand their intercontinental attack forces beyond these figures, but they clearly have the capability for significant further expansion. In an environment where the Soviets see relations with the United States as generally poor and arms control prospects bleak, the number of Soviet intercontinental weapons could grow to over 15,000 in the next five years and some 16,000 by 1998. In all of these cases, the introduction of modernized systems will result in a decline in the number of launchers. (S NF)

We have a projection for an SDI response force that features a greater offensive force expansion (over 18,000 weapons by 1998). The projection is based on a postulated US decision in the early 1990s to deploy land-based ABM interceptors and space-based SDI assets, with actual deployments beginning around 2000. The projection depicts Soviet measures aimed primarily at overwhelming US defenses through sheer numbers of warheads. In addition, Soviet responses could include increased ASAT efforts, BMD deployments, and advanced penetration aids. While increasing the sheer size of their offensive forces would be the Soviets' most viable near-term response, advanced technical countermeasures would be critical to dealing with SDI in the long term. The size of the force could be lower than 18,000, depending on the timing of the introduction of technological countermeasures. Given the uncertain nature of the US program and the potential disruption of Soviet efforts ████████ ████████████████████████████████ we judge that the deployment of significant numbers of countermeasures is unlikely before the year 2000. (S NF)

Strategic Force Objectives and Operations

We judge that, in part, the Soviets view their strategic forces as effectively deterring adversaries from starting a nuclear war with the USSR and as underpinning the USSR's superpower status. The Soviets also have been preparing their strategic nuclear forces to meet two basic military objectives:

- To intimidate NATO from escalating to nuclear use in a conventional war, so that Warsaw Pact conventional forces have some prospect to secure NATO's defeat without such escalation.

- If global nuclear war occurs, to wage it as effectively as possible as mandated by their nuclear warfighting strategy.

[2] *The holder of this view is the Assistant Secretary of State for Intelligence and Research, Department of State.*

Some Soviet public statements now seem to espouse certain longstanding Western strategic theories such as the concept of Mutual Assured Destruction (MAD), which, in part, in order to provide a rationale for emphasizing second-strike nuclear forces and restraining growth in the US strategic force structure, drew sharp distinctions between deterrence and warfighting requirements for strategic forces. The Soviets, in our view, despite some recent public differences on the matter, are continuing to build their forces on the premise that forces that are better prepared to effectively fight a nuclear war are also better able to deter such a war. (S NF)

The Soviets apparently believe that, in the present US-Soviet strategic relationship, each side possesses strategic nuclear capabilities that could devastate the other after absorbing an attack. Thus, the Soviets have strong incentives to avoid risking global nuclear war. Moreover, the Soviets apparently do not believe that this strategic reality will soon change or that either side could acquire a decisive nuclear superiority in the foreseeable future. Nevertheless, they continue to procure weapons and plan force operations intended to secure important combat advantages and goals in the event of nuclear war, including, to the extent possible, limiting damage to Soviet forces and society. (S NF)

In planning for the possibility of actually having to wage a global nuclear war, the Soviets emphasize:
- Massive strikes on enemy forces, passive defenses, and active defenses to limit the damage the enemy can inflict.
- Highly redundant and extensive command, control, and communications (C^3) capabilities and leadership protection to ensure continuity of control of the war effort and the integration and coordination of force operations both at the intercontinental level and in Eurasian theaters.
- In general, preparations for more extended operations after the initial strikes. (S NF)

The Soviets have been increasing the realism in their force training to more fully reflect the complexity of both large-scale conventional and nuclear warfare. Since the late 1970s there has been a continuing Soviet appreciation of the extreme difficulties in prosecuting a nuclear campaign in the European theater. We believe that the Soviets have become more realistic about the problems of conducting military operations in a nuclear environment, but the requirement to carry out nuclear combat operations as effectively as possible is still one of their highest priorities. Indeed, the Soviets continue to prepare their strategic forces to conduct continuing nuclear combat operations for up to a few months following the initial nuclear strikes. (S NF)

Nuclear War Initiation and Escalation
In peacetime, the Soviets' lack of high confidence in accomplishing all of their wartime missions, and their appreciation of the destructiveness of nuclear war, would strongly dissuade them from launching a "bolt-from-the-blue" strategic attack. The Soviets also would probably be inhibited from provoking a direct clash with the United States and its NATO Allies that could potentially escalate to global nuclear war. (S NF)

The Soviets believe that a major nuclear war would be most likely to arise out of a NATO–Warsaw Pact conventional conflict that is preceded by a political crisis. The Soviets see little likelihood that the United States would initiate a surprise nuclear attack from a normal peacetime posture. (S NF)

In a conventional war in which the Soviets were prevailing, they would have strong incentives to keep the war from escalating. Nevertheless, we continue to judge that the Soviets generally assess a NATO–Warsaw Pact war as likely to escalate to the nuclear level; the Soviets recognize, however, that escalation of a NATO–Warsaw Pact conflict would be strongly influenced by the course and perceived outcome of the conventional war in Europe. This Soviet assessment appears to be driven, in large part, by the Soviet expectation that NATO—consistent with official NATO doctrine—is highly likely to resort to nuclear weapons to avoid the defeat of its forces on the continent.

The Soviets are capable of executing a

22. *(Continued)*

preventive/first-strike nuclear option in circumstances where they do not anticipate an imminent NATO nuclear strike. Despite our uncertainties about how this option fits into overall Soviet strike planning, we judge that it would be attractive for the Soviets to consider only if Warsaw Pact forces suffered serious setbacks in a conventional war. The Soviets would not expect, in any case, to be able to forestall a devastating counterstrike by the United States or NATO forces. (S NF)

The Soviets apparently also have developed a limited nuclear option that focuses on the brief use of small numbers of battlefield nuclear weapons. However, this option has not substantially evolved since the early 1970s when it was first developed. Also, we lack clear indications of limited nuclear options involving strategic weapons despite the growth and improvements in the entire array of Soviet nuclear forces, from battlefield weapons to intercontinental weapons. In the event NATO launches a few small-scale nuclear strikes in the theater that do not disrupt a Warsaw Pact conventional offensive, the Soviets might be willing to absorb such strikes without a nuclear response. (S NF)

We judge that, if the Soviets had convincing evidence that the United States intended to launch a large-scale strike with its strategic forces (in, for example, an ongoing theater war in Europe), they would attempt to preempt. It is more difficult to judge whether they would decide to preempt in situations where they see inherently high risks of global nuclear war but have only ambiguous evidence of the United States' intentions to launch its strategic forces. The Soviets have strong incentives to preempt in order to maximize damage to US forces and limit damage to Soviet forces and society. Exercising restraint could jeopardize the Soviets' chances for effectively waging nuclear war. Because preempting on the basis of ambiguous evidence, however, could initiate global nuclear war unnecessarily, the Soviets would also have to consider such factors as: the probable nuclear devastation of their homeland that would result; the reliability of their other nuclear employment options (launching their forces quickly upon warning that a US ICBM attack is under way and retaliating after absorbing enemy strikes); and their prospects for eventual success on the conventional battlefield. We cannot ultimately judge how the Soviets would actually weigh these difficult trade-offs. (S NF)

Strategic Force Capabilities

Because of the Soviets' demanding requirements for force effectiveness, they are likely to rate their capabilities as lower in some areas than we would assess them to be. They are probably apprehensive about the implications of US strategic force modernization programs—including significant improvements in US C³ capabilities—and are especially concerned about the US SDI program and its potential to undercut Soviet military strategy. Although we do not have specific evidence on how the Soviets assess their prospects in a global nuclear war, we judge that they would not have high confidence in the capability of their strategic offensive and defensive forces to accomplish all of their wartime missions—particularly limiting the extent of damage to the Soviet homeland. (S NF)

The Soviets have enough hard-target-capable ICBM reentry vehicles today to attack all US missile silos and launch control centers with at least two warheads each. The projected accuracy and yield improvements for the SS-18 Mod 5 ICBM now being deployed would result in a substantial increase in the effectiveness of a 2-on-1 attack ▮▮▮▮▮▮▮▮▮▮▮▮. We judge that heavy ICBMs will continue to be the primary and most effective weapons against US missile silos during the next 10 years, but some SLBMs and probably other ICBMs are expected to acquire a capability to kill hard targets and thus supplement heavy ICBMs in carrying out the overall hard-target mission. (S NF)

Over the next 10 years, we expect that Soviet offensive forces will not be able to effectively target and destroy patrolling US SSBNs, alert aircraft, aircraft in flight, or dispersed mobile ICBMs. However, we judge that, for a comprehensive Soviet attack against North America, the Soviets currently have enough warheads to meet most and probably all of their other targeting objectives in a preemptive strike. This would also be the case if the Soviets could accomplish a reasonably successful launch-on-tactical-warning (LOTW). However, we judge that the Soviets would have insufficient warheads to achieve high damage goals against US ICBM silos if they were to retaliate

22. *(Continued)*

Secret

after absorbing an initial US attack because of expected Soviet losses in their silo-based ICBMs. On balance, we judge that, even with implementation of the INF Treaty and 50-percent reductions of a START treaty, combined with severe constraints on the deployment of ballistic missile defenses, the Soviets could probably meet their worldwide fixed targeting objectives as effectively as with current forces.

Strategic Policy Issues Under Gorbachev

The Soviets claim that they are reorienting their military doctrine to focus more on defensive operations—the concept of "defensive defense"—and are applying a more stringent criterion of "reasonable sufficiency" in determining military force requirements. The Soviet military appears to be reexamining the nature of a future war. In addition, statements by key political and military leaders indicate that they are examining such issues as the winnability of nuclear war, the basis for a credible strategic deterrent, preemption, and how much is enough for defense. Although we have considerable uncertainty about where these matters stand, we make the following judgments:

- *Nature of a future war.* Nuclear warfare remains a dominant factor in the Soviets' war plans, although they have been devoting more attention over the past several years to the possibility of a prolonged conventional war. Thus far, we see no convincing evidence that the Soviets under Gorbachev are making fundamental changes in their approach to actually fighting nuclear war. Our evidence points to continuing Soviet programs to develop and refine options for both nuclear and conventional war, including longer conventional combat and defensive operations, in order to cope with NATO's improving conventional capabilities—much as the Soviets have worked since the 1970s on improving their options for more extended strategic nuclear operations.

- *Soviet nuclear warfighting objectives.* Among other actions, Soviet leaders have incorporated a "no nuclear victory" position in the recent party program; some military writings, however, have continued to cite the victory objective. There are differences in the US Intelligence Community over what this means. We judge that, in any case, the Soviets continue to be committed to acquiring capabilities that could be important in achieving the best possible outcome in any future war. There is no indication that the Soviets were ever sanguine about the consequences they would expect to suffer in a war no matter which side struck first. At the same time, they have continued to believe that nuclear war is possible, and they have consistently pursued a warfighting strategy that goes beyond deterrence and includes the acquisition of both offensive and defensive warfighting capabilities.

- *Superiority, sufficiency, defensive defense.* We judge that the Soviets continue to place high value on combat advantages in nuclear war, but believe it is highly unlikely that decisive nuclear superiority is achievable by either side in the foreseeable future. There is an ongoing debate among the leadership concerning how much is enough for defense, focused on the concept of "reasonable sufficiency." Although couched in doctrinal terms and aimed in part at Western audiences, the debate at this point appears to be primarily about resource allocations. An alternative view holds that, while Soviet discussions about "reasonable sufficiency" involve, in part, resource allocation issues, they are designed primarily to reduce US/NATO force modernization efforts by proclaiming a less threatening Soviet posture.[3] Much of the Soviet public discussion about "defensive defense" appears aimed at influencing Western opinion, particularly to allay Western concerns about the Soviet conventional threat in the context of nuclear arms reductions. The concept, however, also may be perceived by Soviet military leaders as another device for political leaders to challenge traditional military outlays. To date, as demonstrated in the strategic force programs and resource commitments we have examined, we have not detected changes under Gorbachev that clearly illustrate that either new security concepts or new resource constraints are taking hold.

Resources

Heavy investment in the defense industries since the late 1970s will enable the Soviets to produce the strategic forces projected in this Estimate at least

---

[3] *The holder of this view is the Director, Defense Intelligence Agency.*

through the early-to-middle 1990s. For some basic materials and intermediate goods used in the production process, however, competition within the defense sector and between the military and civilian economies might be stiff during this period. It is possible these factors could somewhat affect the rate at which some strategic systems are introduced and the levels deployed. Nevertheless, the large sunk costs in production for new strategic weapons and the fact that such production facilities cannot readily be converted to civilian uses mean that Gorbachev's industrial modernization goals almost certainly will not have major effects on strategic weapons deployments through the mid-1990s. However, new construction of defense plants and retooling of existing facilities will be required in the late 1980s and early 1990s to produce new weapons for the late 1990s and beyond.

Gorbachev might attempt to save resources by deferring some strategic programs, stretching out procurement rates, and placing more emphasis on replacing older systems on a less than 1-for-1 basis. Major savings could be achieved, in the next several years, only through cutbacks in general purpose forces and programs, which account for the vast majority of Soviet defense spending. Further, for both political as well as military reasons, Gorbachev almost certainly would not authorize unilateral cuts in the size of the strategic forces. We expect, therefore, that Gorbachev will choose to continue his vigorous campaign for deep cuts in both strategic and conventional forces through arms control and for slower growth in defense spending.

Although we do not believe that the Soviets' economic difficulties are the primary reason for their interest in arms control, we believe that concerns over the economy's performance, as well as foreign policy benefits, heighten Moscow's interest in strategic as well as conventional arms control agreements and have contributed to the greater negotiating flexibility evident under Gorbachev's leadership. We judge, however, that Soviet force decisions, including potential arms control agreements, will continue to be more strongly influenced by the requirement to meet military and political objectives than by economic concerns. The Soviets see arms control as a way of avoiding the costs of an escalated military competition with the United States that would, by requiring increased defense spending, force them to reduce the resources scheduled to go elsewhere in the future. Restraining or eliminating SDI, for example, could free enormous amounts of technical and industrial resources vital to other Soviet military and civilian programs, which would otherwise be spent on countermeasures, and the Soviets could pursue advanced technology efforts at their own pace. In addition, they apparently anticipate savings from strategic arms control agreements, which, while small in comparison with the economy's needs, could be used to help alleviate critical bottlenecks and help advance priority programs such as those for industrial modernization. Some of the potential savings, however, might be used for other military purposes. In the near term, the civilian economy would accrue only small benefits from reducing or even eliminating particular strategic systems that are well under development and for which production facilities have been constructed; also, strategic offensive programs account for only about 10 percent of the Soviet military budget.

Arms Control

The Soviets' recent positions on strategic arms control should not be taken as an indicator of whether or not they are implementing a fundamental change in their approach to nuclear war. On the one hand, the asymmetric reductions and acceptance of intrusive on-site inspections entailed by the INF Treaty and apparent Soviet willingness to accept deep strategic force reductions in START do reflect a marked change in political attitude on security issues under Gorbachev. On the other hand, the Soviets' stance on arms control thus far allows them to continue to pursue certain combat advantages, while seeking to constrain US and NATO force modernization—especially in such areas as ballistic missile defense, space warfare, and advanced technology conventional weapons—and at the same time seeking to protect the key capabilities of their own forces. Further, the Soviets see the INF Treaty and a potential START agreement as helping to establish a more predictable environment in which to plan strategic force modernization. Overall, we do not see Moscow's recent arms control positions resulting in strategic forces that the Soviets would perceive as less capable of waging a nuclear war.

23. NIE 11-3/8-91, August 1991, *Soviet Forces and Capabilities for Strategic Nuclear Conflict Through the Year 2000* (Key Judgments)

Director of Central Intelligence

~~Secret~~
~~NOFORN NOCONTRACT~~

Soviet Forces and Capabilities for Strategic Nuclear Conflict Through the Year 2000 ~~(C NF)~~

National Intelligence Estimate

Key Judgments

These Key Judgments represent the views of the Director of Central Intelligence with the advice and assistance of the US Intelligence Community.

~~Secret~~

NIE 11-3/8-91W
8 August 1991
Copy 18

23. *(Continued)*

The following intelligence organizations participated in the preparation of these Key Judgments:

The Central Intelligence Agency
The Defense Intelligence Agency
The National Security Agency
The Assistant Secretary for Intelligence and Research,
Department of State
The Director for Intelligence,
Department of Energy

also participating:

The Deputy Chief of Staff for Intelligence,
Department of the Army
The Director of Naval Intelligence,
Department of the Navy
The Assistant Chief of Staff, Intelligence,
Department of the Air Force
The Director of Intelligence,
Headquarters, Marine Corps

The National Foreign Intelligence Board concurs.

The full text of this Estimate is being published separately with regular distribution.

Warning Notice	Intelligence Sources or Methods Involved (WNINTEL)	
National Security Information	Unauthorized Disclosure Subject to Criminal Sanctions	
Dissemination Control Abbreviations	NOFORN (NF)	Not releasable to foreign nationals
	NOCONTRACT (NC)	Not releasable to contractors or contractor/consultants
	PROPIN (PR)	Caution—proprietary information involved
	ORCON (OC)	Dissemination and extraction of information controlled by originator
	REL...	This information has been authorized for release to...
	WN	WNINTEL—Intelligence sources or methods involved
		Classified by 0594334 Declassify: OADR Derived from multiple sources

All material on this page

23. *(Continued)*

~~Secret~~
~~NOFORN-NOCONTRACT~~

Soviet Forces and Capabilities for Strategic Nuclear Conflict Through the Year 2000 (C NF)

- The decline of the Soviet Union has caused its leaders to view their national security and superpower status as hinging more than ever on strategic nuclear power. Barring a collapse of central authority or the economy, we expect the Soviets to retain and modernize powerful, survivable strategic forces throughout the next decade. ~~(S NF)~~

- We have evidence that five new strategic ballistic missiles are in development—two land based and three sea launched. If these programs continue, four of them would begin deployment in the mid-1990s. ~~(S NF)~~

- Nevertheless, we believe that political upheaval and economic decline will lead to the cancellation or serious delay of one or more of these programs. The Soviet economy will be unable to support a sustained military production and deployment effort in the 1990s comparable to that of the 1980s, even for strategic forces. ~~(S NF)~~

- Production and deployment rates of some new strategic systems have been reduced as the Soviets adjust their programs in expectation of 35- to 40-percent reductions in both launchers and warheads under START. These force cuts would enable them to realize important savings in spending. ~~(S NF)~~

- Soviet nuclear controls appear well suited to prevent the seizure or unauthorized use of nuclear weapons. The ability of the General Staff to maintain its cohesion in the event, for example, of civil war or collapse of the central government, would be a key factor determining whether nuclear controls would break down. ~~(S NF)~~

23. *(Continued)*

~~Secret~~

Soviet Intercontinental Attack Forces Under START [a]

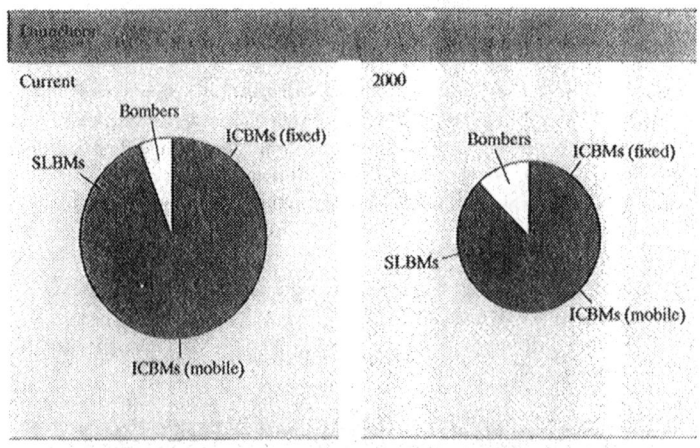

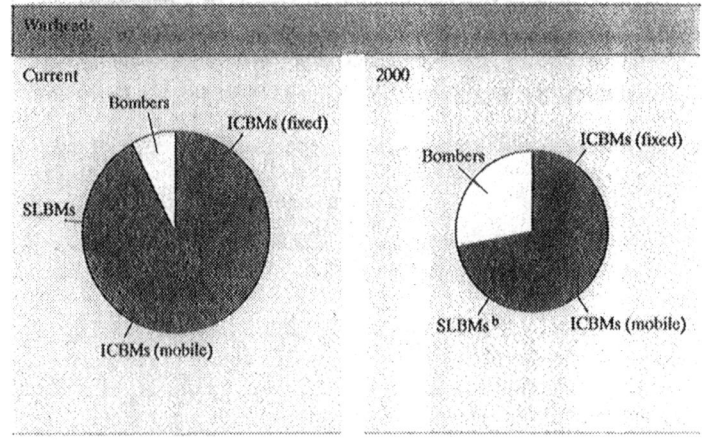

[a] The change in the area of the circles for the year 2000 indicates the projected reduction in the size of the force.

[b] The Director of Naval Intelligence projects that the number of SLBM warheads will continue to comprise about one-third of the number of strategic warheads under START.

23. (*Continued*)

~~Secret~~

Key Judgments

New Policy Context

We confront divergent trends in Soviet strategic nuclear policy. On one hand, the diminished Soviet conventional threat to Western Europe has significantly lessened the chances of East-West conflict and thus of global nuclear war. On the other hand, Soviet strategic nuclear forces remain large and powerful, major modernization programs are in progress, and Soviet nuclear strategy evidently retains its traditional war-fighting orientation. ~~(S-NF)~~

As a result of the crumbling of many other aspects of the Soviet Union's overall superpower position, current Soviet leaders appear to view their security and superpower status as hinging more than ever on strategic nuclear power. Over the past year, statements by various Soviet political and military officials have emphasized the increasing importance of Soviet strategic nuclear power. Barring a collapse of central authority or the economy, it seems clear that Soviet leaders will continue to try to shield their strategic forces and programs from the impact of political unrest and economic decline. At the same time, strategic forces have not been exempt from defense spending cuts since 1988, as procurement spending for both strategic offensive and defensive forces has fallen. ~~(S-NF)~~

We have significant uncertainties about the future roles of reformers, separatists, hardliners, and the Soviet military itself in charting the course of Soviet strategic policy.[1] The possibility remains, therefore, that a reformist regime might challenge the need to maintain strategic nuclear forces comparable to those of the United States to ensure superpower status and might settle for a lower level of force solely for deterrence. ~~(S-NF)~~

In light of the grave economic, political, and social difficulties afflicting the USSR, we are more skeptical than we were last year that the Soviets will be able to implement fully in the coming decade their modernization plans

[1] For discussion of four alternative futures, which the Intelligence Community believes captures the major possibilities for how the Soviet political and economic situation might develop over the next five years, see NIE 11-18-91: *Implications of Alternative Soviet Futures*, ~~(Secret NF NC)~~ July 1991. ~~(S-NF)~~

23. *(Continued)*

~~Secret~~

for their strategic offensive and defensive forces. The Soviet economy will be unable to support a sustained military production and deployment effort in the 1990s comparable to that of the 1980s, even for strategic forces. Indeed, the defense sector is already experiencing some of the disruptions that beset the civilian economy. Some facilities for strategic forces seem to be affected, but these difficulties do not yet appear to have had an appreciable effect on the production or deployment of strategic forces. Observed reductions in Soviet spending on strategic forces appear to be primarily the result of programmatic decisions rather than unplanned disruptions. (S-NF)

Separatist pressure in some republics raises the possibility that the center could lose control over certain strategic production facilities, R&D facilities, and test sites. A loss of control would at least complicate and could severely cripple the overall modernization of strategic forces. Moreover, the ability of the central government to fund defense programs depends on economic revenues from the republics, particularly the Russian Republic, some of which are withholding substantial funds. Separatist problems could also affect the deployment and operation of strategic forces. The Baltic republics, for example, are key to the strategic air defense of the northwestern approach to the USSR. We judge that, even if the central government eventually grants the Baltic republics greater autonomy or independence, it would seek to negotiate basing rights with them to preserve these defenses, at least until they could be relocated or replaced. Gorbachev as well as Yeltsin and other republic leaders are working on arrangements for a new union treaty, but we have large uncertainties about relations between the center and the republics over the long term, and how strategic forces might be affected. (S-NF)

Nuclear Security and Control

The Soviets have established physical security and use-control measures that appear well suited to prevent the seizure or unauthorized use of nuclear weapons. These measures minimize the risk that renegade military officers or other dissidents could gain access to nuclear weapons and threaten to use them. Since the late 1980s, heightened concern about potential internal threats has prompted the Soviets to strengthen security, including removing some warheads from areas of unrest. However, a military coup, the collapse of the central government, or a civil war might threaten the center's ability to maintain these controls. Because of the General Staff's crucial role in controlling nuclear weapons, maintenance of its cohesion in these situations would be a key factor determining whether a breakdown of nuclear controls would occur. (S-NF)

23. *(Continued)*

START

At present, a broad array of both strategic offensive and defensive systems are in various stages of development, production, or deployment. The rates of production and deployment of some new systems, however, have been lower in the past few years than we anticipated from past practices. As a result, strategic force modernization has slowed somewhat. We attribute these trends primarily to programmatic decisions made in the late 1980s, in particular Soviet preparations for an eventual START agreement that would allow savings by not building forces beyond START levels.

Soviet political and military leaders have strong incentives to see START implemented. Political leaders perceive an opportunity to reduce military expenditures and create a climate that fosters foreign economic aid. Military leaders see an opportunity to modernize their forces under a treaty that would preserve the relative strategic balance between the United States and USSR, introduce an element of predictability in strategic force planning, and bolster US incentives to reduce spending on strategic and other military forces.

For several years, Soviet military leaders have been adjusting their strategic programs to fit START limits. Soviet strategic intercontinental nuclear forces currently stand at about 2,400 launchers and 10,500 deployed warheads; under probable Soviet planning assumptions for START, these forces would decline by some 35 to 40 percent to 1,400 launchers and 6,700 warheads to comply with the Treaty.

START II

A force of 3,000 to 4,000 weapons would require the Soviets significantly to revise their targeting strategy, but they still would be able to deliver a devastating countermilitary strike. It is unlikely that the General Staff would gear its long-term strategic planning to such an uncertain prospect as START II, although they probably are preparing contingency plans.

23. *(Continued)*

Strategic Offensive Forces

The Soviets are moving from a force of which nearly half consists of silo-based ICBMs to one consisting mainly of mobile ICBMs, submarine-launched ballistic missiles (SLBMs), and bombers. Under START, well over half of all Soviet deployed warheads would be on mobile systems, although we project some 2,200 warheads would still be on silo-based ICBMs. Five new ballistic missiles are in development—two land based and three sea based. If these programs continue, we project flight-testing of four of them to begin within the next two to three years with deployments beginning in the mid-1990s. In the midst of political upheaval and economic decline, however, we believe that one or more of the five programs is likely to be canceled or seriously delayed:

- *ICBMs*. The Soviets continue to deploy the new SS-18 Mod 5 silo-based ICBM, which enhances capabilities for prompt attack, and the SS-25 road-mobile ICBM, which significantly improves force survivability. They have apparently completed the deployment of the SS-24 Mod 1 rail-mobile ICBM and the Mod 2 silo-based ICBM. Follow-on missiles to both the SS-25 and SS-24 are currently being developed.

- *SLBMs*. The Soviet SSBN force of the future will consist of considerably fewer submarines than today but will be equipped mostly with modern, long-range SLBMs. The Soviets are modifying Typhoon submarines to carry the SS-N-20 follow-on missile, which is being readied for flight-testing within the next year. In addition to the seven Delta-IV submarines already built, four additional submarines, which are probably modified Delta-IVs, probably are under construction. We project that these submarines will carry a new, liquid-propellant SLBM, which we anticipate will be armed with a single warhead. (There is a chance, however, that the Soviets are not building any new modified Delta-IV SSBNs.) There is evidence that a new SSBN is being developed and that it will be armed with a new, solid-propellant SLBM.

- *Bombers*. The Soviets continue to produce the Blackjack, their new strategic bomber, at the rate of three or four a year. We project about 40 will be deployed by 2000, a lower total than we previously had projected. Production of the Bear H cruise missile carrier has slowed and may soon end.

The Soviets have enough warheads to mount a comprehensive attack against fixed targets worldwide (while still retaining weapons in reserve), whether they conducted a preemptive strike or launched on tactical warning. They would retain the same capabilities under proposed START constraints, but they would have fewer weapons in reserve.

23. *(Continued)*

Heavy SS-18 ICBMs will remain the primary and most effective weapons against US missile silos during the next 10 years, but some SLBMs and other ICBMs also will be able to destroy hard targets. The SS-18 Mod 5 is about twice as effective against hard targets as the SS-18 Mod 4 that it is replacing; this difference in effectiveness probably enabled the Soviet military to agree to halve the SS-18 force under START.

Strategic Defensive Forces

The Soviets will continue to devote considerable resources to strategic defense, at least through the early 1990s. Nonetheless, with Soviet military resources declining and arms treaties and budget cuts constraining Western capabilities, pressure is increasing to shrink Soviet strategic defense programs. During the past year, the level of effort has decreased somewhat but with little effect on Soviet strategic defensive capabilities:

- *Antisubmarine Warfare.* The extensive Soviet ASW program has made some gains. The Soviets have an improved, although limited, ability to detect and engage enemy submarines in waters adjacent to the USSR. In the future, the combined effect of multiple layers of ASW systems may constitute a significant challenge to Western submarine operations in Soviet-controlled waters. We judge, however, that through at least the next 15 to 20 years the Soviets will remain incapable of threatening US SSBNs and SSNs in the open ocean.

- *Air Defense.* We project considerably smaller, but heavily modernized strategic air defenses, with a doubling of deployed systems with good capabilities to engage low-altitude vehicles. Modernization programs include deployment of SA-10 surface-to-air-missiles, Foxhound and Flanker interceptors with lookdown/shootdown capabilities, and Mainstay airborne warning and control system aircraft. New versions of these systems also are in development. We judge that, in the event of a major US nuclear attack, the current Soviet air defense system would be unable to prevent large-scale, low-altitude penetration of Soviet airspace. In the coming decade, however, Soviet strategic air defenses will be much more capable of engaging low-altitude vehicles. As a result, penetration by currently deployed US bombers and cruise missiles will become more difficult, particularly in the heavily defended western USSR. If the B-2 bomber and advanced cruise missile achieve the desired level of reduced observability, using tactics appropriate to stealth vehicles they probably would be able to penetrate most of the Soviet Union at low altitude. The capabilities of Soviet air defenses will place some limitations on operations of the B-2 bomber, however.

23. *(Continued)*

- *Ballistic Missile and Space Defense.* The modernized Moscow antiballistic missile (ABM) system, which will eventually have 100 silo-based interceptors, provides an improved intercept capability against small-scale attacks. Through the late 1990s, the Soviets are highly unlikely to undertake widespread ABM deployments that would exceed ABM Treaty limits. Current Soviet antisatellite-capable systems pose a threat to US low-altitude satellites, but the only Soviet capability against high-altitude satellites is electronic warfare.

- *Directed Energy Weapons.* The Soviets are continuing efforts to develop high-energy lasers for air defense, antisatellite, and ballistic missile defense applications. There are large uncertainties and differences of view among agencies, however, about how far the Soviets have advanced, the status and goals of weapon development programs, and the dates for potential prototype or operational capabilities. We judge that within the next two decades the Soviets are likely to develop air defense lasers, ground-based antisatellite lasers, and ground-based radiofrequency antisatellite weapons. The Soviets continue to be interested in developing space-based laser weapons.

- *Leadership Protection.* For 40 years, the Soviet Union has had a vast program under way to ensure the survival of its leaders in the event of nuclear war. This program has involved the construction of an extensive network of deep underground bunkers, tunnels, and secret subway lines in urban and rural areas. There is recent evidence that substantial construction activity continues, and we expect the program to move forward along traditional lines.

24. NIE 11-30-91C, December 1991, *The Winter of the Soviet Military: Cohesion or Collapse?*

Director of Central Intelligence

~~Top Secret~~

The Winter of the Soviet Military: Cohesion or Collapse?

National Intelligence Estimate

This National Intelligence Estimate represents the views of the Director of Central Intelligence with the advice and assistance of the US Intelligence Community.

~~Top Secret~~

NIE 11-30-91C
~~*SC 04222-91*~~
December 1991

Copy 480

23. *(Continued)*

 Director of Central Intelligence

~~Top Secret~~
~~UMBRA~~
~~NOFORN-NOCONTRACT~~
~~ORCON~~

NIE 11-30-91C

The Winter of the Soviet Military: Cohesion or Collapse? ~~(C-NF)~~

Information available as of 5 December 1991 was used in the preparation of this National Intelligence Estimate.

The following intelligence organizations participated in the preparation of this Estimate:
The Central Intelligence Agency
The Defense Intelligence Agency
The National Security Agency
The Bureau of Intelligence and Research,
Department of State

also participating:
The Deputy Chief of Staff for Intelligence,
Department of the Army
The Director of Naval Intelligence,
Department of the Navy
The Assistant Chief of Staff, Intelligence,
Department of the Air Force
The Director of Intelligence,
Headquarters, Marine Corps

This Estimate was approved for publication by the National Foreign Intelligence Board.

~~Handle via COMINT Channels~~

~~Top Secret~~
~~SG 04222-91~~
December 1991

24. *(Continued)*

~~Top Secret~~
~~UMBRA~~
~~NOFORN-NOCONTRACT~~
~~ORCON~~

> This Estimate is one of a series to be published in the coming weeks on various crises facing the former USSR. ▇▇▇▇▇▇▇▇▇▇▇▇▇▇▇▇▇▇▇▇▇▇▇▇ The multiplicity of problems facing the new governments and their limited ability to cope with them make it likely that one or more of these problems will take on "worst case" proportions. This Estimate focuses on the cohesion of the Soviet military only over the winter and does not address all the components that constitute current Soviet military capability (C NF)

24. *(Continued)*

~~Top Secret~~
~~UMBRA~~
~~NOFORN-NOCONTRACT~~
~~ORCON~~

Key Judgments

The Winter of the Soviet Military: Cohesion or Collapse? ~~(C NF)~~

- Forces unleashed by the collapse of the Soviet system are breaking up its premier artifact—the Soviet military; the high command cannot halt this process. While a centralized command and control system continues to operate, political and economic collapse is beginning to fragment the military into elements loyal to the republics or simply devoted to self-preservation. These forces include:

  — Fragmentation:
  - Republic action to take control of units, equipment, and facilities could provoke conflicts of loyalty within the armed forces.
  - Shortages of basic necessities are prompting commanders of major formations to seek ties to local political bodies.
  - Commanders who do not receive local support may act on their own to seize or extort basic necessities.

  — Shortages:
  - Housing shortfalls continue to undermine morale and cohesion.
  - Traditionally first in line for high-tech resources, the military now has difficulty obtaining food and fuel.
  - Triple-digit inflation and the lack of a military budget threaten pay.

~~Handle via COMINT Channels~~

~~Top Secret~~
~~SC 04222-91~~
December 1991

24. *(Continued)*

— Erosion of legitimacy and discipline:

- Since the August coup, questioning of traditional discipline has increased, and officers face difficult decisions about whom to obey.

- The disappearance of an external threat has increased officer disorientation.

- Massive officer cuts further erode discipline and morale. The uncertain future, coupled with a general lack of transferable job skills, heightens officer concern. (S-NF)

- The picture with respect to cohesion in the armed forces is mixed:

  ▬▬▬▬▬▬▬▬▬▬ we have detected little change in the day-to-day activity of much of the force, suggesting unit integrity and nominal responsiveness to the chain of command.

  — On the other hand, senior Soviet officers acknowledge serious problems, and a growing body of anecdotal evidence indicates an increasing tendency for unit commanders to challenge orders that threaten the well-being of their troops.

  The armed forces are likely over the winter to continue to exhibit basic unit integrity and responsiveness, but, as the center fails to provide essential goods and services, the established chain of command will become increasingly irrelevant. (TS-U-NF)

- Moreover, merely getting through the winter will present a false picture of military cohesion and stability. The most likely scenario will be continued decay and breakup of the Soviet armed forces. Halting this trend would require countering the centrifugal forces at work in the former Soviet Union and a major improvement in the economic conditions now affecting the military. (S-NF)

- Although less likely, there is still a significant chance of rapid disintegration and widespread violence if a large number of units seek autonomy or military organization collapses. (S-NF)

- Even less likely is the involvement of the armed forces in a large-scale civil war between or within major republics during the winter. (S-NF)

24. (Continued)

~~Top Secret~~
~~UMBRA~~
~~NOFORN NOCONTRACT~~
~~ORCON~~

Discussion

Armies are microcosms of their societies; often indeed their core.
  Michael Howard
  The Lessons of History

Everything I have devoted my whole life to building is collapsing.
  Suicide Note of Marshal Akhromeyev

Forces unleashed by the collapse of the Soviet system are breaking up its premier artifact—the Soviet military. While a centralized command and control system continues to operate, political and economic collapse threatens to fragment the military into elements loyal to the republics or simply devoted to self-preservation. Widespread shortages are depriving military personnel and their families of basic necessities, damaging morale. The events surrounding the failed coup and the collapse of the Communist Party challenge the moral basis of the officer corps, the authority of the center, and the chain of command. The disappearance of the perceived Western threat and the disintegration of the Warsaw Pact have increased the sense of disorientation among officers. These forces threaten military cohesion, that is, the ability of units at all levels to maintain organizational integrity and respond to orders from an acknowledged chain of command. (S NF)

Stresses on the Military

Fragmentation

Plans by several republic and regional governments to take control of units, facilities, and equipment on their territory will increase pressure on military unity. So far, these plans amount largely to declarations of intent, but, should a republic decide to take control of a major unit, installation, or nuclear weapons, a showdown with the center could provoke conflicts of loyalty within the armed forces. Defense Minister Shaposhnikov and Interior Minister Barannikov, for example, stated in November that force would be used to counter republic attempts to turn such declarations into reality. (S NF)

We believe that through the winter more large military formations will seek ties to local political entities. Many units have longstanding ties to republics or subrepublic areas from which they receive economic essentials. A few Ground Forces units in Byelorussia, Ukraine, and Russia already have offered allegiance to the republics where they are stationed. Failing a local accommodation, some unit commanders may try to take direct control of supplies or, alternatively, engage in warlord-like extortion. (S NF)

The shift in political power to the republics has allowed the nationalist genie to escape from the Stalinist bottle, a condition that hastens fragmentation. Ukraine's situation illustrates one especially dramatic aspect of the pressure of nationalism. Its declaration of independence and demand for its own forces threaten to split the Soviet military. Ukrainians constitute some 30 percent of the officer corps and 17 percent of the conscripts, according to Soviet sources. Many of these personnel may join the Ukrainian armed forces. (S NF)

As a result of the accommodation by the central Ministry of Defense (MOD) to republic demands for a "stay at home" conscription policy, Ground Force units in the republics are becoming more homogeneous (68 percent of Azerbaijan-based units are Azeri). This process, combined with republic concern about possible violence to obtain supplies, may lead to "creeping absorption" of units by local governments. (S NF)

Shortages of Basic Goods and Services

The Soviet military, traditionally first in line for high-tech resources, now finds it difficult to obtain food and fuel (see figure). It can no longer command the

24. (Continued)

delivery of basic items across republic boundaries amid widespread shortages and a growing barter system. Industrial and agricultural enterprises increasingly ignore orders to supply the armed forces in return for "wooden rubles."

Units throughout the military confront worsening shortages:

Housing shortfalls continue to undermine military morale and cohesion:

- Soviet media reported in November that troops in the Baltic states—including an elite airborne unit—refused to leave until "normal social and living conditions are created at their new postings."

Military pay is also threatened. Salary increases have not kept pace with triple-digit inflation. Some units have not been paid on time, a problem that will become more widespread in the absence of a military budget. Yel'tsin recently promised that Russia will pay the military (and double their pay), but in the short run this probably will require printing more money, thereby increasing inflation.

The capacity of the armed forces to deal with these problems is limited. Military command and control, logistics, and personnel systems are designed for central control and have only limited ability to respond to current developments. Despite such resources as military farms and reserves of food, fuel, and other commodities commanders look elsewhere for help. Units get supplies from civilian enterprises in return for labor and sell or rent military equipment. The Chief of the General Staff has asked the Soviet public to donate to a newly created charity for the military. Clearly, such makeshift efforts will not solve the problem. Only improvement in the economy coupled with either interrepublic agreement on military funding or complete breakup into republic armed forces can do that.

Erosion of Legitimacy and Discipline

Soviet officers also face fundamental questions of loyalty and discipline. They are uncertain how to act in the present chaotic political situation. In theory, the armed forces are under control of the central state apparatus, but some officers question its legitimacy and believe that no one is in charge.

Since the August coup attempt, questioning of traditional military discipline has spread within the officer corps. The actions of senior officers—Defense Minister Yazov supported the coup while Air Force Chief Shaposhnikov opposed it—exacerbated splits in the officer corps and further weakened its cohesion.

Officers face increasingly difficult decisions about whom to obey. Those who supported the "right side" while disobeying their superiors—such as the Pacific Fleet officers who supported Yel'tsin—are sometimes praised. Others who followed orders are condemned.

24. *(Continued)*

Traditional obedience to orders is no longer adequate; officers are not to obey a "clearly criminal" order. But they have been given no clear guidance on what constitutes such an order. (S-NF)

Massive officer reductions further erode discipline and morale. Gorbachev's announcement in December 1988 of a unilateral reduction of 500,000 men included a cut of about 100,000 officers, and additional cuts are scheduled. Most Soviet officers, to a much greater degree than Western counterparts, lack transferable skills; the uncertain future intensifies their fear. (S-NF)

Units Become Pressure Points

The effects of these pressures—fragmentation, shortages, and the erosion of legitimacy and discipline—come together at the garrison, divisional, and regimental levels. Individual commanders must deal directly with these new problems. On the whole, they have done a reasonably good job. Whatever their internal problems, most Soviet units retain their basic structure and equipment and, with varying degrees of success, continue some routine operations and training. With no clear alternative, most Soviet officers follow the well-worn patterns of the past. (S-NF)

24. *(Continued)*

Prospects for the Winter

Over the winter it is likely that the armed forces will maintain cohesion. We expect cohesion to hold whether the armed forces continue to decay under the nominal control of central authorities or whether agreements among republics lead to division of the armed forces among them. The latter case would mean the end of the traditional Soviet military. Even in a situation where its basic structures are maintained, however, the military will likely lose control of some units to republics and localities, or even collapse. Such loss of control could lead to incidents of localized violence. (S NF)

Decay will continue. The pressures undermining the military cannot be checked or alleviated over the next several months. The situation—and the military's condition after the winter—will vary by service and from republic to republic. Simultaneous and interdependent outcomes are possible. The ultimate character of the outcome will depend on the military's institutional coherence; its allegiance to civil authorities; its ability to satisfy basic needs; and its willingness to accept increasing hardship and uncertainty. (S NF)

Our conclusion that the armed forces are likely to maintain cohesion over the winter reflects the following:

- Military service, for all its problems, will continue to be more appealing to many than a return to civilian life. The availability of resources in military supply channels and reserve stockpiles, in contrast to bleak civil prospects, will keep many units largely intact.

- Most officers support military subordination to civil authority.

- Yel'tsin has promised to fund the MOD; albeit with major cuts. (S NF)

Getting through the winter relatively peacefully, however, could present a false picture of military cohesion and stability. Spring will find the military under increased pressures and with fewer resources. Absent interrepublic political and economic agreements, there will be even less hope of a solution to the problems facing the military. The reliability of military forces ordered to take unpopular actions, such as suppression of civil unrest, is open to serious question. The effect of such orders probably would be to accelerate the disintegration of the armed forces. (S NF)

Ironically, one of the most disruptive, but least likely, developments—a coup initiated by the military—would require cohesion in the units involved to ensure that orders would be obeyed. The unsettled atmosphere in the officer corps, confusion about the legitimacy of traditional authority, and a reluctance to take action that might accelerate military disintegration inhibit such an act. ▮▮▮▮▮▮▮▮▮▮▮▮▮▮▮▮ Such a coup attempt would reflect a desperate judgment by military leaders that there was no other alternative. A failed coup attempt could precipitate a descent into civil war. (S NF)

Alternative Outcomes

Though unlikely, there is still a significant chance of outcomes involving the severe degradation or destruction of organizational cohesion. These include widespread local unit autonomy and total collapse of the armed forces:

- *Widespread local unit autonomy.* Traditionally strong ties between some units and local civilian authorities and the trend toward local and regional autarky in the economy could produce even more fragmentation in the military structure, leading to autonomous action by units operating in their own interest. The armed forces would retain unit cohesion but fragment on a regional, rayon, or oblast basis. The pressure on military officers to deal with local civilian authorities on a basis of food for

24. *(Continued)*

loyalty or to ensure more military influence in civil affairs could become stronger. Unit accommodations with local authorities would bolster local ties and lead to allegiance to republic or subrepublic governments. On the darker side, where local authorities refused cooperation, units could assume local control or, alternatively, extort supplies from local authorities.

- *Collapse*. Conditions worse than we anticipate—widespread failure to provide military personnel and their families with basic goods and services, collapse of discipline, and lawlessness throughout society—would destroy existing military organization. Large numbers of soldiers would desert. Gangs of deserters would take what they wanted from the civilian population. (S NF)

Even less likely, though most violent, is the involvement of the armed forces in large-scale civil war within or between major republics during the winter. Triggering events could be resistance by the center or Russia to republic efforts to assume control of military forces or equipment on their territory or, alternatively, violence involving Russian minorities in a non-Russian republic. Such conflict would be especially dangerous if the control of nuclear weapons were at stake. Conflicts between republics other than Russia and Ukraine may be more likely but, while violent, probably would remain localized. (S NF)

Least likely are conditions, much better than we anticipate, that could halt the decay and breakup of the Soviet armed forces. Such an outcome would require major improvement in the economic conditions now affecting the military and countering the centrifugal forces at work in the former USSR. (S NF)

www.ingramcontent.com/pod-product-compliance
Lightning Source LLC
Chambersburg PA
CBHW080722230426
43665CB00020B/2584